GRAPHIC ANATOMY ATELIER BOW-WOW

GRAPHIC ANATOMY
ATELIER BOW-WOW

First Published in Japan on March 15th, 2007
Third Published on May 25th, 2007
by TOTO Shuppan (TOTO Ltd.)
TOTO Nogizaka Bldg., 2F, 1-24-3
Minami-aoyama, Minato-ku,
Tokyo 1070062 JAPAN
[Sales] Telephone : +81 3 3402 7138 Facsimile : +81 3 3402 7187
[Editorial] Telephone : +81 3 3497 1010
URL: http://www.toto.co.jp/bookshop/

Planning : GALLERY・MA
Author : Atelier Bow-Wow (Yoshiharu Tsukamoto + Momoyo Kaijima)
Publisher : Nobuyuki Endo

Art Direction : Kan Akita
Design: Kan Akita + Yasuyuki Morita (Akita Design Kan Inc.)

Printing and Binding : Sannichi Printing Co., Ltd.

ISBN978-4-88706-278-8

図解 アトリエ・ワン

GRAPHIC ANATOMY ATELIER BOW-WOW

序文

植物学者や解剖学者など、いくつかの職業では図解することがスキルの一つになっている。彼らが制作する植物図、人体図は科学的なもので、いわゆる絵画作品ではない。むしろ個人の個性というものが出ないように、手法は限られている。そのことが、博物誌の充実に、誰でもどこからでも貢献できる道を拓く。

図解は写真のように写実的であるが、写真とは違った感興を呼ぶ。要素を輪郭によって捉え、その輪郭内を水彩で着彩し、ときに文字を書き込む。その手法の徹底が、驚嘆すべき細部を伴った図を生み、観察する対象の多様性を浮き上がらせる。図解において細部を一つ一つ描き分けることは、人間がそれを見る事ができたという達成の証であると同時に、人間の眼差しが対象によって導かれたという証でもある。

そういう図解の持つ、主体の開放と観察の誠実によって、アトリエ・ワンによる住宅作品を一覧するのがこの本の趣旨である。これまでにも東京のアノニマスな極小ペット建築や、ハイブリッドなダメ建築を収集し、図解してきたアトリエ・ワンだが、今回は自分達のスキルの中で描いてきた、平面詳細図や矩計図などをもとに、そこに空間的な奥行きを与えて住宅を図解している。写真なら何枚も必要となるであろう、部材や室の構成、外部環境との隣接性、振る舞いと居場所、物の関係などが、一枚の絵の中にある。そのことによって、矛盾や対立をはらんだ複数の意図が、特定の建築要素を媒介に有機的に結び付けられる様子や、個々の住宅における物理的な制約に対する応答が、思いがけない光の現象や生活の現象を産む様子などが見えてくることを願っている。それらはどれも、各住宅のそもそもの条件である場所と人を無視してはなかった「いきいきとした空間の実践」である。建築がその多様性に目を開き、耳を澄まし、勇気づけ、手助けすることを通して、建築が再発見されて行く。これがアトリエ・ワンが目指すところである。

PREFACE

In some occupations, such as botanist or anatomist, the ability to make illustrations is a necessary skill. They produce diagrams of plants and human bodies that are scientific works, not so-called artworks. Instead, their technique is restricted so that individual personality is suppressed. This clears the way for anyone, from anywhere, to contribute to the enrichment of our knowledge of natural history.

Although these illustrations have a photograph-like realism, they attract our interest in a way that is unlike photography. Elements are depicted by their outlines, and inscribed within these outlines are the nuanced hues of watercolors and sometimes lettering. The thoroughness of their technique produces drawings with an astonishing level of detail, and the diversity of the objects being studied comes to the fore. Being able to distinguish each detail in an illustration is evidence that people have seen them, and is at the same time evidence that these objects guide the human eye.

Through the liberation from subjectivity and the earnestness of observation in such illustrations, the point of this book is to catalog house designed by Atelier Bow-Wow. Previously, Atelier Bow-Wow have also made illustrated collections of Tokyo's anonymous, tiny pet architecture and hybrid, junky architecture, but now they have used their skills to give house illustrations a spatial depth, based on drawings such as plan details and section details. If they were photographs, probably a great many would be necessary, but contained within a single picture is the composition of rooms and components, the adjacent exterior environments, actions and locations, and the relationships between objects. This provides the appearance of multiple intentions fraught with contradiction and confrontation, organically linked through the medium of specific architectural elements, as well as producing the appearance of unexpected phenomena of light and daily life, in response to the physical constraints on each individual house. Without disregarding the places and people that comprise the initial conditions for each house, these are all the "practice of lively space." Architecture that opens its eyes and strains its ears to this diversity of spatial practice, encouraging and assisting it; this is the rediscovery of architecture itself. That is where the aims of Atelier Bow-Wow lie.

目次 Contents

図解 アトリエ・ワン
GRAPHIC ANATOMY ATELIER BOW-WOW

住宅の振る舞いについて
ON THE BEHAVIOR OF HOUSES

図解 アトリエ・ワン

GRAPHIC ANATOMY ATELIER BOW-WOW

アニ・ハウス
Ani House

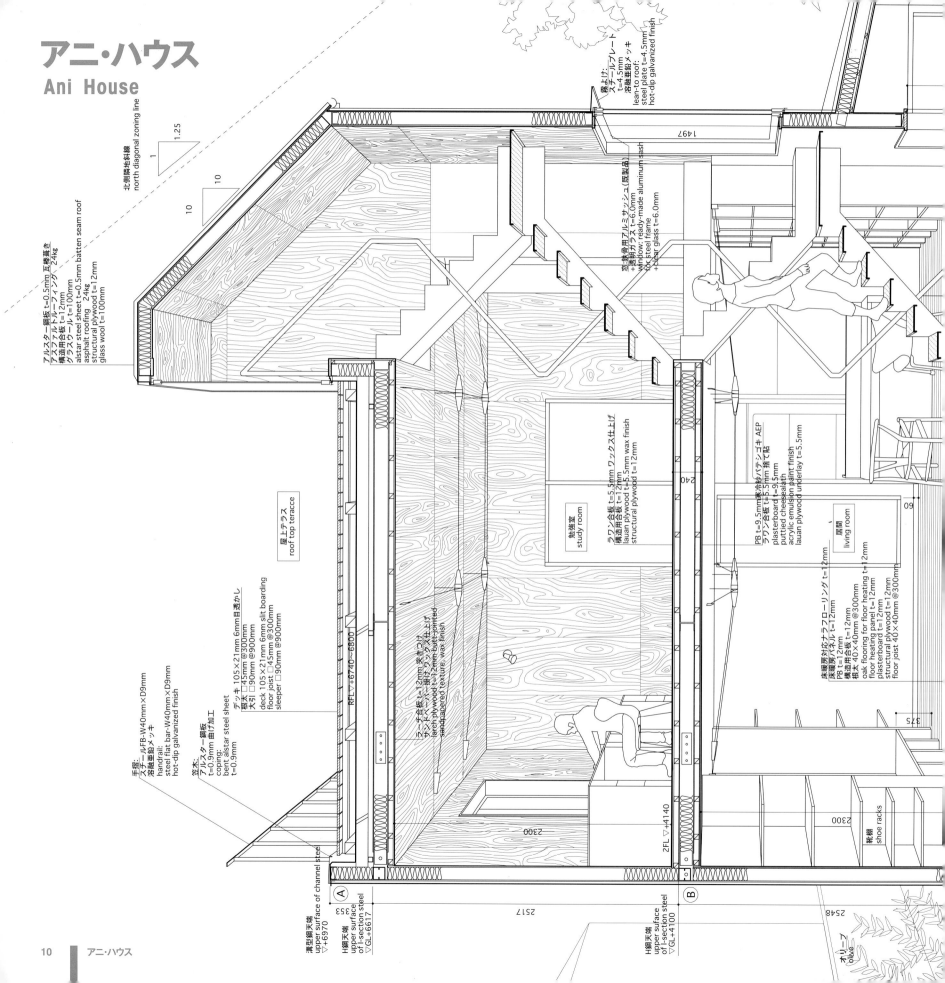

北側隣地斜線
north diagonal zoning line

1.25
1
10
10
10

葺上げ：スチールプレート
t=4.5mm
溶融亜鉛メッキ
lean-to roof:
steel plate t=4.5mm
hot-dip galvanized finish

1497

アルスター鋼板 t=0.5mm 瓦棒葺き
アスファルトルーフィング 24kg
構造用合板 t=12mm
グラスウール t=100mm
alstar steel sheet t=0.5mm batten seam roof
asphalt roofing 24kg
structural plywood t=12mm
glass wool t=100mm

窓枠骨用アルミサッシュ（既製品）
+透明ガラス t=6.0mm
window: ready-made aluminum sash
for steel frame
+clear glass t=6.0mm

手摺：
スチールFB-W40mm×D9mm
溶融亜鉛メッキ
handrail:
steel flat bar-W40mm×D9mm
hot-dip galvanized finish

笠木：
アルスター鋼板
t=0.9mm 曲げ加工
coping:
bent alstar steel sheet
t=0.9mm

屋上テラス
roof top teracce

ラワン合板 t=5.5mm ワックス仕上げ
構造用合板 t=12mm
lauan plywood t=5.5mm wax finish
structural plywood t=12mm

勉強室
study room

デッキ 105×21mm 6mm目透かし
根太 □45mm @300mm
大引 □90mm @900mm
deck 105×21mm 6mm slit boarding
floor joist □45mm @300mm
sleeper □90mm @900mm

ラーチ合板 t=12mm 突きつけ
サンドペーパー掛けワックス仕上げ
larch plywood t=12mm butt-jointed
sandpapered texture, wax finish

PB t=9.5mm寒冷紗パテンゴキ AEP
ラワン合板 t=5.5mm 捨て貼
plasterboard t=9.5mm
puttied cheesecloth
acrylic emulsion paint finish
lauan plywood underlay t=5.5mm

240

居間
living room

床暖房対応ナラフローリング t=12mm
床暖房パネル t=12mm
PB t=12mm
構造用合板 t=12mm
根太 40×40mm @300mm
oak flooring for floor heating t=12mm
floor heating panel t=12mm
plasterboard t=12mm
structural plywood t=12mm
floor joist 40×40mm @300mm

60

09

375

2300

2FL ▽+4140

4140

2300

靴棚
shoe racks

RFL ▽+6740～6800

溝型鋼天端
upper surface of channel steel
▽+6970

H鋼天端
upper surface
of I-section steel
▽GL+6617

353

2517

(A)

H鋼天端
upper suface
of I-section steel
▽GL+4100

(B)

2548

オリーブ
olive

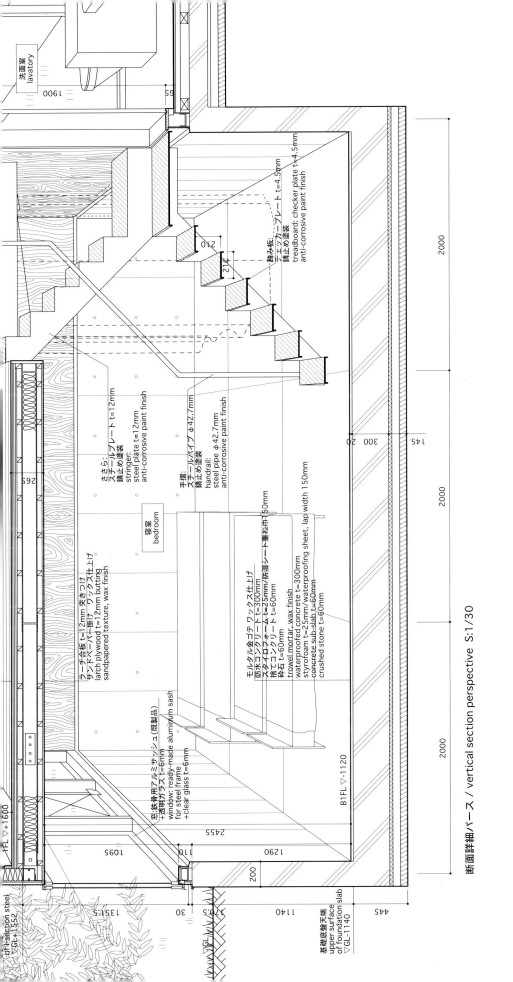

洗面室
lavatory

1900

踏み板：
チェッカープレート t=4.5mm
錆止め塗装
treadboard: checker plate t=4.5mm
anti-corrosive paint finish

2000

2000

2000

145 300 20

265

さきら：
スチールプレート t=12mm
錆止め塗装
stringer:
steel plate t=12mm
anti-corrosive paint finish

手摺：
スチールパイプ φ42.7mm
錆止め塗装
handrail:
steel pipe φ42.7mm
anti-corrosive paint finish

寝室
bedroom

ラーチ合板 t=12mm 突きつけ
サンドペーパー掛け ワックス仕上げ
larch plywood t=12mm butting
sandpapered texture, wax finish

窓：鉄骨用アルミサッシュ（既製品）
＋透明ガラス t=6mm
window: ready-made aluminum sash
for steel frame
＋clear glass t=6mm

モルタル金ゴテ ワックス仕上げ
防水コンクリート t=300mm
スタイロフォーム t=25mm/防湿シート重ね巾150mm
捨てコンクリート t=60mm
砕石 t=60mm
trowel mortar, wax finish
waterproofed concrete t=300mm
styrofoam t=25mm/waterproofing sheet, lap width 150mm
concrete sub-slab t=60mm
crushed stone t=60mm

B1FL ▽-1120

2455

1290

1095

1FL ▽+1600

pit-section steel
▽GL+1352

基礎底盤天端
upper foundation slab
▽GL-1140

110
200
445 1140
30
▽GL
135t/5
1/7.5

断面詳細パース / vertical section perspective S:1/30

240

90

12

窓枠：米栂 20mm OP
window frame:
western hemlock
20mm oil paint finish

ラワン合板 t=5.5mm ワックス仕上げ
構造用台板 t=12mm
lauan plywood t=5.5mm wax finish
structural plywood t=12mm

2FL ▽+4140

12
20
95
23
50
50

L-50×50×5mm

70

43

鉄骨用アルミサッシュ（既製品）
＋網入透明ガラス t=6.8mm
ready-made aluminum sash
for steel frame
＋wired clear glass t=6.8mm

外部
outside

200

霧よけ：
スチールプレート t=4.5mm
溶融亜鉛メッキ
lean-to roof:
steel plate t=4.5mm
hot-dip galvanized finish

Ⓑ 開口部詳細図 / window detail S:1/5

手摺：スチールFB-W40mm×D9mm
溶融亜鉛メッキ
handrail:
steel flat bar-W40mm×D9mm
hot-dip galvanized finish

SUSボルト締め
stainless steel bolt

屋上テラス
roof top teracce

軽歩行用露出塩化ビニルシート
t=2mm
ALCパネル t=100mm
polyvinyl-chloride sheet t=2mm
autoclaved light-weight concrete
t=100mm

ALC薄型パネル
autoclaved light-weight concrete

コーキング
caulking

100
108
48

40

37

214

100

9
41

20

20

笠木：アルスター鋼板大波板 t=0.5mm
t=0.9mm 曲げ加工
coping:
bent alstar steel sheet
t=0.9mm

アルスター鋼板大波板 t=0.5mm
アスファルトルーフィング18kg
構造用台板 t=9mm
グラスウール t=100mm
alstar steel corrugated sheet
t=0.5mm
asphalt roofing 18kg
structural plywood t=9mm
glass wool t=100mm

外部
outside

Ⓐ パラペット詳細図 / parapet detail S:1/5

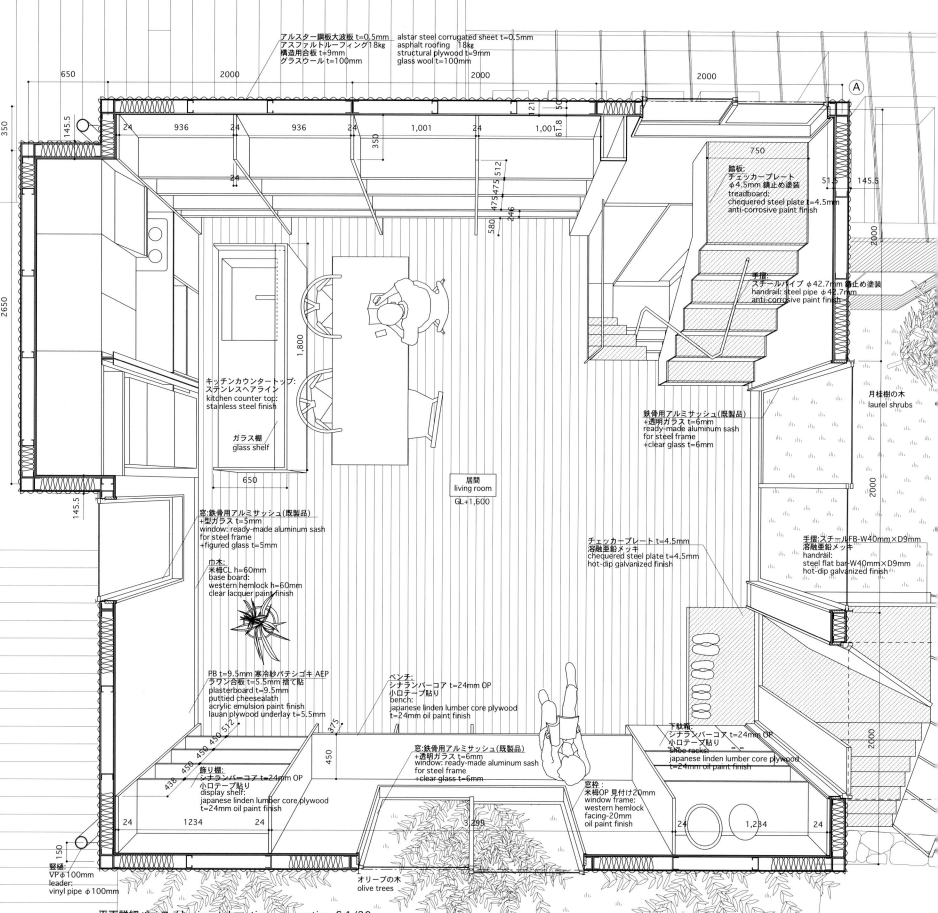

アルスター鋼板大波板 t=0.5mm　alstar steel corrugated sheet t=0.5mm
アスファルトルーフィング18kg　asphalt roofing　18kg
構造用合板 t=9mm　structural plywood t=9mm
グラスウール t=100mm　glass wool t=100mm

650　2000　2000　2000　Ⓐ

350　145.5

24　936　24　936　24　1,001　24　1,001.8

350

2650

512
475

踏板:
チェッカープレート
φ4.5mm 錆止め塗装
treadboard:
chequered steel plate t=4.5mm
anti-corrosive paint finish

750

51.5　145.5

2000

145.5

580　475

246

キッチンカウンタートップ:
ステンレスヘアライン
kitchen counter top:
stainless steel finish

手摺:
スチールパイプ φ42.7mm 錆止め塗装
handrail: steel pipe φ42.7mm
anti-corrosive paint finish

ガラス棚
glass shelf

鉄骨用アルミサッシュ(既製品)
+透明ガラス t=6mm
ready-made aluminum sash
for steel frame
+clear glass t=6mm

月桂樹の木
laurel shrubs

650

居間
living room
GL+1,600

2000

窓:鉄骨用アルミサッシュ(既製品)
+型ガラス t=5mm
window: ready-made aluminum sash
for steel frame
+figured glass t=5mm

145.5

チェッカープレート t=4.5mm
溶融亜鉛メッキ
chequered steel plate t=4.5mm
hot-dip galvanized finish

手摺:スチールFB-W40mm×D9mm
溶融亜鉛メッキ
handrail:
steel flat bar-W40mm×D9mm
hot-dip galvanized finish

巾木:
米栂CL h=60mm
base board:
western hemlock h=60mm
clear lacquer paint finish

PB t=9.5mm 寒冷紗パテシゴキ AEP
ラワン合板 t=5.5mm 捨て貼
plasterboard t=9.5mm
puttied cheesealath
acrylic emulsion paint finish
lauan plywood underlay t=5.5mm

ベンチ:
シナランバーコア t=24mm OP
小口テープ貼り
bench:
japanese linden lumber core plywood
t=24mm oil paint finish

下駄箱:
シナランバーコア t=24mm OP
小口テープ貼り
shoe racks:
japanese linden lumber core plywood
t=24mm oil paint finish

450　450　512

375

450

窓:鉄骨用アルミサッシュ(既製品)
+透明ガラス t=6mm
window: ready-made aluminum sash
for steel frame
+clear glass t=6mm

窓枠:
米栂OP 見付け20mm
window frame:
western hemlock
facing-20mm
oil paint finish

438

飾り棚:
シナランバーコア t=24mm OP
小口テープ貼り
display shelf:
japanese linden lumber core plywood
t=24mm oil paint finish

24　1234　24

3,299

24　1,234　24

2000

150

竪樋:
VPφ100mm
leader:
vinyl pipe φ100mm

オリーブの木
olive trees

平面詳細パース／horizontal section perspective S:1/30

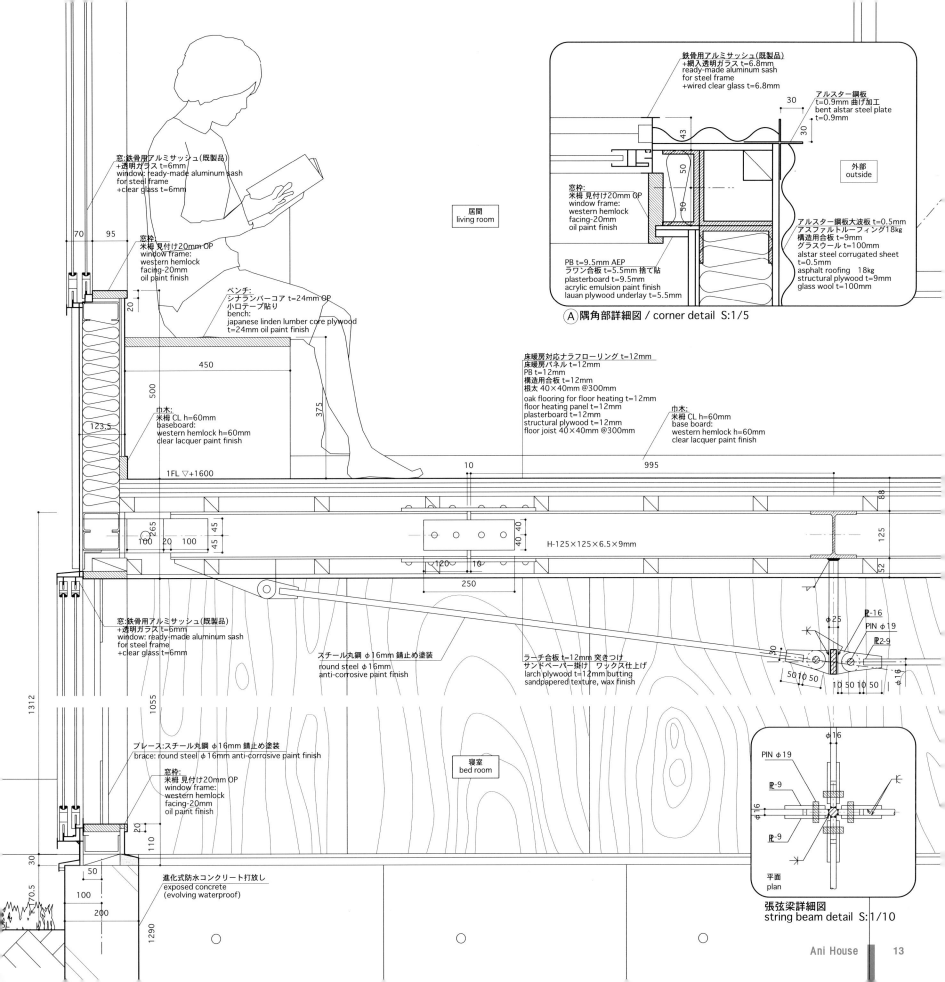

鉄骨用アルミサッシュ(既製品)
+網入透明ガラス t=6.8mm
ready-made aluminum sash
for steel frame
+wired clear glass t=6.8mm

アルスター鋼板
t=0.9mm 曲げ加工
bent alstar steel plate
t=0.9mm

30

30

43

50

50

外部
outside

窓枠:
米栂 見付け20mm OP
window frame:
western hemlock
facing-20mm
oil paint finish

アルスター鋼板大波板 t=0.5mm
アスファルトルーフィング18kg
構造用合板 t=9mm
グラスウール t=100mm
alstar steel corrugated sheet
t=0.5mm
asphalt roofing　18kg
structural plywood t=9mm
glass wool t=100mm

PB t=9.5mm AEP
ラワン合板 t=5.5mm 捨て貼
plasterboard t=9.5mm
acrylic emulsion paint finish
lauan plywood underlay t=5.5mm

Ⓐ 隅角部詳細図 / corner detail S:1/5

窓:鉄骨用アルミサッシュ(既製品)
+透明ガラス t=6mm
window: ready-made aluminum sash
for steel frame
+clear glass t=6mm

窓枠:
米栂 見付け20mm OP
window frame:
western hemlock
facing-20mm
oil paint finish

70   95

20

123.5

居間
living room

床暖房対応ナラフローリング t=12mm
床暖房パネル t=12mm
PB t=12mm
構造用合板 t=12mm
根太 40×40mm @300mm
oak flooring for floor heating t=12mm
floor heating panel t=12mm
plasterboard t=12mm
structural plywood t=12mm
floor joist 40×40mm @300mm

ベンチ:
シナランバーコア t=24mm OP
小口テープ貼り
bench:
japanese linden lumber core plywood
t=24mm oil paint finish

450

500

375

巾木:
米栂 CL h=60mm
baseboard:
western hemlock h=60mm
clear lacquer paint finish

巾木:
米栂 CL h=60mm
base board:
western hemlock h=60mm
clear lacquer paint finish

1FL ▽+1600

10

995

265

45 45

40 40

88

100 20 100

45 45

H-125×125×6.5×9mm

125

120   10

250

52

窓:鉄骨用アルミサッシュ(既製品)
+透明ガラス t=6mm
window: ready-made aluminum sash
for steel frame
+clear glass t=6mm

1312

1055

スチール丸鋼 φ16mm 錆止め塗装
round steel φ16mm
anti-corrosive paint finish

ラーチ合板 t=12mm 突きつけ
サンドペーパー掛け ワックス仕上げ
larch plywood t=12mm butting
sandpapered texture, wax finish

φ25

PIN φ19

PL-16

PL2-9

50 10 50

10 50 10 50

φ16

寝室
bed room

ブレース:スチール丸鋼 φ16mm 錆止め塗装
brace: round steel φ16mm anti-corrosive paint finish

窓枠:
米栂 見付け20mm OP
window frame:
western hemlock
facing-20mm
oil paint finish

20

110

φ16

PIN φ19

PL-9

φ16

PL-9

30

70.5

50

平面
plan

100

200

1290

進化式防水コンクリート打放し
exposed concrete
(evolving waterproof)

張弦梁詳細図
string beam detail S:1/10

ミニ・ハウス
Mini House

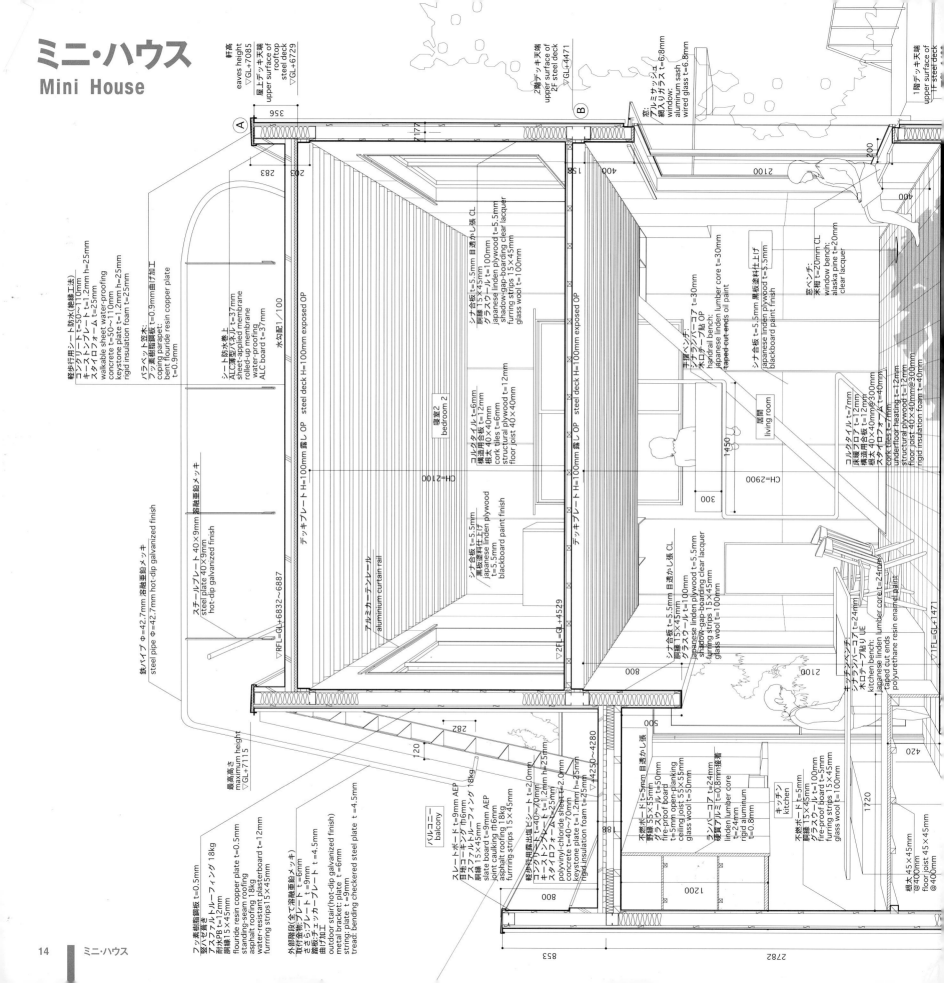

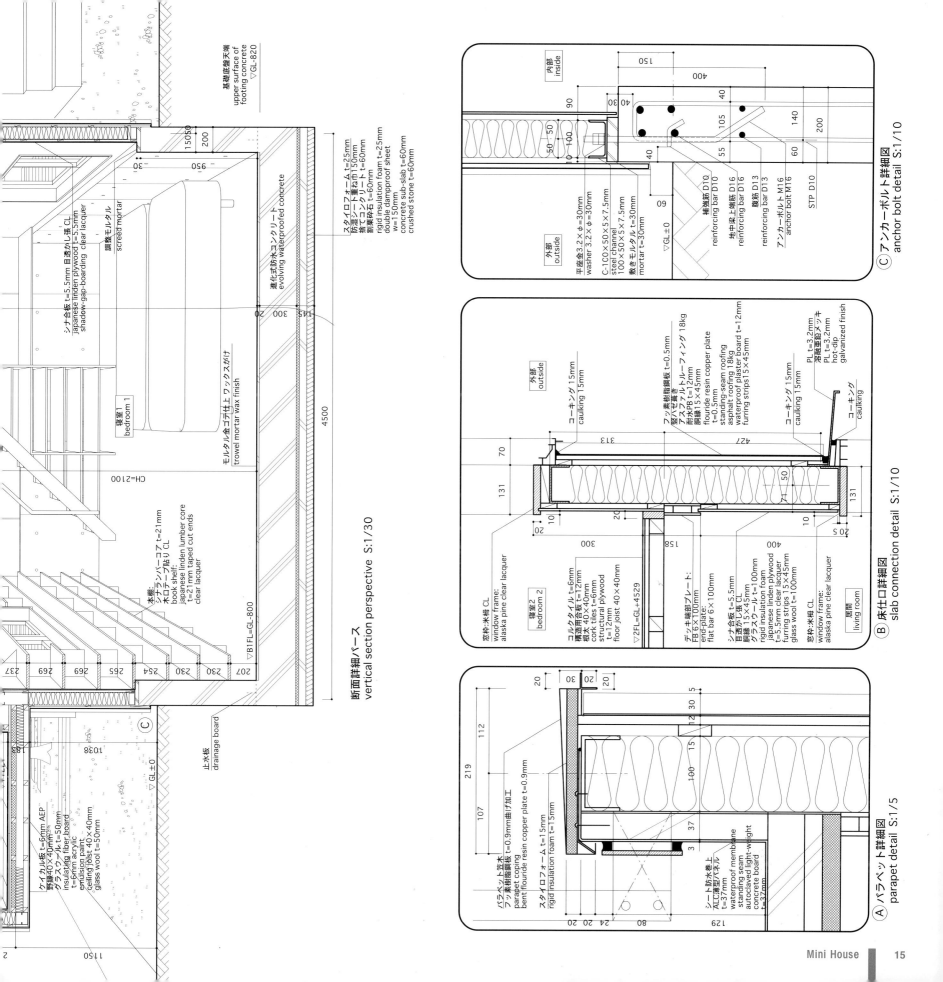

断面詳細パース
vertical section perspective S:1/30

Ⓐ パラペット詳細図 parapet detail S:1/5

Ⓑ 床仕口詳細図 slab connection detail S:1/10

Ⓒ アンカーボルト詳細図 anchor bolt detail S:1/10

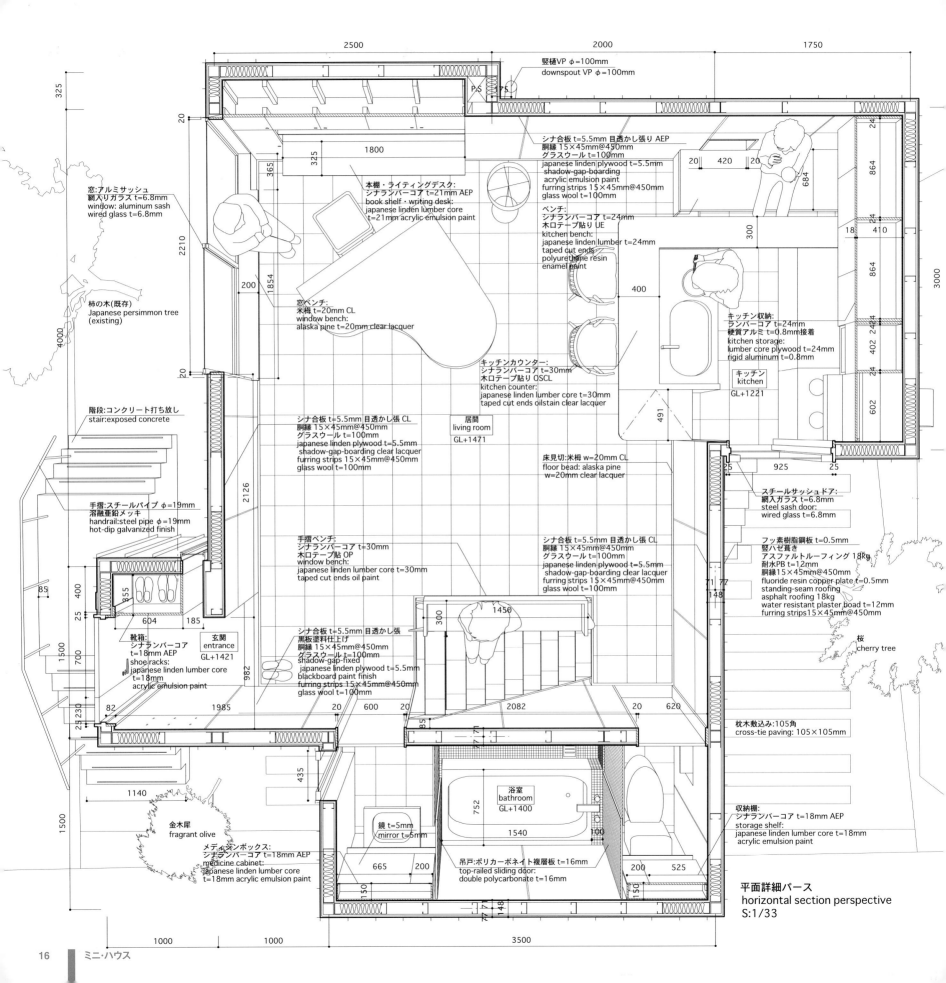

2500　　　2000　　　1750

325

20

325　1800

365

325

竪樋VP φ=100mm
downspout VP φ=100mm

P.S　175

シナ合板 t=5.5mm 目透かし張り AEP
胴縁 15×45mm@450mm
グラスウール t=100mm
japanese linden plywood t=5.5mm
shadow-gap-boarding
acrylic emulsion paint
furring strips 15×45mm@450mm
glass wool t=100mm

20　420　20

864
684

窓:アルミサッシュ
網入りガラス t=6.8mm
window: aluminum sash
wired glass t=6.8mm

2210

200

1854

本棚・ライティングデスク:
シナランバーコア t=21mm AEP
book shelf・writing desk:
japanese linden lumber core
t=21mm acrylic emulsion paint

24
24

18　410

24

ベンチ:
シナランバーコア t=24mm
木口テープ貼り UE
kitchen bench:
japanese linden lumber t=24mm
taped cut ends
polyurethane resin
enamel paint

300

864

4000

柿の木(既存)
Japanese persimmon tree
(existing)

20

窓ベンチ:
米栂 t=20mm CL
window bench:
alaska pine t=20mm clear lacquer

400

3000

キッチンカウンター:
シナランバーコア t=30mm
木口テープ貼り OSCL
kitchen counter:
japanese linden lumber core t=30mm
taped cut ends oilstain clear lacquer

491

キッチン収納:
ランバーコア t=24mm
硬質アルミ t=0.8mm接着
kitchen storage:
lumber core plywood t=24mm
rigid aluminum t=0.8mm

402

24

602

キッチン
kitchen
GL+1221

階段:コンクリート打ち放し
stair:exposed concrete

2126

シナ合板 t=5.5mm 目透かし張 CL
胴縁 15×45mm@450mm
グラスウール t=100mm
japanese linden plywood t=5.5mm
shadow-gap-boarding clear lacquer
furring strips 15×45mm@450mm
glass wool t=100mm

居間
living room
GL+1471

床見切:米栂 w=20mm CL
floor bead: alaska pine
w=20mm clear lacquer

25　925　25

スチールサッシュドア:
網入ガラス t=6.8mm
steel sash door:
wired glass t=6.8mm

手摺:スチールパイプ φ=19mm
溶融亜鉛メッキ
handrail:steel pipe φ=19mm
hot-dip galvanized finish

85

400
25

355

手摺ベンチ:
シナランバーコア t=30mm
木口テープ貼 OP
window bench:
japanese linden lumber core t=30mm
taped cut ends oil paint

シナ合板 t=5.5mm 目透かし張 CL
胴縁 15×45mm@450mm
グラスウール t=100mm
japanese linden plywood t=5.5mm
shadow-gap-boarding clear lacquer
furring strips 15×45mm@450mm
glass wool t=100mm

フッ素樹脂鋼板 t=0.5mm
竪ハゼ葺き
アスファルトルーフィング 18kg
耐水PB t=12mm
胴縁15×45mm@450mm
fluoride resin copper plate t=0.5mm
standing-seam roofing
asphalt roofing 18kg
water resistant plaster board t=12mm
furring strips15×45mm@450mm

71　77
148

1500

604　185

靴箱:
シナランバーコア
t=18mm AEP
shoe racks:
japanese linden lumber core
t=18mm
acrylic emulsion paint

700

982

玄関
entrance
GL+1421

シナ合板 t=5.5mm 目透かし張
黒板塗料仕上げ
胴縁 15×45mm@450mm
グラスウール t=100mm
shadow-gap-fixed
japanese linden plywood t=5.5mm
blackboard paint finish
furring strips 15×45mm@450mm
glass wool t=100mm

300

1450

85

桜
cherry tree

枕木敷込み:105角
cross-tie paving: 105×105mm

1500

25　230

25

82　1985　20　600　20

2082　20　620

1140

435

金木犀
fragrant olive

752

浴室
bathroom
GL+1400

1540

100

収納棚:
シナランバーコア t=18mm AEP
storage shelf:
japanese linden lumber core t=18mm
acrylic emulsion paint

鏡 t=5mm
mirror t=5mm

665　200

メディシンボックス:
シナランバーコア t=18mm AEP
medicine cabinet:
Japanese linden lumber core
t=18mm acrylic emulsion paint

吊戸:ポリカーボネイト複層板 t=16mm
top-railed sliding door:
double polycarbonate t=16mm

200　525

150

150

平面詳細パース
horizontal section perspective
S:1/33

1000　1000　3500

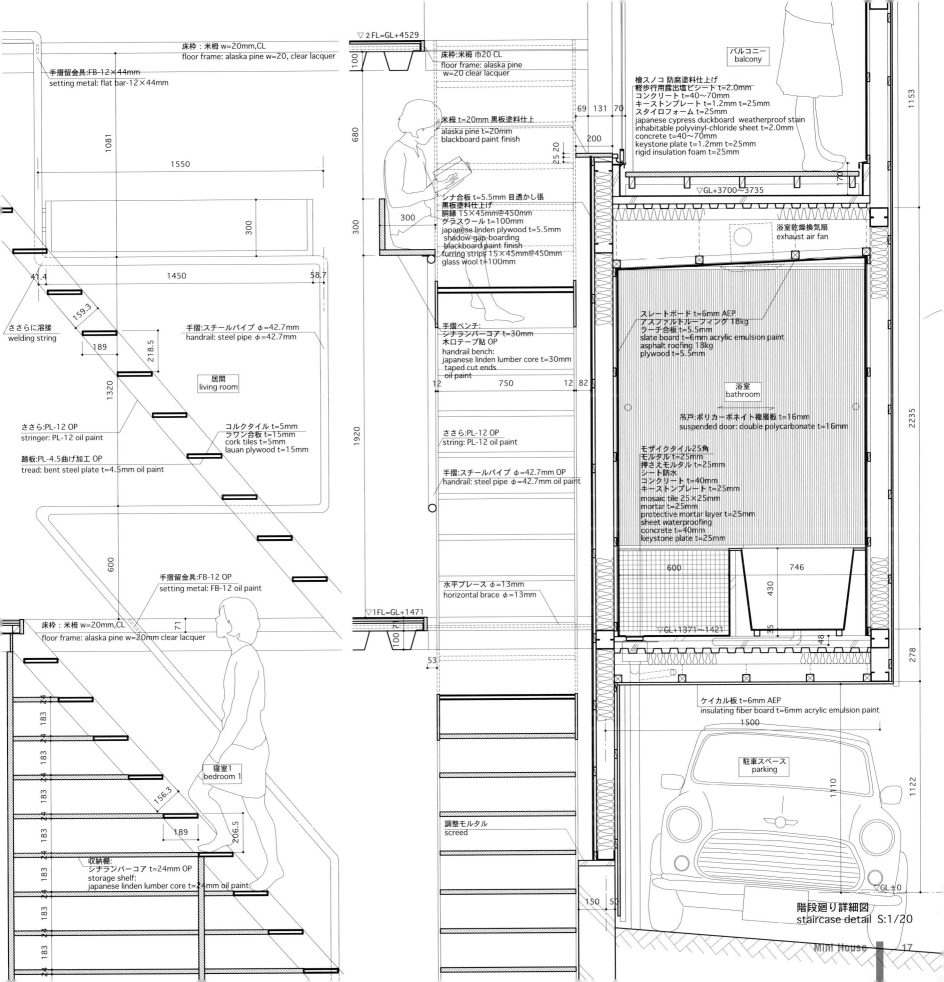

手摺留金具:FB-12×44mm
setting metal: flat bar-12×44mm

床枠：米栂 w=20mm,CL
floor frame: alaska pine w=20, clear lacquer

1081

1550

300

1450

41.4

159.3

189

218.5

58.7

ささらに溶接
welding string

1320

居間
living room

手摺:スチールパイプ φ=42.7mm
handrail: steel pipe φ=42.7mm

ささら:PL-12 OP
stringer: PL-12 oil paint

600

踏板:PL-4.5曲げ加工 OP
tread: bent steel plate t=4.5mm oil paint

コルクタイル t=5mm
ラワン合板 t=15mm
cork tiles t=5mm
lauan plywood t=15mm

手摺留金具:FB-12 OP
setting metal: FB-12 oil paint

床枠：米栂 w=20mm,CL
floor frame: alaska pine w=20mm clear lacquer

71

183
24
183
24
183
24
183
24
183
24
183

寝室1
bedroom 1

156.3

189

206.5

収納棚：
シナランバーコア t=24mm OP
storage shelf:
japanese linden lumber core t=24mm oil paint

▽2FL=GL+4529

100

床枠:米栂 巾20 CL
floor frame: alaska pine
w=20 clear lacquer

680

米栂 t=20mm 黒板塗料仕上
alaska pine t=20mm
blackboard paint finish

300

25 20

300

シナ合板 t=5.5mm 目透かし張
黒板塗料仕上げ
胴縁 T5×45mm@450mm
グラスウール t=100mm
japanese linden plywood t=5.5mm
shadow-gap-boarding
blackboard paint finish
furring strips 15×45mm@450mm
glass wool t=100mm

手摺ベンチ:
シナランバーコア t=30mm
木口テープ貼 OP
handrail bench:
japanese linden lumber core t=30mm
taped cut ends
oil paint

12   750   12 82

ささら:PL-12 OP
string: PL-12 oil paint

手摺:スチールパイプ φ=42.7mm OP
handrail: steel pipe φ=42.7mm oil paint

1920

水平ブレース φ=13mm
horizontal brace φ=13mm

▽1FL=GL+1471

100 7

53

調整モルタル
screed

150 50

69 131 70

200

バルコニー
balcony

1153

檜スノコ 防腐塗料仕上げ
軽歩行用露出塩ビシート t=2.0mm
コンクリート t=40～70mm
キーストンプレート t=1.2mm t=25mm
スタイロフォーム t=25mm
japanese cypress duckboard weatherproof stain
inhabitable polyvinyl-chloride sheet t=2.0mm
concrete t=40～70mm
keystone plate t=1.2mm t=25mm
rigid insulation foam t=25mm

▽GL+3700～3735

170

浴室乾燥換気扇
exhaust air fan

スレートボード t=6mm AEP
アスファルトルーフィング 18kg
ラーチ合板 t=5.5mm
slate board t=6mm acrylic emulsion paint
asphalt roofing 18kg
plywood t=5.5mm

浴室
bathroom

吊戸:ポリカーボネイト複層板 t=16mm
suspended door: double polycarbonate t=16mm

モザイクタイル25角
モルタル t=25mm
押さえモルタル t=25mm
シート防水
コンクリート t=40mm
キーストンプレート t=25mm
mosaic tile 25×25mm
mortar t=25mm
protective mortar layer t=25mm
sheet waterproofing
concrete t=40mm
keystone plate t=25mm

600

746

430

35

48

▽GL+1371～1421

278

ケイカル板 t=6mm AEP
insulating fiber board t=6mm acrylic emulsion paint

1500

駐車スペース
parking

1710

1122

▽GL±0

階段廻り詳細図
staircase detail S:1/20

2235

川西町コテージB
Kawanishi Camping Cottage B

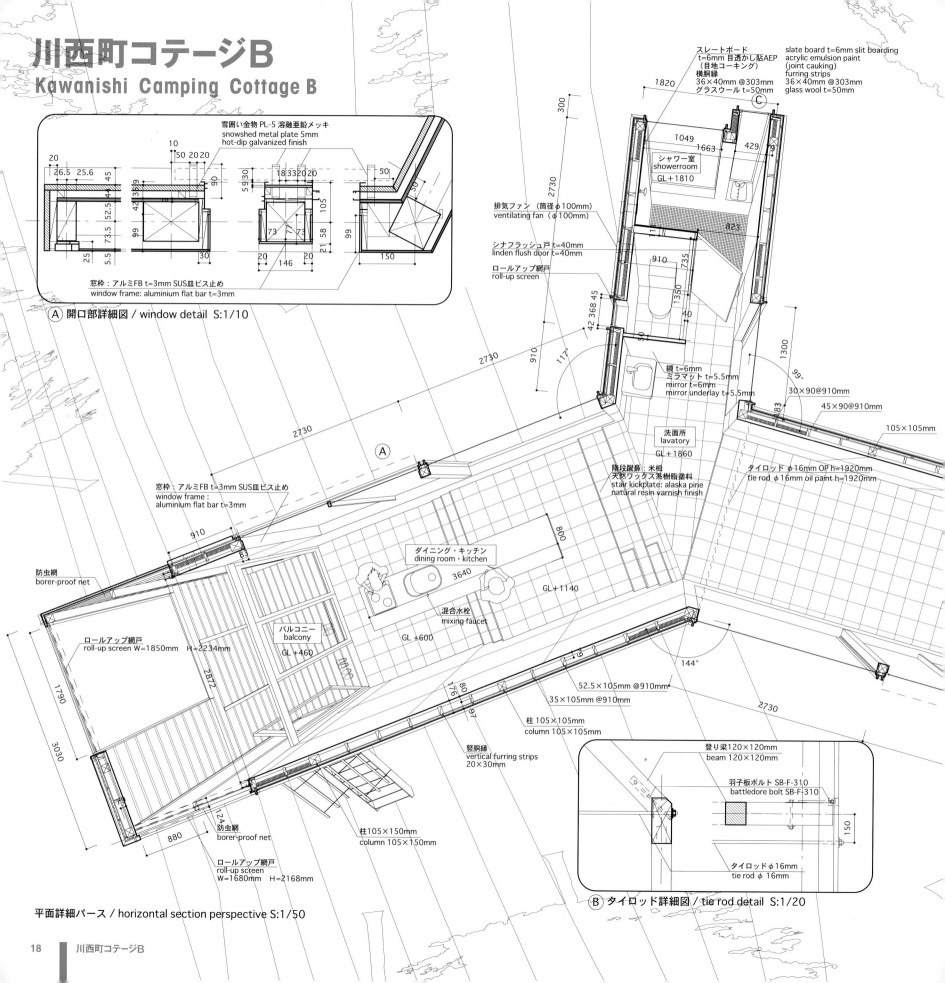

雪囲い金物 PL-5 溶融亜鉛メッキ
snowshed metal plate 5mm
hot-dip galvanized finish

窓枠：アルミ FB t=3mm SUS皿ビス止め
window frame: aluminium flat bar t=3mm

Ⓐ 開口部詳細図 / window detail S:1/10

スレートボード
t=6mm 目透かし貼AEP
（目地コーキング）
横胴縁
36×40mm @303mm
グラスウール t=50mm

slate board t=6mm slit boarding
acrylic emulsion paint
(joint cauking)
furring strips
36×40mm @303mm
glass wool t=50mm

シャワー室
showerroom
GL＋1810

排気ファン（筒径φ100mm）
ventilating fan（φ100mm）

シナフラッシュ戸 t=40mm
linden flush door t=40mm

ロールアップ網戸
roll-up screen

鏡 t=6mm
ミラマット t=5.5mm
mirror t=6mm
mirror underlay t=5.5mm

洗面所
lavatory
GL＋1860

階段蹴鼻：米栂
天然ワックス系樹脂塗料
stair kickplate: alaska pine
natural resin varnish finish

30×90@910mm
45×90@910mm

105×105mm

タイロッド φ16mm OP h=1920mm
tie rod φ16mm oil paint h=1920mm

窓枠：アルミ FB t=3mm SUS皿ビス止め
window frame :
aluminium flat bar t=3mm

防虫網
borer-proof net

ロールアップ網戸
roll-up screen W=1850mm H=2234mm

ダイニング・キッチン
dining room・kitchen

バルコニー
balcony
GL＋460

混合水栓
mixing faucet

GL＋600

GL＋1140

52.5×105mm @910mm
35×105mm @910mm

柱 105×105mm
column 105×105mm

竪胴縁
vertical furring strips
20×30mm

防虫網
borer-proof net

柱105×150mm
column 105×150mm

ロールアップ網戸
roll-up screen
W=1680mm H=2168mm

平面詳細パース / horizontal section perspective S:1/50

登り梁120×120mm
beam 120×120mm

羽子板ボルト SB-F-310
battledore bolt SB-F-310

タイロッド φ16mm
tie rod φ16mm

Ⓑ タイロッド詳細図 / tie rod detail S:1/20

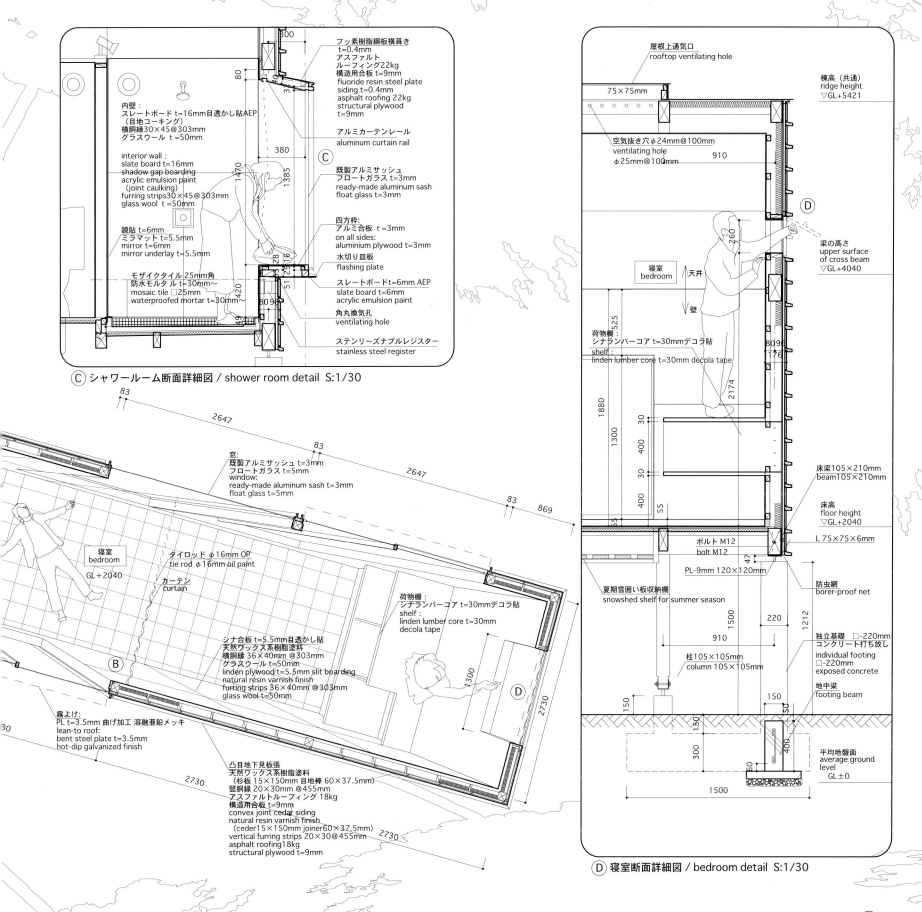

フッ素樹脂鋼板横葺き
t=0.4mm
アスファルト
ルーフィング22kg
構造用合板 t=9mm
fluoride resin steel plate
siding t=0.4mm
asphalt roofing 22kg
structural plywood
t=9mm

アルミカーテンレール
aluminum curtain rail

既製アルミサッシュ
フロートガラス t=3mm
ready-made aluminum sash
float glass t=3mm

四方枠:
アルミ合板 t=3mm
on all sides:
aluminium plywood t=3mm

水切り皿板
flashing plate

スレートボードt=6mm AEP
slate board t=6mm
acrylic emulsion paint

角丸換気孔
ventilating hole

ステンリーズナブルレジスター
stainless steel register

内壁:
スレートボード t=16mm目透かし貼AEP
(目地コーキング)
横胴縁30×45@303mm
グラスウール t=50mm

interior wall :
slate board t=16mm
shadow gap boarding
acrylic emulsion paint
(joint caulking)
furring strips30×45@303mm
glass wool t=50mm

鏡貼 t=6mm
ミラマット t=5.5mm
mirror t=6mm
mirror underlay t=5.5mm

モザイクタイル 25mm角
防水モルタル t=30mm〜
mosaic tile □25mm
waterproofed mortar t=30mm〜

C シャワールーム断面詳細図 / shower room detail S:1/30

窓:
既製アルミサッシュ t=3mm
フロートガラス t=5mm
window:
ready-made aluminum sash t=3mm
float glass t=5mm

タイロッド φ16mm OP
tie rod φ16mm oil paint

カーテン
curtain

寝室
bedroom
GL+2040

霧よけ:
PL t=3.5mm 曲げ加工 溶融亜鉛メッキ
lean-to roof:
bent steel plate t=3.5mm
hot-dip galvanized finish

シナ合板 t=5.5mm目透かし貼
天然ワックス系樹脂塗料
横胴縁 36×40mm @303mm
グラスウール t=50mm
linden plywood t=5.5mm slit boarding
natural resin varnish finish
furring strips 36×40mm @303mm
glass wool t=50mm

荷物棚:
シナランバーコア t=30mmデコラ貼
shelf :
linden lumber core t=30mm
decola tape

凸目地下見板張
天然ワックス系樹脂塗料
(杉板 15×150mm 目地棒 60×37.5mm)
竪胴縁 20×30mm @455mm
アスファルトルーフィング 18kg
構造用合板 t=9mm
convex joint cedar siding
natural resin varnish finish
(ceder15×150mm joiner60×37.5mm)
vertical furring strips 20×30@455mm
asphalt roofing18kg
structural plywood t=9mm

屋根上通気口
rooftop ventilating hole

棟高（共通）
ridge height
▽GL+5421

空気抜き穴φ24mm@100mm
ventilating hole
φ25mm@100mm

寝室
bedroom

天井
壁

荷物棚:
シナランバーコア t=30mmデコラ貼
shelf :
linden lumber core t=30mm decola tape

梁の高さ
upper surface
of cross beam
▽GL+4040

床梁105×210mm
beam105×210mm

床高
floor height
▽GL+2040

L 75×75×6mm

ボルト M12
bolt M12

PL-9mm 120×120mm

防虫網
borer-proof net

夏期雪囲い板収納棚
snowshed shelf for summer season

柱105×105mm
column 105×105mm

独立基礎 □-220mm
コンクリート打ち放し
individual footing
□-220mm
exposed concrete

地中梁
footing beam

平均地盤面
average ground
level
GL±0

D 寝室断面詳細図 / bedroom detail S:1/30

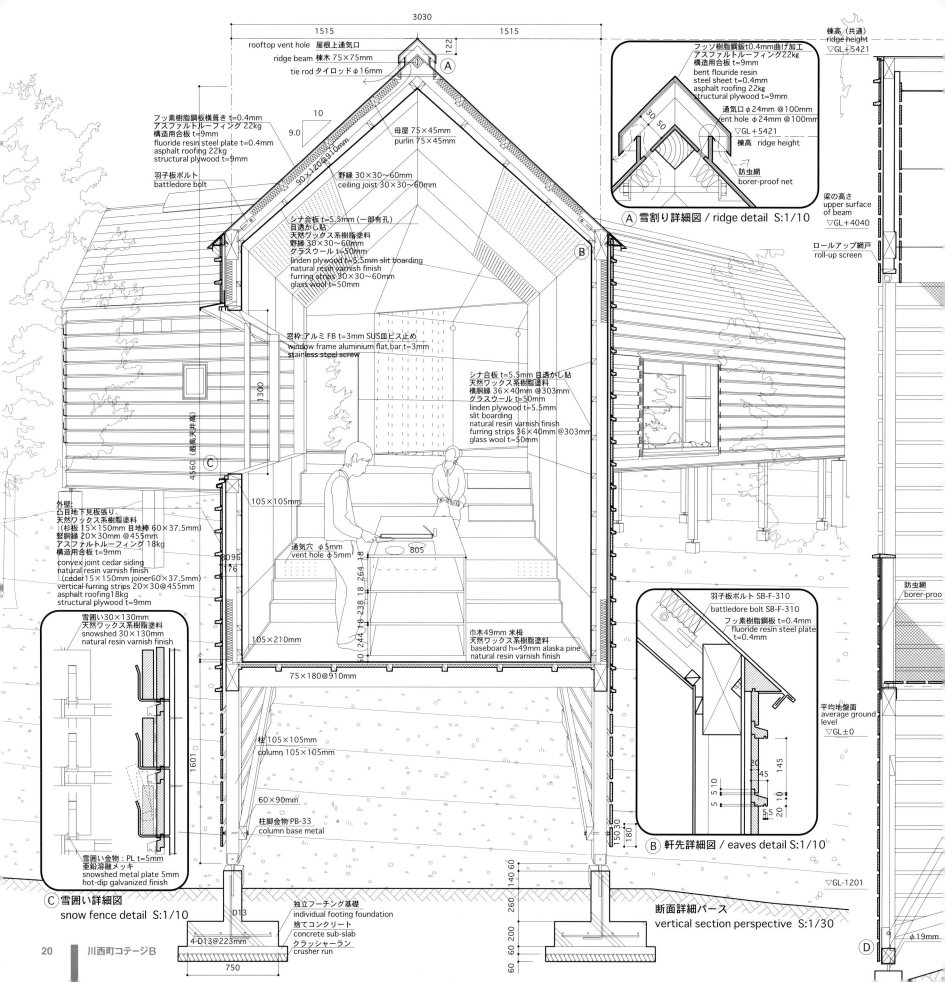

rooftop vent hole 屋根上通気口
ridge beam 棟木 75×75mm
tie rod タイロッドφ16mm

フッソ樹脂鋼鈑t0.4mm曲げ加工
アスファルトルーフィング22kg
構造用合板 t=9mm
bent flouride resin
steel sheet t=0.4mm
asphalt roofing 22kg
structural plywood t=9mm

通気口 φ24mm @100mm
vent hole φ24mm @100mm

▽GL＋5421
棟高　ridge height

防虫網
borer-proof net

A 雪割り詳細図 / ridge detail S:1/10

棟高（共通）
ridge height
▽GL＋5421

梁の高さ
upper surface
of beam
▽GL＋4040

フッ素樹脂鋼板横葺き t=0.4mm
アスファルトルーフィング 22kg
構造用合板 t=9mm
fluoride resin steel plate t=0.4mm
asphalt roofing 22kg
structural plywood t=9mm

羽子板ボルト
battledore bolt

母屋 75×45mm
purlin 75×45mm

野縁 30×30～60mm
ceiling joist 30×30～60mm

シナ合板 t=5.5mm（一部有孔）
目透かし貼
天然ワックス系樹脂塗料
野縁 30×30～60mm
グラスウール t=50mm
linden plywood t=5.5mm slit boarding
natural resin varnish finish
furring strips 30×30～60mm
glass wool t=50mm

ロールアップ網戸
roll-up screen

窓枠:アルミ FB t=3mm SUS皿ビス止め
window frame aluminium flat bar t=3mm
stainless steel screw

シナ合板 t=5.5mm 目透かし貼
天然ワックス系樹脂塗料
横胴縁 36×40mm @303mm
グラスウール t=50mm
linden plywood t=5.5mm
slit boarding
natural resin varnish finish
furring strips 36×40mm @303mm
glass wool t=50mm

外壁:
凸目地下見板張り
天然ワックス系樹脂塗料
（杉板 15×150mm 目地棒 60×37.5mm）
竪胴縁 20×30mm @455mm
アスファルトルーフィング 18kg
構造用合板 t=9mm
convex joint cedar siding
natural resin varnish finish
(ceder15×150mm joiner60×37.5mm)
vertical furring strips 20×30@455mm
asphalt roofing 18kg
structural plywood t=9mm

通気穴 φ5mm
vent hole φ5mm

巾木49mm 米栂
天然ワックス系樹脂塗料
baseboard h=49mm alaska pine
natural resin varnish finish

雪囲い30×130mm
天然ワックス系樹脂塗料
snowshed 30×130mm
natural resin varnish finish

雪囲い金物：PL t=5mm
亜鉛溶融メッキ
snowshed metal plate 5mm
hot-dip galvanized finish

C 雪囲い詳細図
snow fence detail S:1/10

柱 105×105mm
column 105×105mm

柱脚金物 PB-33
column base metal

独立フーチング基礎
individual footing foundation
捨てコンクリート
concrete sub-slab
クラッシャーラン
crusher run

4-D13@223mm
D13

羽子板ボルト SB-F-310
battledore bolt SB-F-310
フッ素樹脂鋼板 t=0.4mm
fluoride resin steel plate
t=0.4mm

B 軒先詳細図 / eaves detail S:1/10

平均地盤面
average ground
level
▽GL±0

防虫網
borer-proof net

断面詳細パース
vertical section perspective S:1/30

▽GL-1201

φ19mm

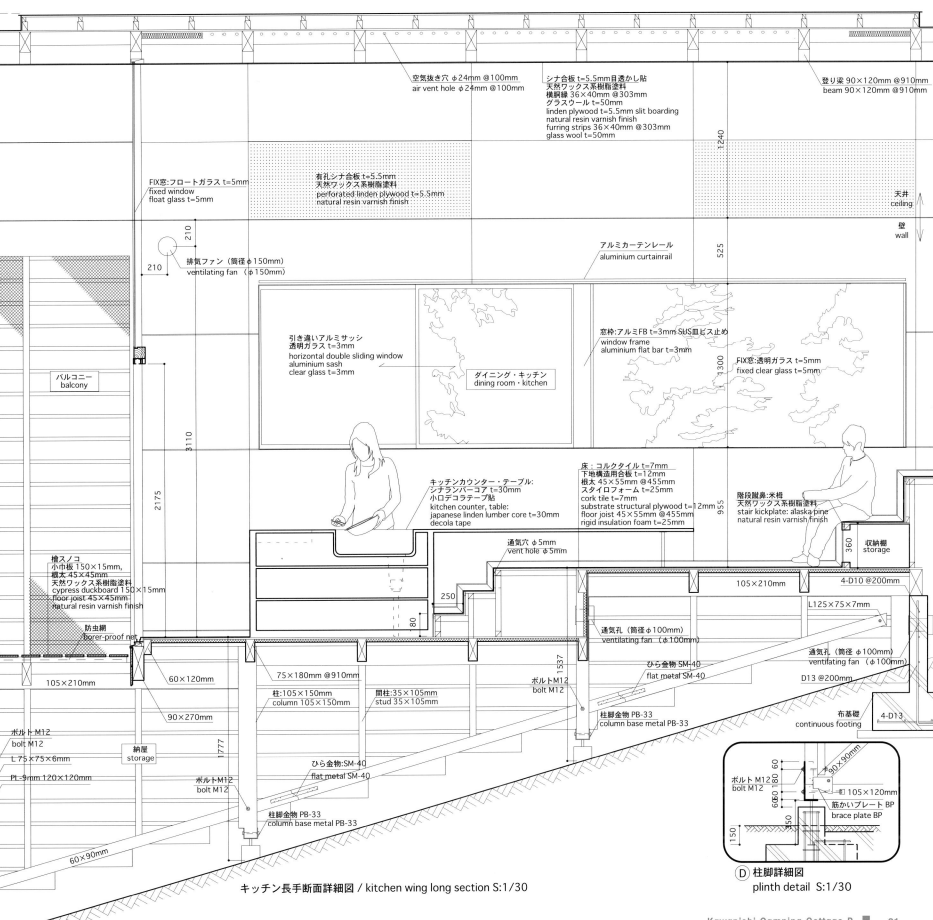

空気抜き穴 φ24mm @100mm
air vent hole φ24mm @100mm

シナ合板 t=5.5mm目透かし貼
天然ワックス系樹脂塗料
横胴縁 36×40mm @303mm
グラスウール t=50mm
linden plywood t=5.5mm slit boarding
natural resin varnish finish
furring strips 36×40mm @303mm
glass wool t=50mm

登り梁 90×120mm @910mm
beam 90×120mm @910mm

240

天井
ceiling

FIX窓:フロートガラス t=5mm
fixed window
float glass t=5mm

有孔シナ合板 t=5.5mm
天然ワックス系樹脂塗料
perforated linden plywood t=5.5mm
natural resin varnish finish

525

壁
wall

210

210

排気ファン（筒径 φ150mm）
ventilating fan （φ150mm）

アルミカーテンレール
aluminium curtainrail

窓枠:アルミFB t=3mm SUS皿ビス止め
window frame
aluminium flat bar t=3mm

引き違いアルミサッシ
透明ガラス t=3mm
horizontal double sliding window
aluminium sash
clear glass t=3mm

ダイニング・キッチン
dining room・kitchen

1300

FIX窓:透明ガラス t=5mm
fixed clear glass t=5mm

バルコニー
balcony

3110

床：コルクタイル t=7mm
下地構造用合板 t=12mm
根太 45×55mm @455mm
スタイロフォーム t=25mm
cork tile t=7mm
substrate structural plywood t=12mm
floor joist 45×55mm @455mm
rigid insulation foam t=25mm

階段蹴鼻:米栂
天然ワックス系樹脂塗料
stair kickplate: alaska pine
natural resin varnish finish

2175

キッチンカウンター・テーブル:
シナランバーコア t=30mm
小口デコラテープ貼
kitchen counter, table:
japanese linden lumber core t=30mm
decola tape

955

360

収納棚
storage

通気穴 φ5mm
vent hole φ5mm

檜スノコ
小巾板 150×15mm,
根太 45×45mm
天然ワックス系樹脂塗料
cypress duckboard 150×15mm
floor joist 45×45mm
natural resin varnish finish

250

80

105×210mm

4-D10 @200mm

L125×75×7mm

防虫網
borer-proof net

通気孔（筒径 φ100mm）
ventilating fan （φ100mm）

105×210mm

60×120mm

75×180mm @910mm

1537

通気孔（筒径 φ100mm）
ventilating fan （φ100mm）

ひら金物 SM-40
flat metal SM-40

D13 @200mm

90×270mm

柱:105×150mm
column 105×150mm

間柱:35×105mm
stud 35×105mm

ボルトM12
bolt M12

柱脚金物 PB-33
column base metal PB-33

ボルト M12
bolt M12

L 75×75×6mm

納屋
storage

1777

ひら金物:SM-40
flat metal SM-40

布基礎
continuous footing

4-D13

PL-9mm 120×120mm

柱脚金物 PB-33
column base metal PB-33

60×90mm

ボルトM12
bolt M12

90×90mm

ボルト M12
bolt M12

60
180
60

60
350

105×120mm

筋かいプレート BP
brace plate BP

150

Ⓓ 柱脚詳細図
plinth detail S:1/30

キッチン長手断面詳細図 / kitchen wing long section S:1/30

モカ・ハウス
Moca House

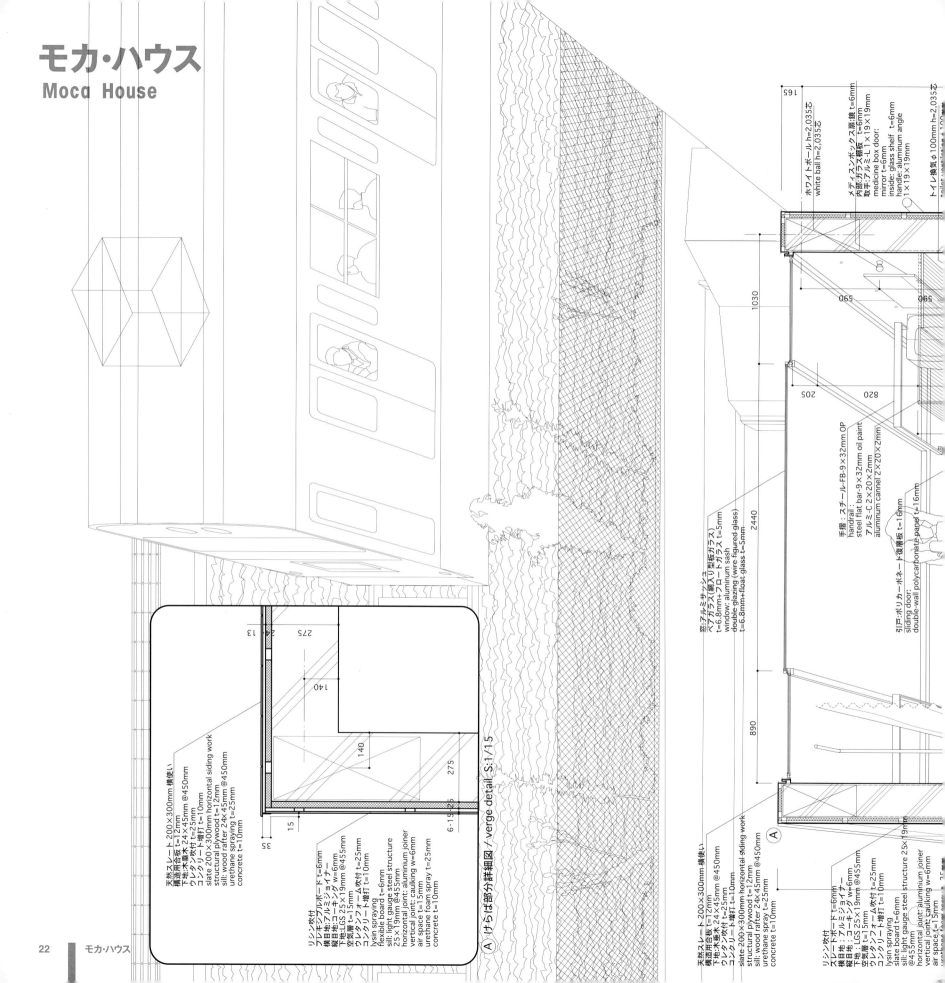

リシン吹付
フレキシブルボード t=6mm
横働目地:アルミジョイナー
縦目地:コーキング w=6mm
下地:LGS 25×19mm @455mm
空気層 t=15mm
ウレタンフォーム吹付 t=25mm
コンクリート増打 t=10mm
lysin spraying
flexible board t=6mm
sill: light gauge steel structure
25×19mm @455mm
horizontal joint: aluminium joiner
vertical joint: caulking w=6mm
air space t=15mm
urethane foam spray t=25mm
concrete t=10mm

天然スレート 200×300mm 横使い
構造用台板 t=12mm
下地:木垂木 24×45mm @450mm
ウレタン吹付 t=25mm
コンクリート増打 t=10mm
slate 200×300mm horizontal siding work
structural plywood t=12mm
sill: wood rafter 24×45mm @450mm
urethane spraying t=25mm
concrete t=10mm

Ⓐ けらば部分詳細図／verge detail S:1/15

天然スレート 200×300mm 横使い
構造用台板 t=12mm
下地:木垂木 24×45mm @450mm
ウレタン吹付 t=25mm
コンクリート増打 t=10mm
slate 200×300mm horizontal siding work
structural plywood t=12mm
sill: wood rafter 24×45mm @450mm
urethane spraying t=25mm
concrete t=10mm

リシン吹付
スレートボード t=6mm
構造用台板 t=12mm
横目地:アルミジョイナー
縦目地:コーキング w=6mm
下地:LGS 25×19mm @455mm
空気層 t=15mm
ウレタン吹付 t=25mm
コンクリート増打 t=10mm
lysin spraying
slate board t=6mm
sill: light gauge steel structure 25×19mm
@455mm
horizontal joint: aluminium joiner
vertical joint: caulking w=6mm
air space t=15mm

窓:アルミサッシュ
ペアガラス(網入り型板ガラス)
t=6.8mm+フロート板ガラス
t=5mm
window: aluminum sash
double glazing (wire figured glass)
t=6.8mm+float glass t=5mm

手摺:スチール FB-9×32mm OP
handrail :
steel flat bar-9×32mm oil paint
アルミ=C 2×20×2mm
aluminum cannel 2×20×2mm

引戸:ポリカーボネート複層板 t=16mm
sliding door:
double-wall polycarbonate paper t=16mm

ホワイトボール h=2,035芯
white ball h=2,035芯

メディスンボックス扉:鏡板 t=6mm
内部:ガラス棚板 t=6mm
取手:アルミ=L 1×19×19mm
medicine box door:
mirror t=6mm
inside: glass shelf t=6mm
handle: aluminum angle
1×19×19mm

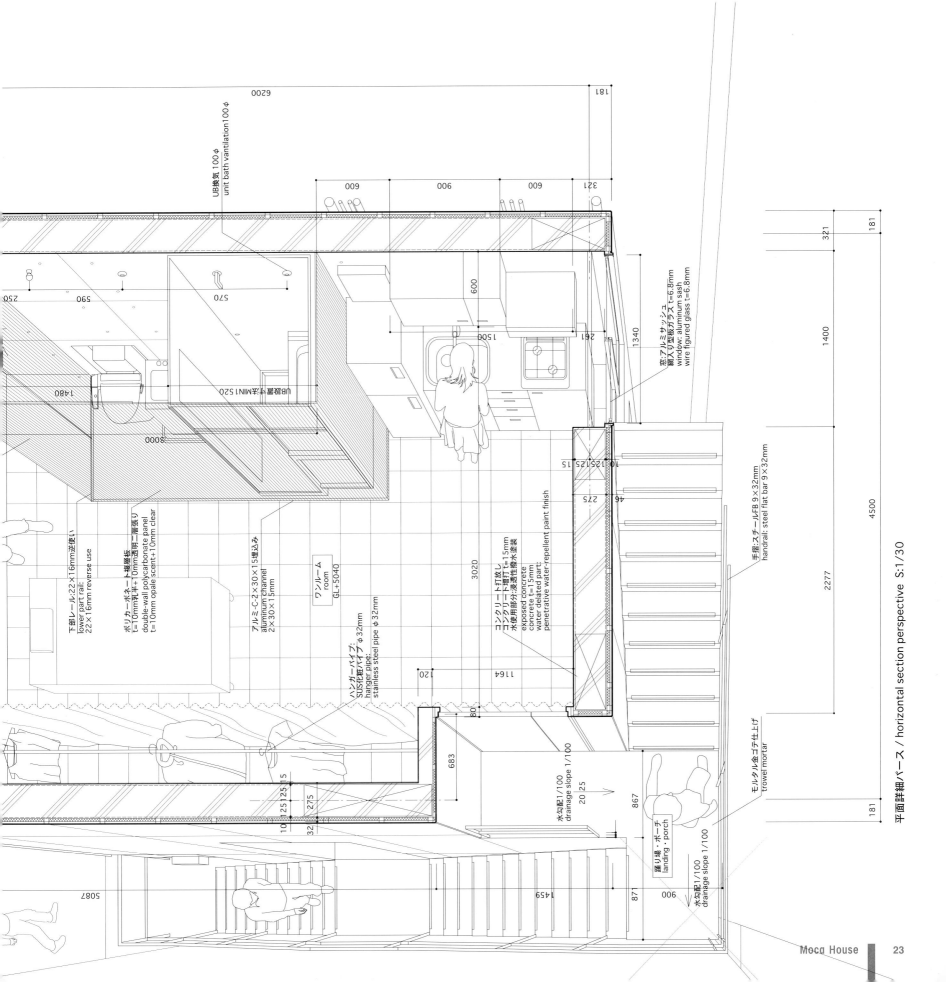

UB換気 100φ
unit bath vantilation 100 φ

6200

181

600
900
600
321

1340

600

1500

261

窓:アルミサッシュ
網入り型板ガラス t=6.8mm
window: aluminum sash
wire figured glass t=6.8mm

321

181

1400

UB浴室 寸法 MIN1 520

10 125125 15

275

46

4500

下部レール:22×16mm逆使い
lower part rail:
22×16mm reverse use

ポリカーボネート複層板
t=10mm乳半+10mm透明二層張り
double-wall polycarbonate panel
t=10mm opale scent+10mm clear

アルミ-C-2×30×15埋込み
aluminum channel
2×30×15mm

ワンルーム
room
GL+5040

ハンガーパイプ:
SUS化粧パイプ φ32mm
hanger pipe:
stainless steel pipe φ32mm

コンクリート打放し
コンクリート撥打ち t=15mm
水使用部分:浸透性撥水塗装
exposed concrete
concrete t=15mm
water delated part:
penetrative water-repellent paint finish

手摺:スチールFB 9×32mm
handrail: steel flat bar 9×32mm

2277

250
590
570

1480

3000

3020

1164

120

80

683

867

25 25 15

10

32

275

水勾配1/100
drainage slope 1/100

20 25

モルタル金ゴテ仕上げ
trowel mortar

181

踊り場・ポーチ
landing・porch

水勾配1/100
drainage slope 1/100

5087

踊り場1/100

1459

871

006

900

水勾配1/100
drainage slope 1/100

平面詳細パース / horizontal section perspective S:1/30

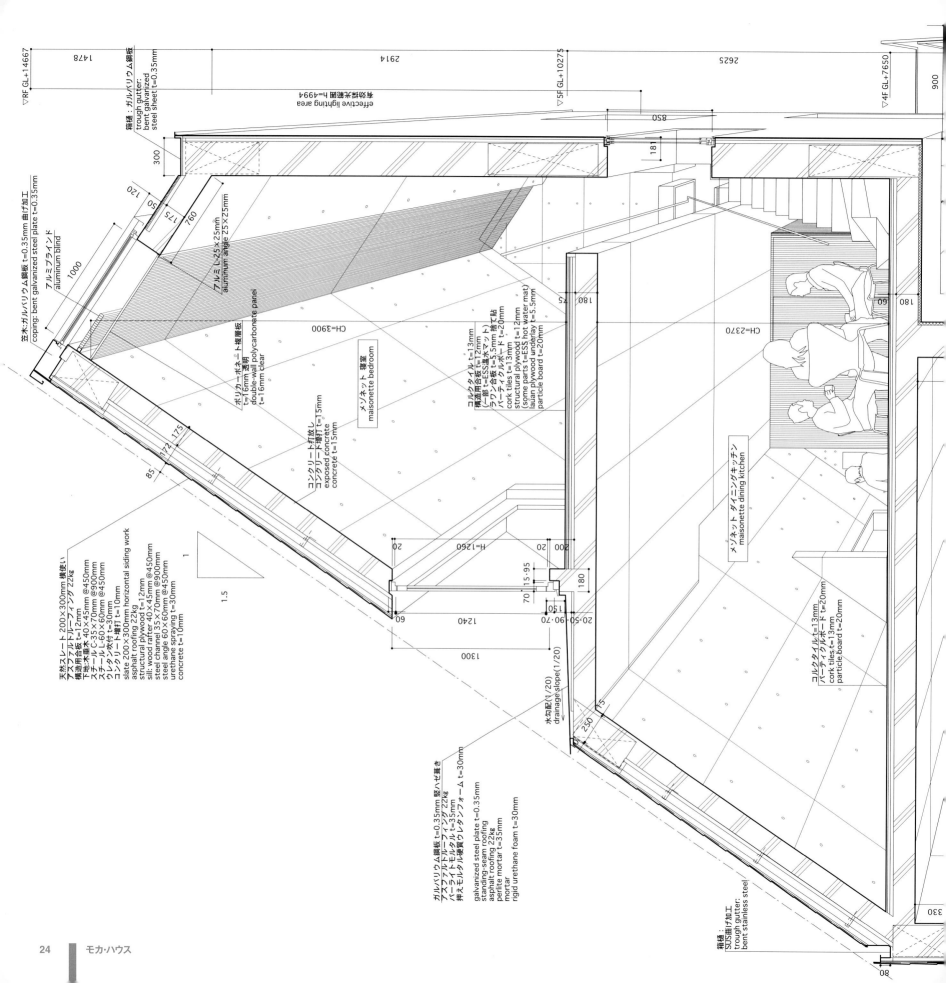

▽RF GL+14667

148

箱樋：ガルバリウム鋼板
trough gutter:
bent galvanized
steel sheet t=0.35mm

2914

effective lighting area
有効採光範囲 h=4994

▽5F GL+10275

2625

181

850

▽4F GL+7650

900

006

300

笠木：ガルバリウム鋼板 t=0.35mm 曲げ加工
coping: bent galvanized steel plate t=0.35mm

120
50
175
760

1000

アルミブラインド
aluminum blind

アルミ L-25×25mm
aluminum angle 25×25mm

ポリカーボネート複層板
t=16mm透明
double-wall polycarbonate panel
t=16mm clear

CH=3900

メゾネット 寝室
maisonette bedroom

コンクリート打放し
コンクリート増打ち t=15mm
exposed concrete
concrete t=15mm

コルクタイル t=13mm
（一部 t=ESS温水マット）
ラワン合板 t=5.5mm 捨て貼
パーティクルボード t=20mm
structural plywood t=12mm
(some parts t=ESS hot water mat)
lauan plywood underlay t=5.5mm
particle board t=20mm

180
25

CH=2370

メゾネット ダイニングキッチン
maisonette dining kitchen

天然スレート 200×300mm 横使い
アスファルトルーフィング 22kg
下地用合板 t=12mm
スチール C-35×45×70mm @450mm
スチール L-60×60mm @450mm
ウレタン吹付 t=30mm
コンクリート増打 t=10mm
slate 200×300mm horizontal siding work
asphalt roofing 22kg
structural plywood t=12mm
sill: wood rafter 40×45mm @450mm
steel channel 35×70mm @900mm
steel angle 60×60mm @450mm
urethane spraying t=30mm
concrete t=10mm

175
172
85

1

1.5

20
200
20
H=1260

70
15・95
180

60
1240
15・95
150
20・50・90・70

1300

250
15

水勾配(1/20)
drainage slope(1/20)

ガルバリウム鋼板 t=0.35mm 竪ハゼ葺き
アスファルトルーフィング 22kg
パーライトモルタル t=35mm
押えモルタル硬質ウレタンフォーム t=30mm
galvanized steel plate t=0.35mm
standing-seam roofing
asphalt roofing 22kg
perlite mortar t=35mm
mortar
rigid urethane foam t=30mm

コルクタイル t=13mm
パーティクルボード t=20mm
cork tiles t=13mm
particle board t=20mm

060

330

箱樋：
SUS曲げ加工
trough gutter:
bent stainless steel

08

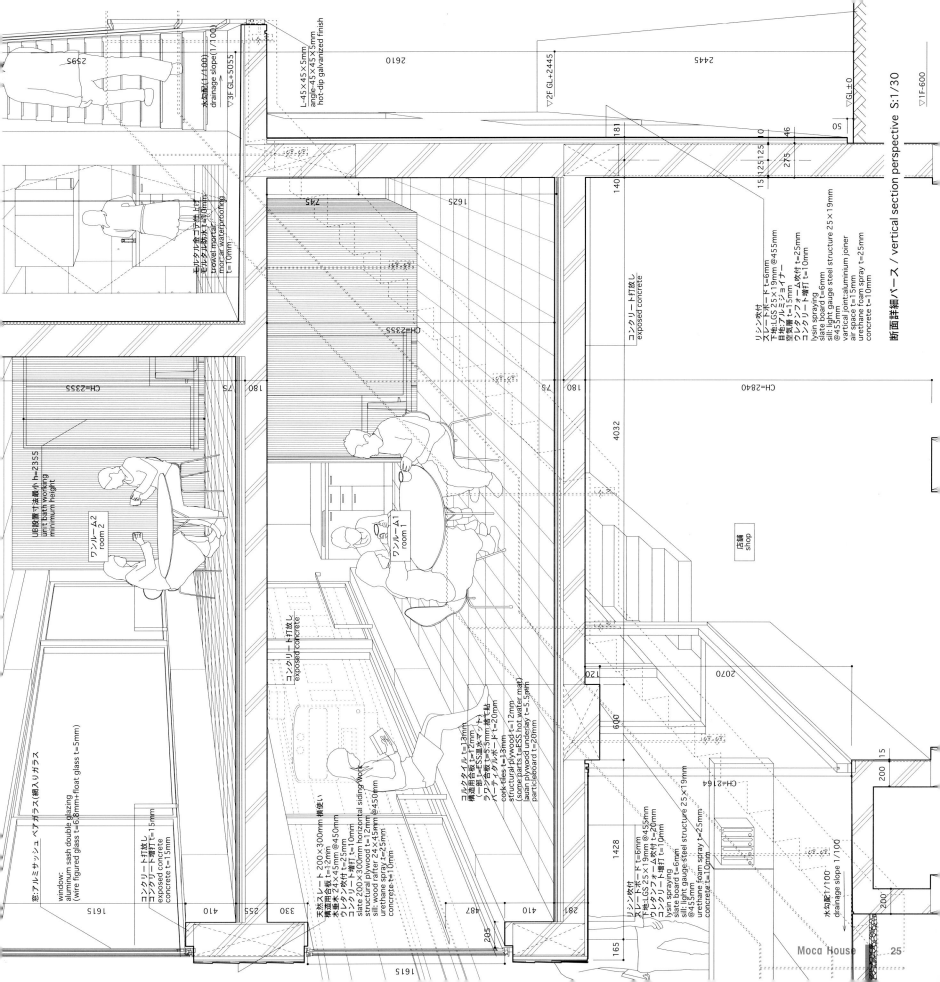

断面詳細パース / vertical section perspective　S:1/30

Moca House　25

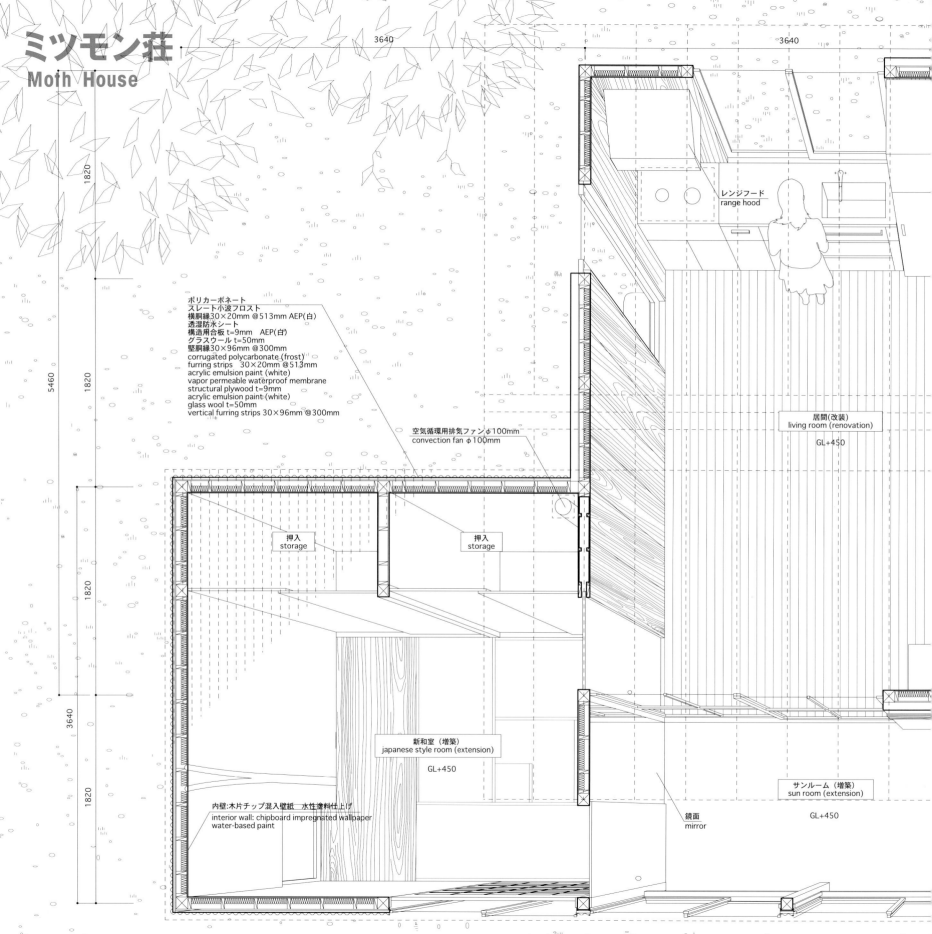

ミツモン荘
Moth House

3640　　　　3640

1820

5460

1820

1820

3640

1820

ポリカーボネート
スレート小波フロスト
横胴縁30×20mm @513mm AEP(白)
透湿防水シート
構造用合板 t=9mm　AEP(白)
グラスウール t=50mm
堅胴縁30×96mm @300mm
corrugated polycarbonate (frost)
furring strips　30×20mm @513mm
acrylic emulsion paint (white)
vapor permeable waterproof membrane
structural plywood t=9mm
acrylic emulsion paint (white)
glass wool t=50mm
vertical furring strips 30×96mm @300mm

空気循環用排気ファンφ100mm
convection fan φ100mm

レンジフード
range hood

押入
storage

押入
storage

居間(改装)
living room (renovation)

GL+450

新和室（増築）
japanese style room (extension)

GL+450

サンルーム（増築）
sun room (extension)

GL+450

内壁:木片チップ混入壁紙　水性塗料仕上げ
interior wall: chipboard impregnated wallpaper
water-based paint

鏡面
mirror

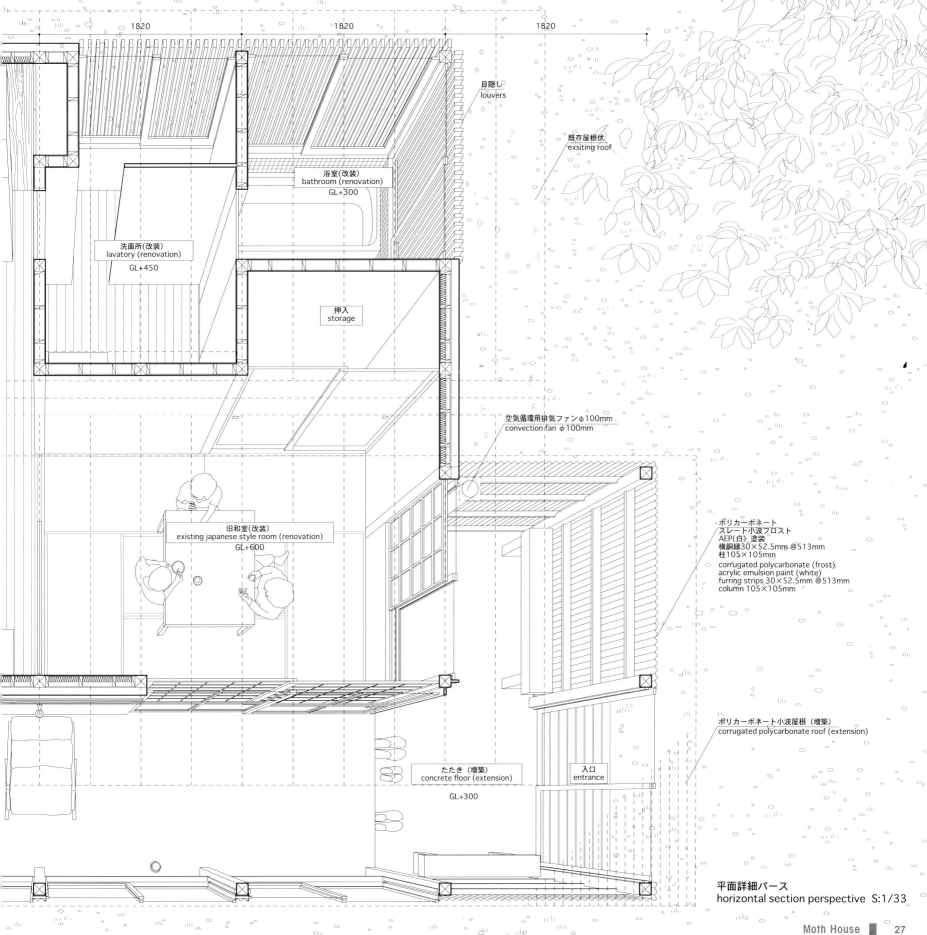

1820　1820　1820

目隠し
louvers

既存屋根伏
exsiting roof

浴室(改装)
bathroom (renovation)
GL+300

洗面所(改装)
lavatory (renovation)
GL+450

押入
storage

空気循環用排気ファンφ100mm
convection fan φ100mm

ポリカーボネート
スレート小波フロスト
AEP(白) 塗装
横胴縁30×52.5mm @513mm
柱105×105mm
corrugated polycarbonate (frost)
acrylic emulsion paint (white)
furring strips 30×52.5mm @513mm
column 105×105mm

旧和室(改装)
existing japanese style room (renovation)
GL+600

ポリカーボネート小波屋根（増築）
corrugated polycarbonate roof (extension)

たたき（増築）
concrete floor (extension)
GL+300

入口
entrance

平面詳細パース
horizontal section perspective S:1/33

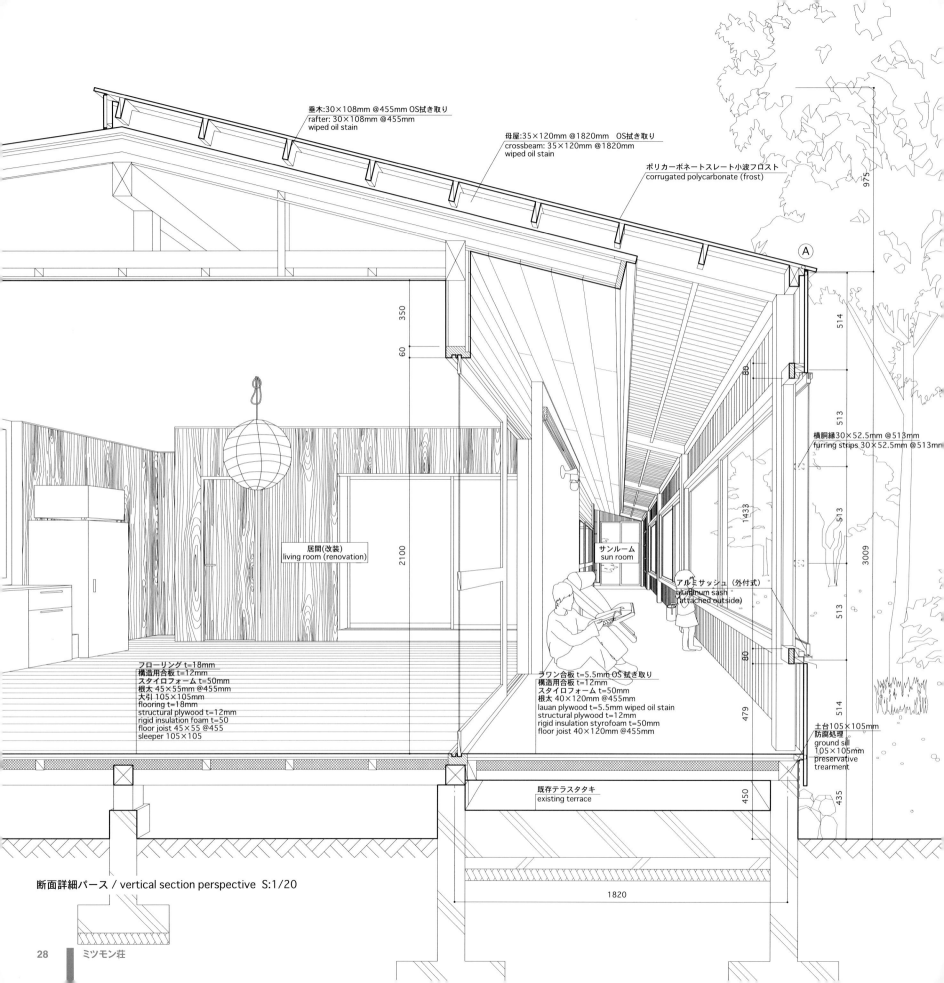

垂木:30×108mm @455mm OS拭き取り
rafter: 30×108mm @455mm
wiped oil stain

母屋:35×120mm @1820mm　OS拭き取り
crossbeam: 35×120mm @1820mm
wiped oil stain

ポリカーボネートスレート小波フロスト
corrugated polycarbonate (frost)

Ⓐ

975

350

60

横胴縁30×52.5mm @513mm
furring strips 30×52.5mm @513mm

513

80

513

2100

1433

3009

居間(改装)
living room (renovation)

サンルーム
sun room

513

アルミサッシュ（外付式）
aluminum sash
(attached outside)

80

フローリング t=18mm
構造用合板 t=12mm
スタイロフォーム t=50mm
根太 45×55mm @455mm
大引 105×105mm
flooring t=18mm
structural plywood t=12mm
rigid insulation foam t=50
floor joist 45×55 @455
sleeper 105×105

ラワン合板 t=5.5mm OS 拭き取り
構造用合板 t=12mm
スタイロフォーム t=50mm
根太 40×120mm @455mm
lauan plywood t=5.5mm wiped oil stain
structural plywood t=12mm
rigid insulation styrofoam t=50mm
floor joist 40×120mm @455mm

514

479

土台105×105mm
防腐処理
ground sill
105×105mm
preservative
trearment

514

既存テラスタタキ
existing terrace

450

435

断面詳細パース / vertical section perspective　S:1/20

1820

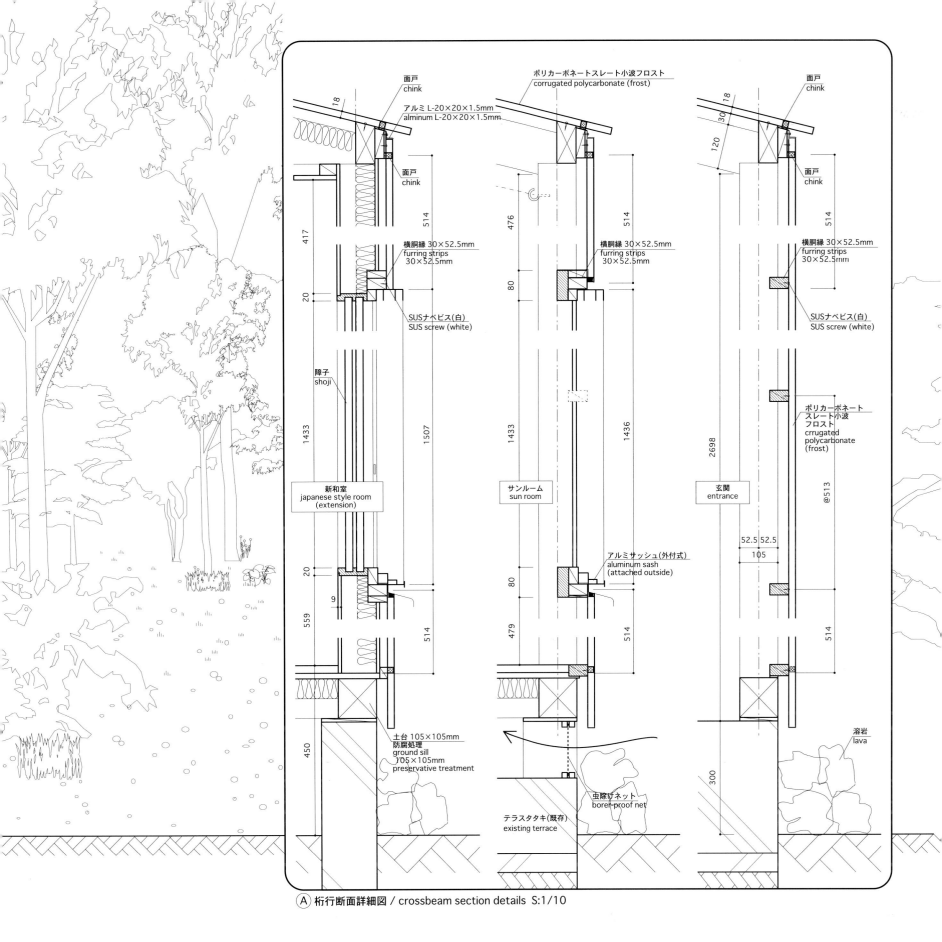

面戸
chink

ポリカーボネートスレート小波フロスト
corrugated polycarbonate (frost)

面戸
chink

アルミ L-20×20×1.5mm
aluminum L-20×20×1.5mm

面戸
chink

面戸
chink

18

18

30

120

417

514

476

514

514

横胴縁 30×52.5mm
furring strips
30×52.5mm

横胴縁 30×52.5mm
furring strips
30×52.5mm

横胴縁 30×52.5mm
furring strips
30×52.5mm

20

80

SUSナベビス(白)
SUS screw (white)

SUSナベビス(白)
SUS screw (white)

障子
shoji

1433

1507

1433

1436

2698

ポリカーボネート
スレート小波
フロスト
crrugated
polycarbonate
(frost)

新和室
japanese style room
(extension)

サンルーム
sun room

玄関
entrance

@513

52.5 52.5

105

20

80

アルミサッシュ(外付式)
aluminum sash
(attached outside)

9

559

514

479

514

514

土台 105×105mm
防腐処理
ground sill
105×105mm
preservative treatment

450

虫除けネット
borer-proof net

溶岩
lava

テラスタタキ(既存)
existing terrace

300

Ⓐ 桁行断面詳細図 / crossbeam section details S:1/10

ハウス・アサマ
House Asama

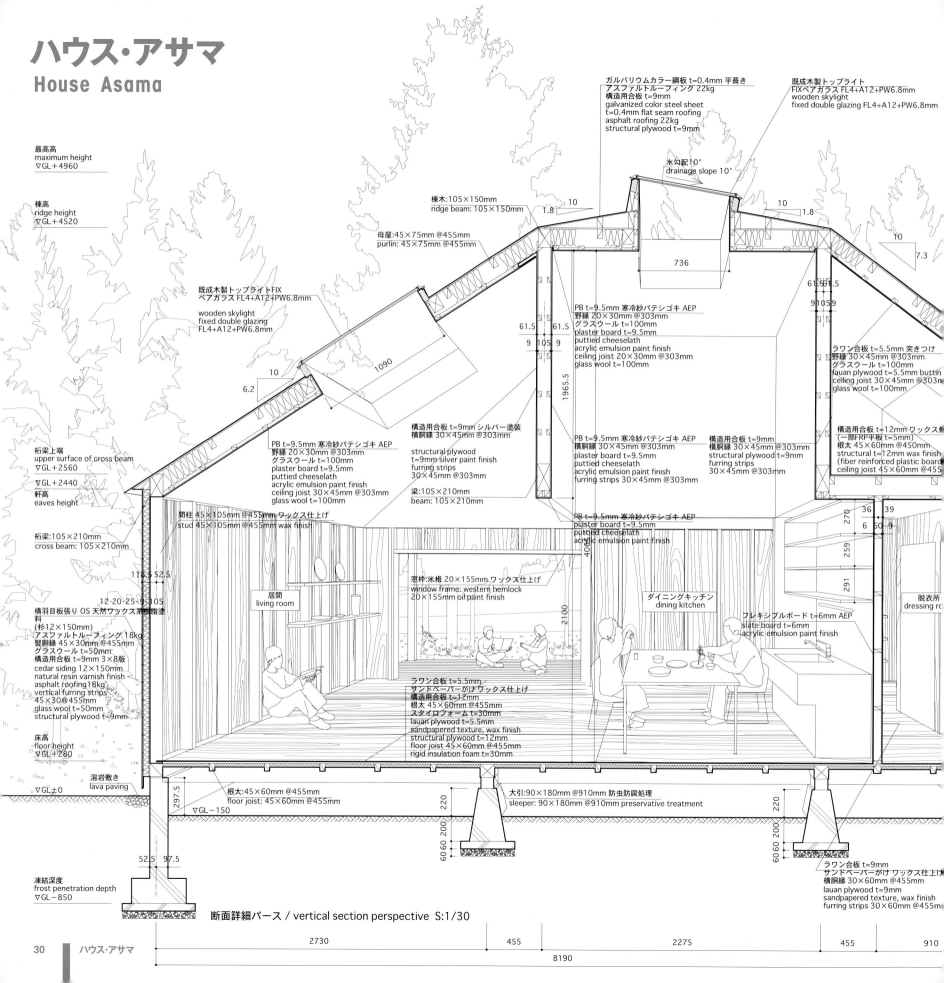

断面詳細パース / vertical section perspective S:1/30

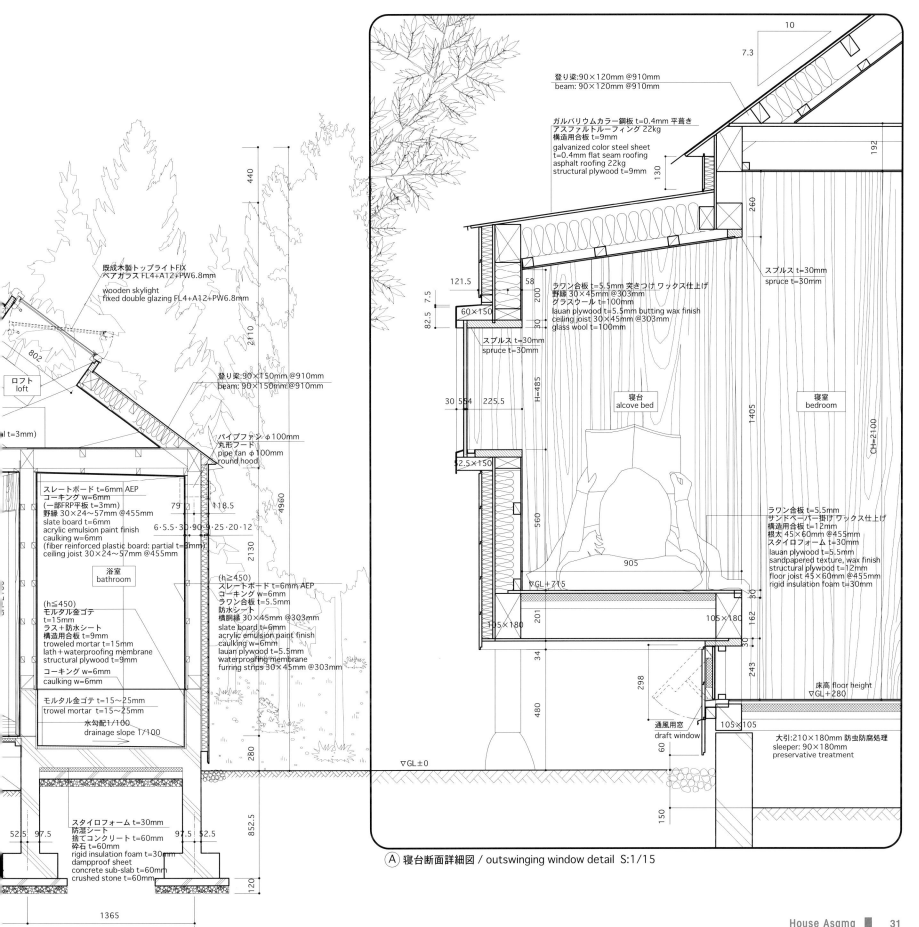

既成木製トップライトFIX
ベアガラス FL4+A12+PW6.8mm
wooden skylight
fixed double glazing FL4+A12+PW6.8mm

ロフト
loft

登り梁:90×150mm @910mm
beam: 90×150mm @910mm

パイプファン φ100mm
丸形フード
pipe fan φ100mm
round hood

スレートボード t=6mm AEP
コーキング w=6mm
(一部FRP平板 t=3mm)
野縁 30×24〜57mm @455mm
slate board t=6mm
acrylic emulsion paint finish
caulking w=6mm
(fiber reinforced plastic board: partial t=3mm)
ceiling joist 30×24〜57mm @455mm

浴室
bathroom

(h≦450)
モルタル金ゴテ
t=15mm
ラス＋防水シート
構造用合板 t=9mm
troweled mortar t=15mm
lath＋waterproofing membrane
structural plywood t=9mm

コーキング w=6mm
caulking w=6mm

モルタル金ゴテ t=15〜25mm
trowel mortar t=15〜25mm

水勾配1/100
drainage slope 1/100

スタイロフォーム t=30mm
防湿シート
捨てコンクリート t=60mm
砕石 t=60mm
rigid insulation foam t=30mm
dampproof sheet
concrete sub-slab t=60mm
crushed stone t=60mm

(h≧450)
スレートボード t=6mm AEP
コーキング w=6mm
ラワン合板 t=5.5mm
防水シート
横胴縁 30×45mm @303mm
slate board t=6mm
acrylic emulsion paint finish
caulking w=6mm
lauan plywood t=5.5mm
waterproofing membrane
furring strips 30×45mm @303mm

登り梁:90×120mm @910mm
beam: 90×120mm @910mm

ガルバリウムカラー鋼板 t=0.4mm 平葺き
アスファルトルーフィング 22kg
構造用合板 t=9mm
galvanized color steel sheet
t=0.4mm flat seam roofing
asphalt roofing 22kg
structural plywood t=9mm

スプルス t=30mm
spruce t=30mm

ラワン合板 t=5.5mm 突きつけ ワックス仕上げ
野縁 30×45mm @303mm
グラスウール t=100mm
lauan plywood t=5.5mm butting wax finish
ceiling joist 30×45mm @303mm
glass wool t=100mm

スプルス t=30mm
spruce t=30mm

寝台
alcove bed

寝室
bedroom

ラワン合板 t=5.5mm
サンドペーパー掛け ワックス仕上げ
構造用合板 t=12mm
根太 45×60mm @455mm
スタイロフォーム t=30mm
lauan plywood t=5.5mm
sandpapered texture, wax finish
structural plywood t=12mm
floor joist 45×60mm @455mm
rigid insulation foam t=30mm

▽GL＋715

通風用窓
draft window

▽GL±0

床高 floor height
▽GL＋280

大引:210×180mm 防虫防腐処理
sleeper: 90×180mm
preservative treatment

Ⓐ 寝台断面詳細図 / outswinging window detail S:1/15

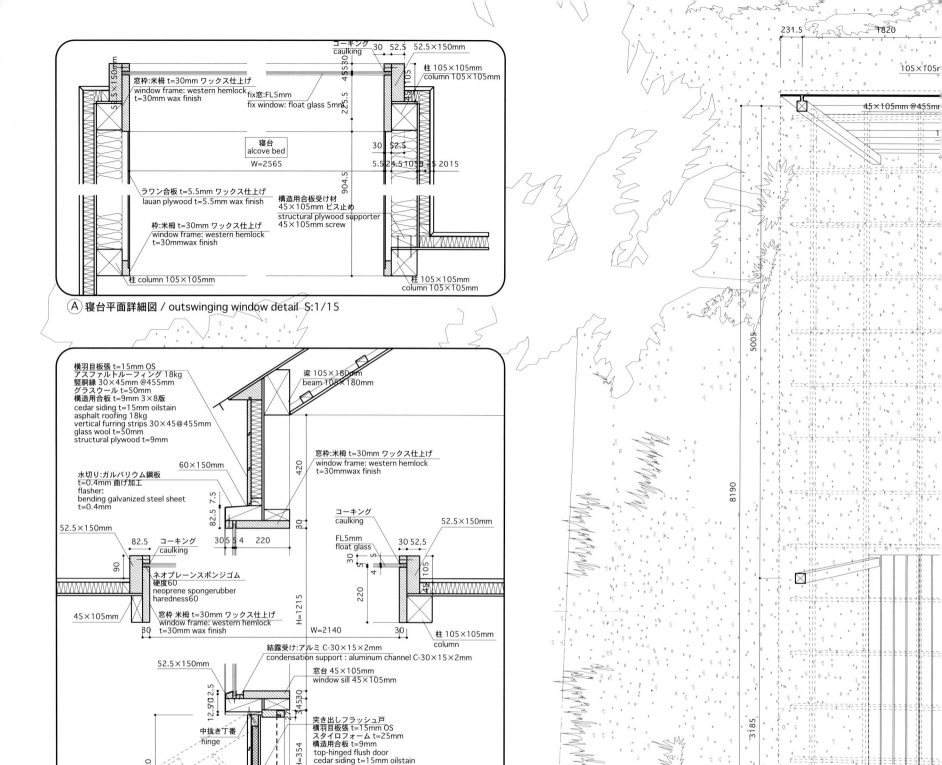

コーキング
caulking

窓枠:米栂 t=30mm ワックス仕上げ
window frame: western hemlock
t=30mm wax finish

30 52.5
52.5×150mm

fix窓:FL5mm
fix window: float glass 5mm

柱 105×105mm
column 105×105mm

45530

22.5

寝台
alcove bed
W=2565

30 52.5

5.5 24.5 105 45 2015

904.5

ラワン合板 t=5.5mm ワックス仕上げ
lauan plywood t=5.5mm wax finish

枠:米栂 t=30mm ワックス仕上げ
window frame: western hemlock
t=30mmwax finish

構造用合板受け材
45×105mm ビス止め
structural plywood supporter
45×105mm screw

柱 column 105×105mm

柱 105×105mm
column 105×105mm

Ⓐ 寝台平面詳細図 / outswinging window detail S:1/15

横羽目板張 t=15mm OS
アスファルトルーフィング 18kg
竪胴縁 30×45mm @455mm
グラスウール t=50mm
構造用合板 t=9mm 3×8版
cedar siding t=15mm oilstain
asphalt roofing 18kg
vertical furring strips 30×45@455mm
glass wool t=50mm
structural plywood t=9mm

梁 105×180mm
beam 105×180mm

60×150mm

420

窓枠:米栂 t=30mm ワックス仕上げ
window frame: western hemlock
t=30mmwax finish

水切り:ガルバリウム鋼板
t=0.4mm 曲げ加工
flasher:
bending galvanized steel sheet
t=0.4mm

82.5 7.5

82.5

30 5 5 4 220

30

52.5×150mm

コーキング
caulking

82.5

90

コーキング
caulking

FL5mm
float glass

30 52.5

30
5
4

52.5×150mm

220

ネオプレーンスポンジゴム
硬度60
neoprene spongerubber
haredness60

H=1215

45×105mm

窓枠 米栂 t=30mm ワックス仕上げ
window frame: western hemlock
t=30mm wax finish

30

W=2140

30

柱 105×105mm
column

結露受け:アルミ C-30×15×2mm
condensation support : aluminum channel C-30×15×2mm

52.5×150mm

窓台 45×105mm
window sill 45×105mm

12.5 70 2.5

34530

中抜き丁番
hinge

27

突き出しフラッシュ戸
横羽目板張 t=15mm OS
スタイロフォーム t=25mm
構造用合板 t=9mm
top-hinged flush door
cedar siding t=15mm oilstain
rigid insulation foam t=25mm
structural plywood t=9mm

H=420

H=354

27

キャッチ錠

つっかえ棒

3

5.5

水切り:ガルバリウム鋼板
t=0.4mm 曲げ加工
flashing:
bending galvanized steel sheet t=0.4mm

15 45 9

30

土台 105×105mm
ground sill 105×105mm

2.5 97.5

砂利敷き gravel paving

Ⓑ 開口部詳細図 / outswinging window detail S:1/15

231.5

1820

105×105r

45×105mm @455mm

5005

8190

3185

105×105mm

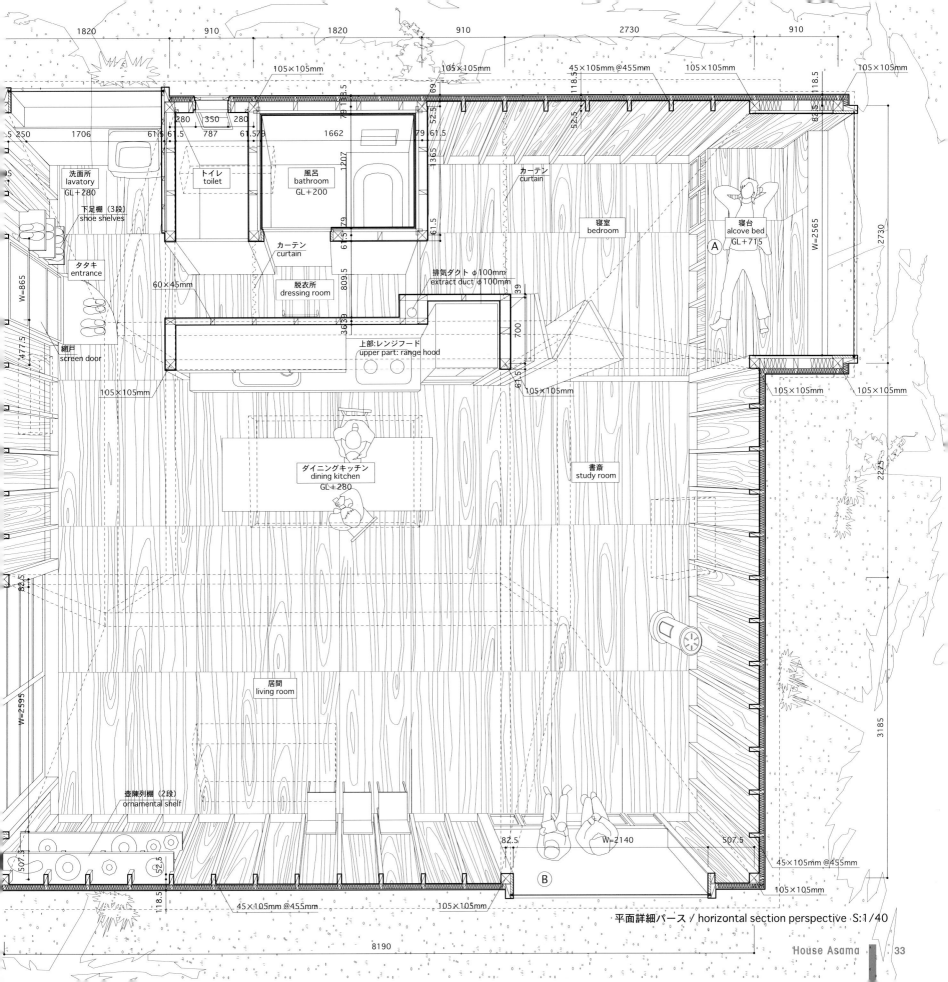

洗面所
lavatory
GL＋280

下足棚（3段）
shoe shelves

タタキ
entrance

網戸
screen door

トイレ
toilet

風呂
bathroom
GL＋200

カーテン
curtain

脱衣所
dressing room

カーテン
curtain

寝室
bedroom

寝台
alcove bed
GL＋715

A

排気ダクト φ100mm
extract duct φ100mm

上部：レンジフード
upper part: range hood

ダイニングキッチン
dining kitchen
GL＋280

書斎
study room

居間
living room

壺陳列棚（2段）
ornamental shelf

B

105×105mm

45×105mm @455mm

105×105mm

105×105mm

105×105mm

60×45mm

105×105mm

105×105mm

105×105mm

45×105mm @455mm

105×105mm

45×105mm @455mm

105×105mm

平面詳細パース / horizontal section perspective S:1/40

ハウス・サイコ
House Saiko

最高高さ maximum height
▽GL+7514

ガルバリウム鋼板大波葺き（長尺）
横胴縁15×45mm@455mm
アスファルトルーフィング22kg
構造用合板 t=9mm
竪胴縁45×45mm@455mm
高性能フェノルフォーム t=35mm
構造用合板 t=9mm
long pitch corrugated galvanized steel sheet
furring strips15×45mm@455mm
asphalt roofing22kg
structural plywood t=9mm
vertical furring strips45×45mm@455mm
high-efficiency phenolic foam t=35mm
structural plywood t=9mm

合板受け：
45×45mm@910mm
plywood support:
45×45mm@910mm

吊柱:2-204@455mm
hanging pillar: 2-204@455mm

構造用合板 t=9mm AEP
structural plywood t=9mm
acrylic emulsion paint

垂木:210@455mm
rafter: 210@455mm

屋根裏部屋2
garret 2

実付きラワン合板 t=24mm 防腐塗料仕上げ
lauan plywood t=24mm weather proof stain

▽2FL=GL+3244

床梁:2-210 @455mm
floor beam: 2-210 @455mm

通気孔 φ=100mm
venthole φ=100mm

水切り金物:
ガルバリウム鋼板葺き
flashing:
galvanized steel sheet

まぐさ:
構造用集成材612
lintel:
structural glue-laminated timber 612

サッシ取付け枠
L-50×50×6mm
window joist
L-50×50×6mm

コーキング
caulking

FIX窓:
ペアガラス FL8+A12+FL8mm
アルミサッシュ
fix window:
double glazing FL8+A12+FL8mm
aluminum sash

額縁:204
casing: 204

D 軒先詳細図 / eaves edge detail S:1/10

杉竪羽目板張り
防腐塗料仕上げ
横胴縁 15×45mm @455mm
防湿シート
竪胴縁 45×45mm @455mm
高性能フェノールフォーム t=25mm
構造用合板 t=9mm
cedar siding
weather proof stain
furring strips15×45mm @455mm
dampproof sheet
vertical furring strips45×45mm@455mm
high-efficiency phenolic foam t=25mm
structural plywood t=9mm

まぐさ:構造用集成材612
lintel:
structural glue-laminated timber 612

FIX窓:
ペアガラス FL8+A12+FL8mm
アルミサッシュ
FIX window:
double glazing FL8+A12+FL8mm
aluminum sash

窓台:109×75mm
window sill: 109×75mm
額縁:204
casing: 204

構造用合板 t=9mm
structural plywood t=9mm

額縁:204
casing:204

網戸
screen

縦枠:206
vertical frame:206

下枠:206
bottom frame: 206

モルタル金ゴテ仕上げ t=30mmワックス塗
シンダーコンクリート t=50mm
ポリエチレン管
ワイヤーメッシュ#150 φ=4mm
スタイロフォーム t=20mm
防湿シート
trowel mortar t=30mm wax finish
cinder concrete t=50mm
polyethylene pipe
wire mesh #150 φ=4mm
rigid insulation foam t=20mm
damp-proof sheet

広間
living room

CH=3435

※ 204:38×89mm
206:38×140mm
208:38×184mm
210:38×235mm
612:140×286mm

**断面詳細パース
vertical section perspective S:1/33**

サッシ取付け枠
L-125×90×10
window joist
L-125×90×10

平均GL
average ground level
▽GL±0

設計GL
▽planned ground level

▽1FL=GL-215

▽2FL=GL-215

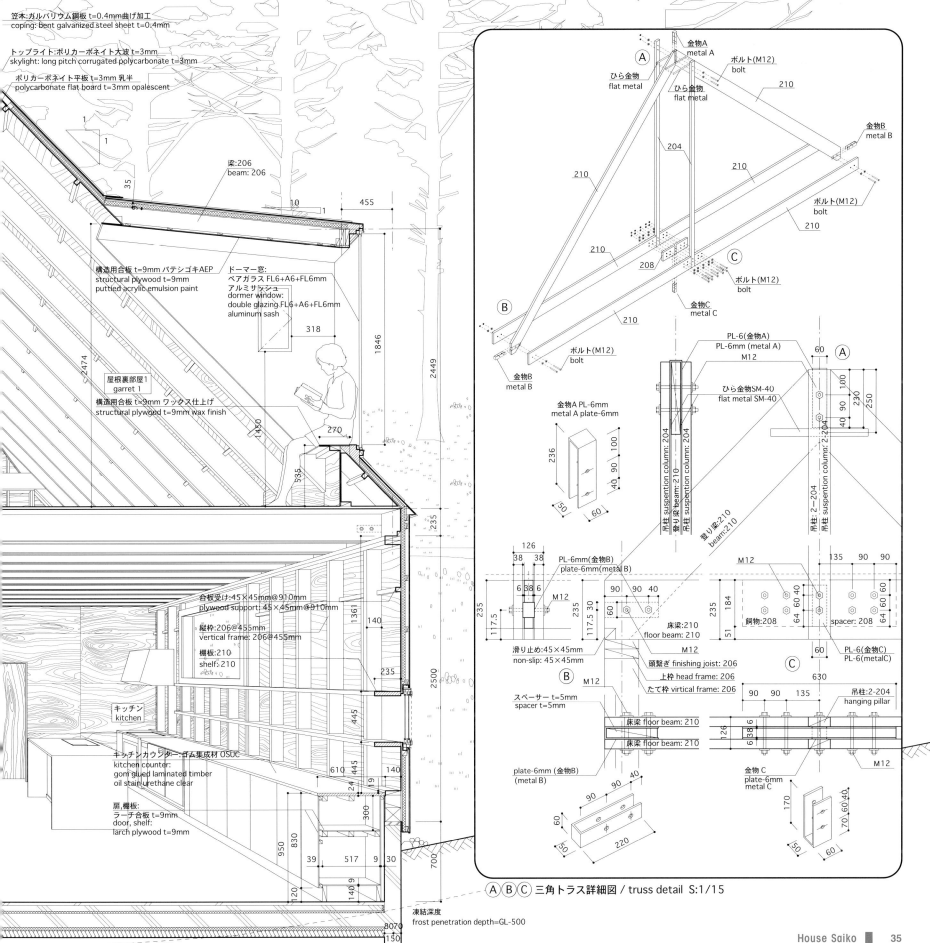

笠木:ガルバリウム鋼板 t=0.4mm曲げ加工
coping: bent galvanized steel sheet t=0.4mm

トップライト:ポリカーボネイト大波 t=3mm
skylight: long pitch corrugated polycarbonate t=3mm

ポリカーボネイト平板 t=3mm 乳半
polycarbonate flat board t=3mm opalescent

梁:206
beam: 206

構造用合板 t=9mm パテシゴキAEP
structural plywood t=9mm
puttied acrylic emulsion paint

ドーマー窓:
ペアガラス FL6+A6+FL6mm
アルミサッシュ
dormer window:
double glazing FL6+A6+FL6mm
aluminum sash

屋根裏部屋1
garret 1

構造用合板 t=9mm ワックス仕上げ
structural plywood t=9mm wax finish

合板受け:45×45mm@910mm
plywood support: 45×45mm@910mm

縦枠:206@455mm
vertical frame: 206@455mm

棚板:210
shelf: 210

キッチン
kitchen

キッチンカウンター:ゴム集成材 OSUC
kitchen counter:
gom glued laminated timber
oil stain urethane clear

扉,棚板:
ラーチ合板 t=9mm
door, shelf:
larch plywood t=9mm

凍結深度
frost penetration depth=GL-500

金物A
metal A

ボルト(M12)
bolt

ひら金物
flat metal

ひら金物
flat metal

金物B
metal B

ボルト(M12)
bolt

金物C
metal C

ボルト(M12)
bolt

金物B
metal B

ボルト(M12)
bolt

PL-6(金物A)
PL-6mm (metal A)
M12

ひら金物SM-40
flat metal SM-40

金物A PL-6mm
metal A plate-6mm

吊柱 suspention column: 204
登り梁 beam: 210
吊柱 suspention column: 204

吊柱:2-204
吊柱 suspention column: 2-204

登り梁:210
beam:210

PL-6mm(金物B)
plate-6mm(metal B)

M12

滑り止め:45×45mm
non-slip: 45×45mm

床梁:210
floor beam: 210

頭繋ぎ finishing joist: 206
上枠 head frame: 206
たて枠 virtical frame: 206

鋼物:208
spacer: 208

PL-6(金物C)
PL-6(metalC)

スペーサー t=5mm
spacer t=5mm

床梁 floor beam: 210

床梁 floor beam: 210

plate-6mm (金物B)
(metal B)

吊柱:2-204
hanging pillar

金物 C
plate-6mm
metal C

M12

ＡＢＣ 三角トラス詳細図 / truss detail S:1/15

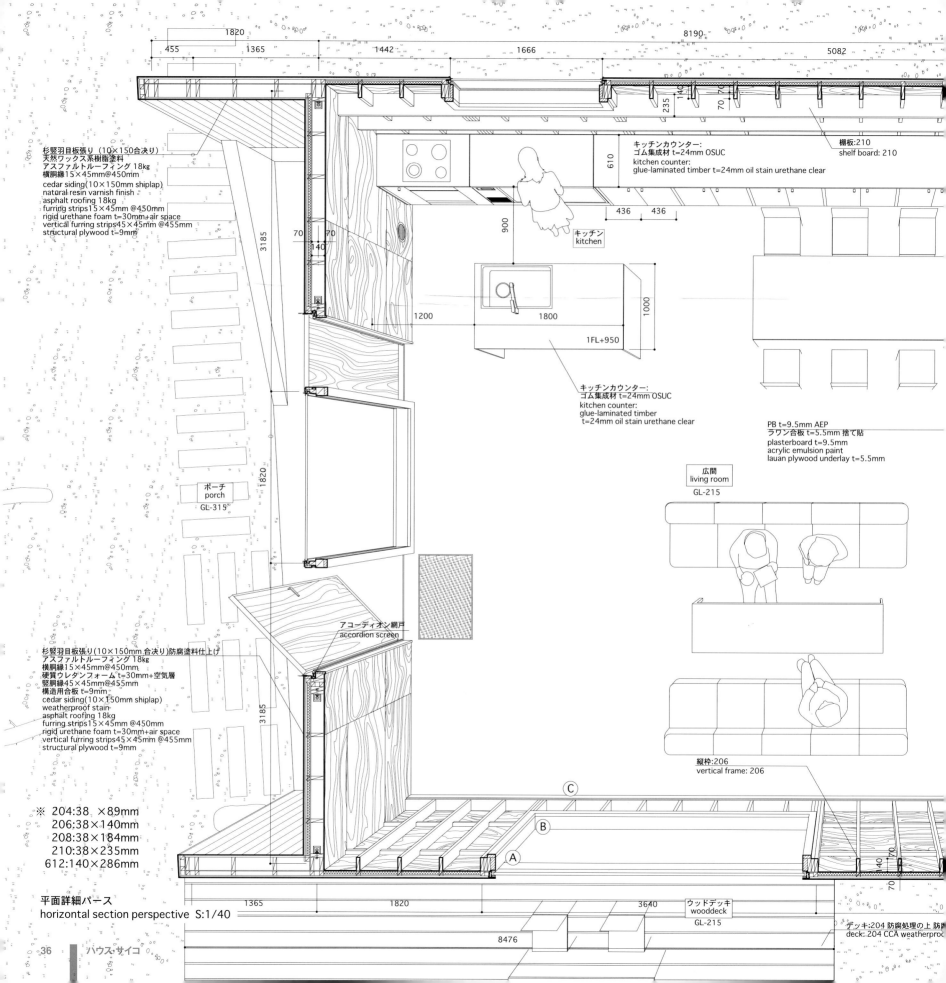

杉竪羽目板張り（10×150合決り）
天然ワックス系樹脂塗料
アスファルトルーフィング 18kg
横胴縁15×45mm@450mm
cedar siding(10×150mm shiplap)
natural resin varnish finish
asphalt roofing 18kg
furring strips15×45mm @450mm
rigid urethane foam t=30mm+air space
vertical furring strips45×45mm @455mm
structural plywood t=9mm

キッチンカウンター:
ゴム集成材 t=24mm OSUC
kitchen counter:
glue-laminated timber t=24mm oil stain urethane clear

棚板:210
shelf board: 210

キッチン
kitchen

1FL+950

キッチンカウンター:
ゴム集成材 t=24mm OSUC
kitchen counter:
glue-laminated timber
t=24mm oil stain urethane clear

PB t=9.5mm AEP
ラワン合板 t=5.5mm 捨て貼
plasterboard t=9.5mm
acrylic emulsion paint
lauan plywood underlay t=5.5mm

広間
living room
GL-215

ポーチ
porch
GL-315

アコーディオン網戸
accordion screen

杉竪羽目板張り(10×150mm 合決り)防腐塗料仕上げ
アスファルトルーフィング 18kg
横胴縁15×45mm@450mm
硬質ウレタンフォーム t=30mm+空気層
竪胴縁45×45mm@455mm
構造用合板 t=9mm
cedar siding(10×150mm shiplap)
weatherproof stain
asphalt roofing 18kg
furring strips15×45mm @450mm
rigid urethane foam t=30mm+air space
vertical furring strips45×45mm @455mm
structural plywood t=9mm

縦枠:206
vertical frame: 206

※ 204:38 ×89mm
　 206:38×140mm
　 208:38×184mm
　 210:38×235mm
　 612:140×286mm

平面詳細パース
horizontal section perspective S:1/40

ウッドデッキ
wooddeck
GL-215

デッキ:204 防腐処理の上 防腐
deck:204 CCA weatherproof

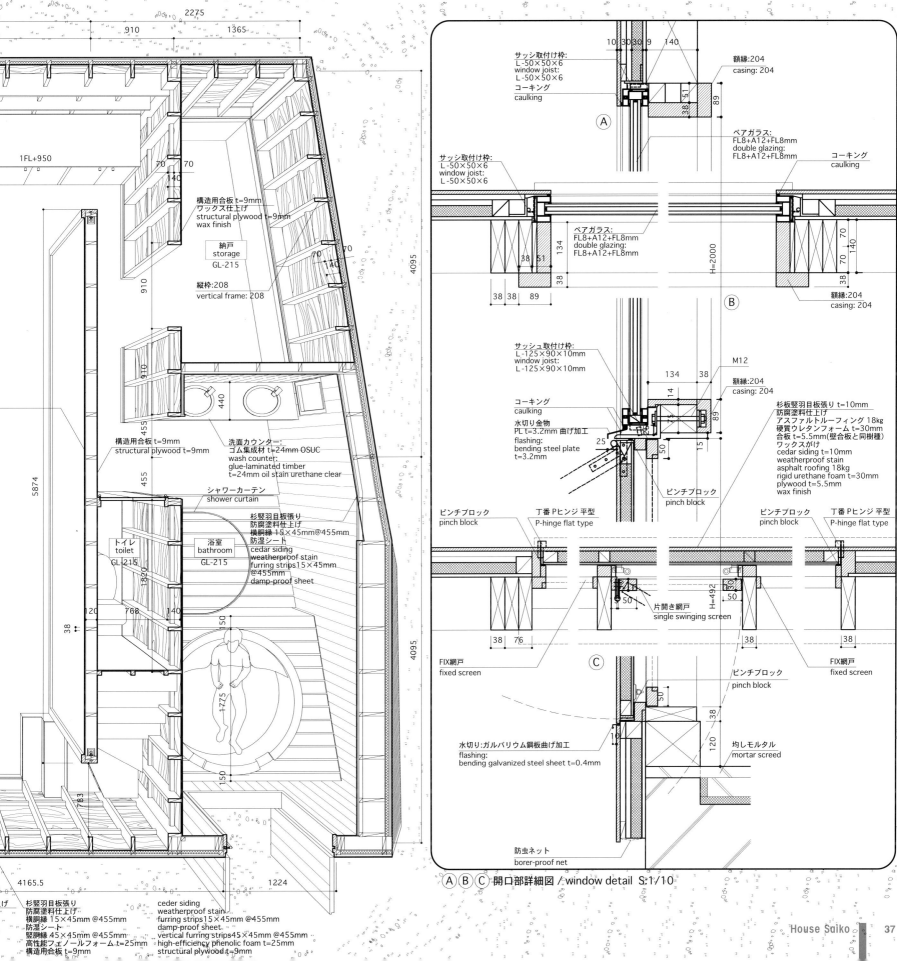

2275

910 1365

1FL+950

70 70

140

構造用合板 t=9mm
ワックス仕上げ
structural plywood t=9mm
wax finish

納戸
storage
GL-215

70 70

縦枠:208
vertical frame: 208

140

910

4095

洗面カウンター:
ゴム集成材 t=24mm OSUC
wash counter:
glue-laminated timber
t=24mm oil stain urethane clear

構造用合板 t=9mm
structural plywood t=9mm

910

シャワーカーテン
shower curtain

440

455

455

杉竪羽目板張り
防腐塗料仕上げ
横胴縁 15×45mm@455mm
防湿シート
cedar siding
weatherproof stain
furring strips15×45mm
@455mm
damp-proof sheet

トイレ
toilet
GL-215

浴室
bathroom
GL-215

5874

1820

1775

38

120 768 140

150

150

783

4095

4165.5 1224

上げ
杉竪羽目板張り   ceder siding
防腐塗料仕上げ   weatherproof stain
横胴縁 15×45mm @455mm   furring strips15×45mm @455mm
防湿シート   damp-proof sheet
竪胴縁 45×45mm @455mm   vertical furring strips45×45mm @455mm
高性能フェノールフォーム t=25mm high-efficiency phenolic foam t=25mm
構造用合板 t=9mm   structural plywood t=9mm

10 30 30 9 140

サッシ取付け枠:
L-50×50×6
window joist:
L-50×50×6
コーキング
caulking

額縁:204
casing: 204

89

38 51

Ⓐ

ベアガラス:
FL8+A12+FL8mm
double glazing:
FL8+A12+FL8mm

コーキング
caulking

サッシ取付け枠:
L-50×50×6
window joist:
L-50×50×6

134

70

70 140

ベアガラス:
FL8+A12+FL8mm
double glazing:
FL8+A12+FL8mm

H=2000

38 51

38

38

38 38 89

Ⓑ

額縁:204
casing: 204

サッシ取付け枠:
L-125×90×10mm
window joist:
L-125×90×10mm

134 38

M12

額縁:204
casing: 204

コーキング
caulking

14

89

水切り金物
PL t=3.2mm 曲げ加工
flashing:
bending steel plate
t=3.2mm

25

50 15

杉板竪羽目板張り t=10mm
防腐塗料仕上げ
アスファルトルーフィング 18kg
硬質ウレタンフォーム t=30mm
合板 t=5.5mm(壁胴板と同樹種)
ワックスがけ
cedar siding t=10mm
weatherproof stain
asphalt roofing 18kg
rigid urethane foam t=30mm
plywood t=5.5mm
wax finish

ピンチブロック
pinch block

ピンチブロック
pinch block

丁番 Pヒンジ 平型
P-hinge flat type

ピンチブロック
pinch block

丁番 Pヒンジ 平型
P-hinge flat type

H=492

50

50

50

片開き網戸
single swinging screen

38 76

Ⓒ

38

38

FIX網戸
fixed screen

FIX網戸
fixed screen

水切り:ガルバリウム鋼板曲げ加工
flashing:
bending galvanized steel sheet t=0.4mm

ピンチブロック
pinch block

10

120

均しモルタル
mortar screed

防虫ネット
borer-proof net

ⒶⒷⒸ 開口部詳細図／window detail S:1/10

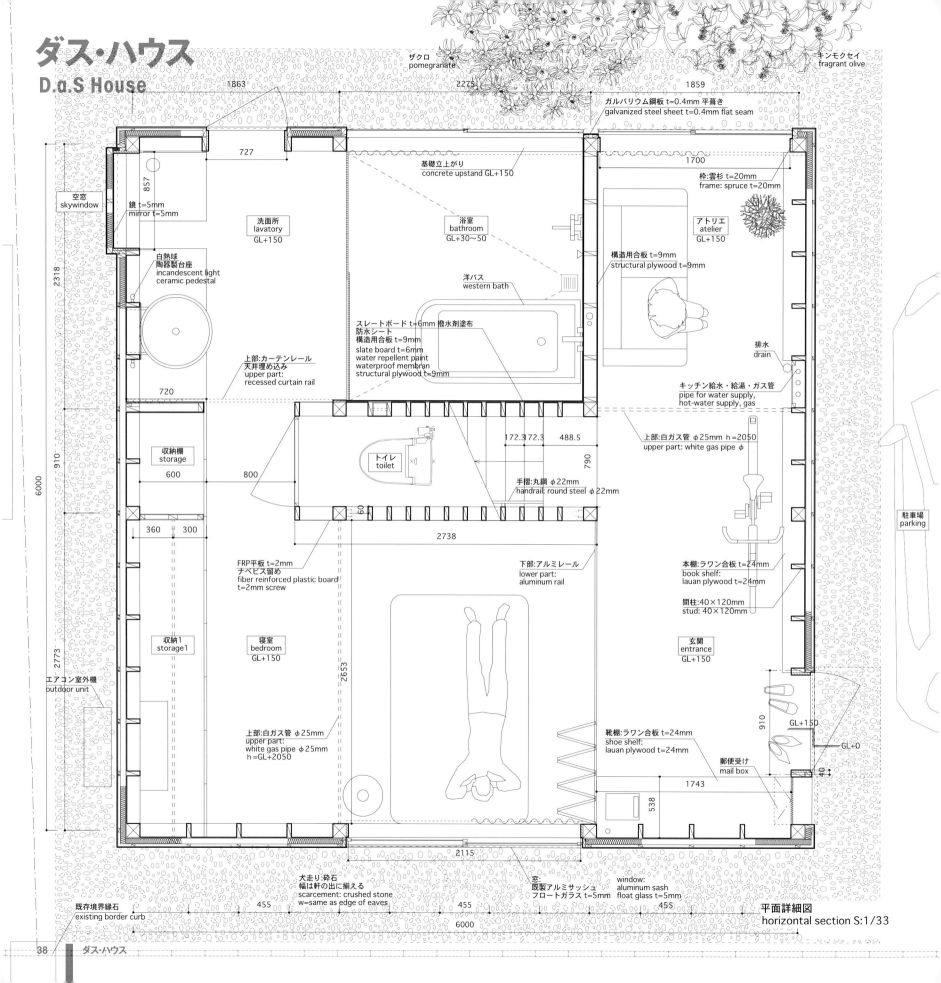

ダス・ハウス
D.a.S House

ザクロ
pomegranate

キンモクセイ
fragrant olive

1863　　　2275　　　1859

ガルバリウム鋼板 t=0.4mm 平葺き
galvanized steel sheet t=0.4mm flat seam

基礎立上がり
concrete upstand GL+150

727

1700

枠:雲杉 t=20mm
frame: spruce t=20mm

空窓
skywindow

857

鏡 t=5mm
mirror t=5mm

洗面所
lavatory
GL+150

浴室
bathroom
GL+30〜50

アトリエ
atelier
GL+150

構造用合板 t=9mm
structural plywood t=9mm

白熱球
陶器製台座
incandescent light
ceramic pedestal

洋バス
western bath

排水
drain

スレートボード t=6mm 撥水剤塗布
防水シート
構造用合板 t=9mm
slate board t=6mm
water repellent paint
waterproof membran
structural plywood t=9mm

上部:カーテンレール
天井埋め込み
upper part:
recessed curtain rail

720

キッチン給水・給湯・ガス管
pipe for water supply,
hot-water supply, gas

2318

172.3 172.3　　488.5

上部:白ガス管 φ25mm h=2050
upper part: white gas pipe φ

収納棚
storage
600

トイレ
toilet

790

6000

910

800

手摺:丸鋼 φ22mm
handrail: round steel φ22mm

本棚:ラワン合板 t=24mm
book shelf:
lauan plywood t=24mm

360　300

2738

下部:アルミレール
lower part:
aluminum rail

間柱:40×120mm
stud: 40×120mm

FRP平板 t=2mm
ナベビス留め
fiber reinforced plastic board
t=2mm screw

収納1
storage1

寝室
bedroom
GL+150

2653

玄関
entrance
GL+150

2773

エアコン室外機
outdoor unit

上部:白ガス管 φ25mm
upper part:
white gas pipe φ25mm
h=GL+2050

靴棚:ラワン合板 t=24mm
shoe shelf:
lauan plywood t=24mm

910

GL+150

GL+0

郵便受け
mail box

538

1743

既存境界縁石
existing border curb

455　　　455　　　455

2115

犬走り:砕石
幅は軒の出に揃える
scarcement: crushed stone
w=same as edge of eaves

窓:
既製アルミサッシュ
フロートガラス t=5mm

window:
aluminum sash
float glass t=5mm

平面詳細図
horizontal section S:1/33

6000

駐車場
parking

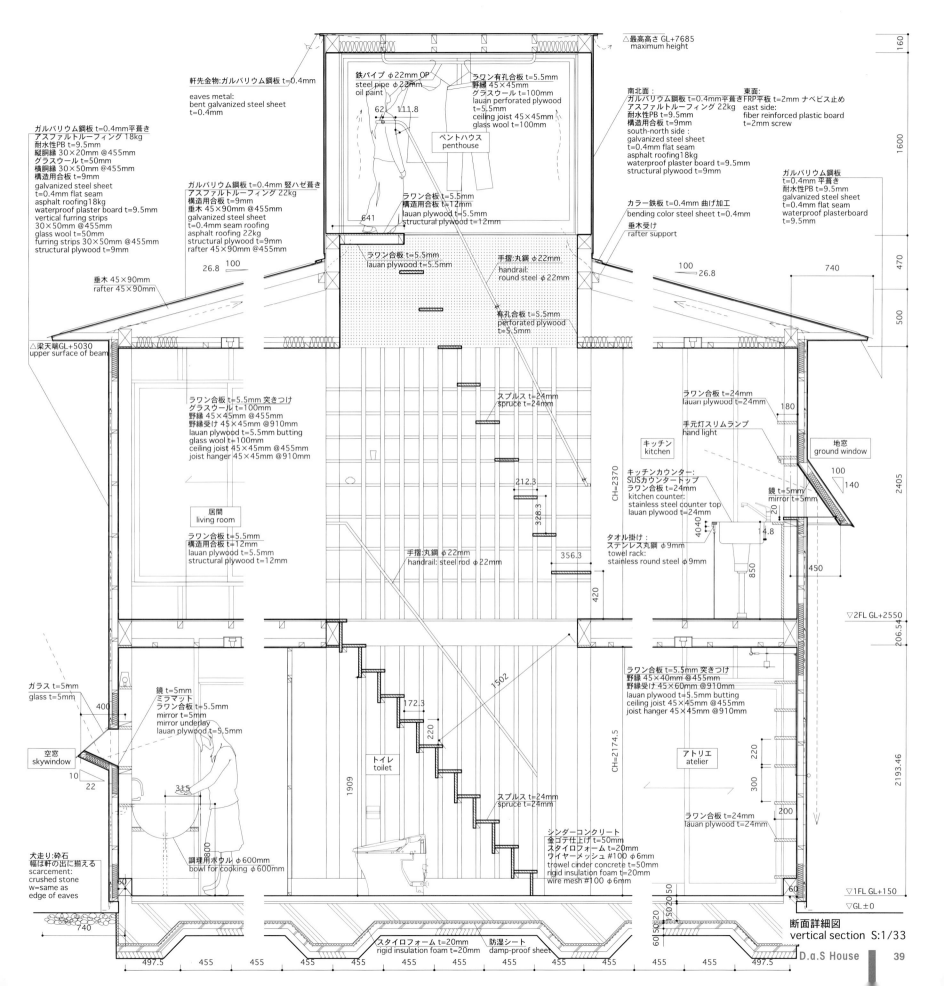

軒先金物：ガルバリウム鋼板 t=0.4mm
eaves metal:
bent galvanized steel sheet
t=0.4mm

鉄パイプ φ22mm OP
steel pipe φ22mm
oil paint

ラワン有孔合板 t=5.5mm
野縁 45×45mm
グラスウール t=100mm
lauan perforated plywood
t=5.5mm
ceiling joist 45×45mm
glass wool t=100mm

南北面：
ガルバリウム鋼板 t=0.4mm平葺き
アスファルトルーフィング 22kg
耐水性PB t=9.5mm
構造用合板 t=9mm
south-north side:
galvanized steel sheet
t=0.4mm flat seam
asphalt roofing18kg
waterproof plaster board t=9.5mm
structural plywood t=9mm

東面：
ガルバリウム鋼板 t=0.4mm平葺き FRP平板 t=2mm ナベビス止め
east side:
fiber reinforced plastic board
t=2mm screw

ベントハウス
penthouse

ガルバリウム鋼板 t=0.4mm平葺き
アスファルトルーフィング 18kg
耐水性PB t=9.5mm
縦胴縁 30×20mm @455mm
グラスウール t=50mm
横胴縁 30×50mm @455mm
構造用合板 t=9mm
galvanized steel sheet
t=0.4mm flat seam
asphalt roofing18kg
waterproof plaster board t=9.5mm
vertical furring strips
30×50mm @455mm
glass wool t=50mm
furring strips 30×50mm @455mm
structural plywood t=9mm

ガルバリウム鋼板 t=0.4mm 竪ハゼ葺き
アスファルトルーフィング 22kg
構造用合板 t=9mm
垂木 45×90mm @455mm
galvanized steel sheet
t=0.4mm seam roofing
asphalt roofing 22kg
structural plywood t=9mm
rafter 45×90mm @455mm

ラワン合板 t=5.5mm
構造用合板 t=12mm
lauan plywood t=5.5mm
structural plywood t=12mm

カラー鉄板 t=0.4mm 曲げ加工
bending color steel sheet t=0.4mm

垂木受け
rafter support

ガルバリウム鋼板
t=0.4mm 平葺き
耐水性PB t=9.5mm
galvanized steel sheet
t=0.4mm flat seam
waterproof plasterboard
t=9.5mm

△最高高さ GL+7685
maximum height

垂木 45×90mm
rafter 45×90mm

ラワン合板 t=5.5mm
lauan plywood t=5.5mm

手摺：丸鋼 φ22mm
handrail:
round steel φ22mm

△梁天端 GL+5030
upper surface of beam

有孔合板 t=5.5mm
perforated plywood
t=5.5mm

ラワン合板 t=5.5mm 突きつけ
グラスウール t=100mm
野縁 45×45mm @455mm
野縁受け 45×45mm @910mm
lauan plywood t=5.5mm butting
glass wool t=100mm
ceiling joist 45×45mm @455mm
joist hanger 45×45mm @910mm

スプルス t=24mm
spruce t=24mm

ラワン合板 t=24mm
lauan plywood t=24mm

手元灯スリムランプ
hand light

キッチン
kitchen

地窓
ground window

居間
living room

ラワン合板 t=5.5mm
構造用合板 t=12mm
lauan plywood t=5.5mm
structural plywood t=12mm

キッチンカウンター：
SUSカウンタートップ
ラワン合板 t=24mm
kitchen counter:
stainless steel counter top
lauan plywood t=24mm

鏡 t=5mm
mirror t=5mm

手摺：丸鋼 φ22mm
handrail: steel rod φ22mm

タオル掛け：
ステンレス丸鋼 φ9mm
towel rack:
stainless round steel φ9mm

ガラス t=5mm
glass t=5mm

鏡 t=5mm
ミラマット
ラワン合板 t=5.5mm
mirror t=5mm
mirror underlay
lauan plywood t=5.5mm

空窓
skywindow

トイレ
toilet

スプルス t=24mm
spruce t=24mm

ラワン合板 t=5.5mm 突きつけ
野縁 45×40mm @455mm
野縁受け 45×60mm @910mm
lauan plywood t=5.5mm butting
ceiling joist 45×45mm @455mm
joist hanger 45×45mm @910mm

アトリエ
atelier

調理用ボウル φ600mm
bowl for cooking φ600mm

シンダーコンクリート
金ゴテ仕上げ t=50mm
スタイロフォーム t=20mm
ワイヤーメッシュ #100 φ6mm
trowel cinder concrete t=50mm
rigid insulation foam t=20mm
wire mesh #100 φ6mm

ラワン合板 t=24mm
lauan plywood t=24mm

犬走り：砕石
幅は軒の出に揃える
scarement:
crushed stone
w=same as
edge of eaves

▽2FL GL+2550

▽1FL GL+150
▽GL±0

スタイロフォーム t=20mm
rigid insulation foam t=20mm

防湿シート
damp-proof sheet

断面詳細図
vertical section S:1/33

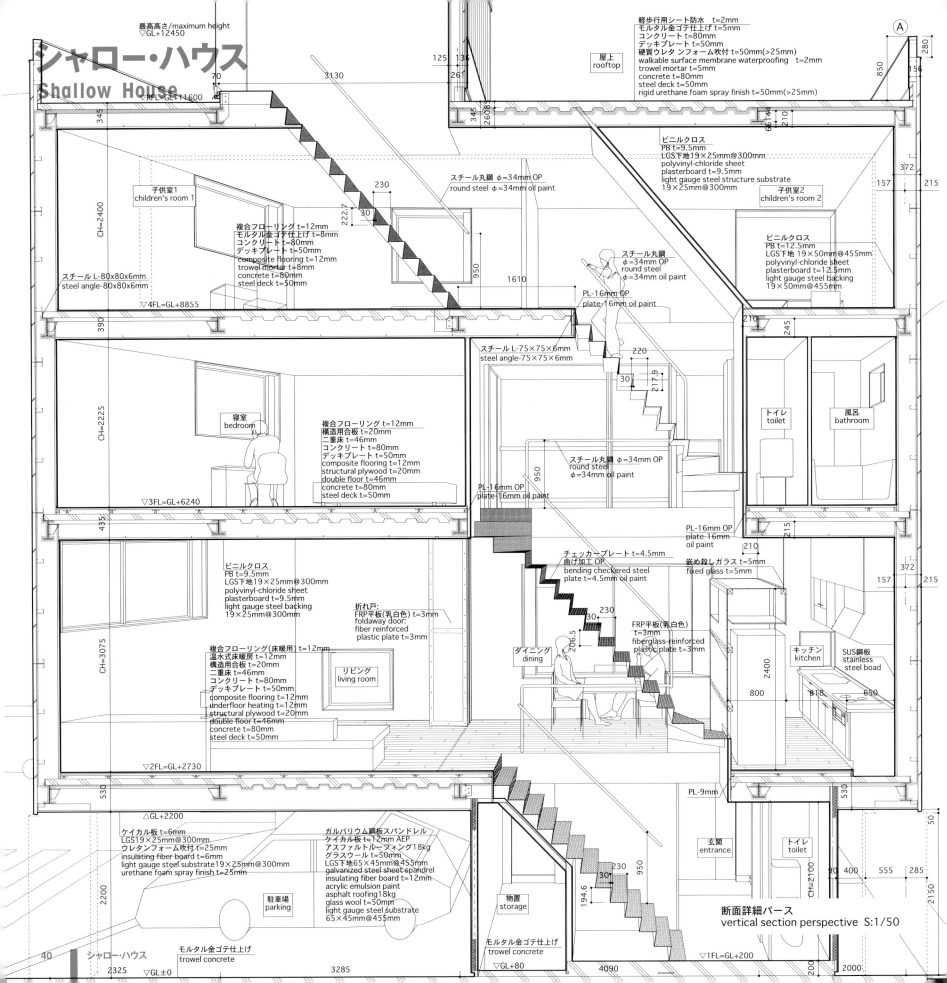

シャロー・ハウス
Shallow House

断面詳細パース
vertical section perspective S:1/50

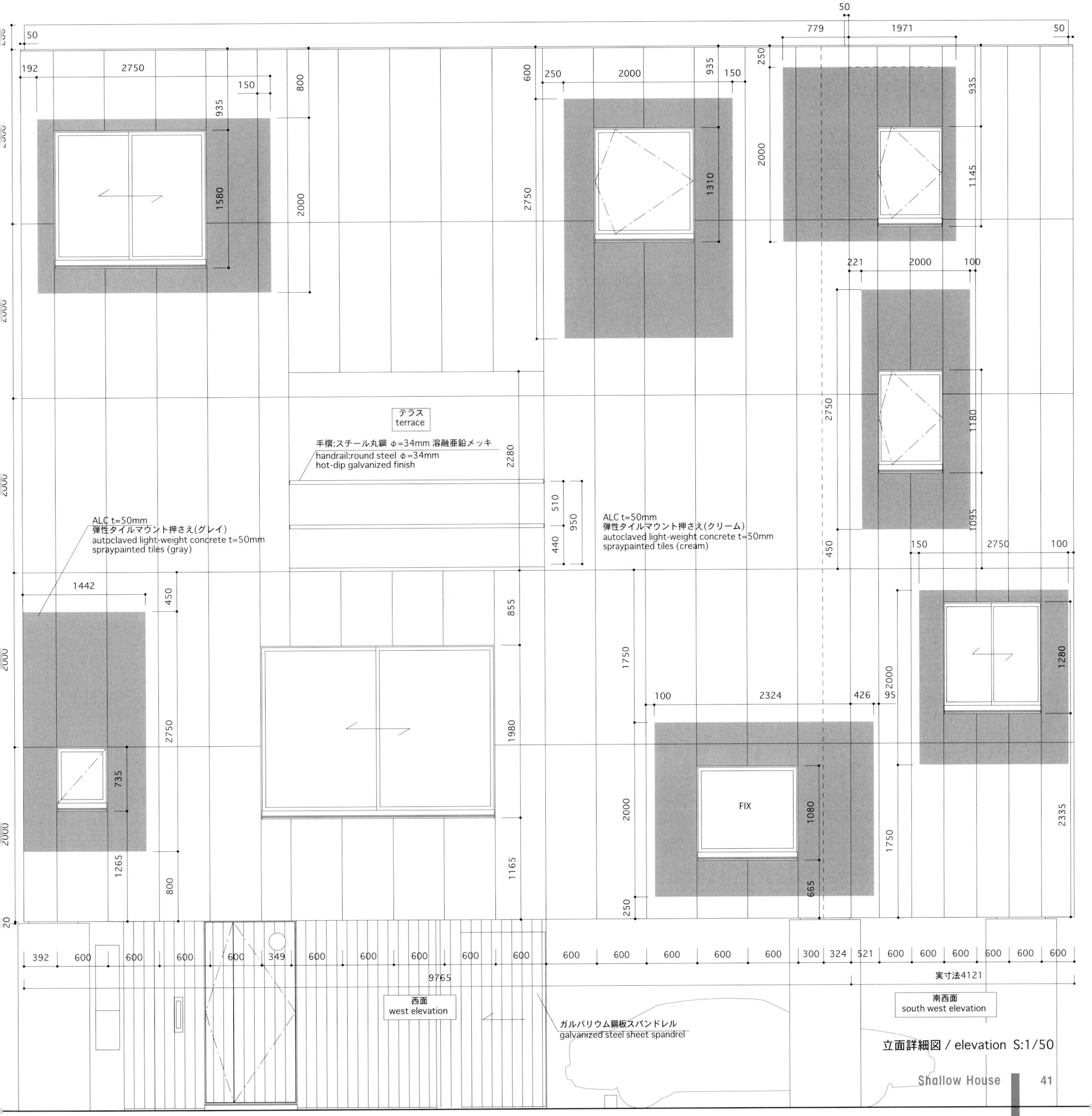

50

50

779 1971 50

192 2750 150 800 600 250 2000 935 150 250 935

935 1580 2750 2000 1310 2000 1145

テラス
terrace

221 2000 100

手摺:スチール丸鋼 φ=34mm 溶融亜鉛メッキ
handrail:round steel φ=34mm
hot-dip galvanized finish

2280 2750 1180

510 1095

950 440

ALC t=50mm
弾性タイルマウント押さえ(グレイ)
autoclaved light-weight concrete t=50mm
spraypainted tiles (gray)

ALC t=50mm
弾性タイルマウント押さえ(クリーム)
autoclaved light-weight concrete t=50mm
spraypainted tiles (cream)

450 150 2750 100

1442 450 855

1750 1280

2750 1980 100 2324 426 2000 95 2335

735 1750

1080

2000

FIX

665

250

1265 1165

800 250

392 600 600 600 600 349 600 600 600 600 600 600 600 600 600 600 300 324 521 600 600 600 600 600 600

9765 実寸法4121

ガルバリウム鋼板スパンドレル
galvanized steel sheet spandrel

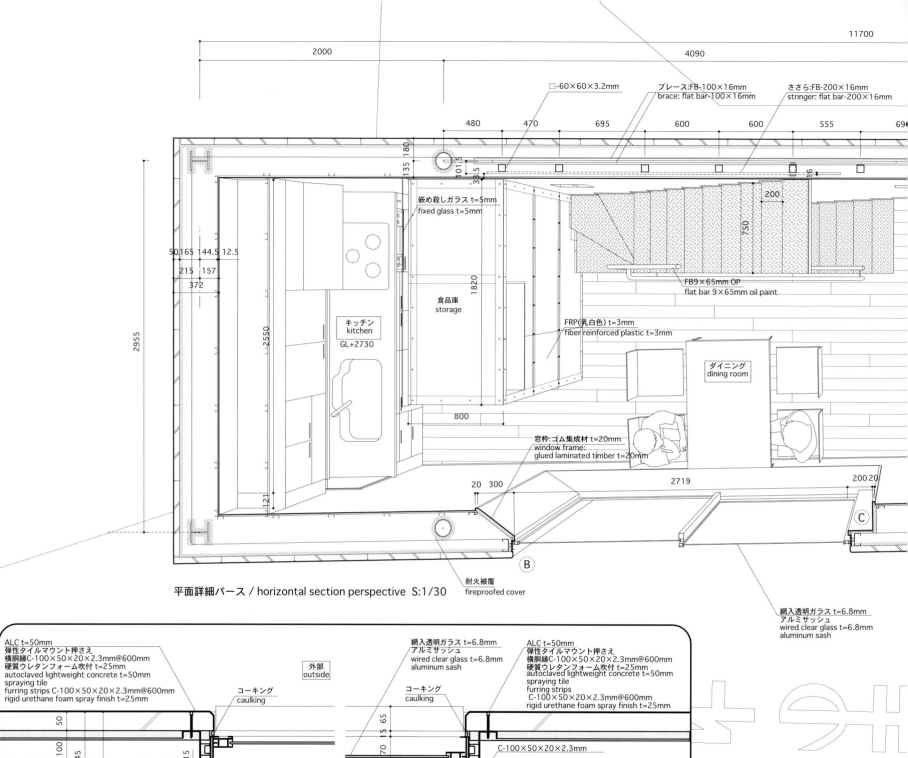

□-60×60×3.2mm

ブレース:FB-100×16mm
brace: flat bar-100×16mm

ささら:FB-200×16mm
stringer: flat bar-200×16mm

11700

2000

4090

480 470 695 600 600 555 69

180

135

1015

33.5

200

750

6

嵌め殺しガラス t=5mm
fixed glass t=5mm

食品庫
storage

1820

FB9×65mm OP
flat bar 9×65mm oil paint

FRP(乳白色) t=3mm
fiber reinforced plastic t=3mm

50 165 144.5 12.5

215 157

372

2955

2550

キッチン
kitchen

GL+2730

ダイニング
dining room

1121

窓枠:ゴム集成材 t=20mm
window frame:
glued laminated timber t=20mm

800

20 300

2719

200 20

C

B

耐火被覆
fireproofed cover

平面詳細パース / horizontal section perspective S:1/30

網入透明ガラス t=6.8mm
wired clear glass t=6.8mm
アルミサッシュ
aluminum sash

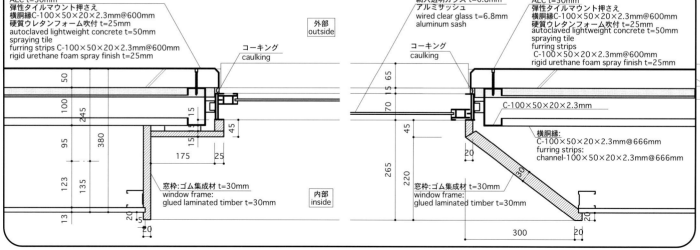

ALC t=50mm
弾性タイルマウント押さえ
横胴縁C-100×50×20×2.3mm@600mm
硬質ウレタンフォーム吹付 t=25mm
autoclaved lightweight concrete t=50mm
spraying tile
furring strips C-100×50×20×2.3mm@600mm
rigid urethane foam spray finish t=25mm

網入透明ガラス t=6.8mm
アルミサッシュ
wired clear glass t=6.8mm
aluminum sash

ALC t=50mm
弾性タイルマウント押さえ
横胴縁C-100×50×20×2.3mm@600mm
硬質ウレタンフォーム吹付 t=25mm
autoclaved lightweight concrete t=50mm
spraying tile
furring strips
C-100×50×20×2.3mm@600mm
rigid urethane foam spray finish t=25mm

外部
outside

コーキング
caulking

コーキング
caulking

C-100×50×20×2.3mm

50

100

245

95

380

15

45

175 25

123 135

13

20 5

20

窓枠:ゴム集成材 t=30mm
window frame:
glued laminated timber t=30mm

内部
inside

横胴縁:
C-100×50×20×2.3mm@666mm
furring strips:
channel-100×50×20×2.3mm@666mm

65

15

70

45

20

265

220

30

窓枠:ゴム集成材 t=30mm
window frame:
glued laminated timber t=30mm

300

20

20

B C 開口部詳細図 / window detail S:1/10

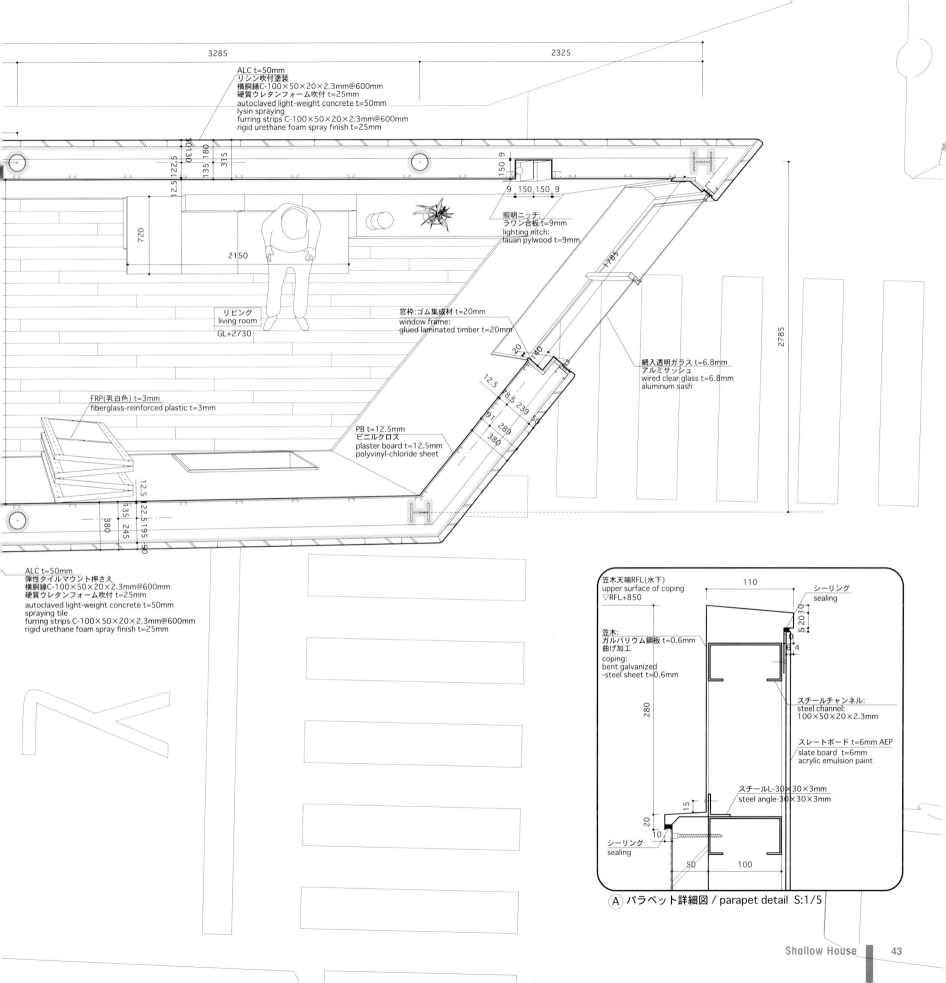

ALC t=50mm
リシン吹付塗装
横胴縁C-100×50×20×2.3mm@600mm
硬質ウレタンフォーム吹付 t=25mm
autoclaved light-weight concrete t=50mm
lysin spraying
furring strips C-100×50×20×2.3mm@600mm
rigid urethane foam spray finish t=25mm

照明ニッチ:
ラワン合板 t=9mm
lighting nitch:
lauan pylwood t=9mm

窓枠:ゴム集成材 t=20mm
window frame:
glued laminated timber t=20mm

網入透明ガラス t=6.8mm
アルミサッシ
wired clear glass t=6.8mm
aluminum sash

リビング
living room
GL+2730

FRP(乳白色) t=3mm
fiberglass-reinforced plastic t=3mm

PB t=12.5mm
ビニルクロス
plaster board t=12.5mm
polyvinyl-chloride sheet

2150

720

3285

2325

ALC t=50mm
弾性タイルマウント押さえ
横胴縁C-100×50×20×2.3mm@600mm
硬質ウレタンフォーム吹付 t=25mm
autoclaved light-weight concrete t=50mm
spraying tile
furring strips C-100×50×20×2.3mm@600mm
rigid urethane foam spray finish t=25mm

笠木天端RFL(水下)
upper surface of coping
▽RFL+850

シーリング
sealing

笠木:
ガルバリウム鋼板 t=0.6mm
曲げ加工
coping:
bent galvanized
-steel sheet t=0.6mm

スチールチャンネル:
steel channel:
100×50×20×2.3mm

スレートボード t=6mm AEP
slate board t=6mm
acrylic emulsion paint

スチールL-30×30×3mm
steel angle-30×30×3mm

シーリング
sealing

110
280
50   100
15
20
10

Ⓐ パラペット詳細図 / parapet detail S:1/5

ジグ
Jig

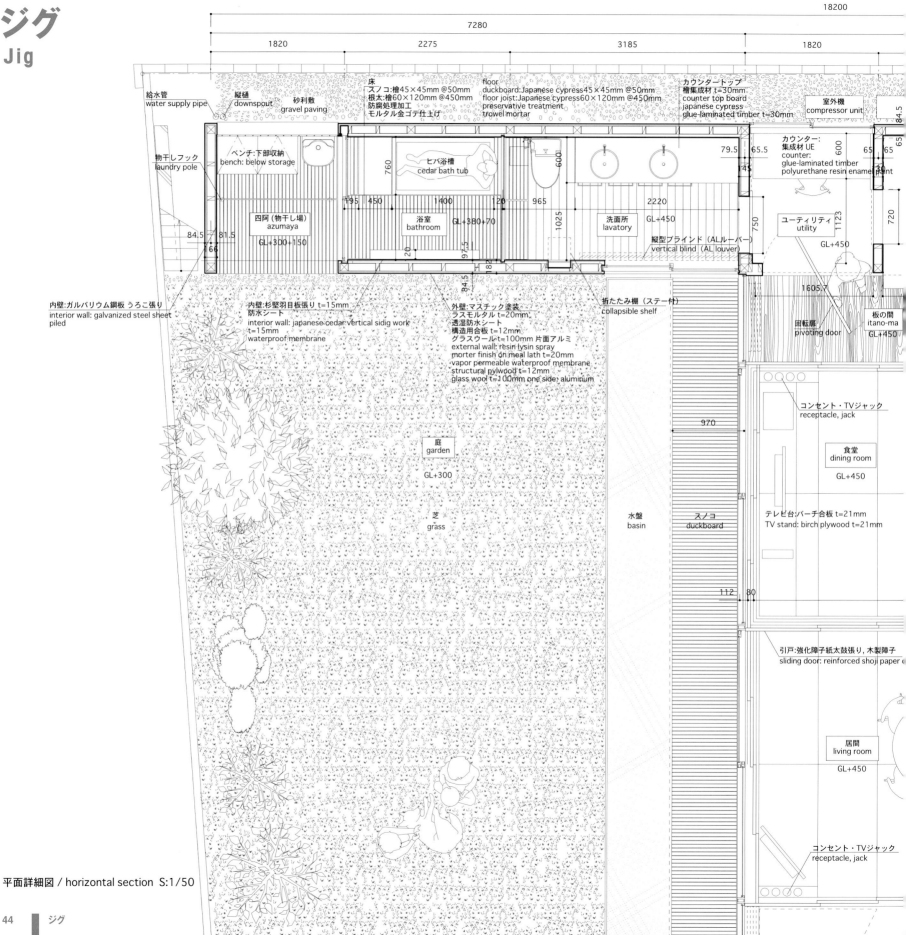

18200

7280

| 1820 | 2275 | 3185 | 1820 |

給水管
water supply pipe

縦樋
downspout

砂利敷
gravel paving

床
スノコ:檜45×45mm @50mm
根太:檜60×120mm @450mm
防腐処理加工
モルタル金ゴテ仕上げ

floor
duckboard:Japanese cypress45×45mm @50mm
floor joist:Japanese cypress60×120mm @450mm
preservative treatment
trowel mortar

カウンタートップ
檜集成材 t=30mm
counter top board
japanese cypress
glue-laminated timber t=30mm

室外機
compressor unit

物干しフック
laundry pole

ベンチ:下部収納
bench: below storage

ヒバ浴槽
cedar bath tub

79.5　65.5

カウンター:
集成材 UE
counter:
glue-laminated timber
polyurethane resin enamel paint

600

四阿（物干し場）
azumaya

GL+300+150

760

浴室
bathroom
GL+380+70

195　450　1400　120　965

1025

洗面所
lavatory　GL+450

2220

750

600

ユーティリティ
utility

GL+450

1123

720

84.5　81.5

66

20

97.5　182

84.5

縦型ブラインド（ALルーバー）
vertical blind（AL louver）

1605.7

内壁:ガルバリウム鋼板 うろこ張り
interior wall: galvanized steel sheet
piled

内壁:杉堅羽目板張り t=15mm
防水シート
interior wall: japanese cedar vertical sidig work
t=15mm
waterproof membrane

外壁:マスチック塗装
ラスモルタル t=20mm
透湿防水シート
構造用合板 t=12mm
グラスウール t=100mm 片面アルミ
external wall: resin lysin spray
morter finish on meal lath t=20mm
vapor permeable waterproof membrane
structural pylwood t=12mm
glass wool t=100mm one side: aluminum

折たたみ棚（ステー付）
collapsible shelf

回転扉
pivoting door

板の間
itano-ma
GL+450

970

コンセント・TVジャック
receptacle, jack

食堂
dining room
GL+450

庭
garden

GL+300

芝
grass

水盤
basin

スノコ
duckboard

テレビ台:バーチ合板 t=21mm
TV stand: birch plywood t=21mm

112　80

引戸:強化障子紙太鼓張り，木製障子
sliding door: reinforced shoji paper

居間
living room
GL+450

コンセント・TVジャック
receptacle, jack

平面詳細図 / horizontal section S:1/50

720

5460

5460

2620 | 1020 | 5160 | 300

引込みポール
pole for incoming line

910 910

665

514 100 50

給湯器
boiler

プロパンガス置場
place for propane gas

砂利敷
gravel paving

92

84.5

7.5

690

棚
shelf

550

28

床:モルタル金ゴテ仕上げ
floor: trowel mortar

外部階段:
セランガンバツ t=20mm
受け:スチールPL t=4.5 曲げ加工
L-40×40×3
exterior stairs:
selanganbatu t=20mm
support parts: bent steel plate t=4.5mm
L-40×40×3

1900

950

38

1703

892

倉庫
storage

GL-200

100

265

1820

2030

2850

分電盤
switch board

900

キッチン
kitchen

GL+450

943

803

781

棚
shelf

262

58.5

43

210

カウンター: 集成材 UE
er: glue-laminated timber
rethane resin enamel paint

590

棚
shelf

395

勝手口
GL+300
service entrance

84.5

ブロアー
convection fan

2445

135

270

786

排水溝
drainage gutter

890

135

900

220

150

600

床:バーチ合板 t=6.5mm OSCL
floor: birch plywood t=6.5mm oilstain clearlacquer

120

210

1785

150

合併処理浄化槽 (7人槽)
individual sewage treatment tank (for 7 people)

1150

郵便受:FRP t=1.5mm
SUS パンチングメタル
mailbox: fiber reinforced plastic t=1.5mm
stainless steel perforated metal

115

110 110

110 100

90 220 800 210 56

3245

床:縁なし畳 t=15mm (床暖房用)
floor: tatami without frame
t=15mm(for floor heating)

床:構造用合板 t=12mm
floor: structural plywood t=12mm

床:コンクリート金ゴテ仕上げ
floor: trowel concrete

4104

押入
closet

車止め
stopper

270 200

135

neling

894

129

押入
closet

PS

駐車場
parking

GL±0〜+300

L字側溝
L-shaped gutter

アスファルト
asphalt

6.9 15.9

6.9

1200

20 56

20 100

上部:飾棚
ornamental
shelf above

135

270

135

7280

1095

2545

980

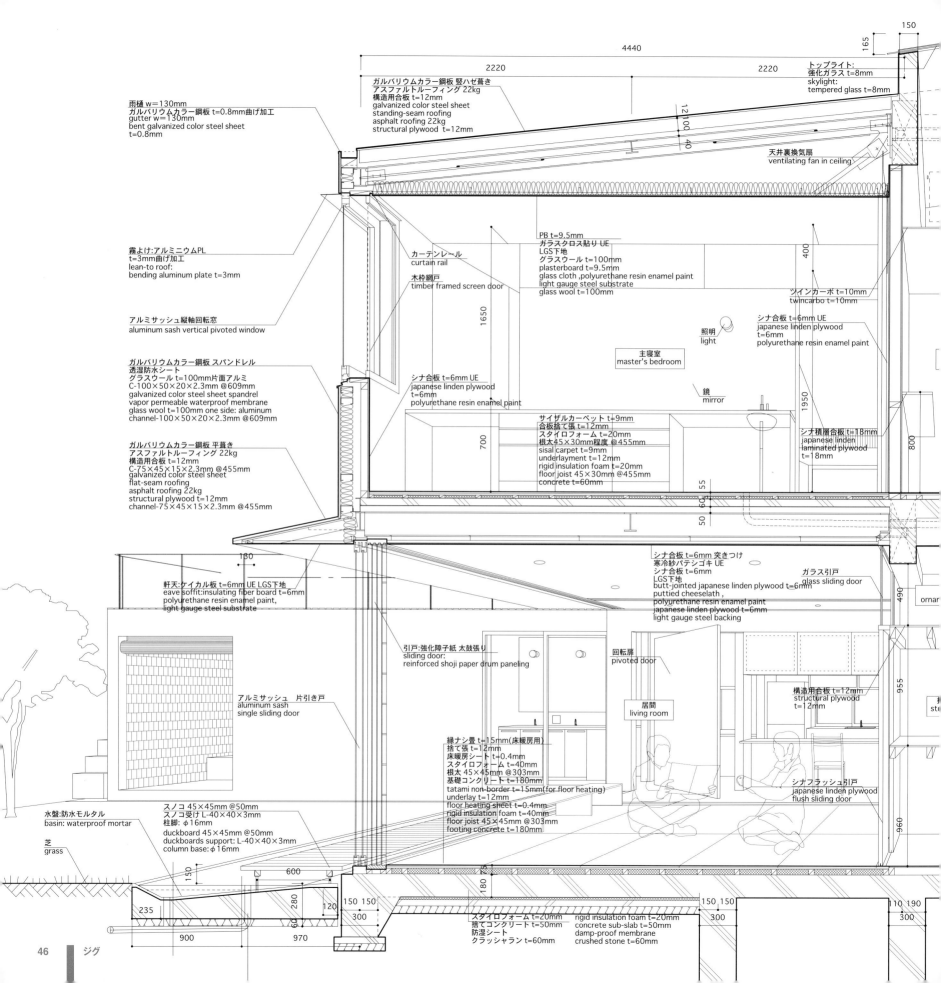

雨樋 w=130mm
ガルバリウムカラー鋼板 t=0.8mm曲げ加工
gutter w=130mm
bent galvanized color steel sheet
t=0.8mm

ガルバリウムカラー鋼板 竪ハゼ葺き
アスファルトルーフィング 22kg
構造用合板 t=12mm
galvanized color steel sheet
standing-seam roofing
asphalt roofing 22kg
structural plywood t=12mm

トップライト:
強化ガラス t=8mm
skylight:
tempered glass t=8mm

4440
2220
2220
150
165

天井裏換気扇
ventilating fan in ceiling

霧よけ:アルミニウムPL
t=3mm曲げ加工
lean-to roof:
bending aluminum plate t=3mm

PB t=9.5mm
ガラスクロス貼り UE
LGS下地
グラスウール t=100mm
plasterboard t=9.5mm
glass cloth ,polyurethane resin enamel paint
light gauge steel substrate
glass wool t=100mm

400

カーテンレール
curtain rail

木枠網戸
timber framed screen door

ツインカーボ t=10mm
twincarbo t=10mm

アルミサッシ 縦軸回転窓
aluminum sash vertical pivoted window

1650

照明
light

シナ合板 t=6mm UE
japanese linden plywood
t=6mm
polyurethane resin enamel paint

ガルバリウムカラー鋼板 スパンドレル
透湿防水シート
グラスウール t=100mm片面アルミ
C-100×50×20×2.3mm @609mm
galvanized color steel sheet spandrel
vapor permeable waterproof membrane
glass wool t=100mm one side: aluminum
channel-100×50×20×2.3mm @609mm

主寝室
master's bedroom

鏡
mirror

シナ合板 t=6mm UE
japanese linden plywood
t=6mm
polyurethane resin enamel paint

1950

シナ積層合板 t=18mm
japanese linden
laminated plywood
t=18mm

ガルバリウムカラー鋼板 平葺き
アスファルトルーフィング 22kg
構造用合板 t=12mm
C-75×45×15×2.3mm @455mm
galvanized color steel sheet
flat-seam roofing
asphalt roofing 22kg
structural plywood t=12mm
channel-75×45×15×2.3mm @455mm

サイザルカーペット t=9mm
合板捨て張り t=12mm
スタイロフォーム t=20mm
根太45×30mm程度 @455mm
sisal carpet t=9mm
underlayment t=12mm
rigid insulation foam =20mm
floor joist 45×30mm @455mm
concrete t=60mm

700

800

55
50
50

130

シナ合板 t=6mm 突きつけ
寒冷紗パテシゴキ UE
シナ合板 t=6mm
LGS下地
butt-jointed japanese linden plywood t=6mm
puttied cheeselath ,
polyurethane resin enamel paint
japanese linden plywood t=6mm
light gauge steel backing

ガラス引戸
glass sliding door

軒天:ケイカル板 t=6mm UE LGS下地
eave soffit:insulating fiber board t=6mm
polyurethane resin enamel paint,
light gauge steel substrate

490

ornar

引戸:強化障子紙 太鼓張り
sliding door:
reinforced shoji paper drum paneling

回転扉
pivoted door

955

アルミサッシ 片引き戸
aluminum sash
single sliding door

居間
living room

構造用合板 t=12mm
structural plywood
t=12mm

構造
ste

縁ナシ畳 t=15mm(床暖房用)
捨て張り t=12mm
床暖房シート t=0.4mm
スタイロフォーム t=40mm
根太 45×45mm @303mm
基礎コンクリート t=180mm
tatami non-border t=15mm(for floor heating)
underlay t=12mm
floor heating sheet t=0.4mm
rigid insulation foam =40mm
floor joist 45×45mm @303mm
footing concrete t=180mm

シナフラッシュ引戸
japanese linden plywood
flush sliding door

960

水盤:防水モルタル
basin: waterproof mortar

スノコ 45×45mm @50mm
スノコ受け L-40×40×3mm
柱脚:φ16mm
duckboard 45×45mm @50mm
duckboards support: L-40×40×3mm
column base:φ16mm

芝
grass

150
600
280
120
235
60
300
150 150
180
75
300
110 190
150 150
300
900
970

スタイロフォーム t=20mm
捨てコンクリート t=50mm
防湿シート
クラッシャラン t=60mm
rigid insulation foam =20mm
concrete sub-slab =50mm
damp-proof membrane
crushed stone t=60mm

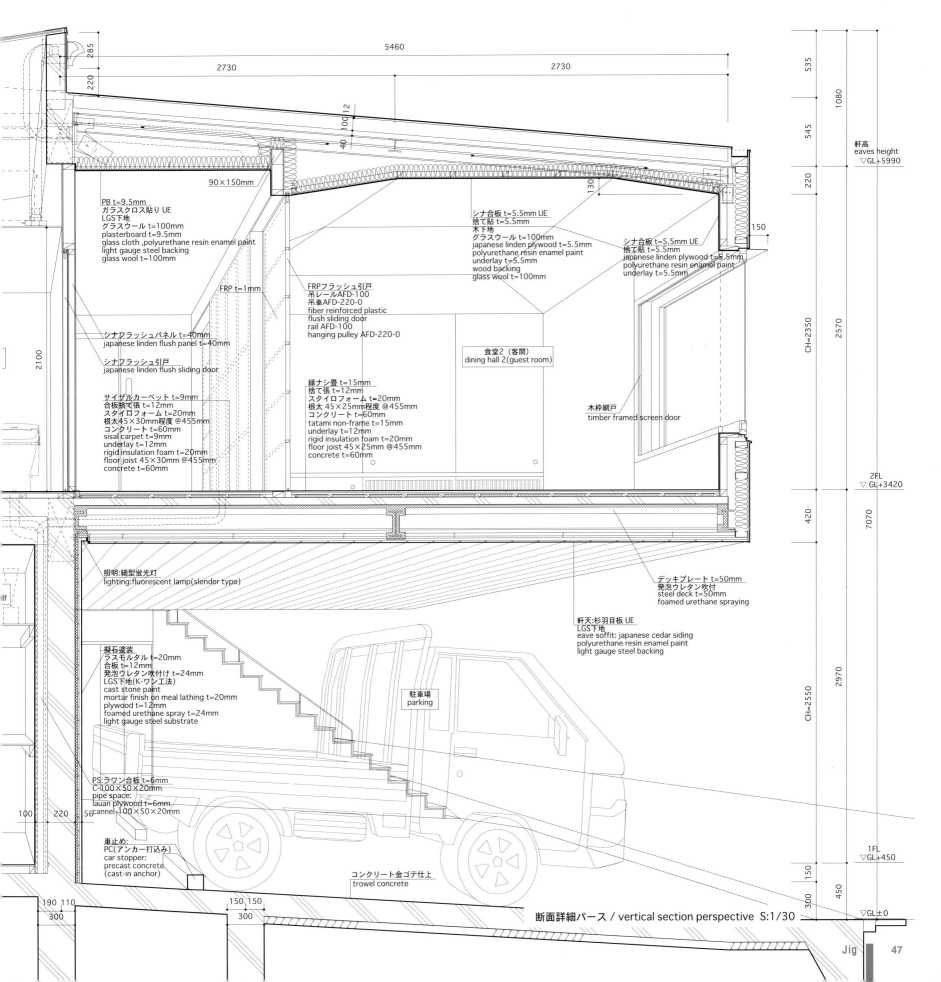

5460

2730 2730

285

220

535

1080

545

軒高
eaves height
▽GL+5990

220

90×150mm

PB t=9.5mm
ガラスクロス貼り UE
LGS下地
グラスウール t=100mm
plasterboard t=9.5mm
glass cloth ,polyurethane resin enamel paint
light gauge steel backing
glass wool t=100mm

シナ合板 t=5.5mm UE
捨て貼 t=5.5mm
木下地
グラスウール t=100mm
japanese linden plywood t=5.5mm
polyurethane resin enamel paint
underlay=5.5mm
wood backing
glass wool t=100mm

シナ合板 t=5.5mm UE
捨て貼 t=5.5mm
japanese linden plywood t=5.5mm
polyurethane resin enamel paint
underlay t=5.5mm

150

130

FRP t=1mm

FRPフラッシュ引戸
吊レールAFD-100
吊車AFD-220-0
fiber reinforced plastic
flush sliding door
rail AFD-100
hanging pulley AFD-220-0

CH=2350

2570

シナフラッシュパネル t=40mm
japanese linden flush panel t=40mm

シナフラッシュ引戸
japanese linden flush sliding door

食堂2（客間）
dining hall 2(guest room)

木枠網戸
timber framed screen door

サイザルカーペット t=9mm
合板捨て張 t=12mm
スタイロフォーム t=20mm
根太45×30mm程度 @455mm
コンクリート t=60mm
sisal carpet t=9mm
underlay t=12mm
rigid insulation foam t=20mm
floor joist 45×30mm @455mm
concrete t=60mm

縁ナシ畳 t=15mm
捨て張 t=12mm
スタイロフォーム t=20mm
根太 45×25mm程度 @455mm
コンクリート t=60mm
tatami non-frame t=15mm
underlay t=12mm
rigid insulation foam t=20mm
floor joist 45×25mm @455mm
concrete t=60mm

2100

2FL
▽GL+3420

420

7070

照明:細型蛍光灯
lighting:fluorescent lamp(slender type)

デッキプレート t=50mm
発泡ウレタン吹付
steel deck t=50mm
foamed urethane spraying

軒天:杉羽目板 UE
LGS下地
eave soffit: japanese cedar siding
polyurethane resin enamel paint
light gauge steel backing

凝石塗装
ラスモルタル t=20mm
合板 t=12mm
発泡ウレタン吹付け t=24mm
LGS下地(K-ワン工法)
cast stone paint
mortar finish on meal lathing t=20mm
plywood t=12mm
foamed urethane spray t=24mm
light gauge steel substrate

駐車場
parking

CH=2550

2970

PS:ラワン合板 t=6mm
C-100×50×20mm
pipe space:
lauan plywood t=6mm
cannel 100×50×20mm

車止め:
PC(アンカー打込み)
car stopper:
precast concrete
(cast-in anchor)

コンクリート金ゴテ仕上
trowel concrete

1FL
▽GL+450

150

450

100 220

190 110

300

150 150

300

300

断面詳細パース / vertical section perspective S:1/30

▽GL±0

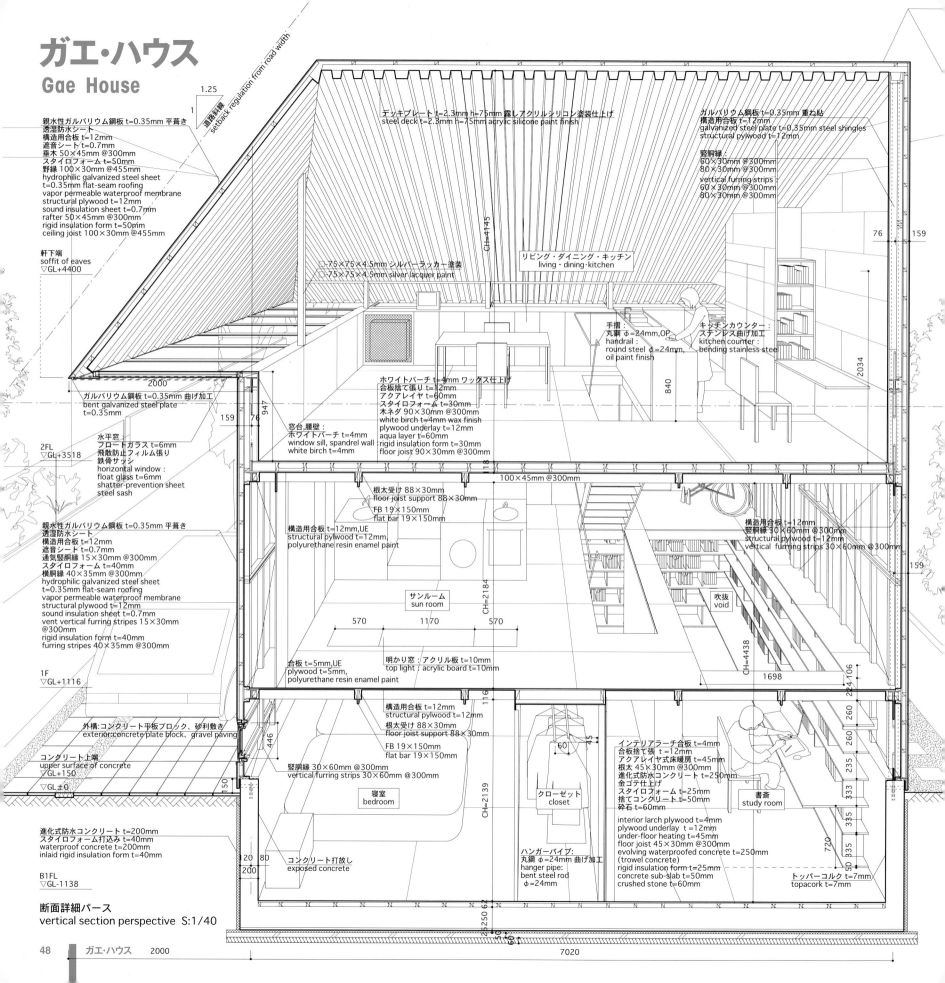

ガエ・ハウス
Gae House

道路斜線
setback regulation from road width
1.25
1

親水性ガルバリウム鋼板 t=0.35mm 平葺き
透湿防水シート
構造用合板 t=12mm
遮音シート t=0.7mm
垂木 50×45mm @300mm
スタイロフォーム t=50mm
野縁 100×30mm @455mm
hydrophilic galvanized steel sheet
t=0.35mm flat-seam roofing
vapor permeable waterproof membrane
structural plywood t=12mm
sound insulation sheet t=0.7mm
rafter 50×45mm @300mm
rigid insulation form t=50mm
ceiling joist 100×30mm @455mm

軒下端
soffit of eaves
▽GL+4400

2000

ガルバリウム鋼板 t=0.35mm 曲げ加工
bent galvanized steel plate
t=0.35mm

159 76 947

水平窓
フロートガラス t=6mm
飛散防止フィルム張り
鉄骨サッシ
horizontal window :
float glass t=6mm
shatter-prevention sheet
steel sash

2FL
▽GL+3518

親水性ガルバリウム鋼板 t=0.35mm 平葺き
透湿防水シート
構造用合板 t=12mm
遮音シート t=0.7mm
通気竪胴縁 15×30mm @300mm
スタイロフォーム t=40mm
横胴縁 40×35mm @300mm
hydrophilic galvanized steel sheet
t=0.35mm flat-seam roofing
vapor permeable waterproof membrane
structural plywood t=12mm
sound insulation sheet t=0.7mm
vent vertical furring stripes 15×30mm
@300mm
rigid insulation form t=40mm
furring stripes 40×35mm @300mm

1F
▽GL+1116

外構:コンクリート平板ブロック、砂利敷き
exterior:concrete plate block, gravel paving

コンクリート上端
upper surface of concrete
▽GL+150
▽GL±0

進化式防水コンクリート t=200mm
スタイロフォーム打込み t=40mm
waterproof concrete t=200mm
inlaid rigid insulation form t=40mm

B1FL
▽GL-1138

断面詳細パース
vertical section perspective S:1/40

デッキプレート t=2.3mm h=75mm 露しアクリルシリコン塗装仕上げ
steel deck t=2.3mm h=75mm acrylic silicone paint finish

ガルバリウム鋼板 t=0.35mm 重ね貼
構造用合板 t=12mm
galvanized steel plate t=0.35mm steel shingles
structural pylwood t=12mm

竪胴縁：
60×30mm @300mm
80×30mm @300mm
vertical furring strips
60×30mm @300mm
80×30mm @300mm

CH=4145

リビング・ダイニング・キッチン
living・dining・kitchen

76 159

□-75×75×4.5mm シルバーラッカー塗装
□-75×75×4.5mm silver lacquer paint

手摺：
丸鋼 φ=24mm,OP
handrail :
round steel φ=24mm,
oil paint finish

キッチンカウンター：
ステンレス曲げ加工
kitchen counter :
bending stainless steel

840 2034

ホワイトバーチ t=4mm ワックス仕上げ
合板捨て張り t=12mm
アクアレイヤ t=60mm
スタイロフォーム t=30mm
木ネダ 90×30mm @300mm
white birch t=4mm wax finish
plywood underlay t=12mm
aqua layer t=60mm
rigid insulation form t=30mm
floor joist 90×30mm @300mm

窓台,腰壁：
ホワイトバーチ t=4mm
window sill, spandrel wall
white birch t=4mm

根太受け 88×30mm
floor joist support 88×30mm
FB 19×150mm
flat bar 19×150mm

100×45mm @300mm

構造用合板 t=12mm,UE
structural pylwood t=12mm,
polyurethane resin enamel paint

構造用合板 t=12mm
竪胴縁 30×60mm @300mm
structural pylwood t=12mm
vertical furring strips 30×60mm @300mm

159

サンルーム
sun room

CH=2184

吹抜
void

CH=4438

570 1170 570

1698

24-106
260 260

合板 t=5mm,UE
plywood t=5mm,
polyurethane resin enamel paint

明かり窓：アクリル板 t=10mm
top light : acrylic board t=10mm

構造用合板 t=12mm
structural pylwood t=12mm
根太受け 88×30mm
floor joist support 88×30mm
FB 19×150mm
flat bar 19×150mm

竪胴縁 30×60mm @300mm
vertical furring strips 30×60mm @300mm

60 45

インテリアラーチ合板 t=4mm
合板捨て張り t=12mm
アクアレイヤ式床暖房 t=45mm
根太 45×30mm @300mm
進化式防水コンクリート t=250mm
金ゴテ仕上げ
スタイロフォーム t=25mm
捨てコンクリート t=50mm
砕石 t=60mm
interior larch plywood t=4mm
plywood underlay t=12mm
under-floor heating t=45mm
floor joist 45×30mm @300mm
evolving waterproofed concrete t=250mm
(trowel concrete)
rigid insulation form t=25mm
concrete sub-slab t=50mm
crushed stone t=60mm

116

寝室
bedroom

CH=2139

クローゼット
closet

書斎
study room

235 333 335 335 720 50

20 80
200

コンクリート打放し
exposed concrete

ハンガーパイプ：
丸鋼 φ=24mm 曲げ加工
hanger pipe:
bent steel rod
φ=24mm

トッパーコルク t=7mm
topacork t=7mm

250 62

446 150

7020

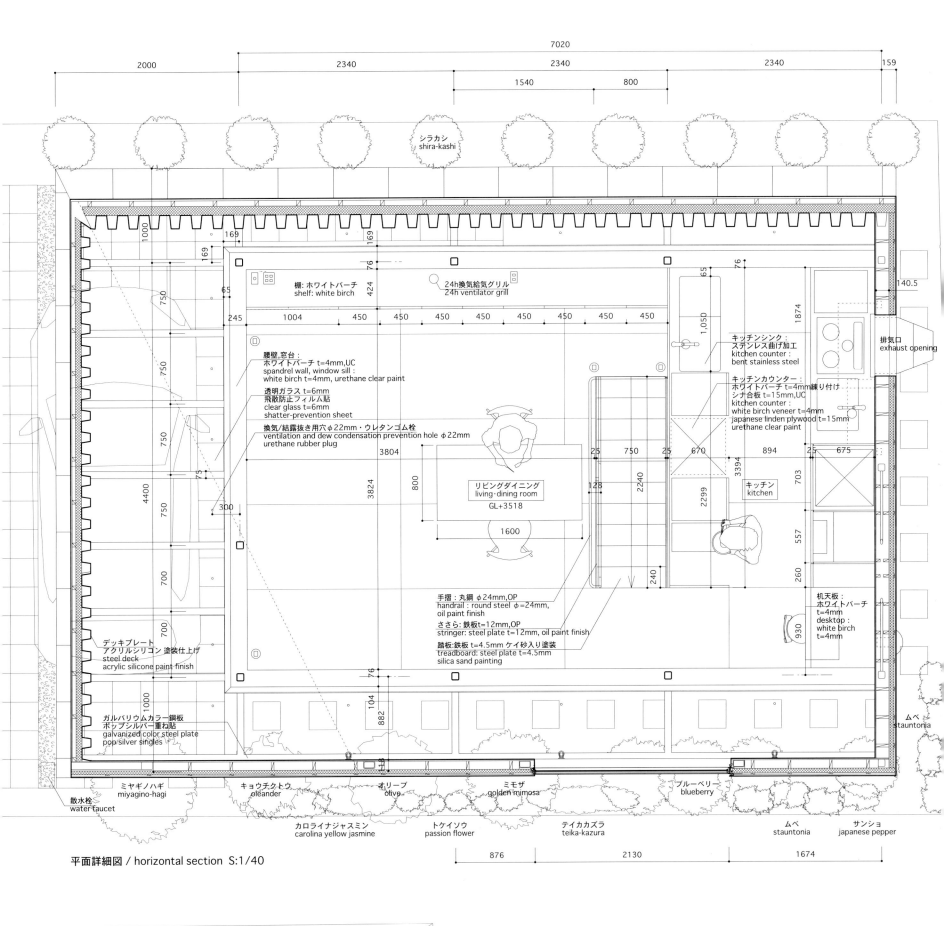

シラカシ
shira-kashi

7020
2000
2340
2340
2340
159
1540
800

169
169
76
76
140.5

棚：ホワイトバーチ
shelf: white birch

24h換気給気グリル
24h ventilator grill

キッチンシンク：
ステンレス曲げ加工
kitchen counter :
bent stainless steel

1000
169
169

65

750

245
1004
450
450
450
450
450
450
450
450

750

腰壁,窓台
ホワイトバーチ t=4mm,UC
spandrel wall, window sill :
white birch t=4mm, urethane clear paint

透明ガラス t=6mm
飛散防止フィルム貼
clear glass t=6mm
shatter-prevention sheet

換気/結露抜き用穴φ22mm・ウレタンゴム栓
ventilation and dew condensation prevention hole φ22mm
urethane rubber plug

1,050
65
1874

キッチンカウンター：
ホワイトバーチ t=4mm練り付け
シナ合板 t=15mm,UC
kitchen counter :
white birch veneer t=4mm
japanese linden plywood t=15mm
urethane clear paint

排気口
exhaust opening

4400
750

750

75

300

3804

3824
800

リビングダイニング
living・dining room
GL+3518

25
750
25
670
894
25
675

128
2240
2299

キッチン
kitchen

3394
703

1600

240
557

手摺：丸鋼 φ24mm,OP
handrail : round steel φ24mm,
oil paint finish

ささら：鉄板t=12mm,OP
stringer: steel plate t=12mm, oil paint finish

踏板：鉄板 t=4.5mm ケイ砂入り塗装
treadboard: steel plate t=4.5mm
silica sand painting

700

700

デッキプレート
アクリルシリコン 塗装仕上げ
steel deck
acrylic silicone paint finish

260

机天板：
ホワイトバーチ
t=4mm
desktop :
white birch
t=4mm

930

1000

ガルバリウムカラー鋼板
ポップシルバー重ね貼
galvanized color steel plate
pop silver singles

76
104
882

ムベ
stauntonia

ミヤギノハギ
miyagino-hagi

散水栓
water faucet

キョウチクトウ
oleander

オリーブ
olive

ミモザ
golden mimosa

ブルーベリー
blueberry

カロライナジャスミン
carolina yellow jasmine

トケイソウ
passion flower

テイカカズラ
teika-kazura

ムベ
stauntonia

サンショ
japanese pepper

876
2130
1674

平面詳細図 / horizontal section S:1/40

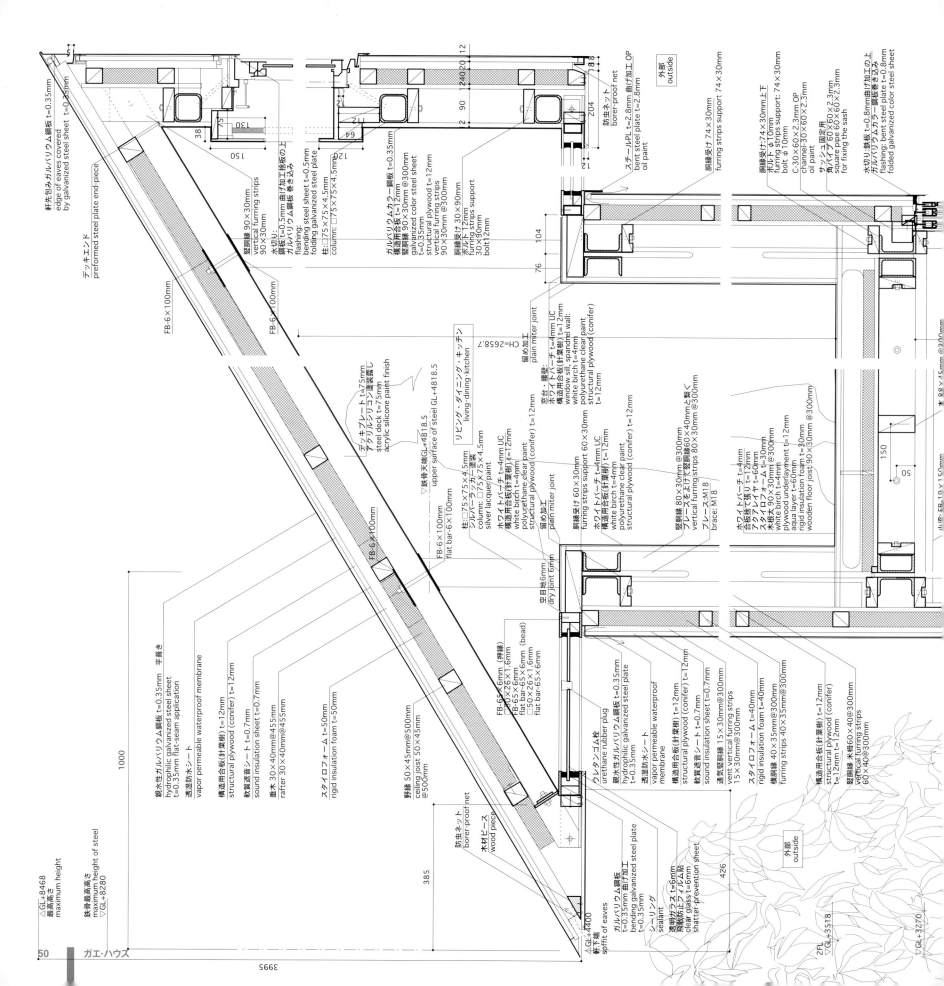

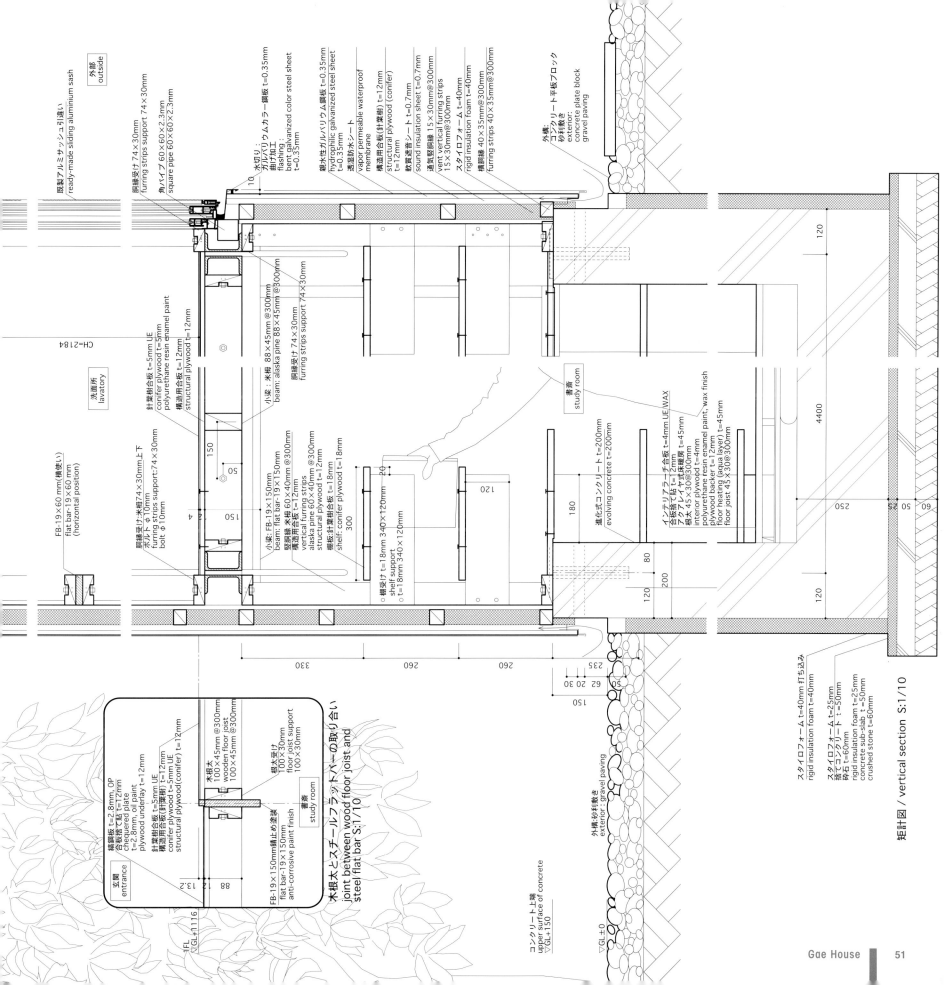

既製アルミサッシュ引違い
ready-made sliding aluminium sash

外部
outside

胴縁受け 74×30mm
furring strips support 74×30mm

角パイプ 60×60×2.3mm
square pipe 60×60×2.3mm

水切り
ガルバリウムカラー鋼板 t=0.35mm
曲げ加工
flashing：
bent galvanized color steel sheet
t=0.35mm

親水性ガルバリウム鋼板 t=0.35mm
hydrophilic galvanized steel sheet
t=0.35mm

透湿防水シート
vapor permeable waterproof
membrane

構造用合板(針葉樹) t=12mm
structural plywood (conifer)
t=12mm

軟質遮音シート t=0.7mm
sound insulation sheet t=0.7mm

通気竪胴縁 15×30mm@300mm
vent vertical furring strips
15×30mm@300mm

スタイロフォーム t=40mm
rigid insulation foam t=40mm

横胴縁 40×35mm@300mm
furring strips 40×35mm@300mm

外構：
コンクリート平板ブロック
concrete plate block

外構：
コンクリート平板ブロック
砂利敷き
exterior:
concrete plate block
gravel paving

既製アルミサッシュ引違い
ready-made sliding aluminium sash

CH=2184

洗面所
lavatory

FB-19×60mm(横使い)
flat bar-19×60 mm
(horizontal position)

針葉樹合板 t=5mm UE
conifer plywood t=5mm
ポリウレタン樹脂エナメル塗装
polyurethane resin enamel paint
構造用合板 t=12mm
structural plywood t=12mm

胴縁受け:米栂74×30mm上下
furring strips support:74×30mm
ボルト φ10mm
bolt φ10mm

小梁：米栂 88×45mm @300mm
beam: alaska pine 88×45mm @300mm
胴縁受け 74×30mm
furring strips support 74×30mm

小梁:FB-19×150mm
beam: flat bar-19×150mm
竪胴縁 米栂 60×40mm @300mm
vertical furring strips
alaska pine 60×40mm @300mm
構造用合板 t=12mm
structural plywood t=12mm
棚板:針葉樹合板 t=18mm
shelf: conifer plywood t=18mm

棚受け t=18mm 340×120mm
shelf support
t=18mm 340×120mm

書斎
study room

進化式コンクリート t=200mm
evolving concrete t=200mm

インテリアラーチ合板 t=4mm UE/WAX
合板捨て貼 t=12mm
アクアレイヤ式床暖房 t=45mm
根太 45×30@300mm
interior plywood t=4mm
polyurethane resin enamel paint, wax finish
plywood backer t=12mm
floor heating (aqua layer) t=45mm
floor joist 45×30@300mm

スタイロフォーム t=40mm打ち込み
rigid insulation foam t=40mm

スタイロフォーム t=25mm
捨てコンクリート t=50mm
砕石 t=60mm
rigid insulation foam t=25mm
concrete sub-slab t=50mm
crushed stone t=60mm

外構:砂利敷き
exterior : gravel paving

矩計図 / vertical section S:1/10

縞鋼板 t=2.8mm, OP
合板捨て貼 t=12mm
t=2.8mm, oil paint
plywood underlay t=12mm
針葉樹合板 t=5mm UE
構造用合板(針葉樹) t=12mm
conifer plywood t=5mm UE
structural plywood(conifer) t=12mm

木根太
100×45mm @300mm
wooden floor joist
100×45mm@300mm

根太受け
100×30mm
floor joist support
100×30mm

書斎
study room

FB-19×150mm鎖止め塗装
flat bar-19×150mm
anti-corrosive paint finish

縞鋼板 t=2.8mm, OP
chequered plate

玄関
entrance

コンクリート上端
upper surface of concrete
▽GL+150

1FL
▽GL+1116

木根太とスチールフラットバーの取り合い
joint between wood floor joist and
steel flat bar S:1/10

外構:砂利敷き
exterior : gravel paving

コンクリート上端
upper surface of concrete
▽GL+150

▽GL±0

クス・ハウス
Kus House

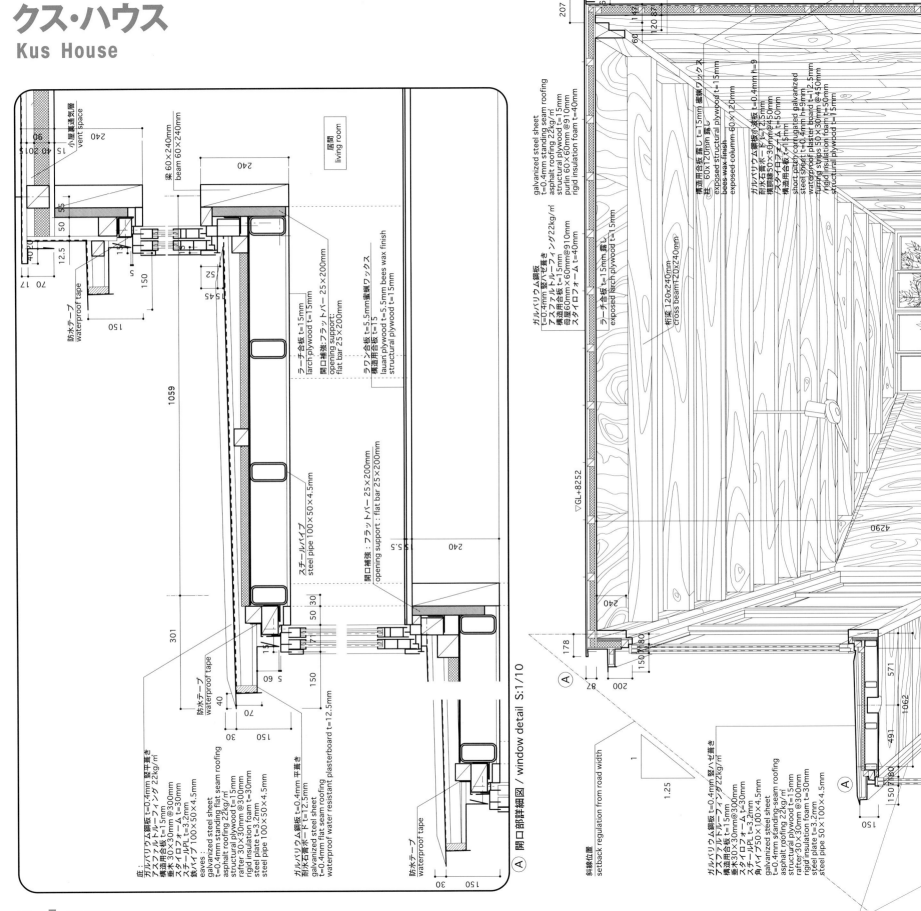

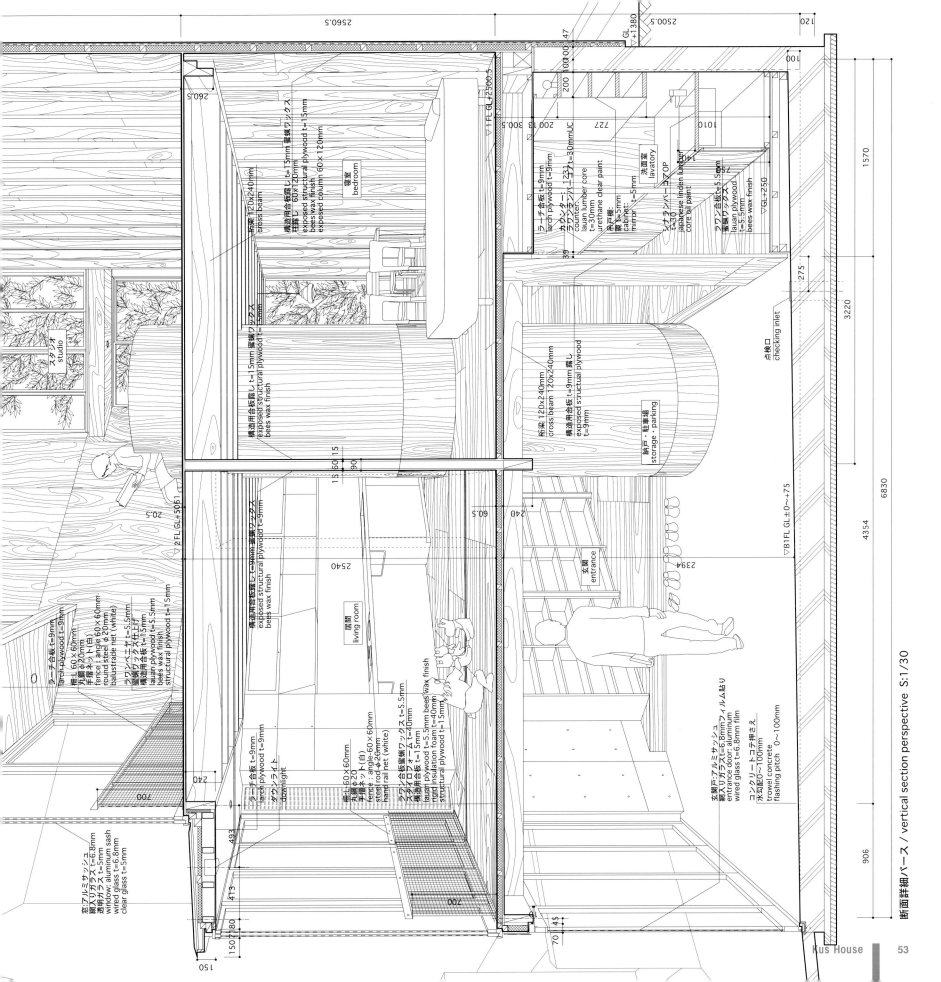

断面詳細パース / vertical section perspective S:1/30

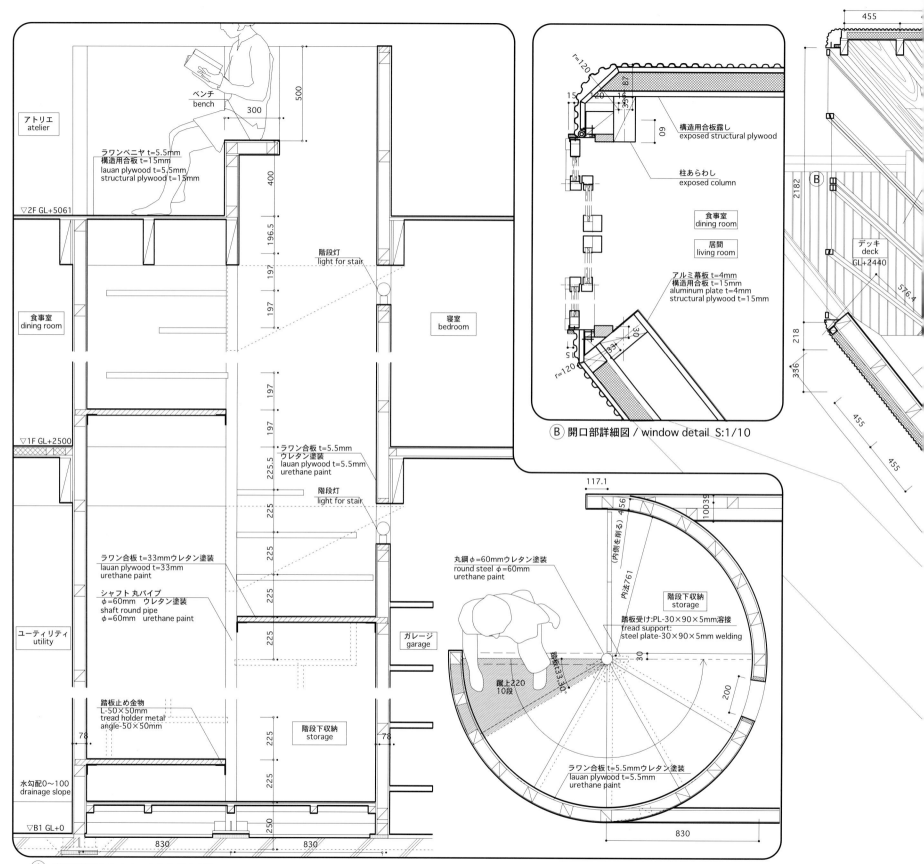

アトリエ
atelier

ベンチ
bench

500

300

ラワンベニヤ t=5.5mm
構造用合板 t=15mm
lauan plywood t=5.5mm
structural plywood t=15mm

400

▽2F GL+5061

196.5

197

食事室
dining room

197

階段灯
light for stair

寝室
bedroom

▽1F GL+2500

ラワン合板 t=5.5mm
ウレタン塗装
lauan plywood t=5.5mm
urethane paint

225.5

階段灯
light for stair

ラワン合板 t=33mmウレタン塗装
lauan plywood t=33mm
urethane paint

225

シャフト 丸パイプ
φ=60mm ウレタン塗装
shaft round pipe
φ=60mm urethane paint

225

ユーティリティ
utility

225

ガレージ
garage

踏板止め金物
L-50×50mm
tread holder metal
angle-50×50mm

225

階段下収納
storage

78

78

水勾配0〜100
drainage slope

225

▽B1 GL+0

830

250

830

Ⓐ 階段詳細図 / stairs detail S:1/20

r=120

15 120

87

336

60

構造用合板露し
exposed structural plywood

柱あらわし
exposed column

食事室
dining room

居間
living room

アルミ幕板 t=4mm
構造用合板 t=15mm
aluminum plate t=4mm
structural plywood t=15mm

334

r=120

Ⓑ 開口部詳細図 / window detail S:1/10

455

Ⓑ

2182

576.4

デッキ
deck
GL+2440

218

336

455

455

117.1

456

100 39

(内側を前名)

内法761

階段下収納
storage

丸鋼φ=60mmウレタン塗装
round steel φ=60mm
urethane paint

踏板受け:PL-30×90×5mm溶接
tread support:
steel plate-30×90×5mm welding

30

200

踏板t33.30

蹴上220
10段

ラワン合板 t=5.5mmウレタン塗装
lauan plywood t=5.5mm
urethane paint

830

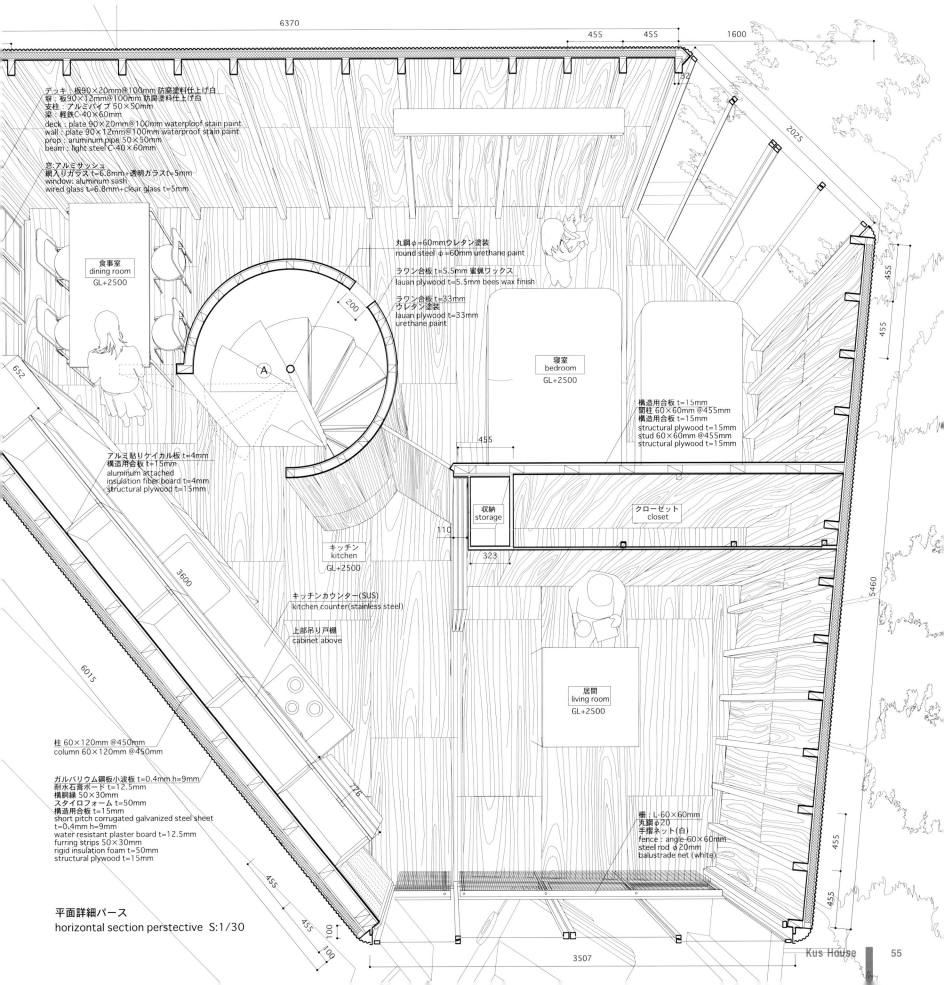

デッキ：板90×20mm@100mm 防腐塗料仕上げ白
塀：板90×12mm@100mm 防腐塗料仕上げ白
支柱：アルミパイプ 50×50mm
梁：軽鉄C-40×60mm
deck : plate 90×20mm@100mm waterploof stain paint
wall : plate 90×12mm@100mm waterproof stain paint
prop : aruminum pipe 50×50mm
beam : light steel C-40×60mm

窓：アルミサッシュ
網入りガラス t=6.8mm+透明ガラスt=5mm
window: aluminum sash
wired glass t=6.8mm+clear glass t=5mm

丸鋼φ=60mmウレタン塗装
round steel φ=60mm urethane paint

ラワン合板 t=5.5mm 蜜蝋ワックス
lauan plywood t=5.5mm bees wax finish

ラワン合板 t=33mm
ウレタン塗装
lauan plywood t=33mm
urethane paint

食事室
dining room
GL+2500

寝室
bedroom
GL+2500

構造用合板 t=15mm
間柱 60×60mm @455mm
構造用合板 t=15mm
structural plywood t=15mm
stud 60×60mm @455mm
structural plywood t=15mm

アルミ貼りケイカル板 t=4mm
構造用合板 t=15mm
aluminum attached
insulation fiber board t=4mm
structural plywood t=15mm

収納
storage

クローゼット
closet

キッチン
kitchen
GL+2500

キッチンカウンター(SUS)
kitchen counter(stainless steel)

上部吊り戸棚
cabinet above

居間
living room
GL+2500

柱 60×120mm @450mm
column 60×120mm @450mm

ガルバリウム鋼板小波板 t=0.4mm.h=9mm
耐水石膏ボード t=12.5mm
横胴縁 50×30mm
スタイロフォーム t=50mm
構造用合板 t=15mm
short pitch corrugated galvanized steel sheet
t=0.4mm h=9mm
water resistant plaster board t=12.5mm
furring strips 50×30mm
rigid insulation foam t=50mm
structural plywood t=15mm

柵：L-60×60mm
丸鋼φ20
手摺ネット(白)
fence : angle-60×60mm
steel rod φ20mm
balustrade net (white)

平面詳細パース
horizontal section perstective S:1/30

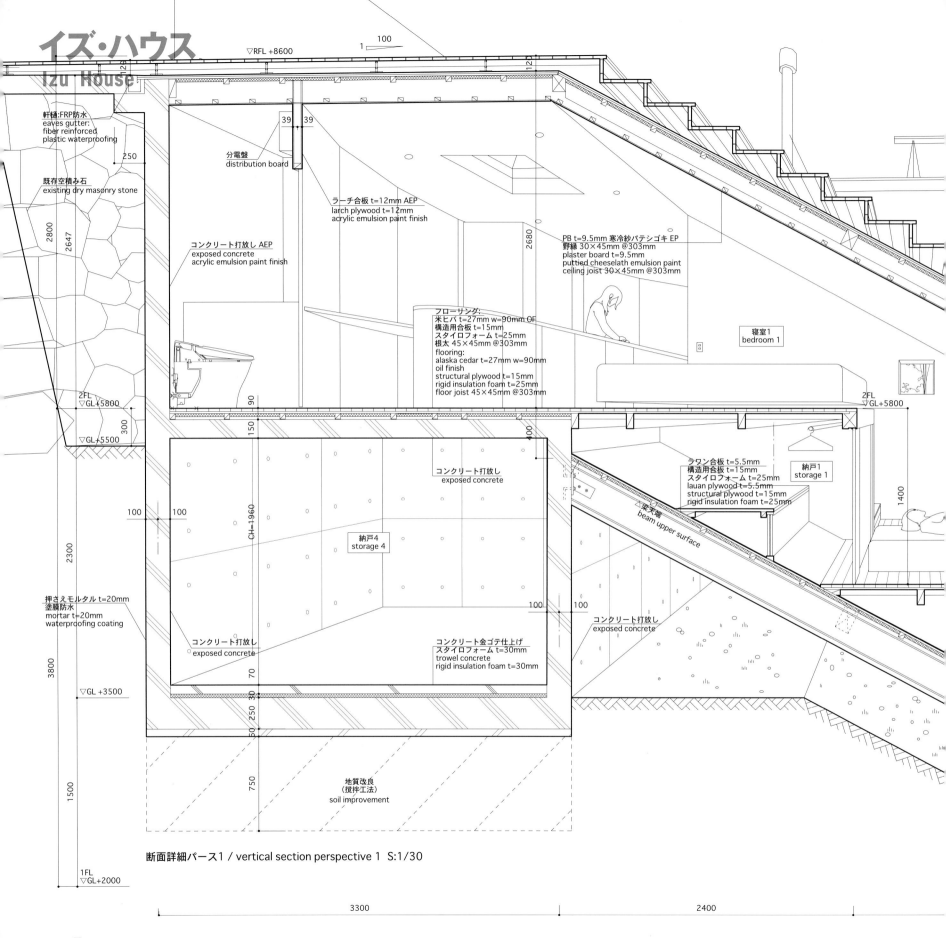

イズ・ハウス
Izu House

▽RFL +8600

1 : 100

軒樋:FRP防水
eaves gutter:
fiber reinforced
plastic waterproofing

250

既存空積み石
existing dry masonry stone

2800
2647

分電盤
distribution board

39 39

ラーチ合板 t=12mm AEP
larch plywood t=12mm
acrylic emulsion paint finish

コンクリート打放し AEP
exposed concrete
acrylic emulsion paint finish

2680

PB t=9.5mm 寒冷紗パテシゴキ EP
野縁 30×45mm @303mm
plaster board t=9.5mm
puttied cheeselath emulsion paint
ceiling joist 30×45mm @303mm

フローリング:
米ヒバ t=27mm w=90mm OF
構造用合板 t=15mm
スタイロフォーム t=25mm
根太 45×45mm @303mm
flooring:
alaska cedar t=27mm w=90mm
oil finish
structural plywood t=15mm
rigid insulation foam t=25mm
floor joist 45×45mm @303mm

寝室1
bedroom 1

2FL
▽GL +5800

2FL
▽GL +5800

2FL
▽GL +5800

300

▽GL +5500

150

90

400

コンクリート打放し
exposed concrete

納戸1
storage 1

ラワン合板 t=5.5mm
構造用合板 t=15mm
スタイロフォーム t=25mm
lauan plywood t=5.5mm
structural plywood t=15mm
rigid insulation foam t=25mm

1400

2300

100

100

CH=1960

納戸4
storage 4

梁天端
beam upper surface

100

100

押さえモルタル t=20mm
塗膜防水
mortar t=20mm
waterproofing coating

コンクリート打放し
exposed concrete

コンクリート打放し
exposed concrete

3800

コンクリート金ゴテ仕上げ
スタイロフォーム t=30mm
trowel concrete
rigid insulation foam t=30mm

70

▽GL +3500

30
250
50

地質改良
(撹拌工法)
soil improvement

1500

750

1FL
▽GL +2000

断面詳細パース1 / vertical section perspective 1 S:1/30

3300

2400

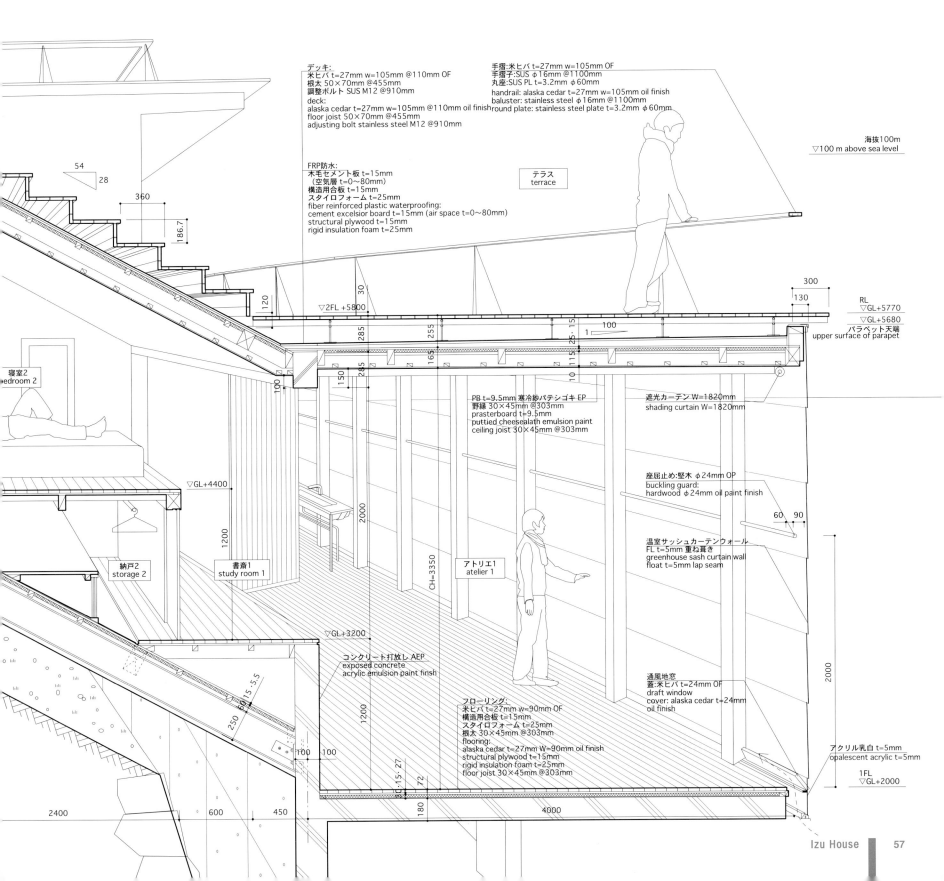

デッキ:
米ヒバ t=27mm w=105mm @110mm OF
根太 50×70mm @455mm
調整ボルト SUS M12 @910mm
deck:
alaska cedar t=27mm w=105mm @110mm oil finish
floor joist 50×70mm @455mm
adjusting bolt stainless steel M12 @910mm

手摺:米ヒバ t=27mm w=105mm OF
手摺子:SUS φ16mm @1100mm
丸座:SUS PL t=3.2mm φ60mm
handrail: alaska cedar t=27mm w=105mm oil finish
baluster: stainless steel φ16mm @1100mm
round plate: stainless steel plate t=3.2mm φ60mm

海抜100m
▽100 m above sea level

FRP防水:
木毛セメント板 t=15mm
(空気層 t=0〜80mm)
構造用合板 t=15mm
スタイロフォーム t=25mm
fiber reinforced plastic waterproofing:
cement excelsior board t=15mm (air space t=0〜80mm)
structural plywood t=15mm
rigid insulation foam t=25mm

テラス
terrace

54
28

360

186.7

120
30

▽2FL +5800

285
255

RL
▽GL+5770
▽GL+5680
300
130

100
1

パラペット天端
upper surface of parapet

寝室2
bedroom 2

165
285
150
100

115·25·15
10

PB t=9.5mm 寒冷紗パテシゴキ EP
野縁 30×45mm @303mm
prasterboard t=9.5mm
puttied cheesealath emulsion paint
ceiling joist 30×45mm @303mm

遮光カーテン W=1820mm
shading curtain W=1820mm

▽GL+4400

2000

CH=3350

1200

書斎1
study room 1

アトリエ1
atelier 1

座屈止め:堅木 φ24mm OP
buckling guard:
hardwood φ24mm oil paint finish

60 90

温室サッシュカーテンウォール
FL t=5mm 重ね葺き
greenhouse sash curtain wall
float t=5mm lap seam

納戸2
storage 2

▽GL+3200

コンクリート打放し AEP
exposed concrete
acrylic emulsion paint finish

2000

60·15·5.5

250

100 100

1200

フローリング:
米ヒバ t=27mm w=90mm OF
構造用合板 t=15mm
スタイロフォーム t=25mm
根太 30×45mm @303mm
flooring:
alaska cedar t=27mm W=90mm oil finish
structural plywood t=15mm
rigid insulation foam t=25mm
floor joist 30×45mm @303mm

通風地窓
蓋:米ヒバ t=24mm OF
draft window
cover: alaska cedar t=24mm
oil finish

アクリル乳白 t=5mm
opalescent acrylic t=5mm

30·15·27
72

180

1FL
▽GL+2000

2400
600
450
4000

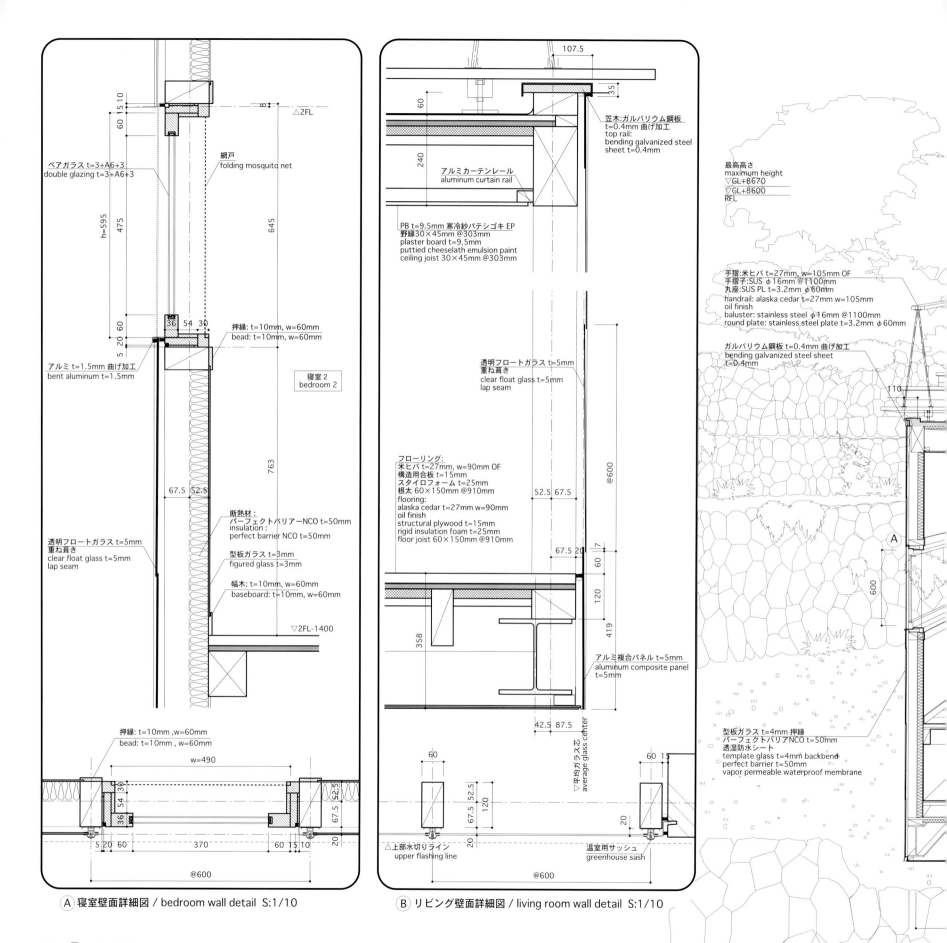

ベアガラス t=3+A6+3
double glazing t=3+A6+3

網戸
folding mosquito net

押縁: t=10mm, w=60mm
bead: t=10mm, w=60mm

アルミ t=1.5mm 曲げ加工
bent aluminum t=1.5mm

寝室 2
bedroom 2

透明フロートガラス t=5mm
重ね葺き
clear float glass t=5mm
lap seam

断熱材：
パーフェクトバリアーNCO t=50mm
insulation :
perfect barrier NCO t=50mm

型板ガラス t=3mm
figured glass t=3mm

幅木: t=10mm, w=60mm
baseboard: t=10mm, w=60mm

▽2FL-1400

押縁: t=10mm ,w=60mm
bead: t=10mm , w=60mm

w=490

@600

Ⓐ 寝室壁面詳細図 / bedroom wall detail S:1/10

△2FL

笠木:ガルバリウム鋼板
t=0.4mm 曲げ加工
top rail:
bending galvanized steel
sheet t=0.4mm

アルミカーテンレール
aluminum curtain rail

PB t=9.5mm 寒冷紗パテシゴキ EP
野縁30×45mm @303mm
plaster board t=9.5mm
puttied cheeselath emulsion paint
ceiling joist 30×45mm @303mm

透明フロートガラス t=5mm
重ね葺き
clear float glass t=5mm
lap seam

フローリング:
米ヒバ t=27mm, w=90mm OF
構造用合板 t=15mm
スタイロフォーム t=25mm
根太 60×150mm @910mm
flooring:
alaska cedar t=27mm w=90mm
oil finish
structural plywood t=15mm
rigid insulation foam t=25mm
floor joist 60×150mm @910mm

アルミ複合パネル t=5mm
aluminum composite panel
t=5mm

▽平均ガラス芯
average glass center

△上部水切りライン
upper flashing line

温室用サッシュ
greenhouse sash

@600

Ⓑ リビング壁面詳細図 / living room wall detail S:1/10

最高高さ
maximum height
▽GL+8670
▽GL+8600
RFL

手摺:米ヒバ t=27mm, w=105mm OF
手摺子:SUS φ16mm @1100mm
丸座:SUS PL t=3.2mm φ60mm
handrail: alaska cedar t=27mm w=105mm
oil finish
baluster: stainless steel φ16mm @1100mm
round plate: stainless steel plate t=3.2mm φ60mm

ガルバリウム鋼板 t=0.4mm 曲げ加工
bending galvanized steel sheet
t=0.4mm

型板ガラス t=4mm 押縁
パーフェクトバリアNCO t=50mm
透湿防水シート
template glass t=4mm backbend
perfect barrier t=50mm
vapor permeable waterproof membrane

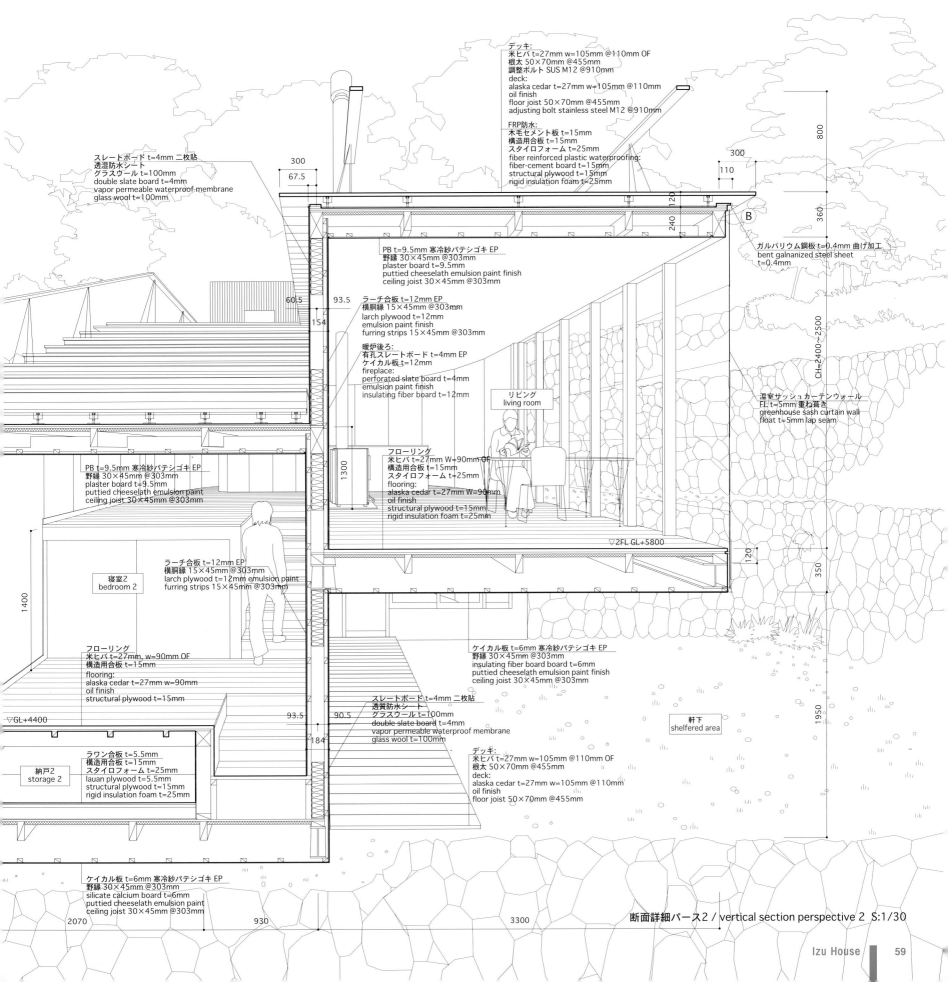

スレートボード t=4mm 二枚貼
透湿防水シート
グラスウール t=100mm
double slate board t=4mm
vapor permeable waterproof membrane
glass wool t=100mm

デッキ:
米ヒバ t=27mm w=105mm @110mm OF
根太 50×70mm @455mm
調整ボルト SUS M12 @910mm
deck:
alaska cedar t=27mm w=105mm @110mm
oil finish
floor joist 50×70mm @455mm
adjusting bolt stainless steel M12 @910mm

FRP防水:
木毛セメント板 t=15mm
構造用合板 t=15mm
スタイロフォーム t=25mm
fiber reinforced plastic waterproofing:
fiber-cement board t=15mm
structural plywood t=15mm
rigid insulation foam t=25mm

300
67.5
300
110

800
360

B

ガルバリウム鋼板 t=0.4mm 曲げ加工
bent galnanized steel sheet
t=0.4mm

PB t=9.5mm 寒冷紗パテシゴキ EP
野縁 30×45mm @303mm
plaster board t=9.5mm
puttied cheeselath emulsion paint finish
ceiling joist 30×45mm @303mm

ラーチ合板 t=12mm EP
横胴縁 15×45mm @303mm
larch plywood t=12mm
emulsion paint finish
furring strips 15×45mm @303mm

暖炉後ろ
有孔スレートボード t=4mm EP
ケイカル板 t=12mm
fireplace:
perforated slate board t=4mm
emulsion paint finish
insulating fiber board t=12mm

60.5
93.5
154

リビング
living room

CH=2400～2500

温室サッシュカーテンウォール
FL t=5mm 重ね葺き
greenhouse sash curtain wall
float t=5mm lap seam

PB t=9.5mm 寒冷紗パテシゴキ EP
野縁 30×45mm @303mm
plaster board t=9.5mm
puttied cheeselath emulsion paint
ceiling joist 30×45mm @303mm

フローリング
米ヒバ t=27mm W=90mm OF
構造用合板 t=15mm
スタイロフォーム t=25mm
flooring:
alaska cedar t=27mm W=90mm
oil finish
structural plywood t=15mm
rigid insulation foam t=25mm

1300

寝室2
bedroom 2

ラーチ合板 t=12mm EP
横胴縁 15×45mm @303mm
larch plywood t=12mm emulsion paint
furring strips 15×45mm @303mm

▽2FL GL+5800

120
350

1400

フローリング
米ヒバ t=27mm, w=90mm OF
構造用合板 t=15mm
flooring:
alaska cedar t=27mm w=90mm
oil finish
structural plywood t=15mm

ケイカル板 t=6mm 寒冷紗パテシゴキ EP
野縁 30×45mm @303mm
insulating fiber board board t=6mm
puttied cheeselath emulsion paint finish
ceiling joist 30×45mm @303mm

軒下
shelfered area

1950

▽GL+4400

93.5
90.5

184

納戸2
storage 2

ラワン合板 t=5.5mm
構造用合板 t=15mm
スタイロフォーム t=25mm
lauan plywood t=5.5mm
structural plywood t=15mm
rigid insulation foam t=25mm

スレートボード t=4mm 二枚貼
透質防水シート
グラスウール t=100mm
double slate board t=4mm
vapor permeable waterproof membrane
glass wool t=100mm

デッキ:
米ヒバ t=27mm w=105mm @110mm OF
根太 50×70mm @455mm
deck:
alaska cedar t=27mm w=105mm @110mm
oil finish
floor joist 50×70mm @455mm

ケイカル板 t=6mm 寒冷紗パテシゴキ EP
野縁 30×45mm @303mm
silicate calcium board t=6mm
puttied cheeselath emulsion paint
ceiling joist 30×45mm @303mm

2070
930
3300

断面詳細パース2 / vertical section perspective 2 S:1/30

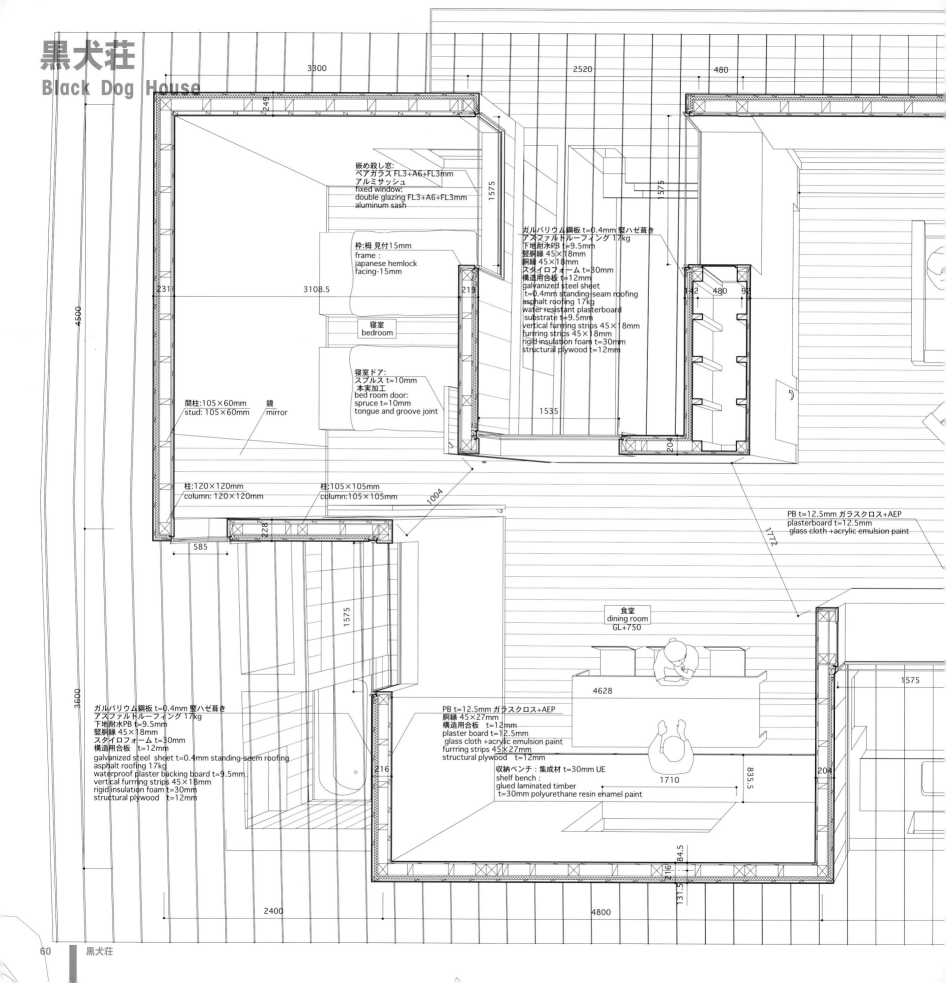

嵌め殺し窓:
ペアガラス FL3+A6+FL3mm
アルミサッシ
fixed window:
double glazing FL3+A6+FL3mm
aluminum sash

枠:栂 見付15mm
frame :
japanese hemlock
facing-15mm

寝室
bedroom

寝室ドア:
スプルス t=10mm
本実加工
bed room door:
spruce t=10mm
tongue and groove joint

ガルバリウム鋼板 t=0.4mm 竪ハゼ葺き
アスファルトルーフィング 17kg
下地耐水PB t=9.5mm
竪胴縁 45×18mm
胴縁 45×18mm
スタイロフォーム t=30mm
構造用合板 t=12mm
galvanized steel sheet
t=0.4mm standing-seam roofing
asphalt roofing 17kg
water resistant plasterboard
substrate t=9.5mm
vertical furring strips 45×18mm
furring strips 45×18mm
rigid insulation foam t=30mm
structural plywood t=12mm

間柱:105×60mm
stud: 105×60mm

鏡
mirror

柱:120×120mm
column: 120×120mm

柱:105×105mm
column:105×105mm

PB t=12.5mm ガラスクロス+AEP
plasterboard t=12.5mm
glass cloth +acrylic emulsion paint

食堂
dining room
GL+750

ガルバリウム鋼板 t=0.4mm 竪ハゼ葺き
アスファルトルーフィング 17kg
下地耐水PB t=9.5mm
竪胴縁 45×18mm
スタイロフォーム t=30mm
構造用合板 t=12mm
galvanized steel sheet t=0.4mm standing-seam roofing
asphalt roofing 17kg
waterproof plaster backing board t=9.5mm
vertical furring strips 45×18mm
rigid insulation foam t=30mm
structural plywood t=12mm

PB t=12.5mm ガラスクロス+AEP
胴縁 45×27mm
構造用合板 t=12mm
plaster board t=12.5mm
glass cloth +acrylic emulsion paint
furrring strips 45×27mm
structural plywood t=12mm

収納ベンチ:集成材 t=30mm UE
shelf bench :
glued laminated timber
t=30mm polyurethane resin enamel paint

3300
2520
480
2249
1575
1575
231
3108.5
219
142 480 92
4500
204
1535
3600
585
228
1004
1575
216
1772
4628
1710
835.5
204
1575
2400
216
84.5
131.5
4800

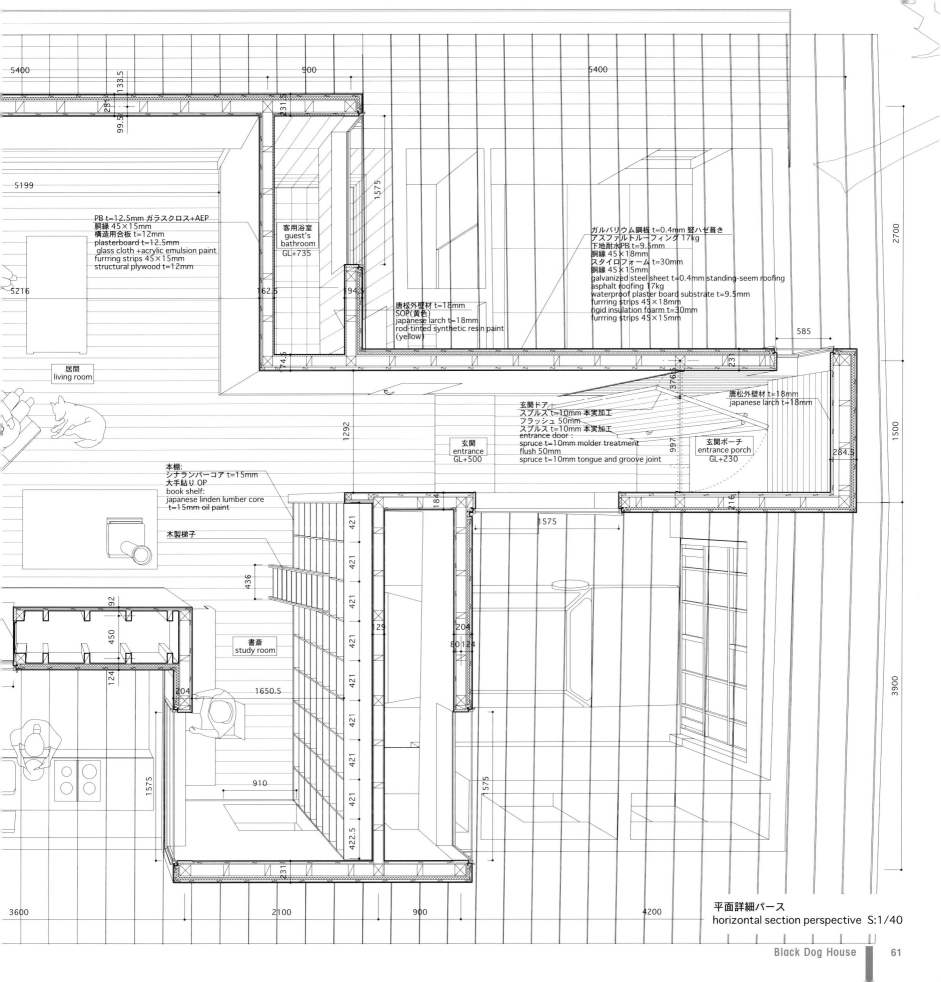

5400
133.5
28
99.5
900
5400
2700
231

5199

231

PB t=12.5mm ガラスクロス+AEP
胴縁 45×15mm
構造用合板 t=12mm
plasterboard t=12.5mm
glass cloth +acrylic emulsion paint
furrring strips 45×15mm
structural plywood t=12mm

客用浴室
guest's
bathroom
GL+735

1575

5216

162.5

194.5

ガルバリウム鋼板 t=0.4mm 竪ハゼ葺き
アスファルトルーフィング 17kg
下地耐水PB t=9.5mm
胴縁 45×18mm
スタイロフォーム t=30mm
胴縁 45×15mm
galvanized steel sheet t=0.4mm standing-seem roofing
asphalt roofing 17kg
waterproof plaster board substrate t=9.5mm
furrring strips 45×18mm
rigid insulation foarm t=30mm
furrring strips 45×15mm

585

唐松外壁材 t=18mm
SOP(黄色)
japanese larch t=18mm
rod-tinted synthetic resin paint
(yellow)

居間
living room

23

74.5

376.5

唐松外壁材 t=18mm
japanese larch t=18mm

1500

玄関ドア
スプルス t=10mm 本実加工
フラッシュ 50mm
スプルス t=10mm 本実加工
entrance door :
spruce t=10mm molder treatment
flush 50mm
spruce t=10mm tongue and groove joint

997

玄関ポーチ
entrance porch
GL+230

284.5

1292

玄関
entrance
GL+500

184

本棚:
シナランバーコア t=15mm
大手貼り OP
book shelf:
japanese linden lumber core
t=15mm oil paint

216

1575

木製梯子

421

436

421

92

450

124

204

421

書斎
study room

29

421

204

80 124

421

1650.5

421

1575

910

421

422.5

231

1575

3600
2100
900
4200

平面詳細パース
horizontal section perspective S:1/40

3900

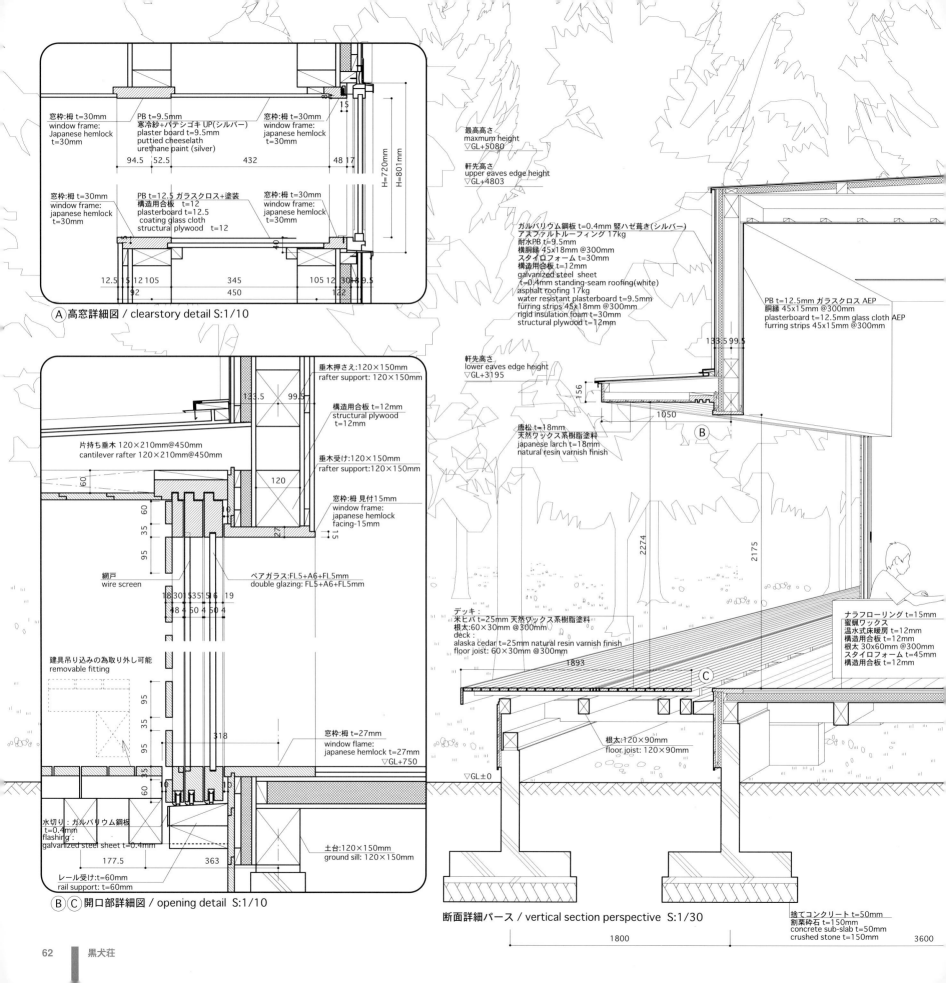

窓枠:栂 t=30mm
window frame:
Japanese hemlock
t=30mm

PB t=9.5mm
寒冷紗+パテシゴキ UP(シルバー)
plaster board t=9.5mm
puttied cheeselath
urethane paint (silver)

窓枠:栂 t=30mm
window frame:
japanese hemlock
t=30mm

94.5 52.5 | 432 | 48 17

H=720mm
H=801mm

15

窓枠:栂 t=30mm
window frame:
japanese hemlock
t=30mm

PB t=12.5 ガラスクロス+塗装
構造用合板 t=12
plasterboard t=12.5
coating glass cloth
structural plywood t=12

窓枠:栂 t=30mm
window frame:
japanese hemlock
t=30mm

12.5 15 12 105 | 345 | 105 12 30 8 9.5
92 | 450 | 122

Ⓐ 高窓詳細図 / clearstory detail S:1/10

最高高さ
maxmum height
▽GL+5080

軒先高さ
upper eaves edge height
▽GL+4803

ガルバリウム鋼板 t=0.4mm 竪ハゼ葺き(シルバー)
アスファルトルーフィング 17kg
耐水PB t=9.5mm
横胴縁 45x18mm @300mm
スタイロフォーム t=30mm
構造用合板 t=12mm
galvanized steel sheet
(t=0.4mm standing-seam roofing(white)
asphalt roofing 17kg
water resistant plasterboard t=9.5mm
furring strips 45x18mm @300mm
rigid insulation foam t=30mm
structural plywood t=12mm

PB t=12.5mm ガラスクロス AEP
胴縁 45x15mm @300mm
plasterboard t=12.5mm glass cloth AEP
furring strips 45x15mm @300mm

133.5 99.5

軒先高さ
lower eaves edge height
▽GL+3195

垂木押さえ:120×150mm
rafter support: 120×150mm

構造用合板 t=12mm
structural plywood
t=12mm

垂木受け:120×150mm
rafter support:120×150mm

窓枠:栂 見付15mm
window frame:
japanese hemlock
facing-15mm

133.5 | 99.5

片持ち垂木 120×210mm@450mm
cantilever rafter 120×210mm@450mm

120

60

60

35

95

27

15

156

1050

唐松 t=18mm
天然ワックス系樹脂塗料
japanese larch t=18mm
natural resin varnish finish

Ⓑ

網戸
wire screen

ペアガラス:FL5+A6+FL5mm
double glazing: FL5+A6+FL5mm

18 30 15 35 5 6 19
48 4 50 4 50 4

建具吊り込みの為取り外し可能
removable fitting

95

35

95

318

窓枠:栂 t=27mm
window flame:
japanese hemlock t=27mm
▽GL+750

95

35

60

水切り:ガルバリウム鋼板
t=0.4mm
flashing :
galvanized steel sheet t=0.4mm

177.5 | 363

土台:120×150mm
ground sill: 120×150mm

レール受け:t=60mm
rail support: t=60mm

ⒷⒸ 開口部詳細図 / opening detail S:1/10

2274

2175

デッキ:
米ヒバ t=25mm 天然ワックス系樹脂塗料
根太:60×30mm @300mm
deck :
alaska cedar t=25mm natural resin varnish finish
floor joist: 60×30mm @300mm

ナラフローリング t=15mm
蜜蝋ワックス
温水式床暖房 t=12mm
構造用合板 t=12mm
根太 30×60mm @300mm
スタイロフォーム t=45mm
構造用合板 t=12mm

1893

Ⓒ

根太:120×90mm
floor joist: 120×90mm

▽GL±0

断面詳細パース / vertical section perspective S:1/30

捨てコンクリート t=50mm
割栗砕石 t=150mm
concrete sub-slab t=50mm
crushed stone t=150mm

1800

3600

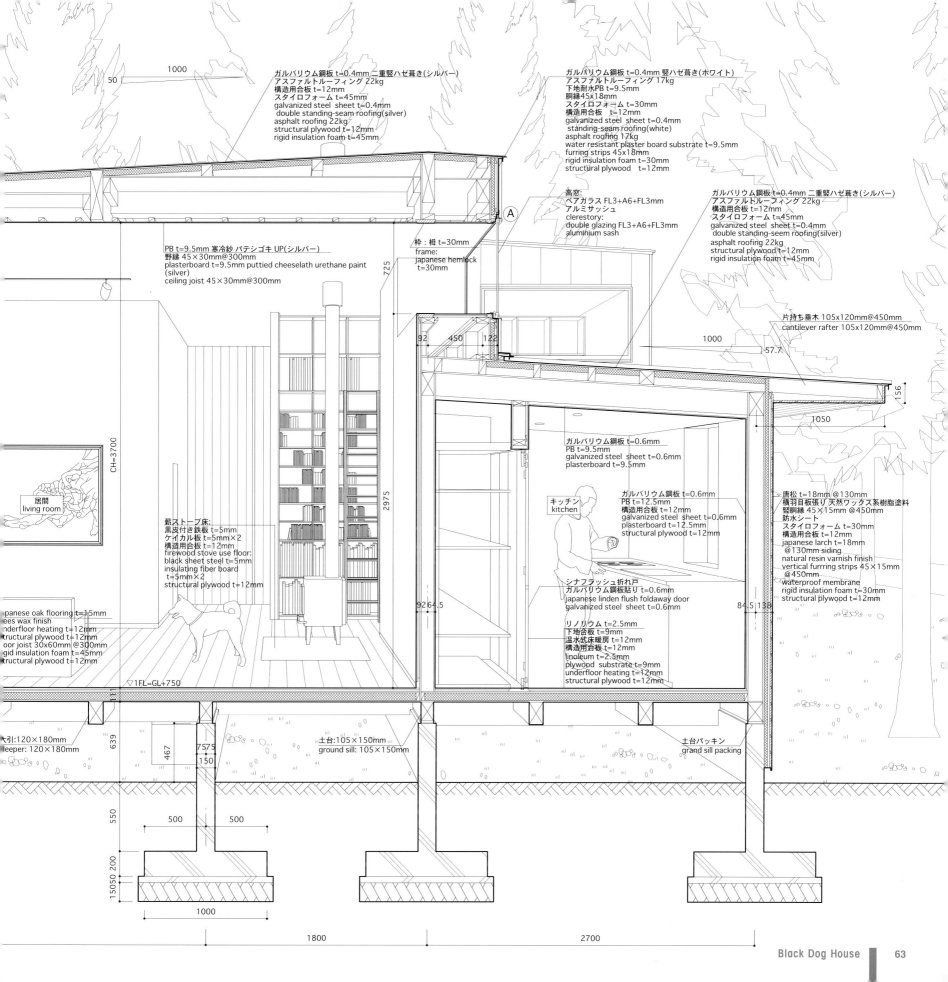

ガルバリウム鋼板 t=0.4mm 二重竪ハゼ葺き(シルバー)
アスファルトルーフィング 22kg
構造用合板 t=12mm
スタイロフォーム t=45mm
galvanized steel sheet t=0.4mm
double standing-seam roofing(silver)
asphalt roofing 22kg
structural plywood t=12mm
rigid insulation foam t=45mm

ガルバリウム鋼板 t=0.4mm 竪ハゼ葺き(ホワイト)
アスファルトルーフィング 17kg
下地耐水PB t=9.5mm
胴縁45x18mm
スタイロフォーム t=30mm
構造用合板 t=12mm
galvanized steel sheet t=0.4mm
standing-seam roofing(white)
asphalt roofing 17kg
water resistant plaster board substrate t=9.5mm
furring strips 45x18mm
rigid insulation foam t=30mm
structural plywood t=12mm

高窓:
ペアガラス FL3+A6+FL3mm
アルミサッシュ
clerestory:
double glazing FL3+A6+FL3mm
aluminium sash

ガルバリウム鋼板 t=0.4mm 二重竪ハゼ葺き(シルバー)
アスファルトルーフィング 22kg
構造用合板 t=12mm
スタイロフォーム t=45mm
galvanized steel sheet t=0.4mm
double standing-seem roofing(silver)
asphalt roofing 22kg
structural plywood t=12mm
rigid insulation foam t=45mm

枠：栂 t=30mm
frame:
japanese hemlock
t=30mm

PB t=9.5mm 寒冷紗 パテシゴキ UP(シルバー)
野縁 45×30mm@300mm
plasterboard t=9.5mm puttied cheeselath urethane paint
(silver)
ceiling joist 45×30mm@300mm

片持ち垂木 105x120mm@450mm
cantilever rafter 105x120mm@450mm

ガルバリウム鋼板 t=0.6mm
PB t=9.5mm
galvanized steel sheet t=0.6mm
plasterboard t=9.5mm

ガルバリウム鋼板 t=0.6mm
PB t=12.5mm
構造用合板 t=12mm
galvanized steel sheet t=0.6mm
plasterboard t=12.5mm
structural plywood t=12mm

唐松 t=18mm @130mm
横羽目板張り 天然ワックス系樹脂塗料
竪胴縁 45×15mm @450mm
防水シート
スタイロフォーム t=30mm
構造用合板 t=12mm
japanese larch t=18mm
@130mm siding
natural resin varnish finish
vertical furrring strips 45×15mm
@450mm
waterproof membrane
rigid insulation foam t=30mm
structural plywood t=12mm

薪ストーブ床:
黒皮付き鉄板 t=5mm
ケイカル板 t=5mm×2
構造用合板 t=12mm
firewood stove use floor:
black sheet steel t=5mm
insulating fiber board
t=5mm×2
structural plywood t=12mm

シナフラッシュ折れ戸
ガルバリウム鋼板貼り t=0.6mm
japanese linden flush foldaway door
galvanized steel sheet t=0.6mm

リノリウム t=2.5mm
下地合板 t=9mm
温水式床暖房 t=12mm
構造用合板 t=12mm
linoleum t=2.5mm
plywood substrate t=9mm
underfloor heating t=12mm
structural plywood t=12mm

居間
living room

キッチン
kitchen

japanese oak flooring t=15mm
bees wax finish
underfloor heating t=12mm
structural plywood t=12mm
floor joist 30x60mm @300mm
rigid insulation foam t=45mm
structural plywood t=12mm

▽1FL=GL+750

大引:120×180mm
sleeper:120×180mm

土台:105×150mm
ground sill: 105×150mm

土台パッキン
grand sill packing

CH=3700

ロコ・ハウス
Loco House

FRP防水
スレートボード t=4mm
下地合板 t=12mm
母屋 60×30mm@300mm
スタイロフォーム t=50mm
構造用合板 t=12mm
fiber reinforced plastic waterproofing
slate board t=4mm
substrate plywood t=12mm
purlin 60×30mm@300mm
rigid insulation foam t=50mm
structural plywood t=12mm

梁:38×140mm@450mm
beam: 38×140mm@450mm

最高高さ
maximum height
▽GL+5740

横架材上端
upper surface of
horizontal member
▽ GL+5550

88

140

150

梁・野地合板あらわし
exposed beam, plywood

寝室2
bedroom 2

通気用すかし目地
shadow gap joint

Ⓐ

珪酸カルシウム板 t=6mm
リシン吹き付け
insulating fiber board t=6mm
lysin spraying

ラワン合板 t=5.5mm（3×8判）
合板捨貼 t=9mm
lauan plywood t=5.5mm
plywood underlay t=9mm

PB t=12.5mm 壁紙
plaster board
t=12.5mm wallpaper

手すり：ヒバ　φ=36mm
coping: cypress φ=36mm

ラワン合板 t=5.5mm
合板 t=12mm
根太 44.5mm×30mm@300
グラスウール充填
遮音シート t=1mm
ラワン合板 t=12mm
lauan plywood t=5.5mm
plywood t=12mm
floor joist 44.5mm×30mm@300
infill glasswool
sound insulation sheet t=1mm
lauan plywood t=12mm

92

67

67

96

横架材上端
upper surface of
horizontal member
▽GL+2975

2FL ▽GL+3050

275

184

180

モルタル t=15mm リシン吹き付け
ラス網
防水シート
構造用合板 t=12mm
mortar t=15mm lysin spraying
furring strips t=15mm
waterproofing sheet
structural plywood t=12mm

スカイルーム
sky room

5100

スレートボード t=4mm
防水シート
耐水ベニヤ t=5.5mm
slate board t=4mm
waterploof membrane
water-resistant veneer t=5.5mm

92

100

100

96

踏面:米ヒバ t=36mm
tread: alaska cedar t=36mm

スレートボード t=4mmOP
防水シート
耐水ベニヤ t=5mm
胴縁 t=15mm
slate board t=4mm oil paint
waterploof membrane
water-resistant veneer t=5mm
furring strips t=15mm

浴室
bathroom

1975

浴室基礎立ち上がり
rise of bathroom
▽GL+800

簀子:米ヒバ t=20mm
根太:70×30mm@300mm
モルタル金コテ仕上げ
drainboard: alaska cedar
t=20mm
floor joist:
70×30mm@300mm
troweled mortar

米ヒバ t=20mm
根太 70×30mm@300mm
デッキ材用水性塗料
alaska cedar t=20mm
floor joist 70×30mm@300mm

1FL ▽GL+450

1FL ▽GL+45

基礎立ち上がり
concrete upstand
▽GL+235

150

150

1059

▽ GL±0

150

294

60

60

60

60

400

229

300

400

400

1100

900

900

1100

2250

1750

2250

877

9400

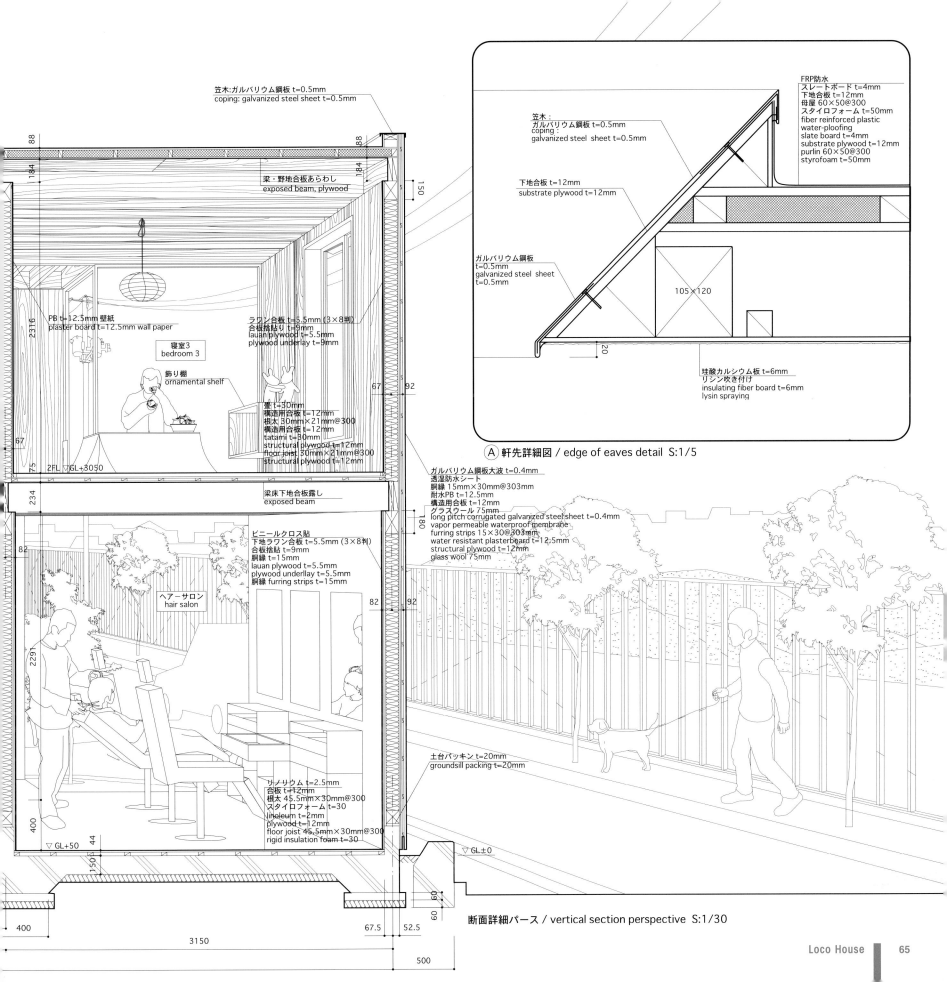

笠木:ガルバリウム鋼板 t=0.5mm
coping: galvanized steel sheet t=0.5mm

梁・野地合板あらわし
exposed beam, plywood

PB t=12.5mm 壁紙
plaster board t=12.5mm wall paper

寝室3
bedroom 3

飾り棚
ornamental shelf

ラワン合板 t=5.5mm（3×8判）
合板捨貼り t=9mm
lauan plywood t=5.5mm
plywood underlay t=9mm

畳 t=30mm
構造用合板 t=12mm
根太 30mm×21mm@300
構造用合板 t=12mm
tatami t=30mm
structural plywood t=12mm
floor joist 30mm×21mm@300
structural plywood t=12mm

2FL ▽GL+3050

梁床下地合板露し
exposed beam

ビニールクロス貼
下地ラワン合板 t=5.5mm（3×8判）
合板捨貼 t=9mm
胴縁 t=15mm
lauan plywood t=5.5mm
plywood underllay t=5.5mm
胴縁 furring strips t=15mm

ヘアーサロン
hair salon

リノリウム t=2.5mm
合板 t=12mm
根太 45.5mm×30mm@300
スタイロフォーム t=30
linoleum t=2mm
plywood t=12mm
floor joist 45.5mm×30mm@300
rigid insulation foam t=30

土台パッキン t=20mm
groundsill packing t=20mm

▽GL+50

▽GL±0

A 軒先詳細図 / edge of eaves detail S:1/5

FRP防水
スレートボード t=4mm
下地合板 t=12mm
母屋 60×50@300
スタイロフォーム t=50mm
fiber reinforced plastic
water-ploofing
slate board t=4mm
substrate plywood t=12mm
purlin 60×50@300
styrofoam t=50mm

笠木：
ガルバリウム鋼板 t=0.5mm
coping：
galvanized steel sheet t=0.5mm

下地合板 t=12mm
substrate plywood t=12mm

ガルバリウム鋼板
t=0.5mm
galvanized steel sheet
t=0.5mm

105×120

珪酸カルシウム板 t=6mm
リシン吹き付け
insulating fiber board t=6mm
lysin spraying

ガルバリウム鋼板大波 t=0.4mm
透湿防水シート
胴縁 15mm×30mm@303mm
耐水PB t=12.5mm
構造用合板 t=12mm
グラスウール 75mm
long pitch corrugated galvanized steel sheet t=0.4mm
vapor permeable waterproof membrane
furring strips 15×30@303mm
water resistant plasterboard t=12.5mm
structural plywood t=12mm
glass wool 75mm

断面詳細パース / vertical section perspective S:1/30

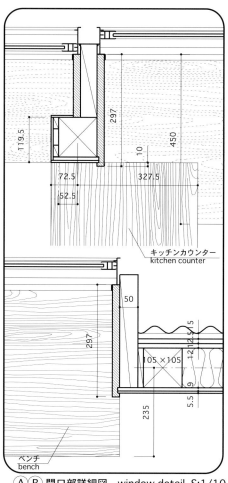

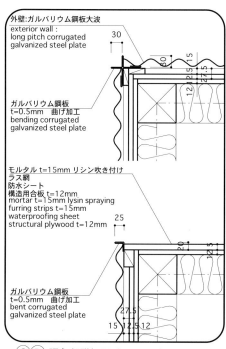

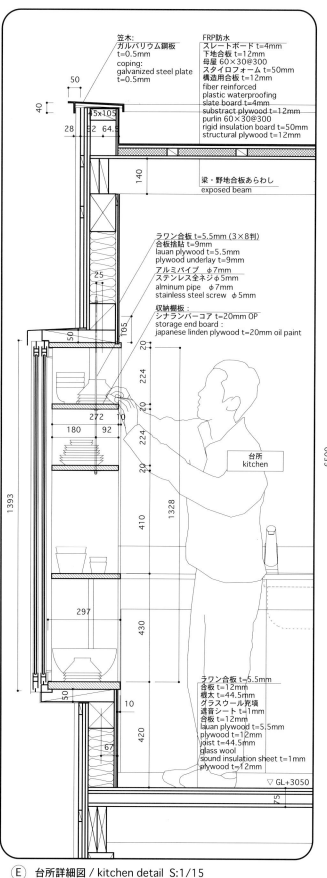

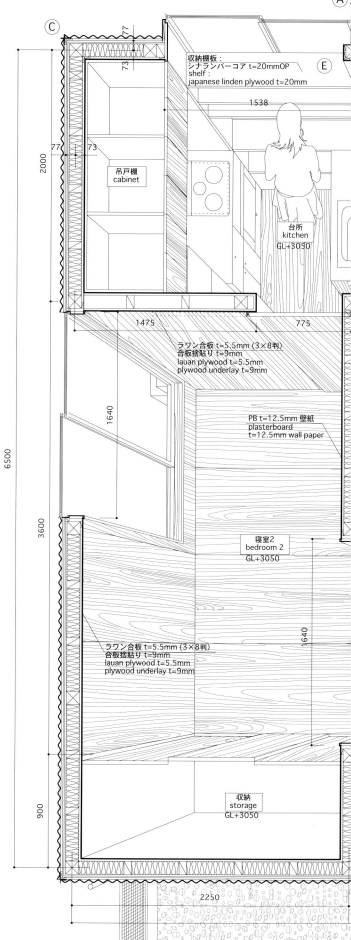

Ⓐ

Ⓒ

Ⓔ

笠木：
ガルバリウム鋼板
t=0.5mm
coping:
galvanized steel plate
t=0.5mm

FRP防水
スレートボード t=4mm
下地合板 t=12mm
母屋 60×30@300
スタイロフォーム t=50mm
構造用合板 t=12mm
fiber reinforced
plastic waterproofing
slate board t=4mm
substract plywood t=12mm
purlin 60×30@300
rigid insulation board t=50mm
structural plywood t=12mm

45×105

梁・野地合板あらわし
exposed beam

ラワン合板 t=5.5mm（3×8判）
合板捨貼 t=9mm
lauan plywood t=5.5mm
plywood underlay t=9mm

アルミパイプ φ7mm
ステンレス全ネジφ5mm
aluminum pipe φ7mm
stainless steel screw φ5mm

収納棚板：
シナランバーコア t=20mm OP
storage end board :
japanese linden plywood t=20mm oil paint

ラワン合板 t=5.5mm
合板 t=12mm
根太 t=44.5mm
グラスウール充填
遮音シート t=1mm
合板 t=12mm
lauan plywood t=5.5mm
plywood t=12mm
joist t=44.5mm
glass wool
sound insulation sheet t=1mm
plywood t=12mm

台所
kitchen

▽ GL+3050

収納棚板：
シナランバーコア t=20mmOP
shelf :
japanese linden plywood t=20mm

吊戸棚
cabinet

台所
kitchen
GL+3050

ラワン合板 t=5.5mm（3×8判）
合板捨貼り t=9mm
lauan plywood t=5.5mm
plywood underlay t=9mm

PB t=12.5mm 壁紙
plasterboard
t=12.5mm wall paper

寝室2
bedroom 2
GL+3050

ラワン合板 t=5.5mm（3×8判）
合板捨貼り t=9mm
lauan plywood t=5.5mm
plywood underlay t=9mm

収納
storage
GL+3050

キッチンカウンター
kitchen counter

ベンチ
bench

ⒶⒷ 開口部詳細図　window detail　S:1/10

外壁：ガルバリウム鋼板大波
exterior wall :
long pitch corrugated
galvanized steel plate

ガルバリウム鋼板
t=0.5mm　曲げ加工
bending corrugated
galvanized steel plate

モルタル t=15mm リシン吹き付け
ラス網
防水シート
構造用合板 t=12mm
mortar t=15mm lysin spraying
furring strips t=15mm
waterproofing sheet
structural plywood t=12mm

ガルバリウム鋼板
t=0.5mm　曲げ加工
bent corrugated
galvanized steel plate

ⒸⒹ 隅角部詳細図 / corner detail　S:1/10

Ⓔ 台所詳細図 / kitchen detail　S:1/15

メラミン合板 t=1.2mm
ラワンランバーコア t=20mm
melamine resin plywood t=1.2mm
lauan lumber core t=20mm

キッチンカウンター：
ラワンランバーコア t=20mm
kitchen counter：
lauan lumber core t=20mm

窓台：
ラワン合板 t=20mm
window sill：
lauan plywood t=20mm

3380

1640

居間食堂
living・dining room
GL+3050

PB t=12.5mm 壁紙
PB t=12.5mm wallpaper

ラワン合板 t=5.5mm(3×8判)
合板捨貼 t=9mm
lauan plywood t=5.5mm
plywood underlay t=9mm

ガルバリウム鋼板大波
透湿防水シート
胴縁 t=15mm
耐水PB t=12.5mm
構造用合板 t=12mm
グラスウール 75mm
long pitch corrugated galvanized steel plate
vapor permeable waterproofing sheet
furring strips t=15mm
waterproof plaster board t=12.5mm
structural plywood t=12mm
glass wool 75mm

172
77
73

縦軸回転扉
vertical pivoted door

920
365

ラワン合板 t=5.5mm(3×8判)
合板捨貼 t=9mm
lauan plywood t=5.5mm
plywood underlayment t=9mm

67
92

飾り棚
ornamental shelf

手すり：ヒバ φ=36mm
coping: cypress φ=36mm

踏面:米ヒバ t=36mm
tread: alaska cedar t=36mm

150

1640

1640

モルタル t=15mm リシン吹き付け
ラス網
防水シート
構造用合板 t=12mm
mortar t=15mm lysin spraying
furring strips t=15mm
waterproofing sheet
structural plywood t=12mm

スカイルーム
sky room
GL+450

寝室3
bedroom 3
GL+3050

PB t=12.5mm 壁紙
plasterboard t=12.5mm wall paper

上部天窓
skylight above

2000

6500

4500

1640

カーテン
curtain

収納
storage
GL+3050

1600

2400

9400

1350

1800

雨樋
rain gutter

D

B

平面詳細パース / horizontal section perspective S:1/30

Loco House

67

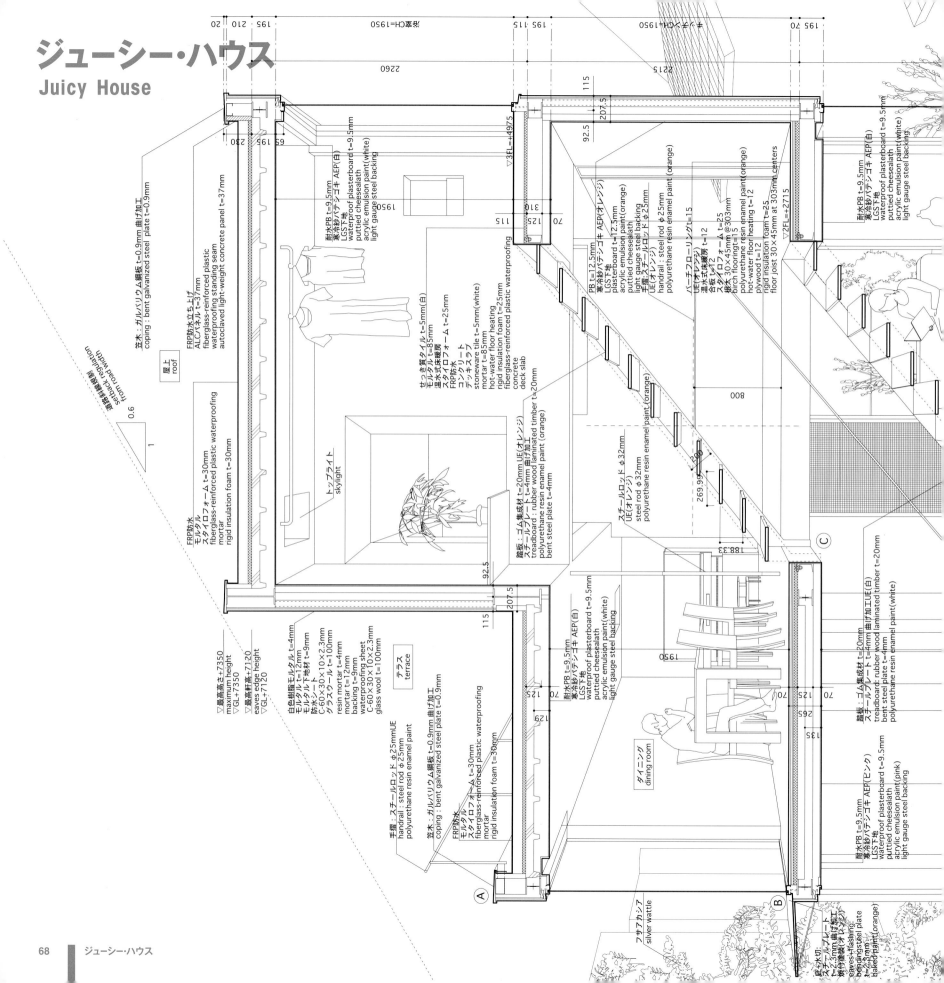

ジューシー・ハウス
Juicy House

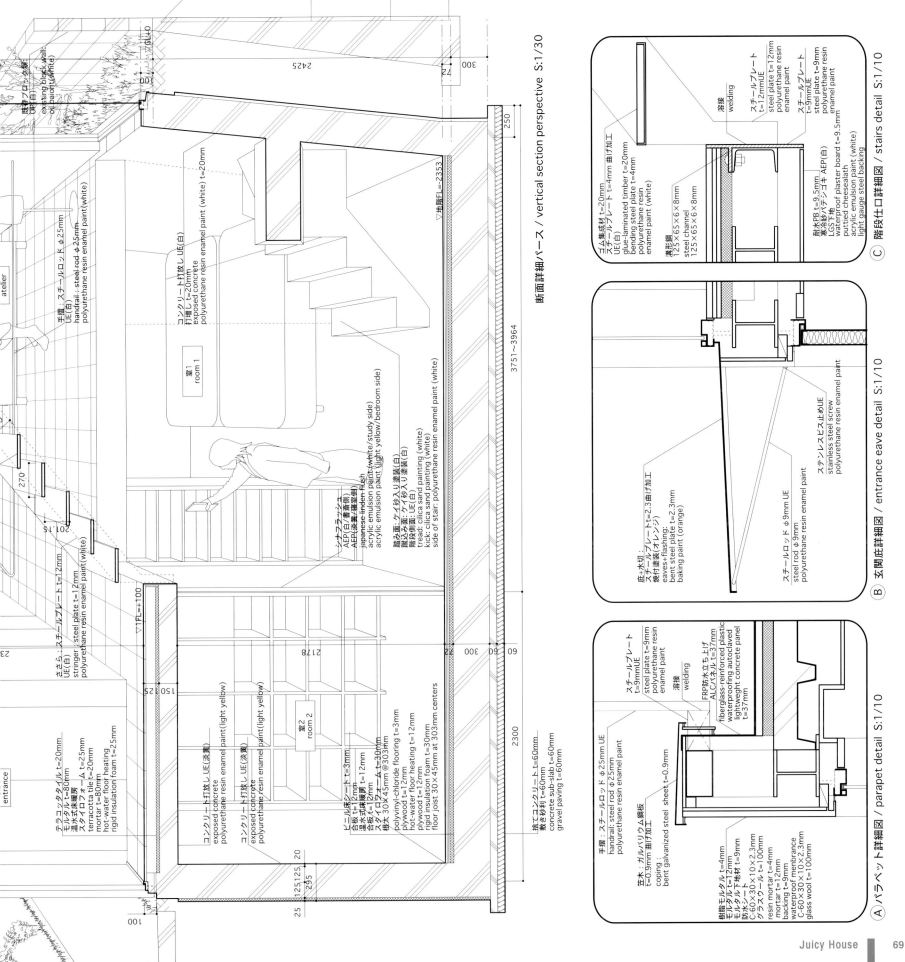

断面詳細パース / vertical section perspective S:1/30

C 階段仕口詳細図 / stairs detail S:1/10

B 玄関庇詳細図 / entrance eave detail S:1/10

A パラペット詳細図 / parapet detail S:1/10

ゴム集成材 t=20mm
スチールプレート t=4mm 曲げ加工
UE(白)
glue-laminated timber t=20mm
bending steel plate t=4mm
polyurethane resin
enamel paint (white)

溶接
welding

スチールプレート t=12mmUE
steel plate t=12mm
polyurethane resin
enamel paint (white)

スチールプレート
t=9mmUE
steel plate t=9mm
polyurethane resin
enamel paint

溝形鋼
125×65×6×8mm
steel channel
125×65×6×8mm

耐水PB t=9.5mm
塗込パテシゴキ AEP(白)
LGST下地
waterproof plaster board t=9.5mm
puttied cheesealath
acrylic emulsion paint (white)
light gauge steel backing

庇+水切
スチールプレート t=2.3 曲げ加工
焼付塗装(オレンジ)
eaves+flashing:
bent steel plate t=2.3mm
baking paint (orange)

スチールロッド φ9mm UE
steel rod φ9mm
polyurethane resin enamel paint

ステンレスビス止めUE
stainless steel screw
polyurethane resin enamel paint

スチールプレート
t=9mmUE
steel plate t=9mm
polyurethane resin
enamel paint

溶接
welding

FRP防水立ち上げ
ALCパネル t=37mm
fiberglass-reinforced plastic
waterproofing autoclaved
lightweight concrete panel
t=37mm

手摺：スチールロッド φ25mm UE
handrail: steel rod φ25mm
polyurethane resin enamel paint

笠木：ガルバリウム鋼板
t=0.9mm 曲げ加工
coping:
bent galvanized steel sheet t=0.9mm

樹脂モルタル t=4mm
モルタル t=12mm
防水シート
C-60×30×10×2.3mm
グラスウール t=100mm
resin mortar t=4mm
mortar t=12mm
waterproof membrance
C-60×30×10×2.3mm
glass wool t=100mm

existing block wall
UE(白)
existing block wall
oil paint(white)

手摺：スチールロッド φ25mm
handrail：steel rod φ25mm
UE(白)
polyurethane resin enamel paint (white)

ささら：スチールプレート t=12mm
UE(白)
stringer: steel plate t=12mm
polyurethane resin enamel paint(white)

デラコッタタイル t=20mm
モルタル t=80mm
温水式床暖房
スタイロフォーム t=25mm
terracotta tile t=20mm
mortar t=80mm
hot-water floor heating
rigid insulation foam t=25mm

コンクリート打放し UE(白)
打増し t=20mm
exposed concrete
polyurethane resin enamel paint (white)

室1
room 1

atelier

entrance

シナフラッシュ
AEP(白/書斎側)
AEP(淡黄/寝室側)
japanese-linden flush
acrylic emulsion paint(white/study side)
acrylic emulsion paint (light yellow/bedroom side)

踏み面：ケイ砂入り塗装(白)
蹴込み面：ケイ砂入り塗装(白)
階段側面：UE(白)
tread: cilica sand painting (white)
kick: cilica sand painting (white)
side of stair: polyurethane resin enamel paint (white)

コンクリート打放し UE(淡黄)
exposed concrete
polyurethane resin enamel paint(light yellow)

コンクリート打放し UE(淡黄)
exposed concrete
polyurethane resin enamel paint (light yellow)

ビニル床シート t=2mm
合板 t=3mm
合板 t=12mm
温水式床暖房 t=12mm
スタイロフォーム t=30mm
根太 30×45mm @303mm
polyvinyl-chloride flooring t=3mm
plywood t=12mm
hot-water floor heating t=12mm
plywood t=12mm
rigid insulation foam t=30mm
floor joist 30×45mm at 303mm centers

室2
room 2

捨てコンクリート t=60mm
敷き砂利 t=60mm
concrete sub-slab t=60mm
gravel paving t=60mm

▽1FL=+100

▽地階FL=-2353

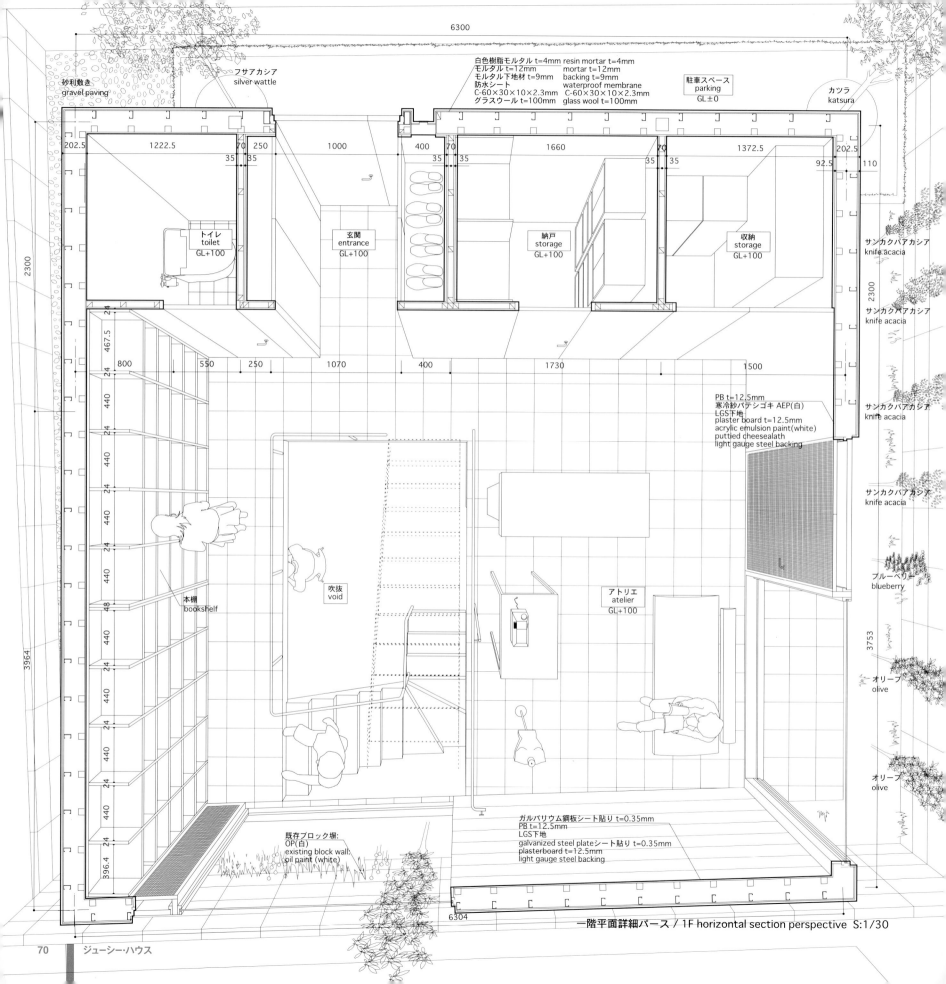

6300

砂利敷き
gravel paving

フサアカシア
silver wattle

白色樹脂モルタル t=4mm　resin mortar t=4mm
モルタル t=12mm　　　mortar t=12mm
モルタル下地材 t=9mm　backing t=9mm
防水シート　　　　　　waterproof membrane
C-60×30×10×2.3mm　C-60×30×10×2.3mm
グラスウール t=100mm　glass wool t=100mm

駐車スペース
parking
GL±0

カツラ
katsura

202.5　1222.5　70　250　　1000　　400　70　　1660　　70　　1372.5　　202.5
　　　　　　35 35　　　　　　　　35 35　　　　　　　35 35　　　　92.5　110

トイレ
toilet
GL+100

玄関
entrance
GL+100

納戸
storage
GL+100

収納
storage
GL+100

サンカクバアカシア
knife acacia

サンカクバアカシア
knife acacia

2300

2300

467.5
24

800　550　250　　1070　　400　　　1730　　　　1500

サンカクバアカシア
knife acacia

PB t=12.5mm
寒冷紗パテシゴキ AEP(白)
LGS下地
plaster board t=12.5mm
acrylic emulsion paint(white)
puttied cheesealath
light gauge steel backing

24
440
24
440
24
440
24
440

サンカクバアカシア
knife acacia

3964

24
440
48
440

本棚
bookshelf

吹抜
void

アトリエ
atelier
GL+100

ブルーベリー
blueberry

24
440
24
440
24
440

3753

24
440
24

オリーブ
olive

既存ブロック塀:
OP(白)
existing block wall:
oil paint (white)

ガルバリウム鋼板シート貼り t=0.35mm
PB t=12.5mm
LGS下地
galvanized steel plateシート貼り t=0.35mm
plasterboard t=12.5mm
light gauge steel backing

オリーブ
olive

396.4

6304

一階平面詳細パース / 1F horizontal section perspective　S:1/30

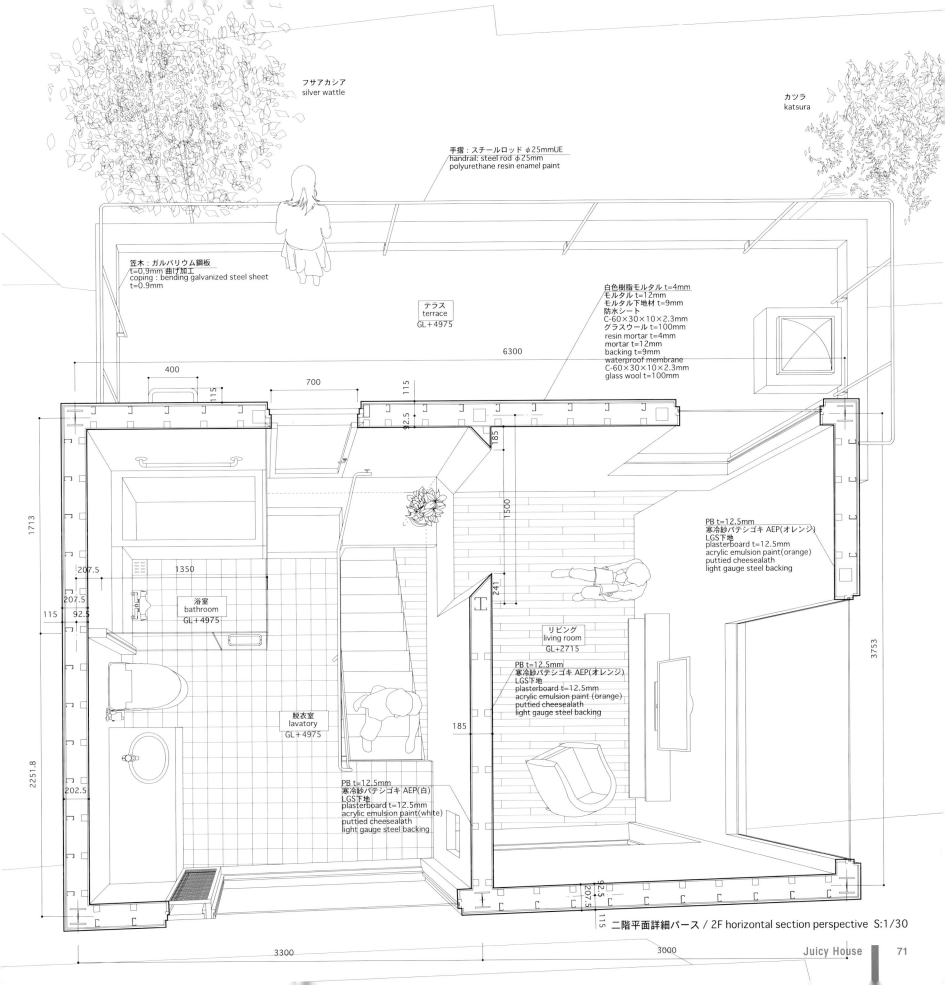

フサアカシア
silver wattle

カツラ
katsura

手摺：スチールロッド φ25mmUE
handrail: steel rod φ25mm
polyurethane resin enamel paint

笠木：ガルバリウム鋼板
t=0.9mm 曲げ加工
coping : bending galvanized steel sheet
t=0.9mm

テラス
terrace
GL＋4975

白色樹脂モルタル t=4mm
モルタル t=12mm
モルタル下地材 t=9mm
防水シート
C-60×30×10×2.3mm
グラスウール t=100mm
resin mortar t=4mm
mortar t=12mm
backing t=9mm
waterproof membrane
C-60×30×10×2.3mm
glass wool t=100mm

6300

400

700

115

115

92.5

185

1500

PB t=12.5mm
寒冷紗パテシゴキ AEP(オレンジ)
LGS下地
plasterboard t=12.5mm
acrylic emulsion paint(orange)
puttied cheesealath
light gauge steel backing

1713

207.5

1350

207.5

浴室
bathroom
GL＋4975

115

92.5

241

リビング
living room
GL＋2715

PB t=12.5mm
寒冷紗パテシゴキ AEP(オレンジ)
LGS下地
plasterboard t=12.5mm
acrylic emulsion paint (orange)
puttied cheesealath
light gauge steel backing

3753

2251.8

脱衣室
lavatory
GL＋4975

185

202.5

PB t=12.5mm
寒冷紗パテシゴキ AEP(白)
LGS下地
plasterboard t=12.5mm
acrylic emulsion paint(white)
puttied cheesealath
light gauge steel backing

92.5

207.5

115

二階平面詳細パース / 2F horizontal section perspective S:1/30

3300

3000

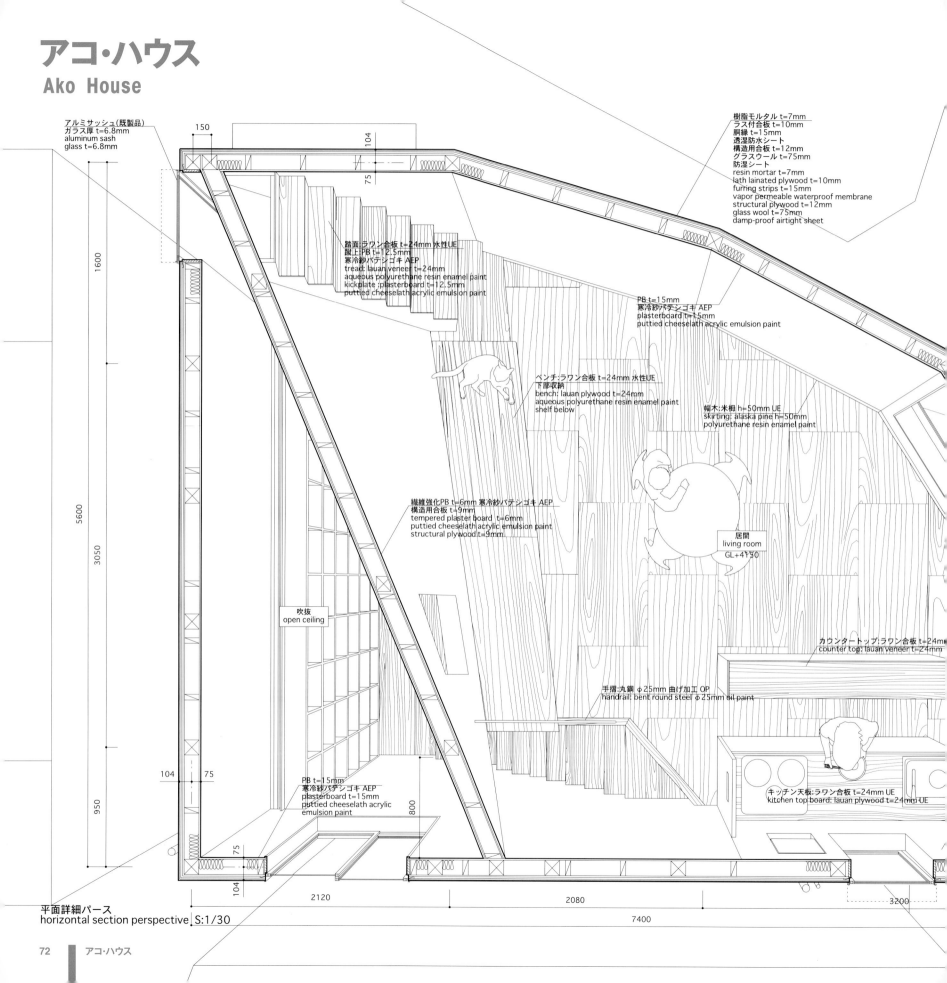

アコ・ハウス
Ako House

アルミサッシュ(既製品)
ガラス厚 t=6.8mm
aluminum sash
glass t=6.8mm

150

104

樹脂モルタル t=7mm
ラス付合板 t=10mm
胴縁 t=15mm
透湿防水シート
構造用合板 t=12mm
グラスウール t=75mm
防湿シート
resin mortar t=7mm
lath lainated plywood t=10mm
furring strips t=15mm
vapor permeable waterproof membrane
structural plywood t=12mm
glass wool t=75mm
damp-proof airtight sheet

75

1600

踏面:ラワン合板 t=24mm 水性UE
蹴上:PB t=12.5mm
寒冷紗パテシゴキ AEP
tread: lauan veneer t=24mm
aqueous polyurethane resin enamel paint
kickplate :plasterboard t=12.5mm
puttied cheeselath acrylic emulsion paint

PB t=15mm
寒冷紗パテシゴキ AEP
plasterboard t=15mm
puttied cheeselath acrylic emulsion paint

ベンチ:ラワン合板 t=24mm 水性UE
下部収納
bench: lauan plywood t=24mm
aqueous polyurethane resin enamel paint
shelf below

幅木:米栂 h=50mm UE
skirting: alaska pine h=50mm
polyurethane resin enamel paint

5600

3050

繊維強化PB t=6mm 寒冷紗パテシゴキ AEP
構造用合板 t=9mm
tempered plaster board t=6mm
puttied cheeselath acrylic emulsion paint
structural plywood t=9mm

居間
living room
GL+4150

吹抜
open ceiling

カウンタートップ:ラワン合板 t=24mm
counter top: lauan veneer t=24mm

手摺:丸鋼 φ25mm 曲げ加工 OP
handrail: bent round steel φ25mm oil paint

104   75

950

PB t=15mm
寒冷紗パテシゴキ AEP
plasterboard t=15mm
puttied cheeselath acrylic
emulsion paint

800

75

キッチン天板:ラワン合板 t=24mm UE
kitchen top board: lauan plywood t=24mm UE

104

2120

2080

3200

平面詳細パース
horizontal section perspective S:1/30

7400

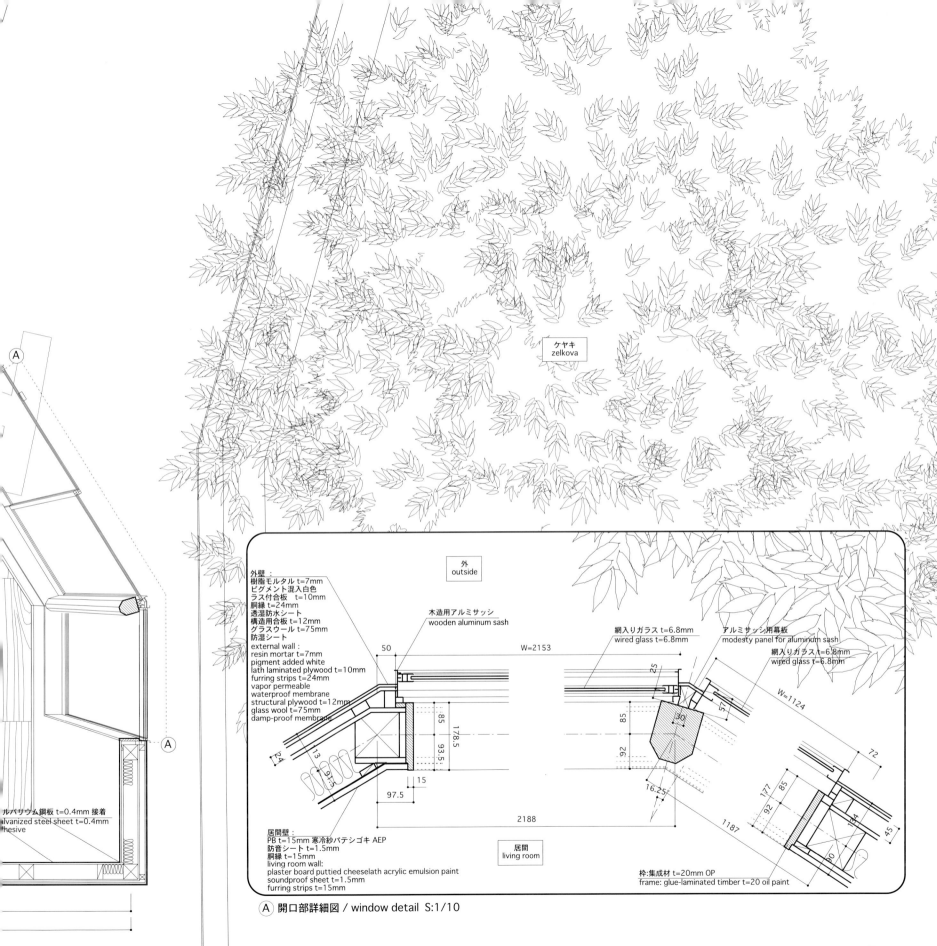

ケヤキ
zelkova

外壁：
樹脂モルタル t=7mm
ピグメント混入白色
ラス付合板　t=10mm
胴縁 t=24mm
透湿防水シート
構造用合板 t=12mm
グラスウール t=75mm
防湿シート
external wall :
resin mortar t=7mm
pigment added white
lath laminated plywood t=10mm
furring strips t=24mm
vapor permeable
waterproof membrane
structural plywood t=12mm
glass wool t=75mm
damp-proof membrane

外
outside

木造用アルミサッシ
wooden aluminum sash

網入りガラス t=6.8mm
wired glass t=6.8mm

アルミサッシ用幕板
modesty panel for aluminum sash

網入りガラス t=6.8mm
wired glass t=6.8mm

50

W=2153

25

85

178.5

93.5

85

92

30

5

W=1124

24

3

91.5

15

97.5

2188

16.25

1187

72

177

85

92

54

45

90

居間壁：
PB t=15mm 寒冷紗パテシゴキ AEP
防音シート t=1.5mm
胴縁 t=15mm
living room wall:
plaster board puttied cheeselath acrylic emulsion paint
soundproof sheet t=1.5mm
furring strips t=15mm

居間
living room

枠:集成材 t=20mm OP
frame: glue-laminated timber t=20 oil paint

ルバサリウム鋼板 t=0.4mm 接着
lvanized steel sheet t=0.4mm
hesive

Ⓐ 開口部詳細図 / window detail S:1/10

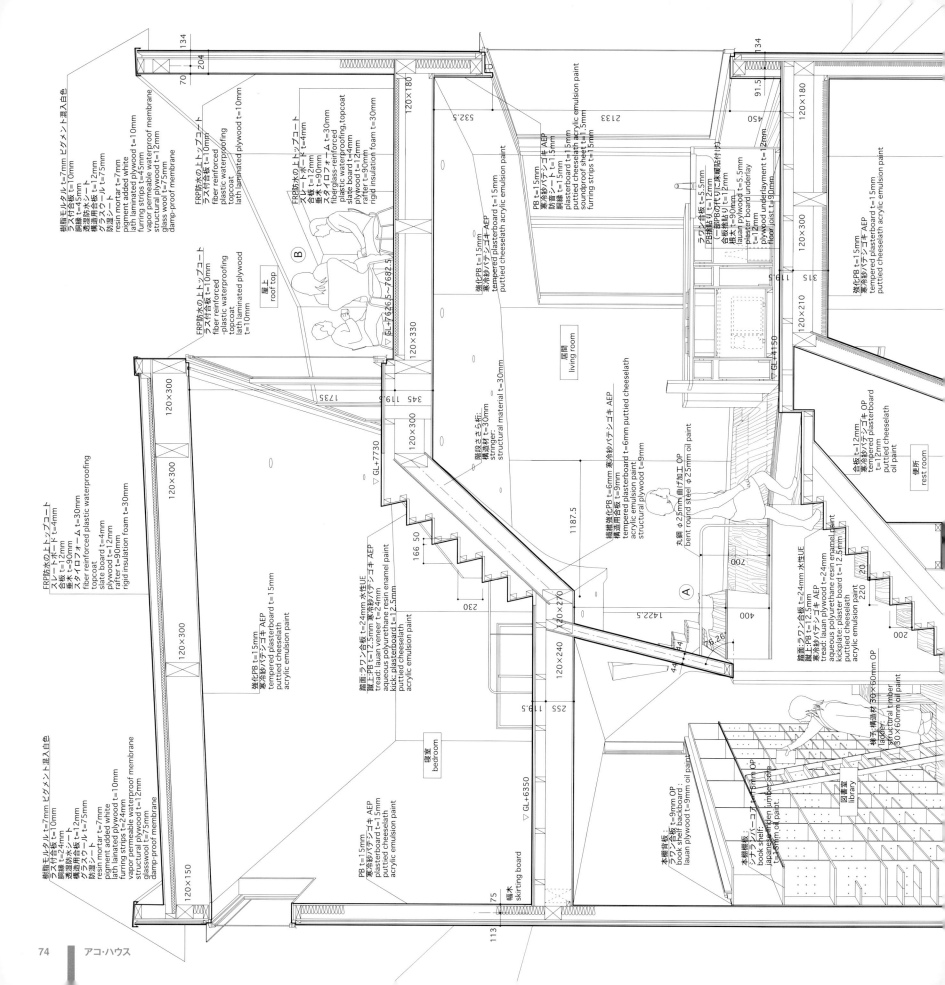

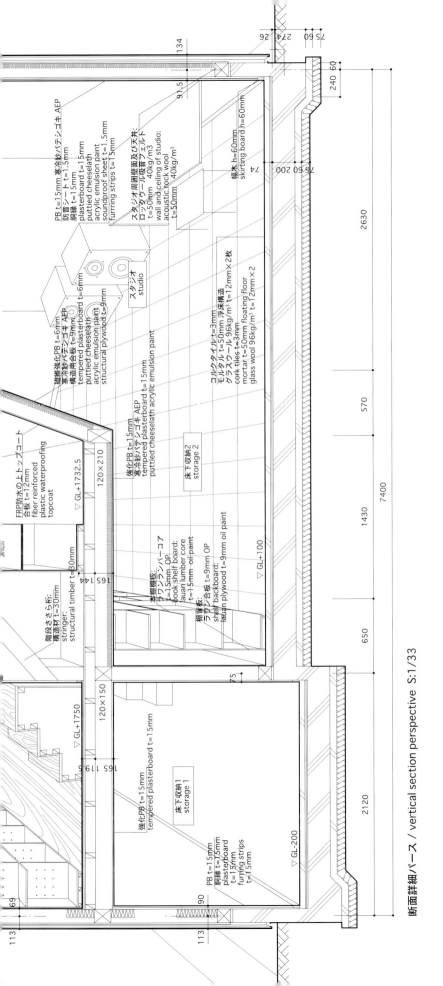

断面詳細パース / vertical section perspective S:1/33

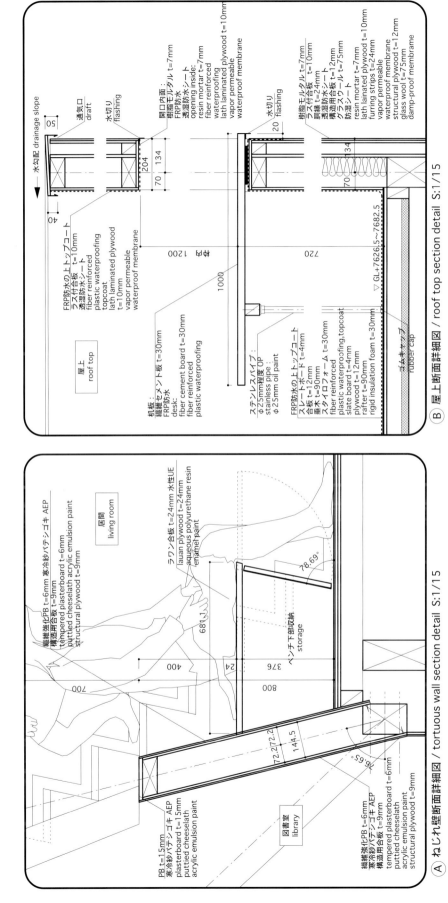

Ⓐ ねじれ壁断面詳細図 / tortuous wall section detail S:1/15

Ⓑ 屋上断面詳細図 / roof top section detail S:1/15

ガク・ハウス
Gak House

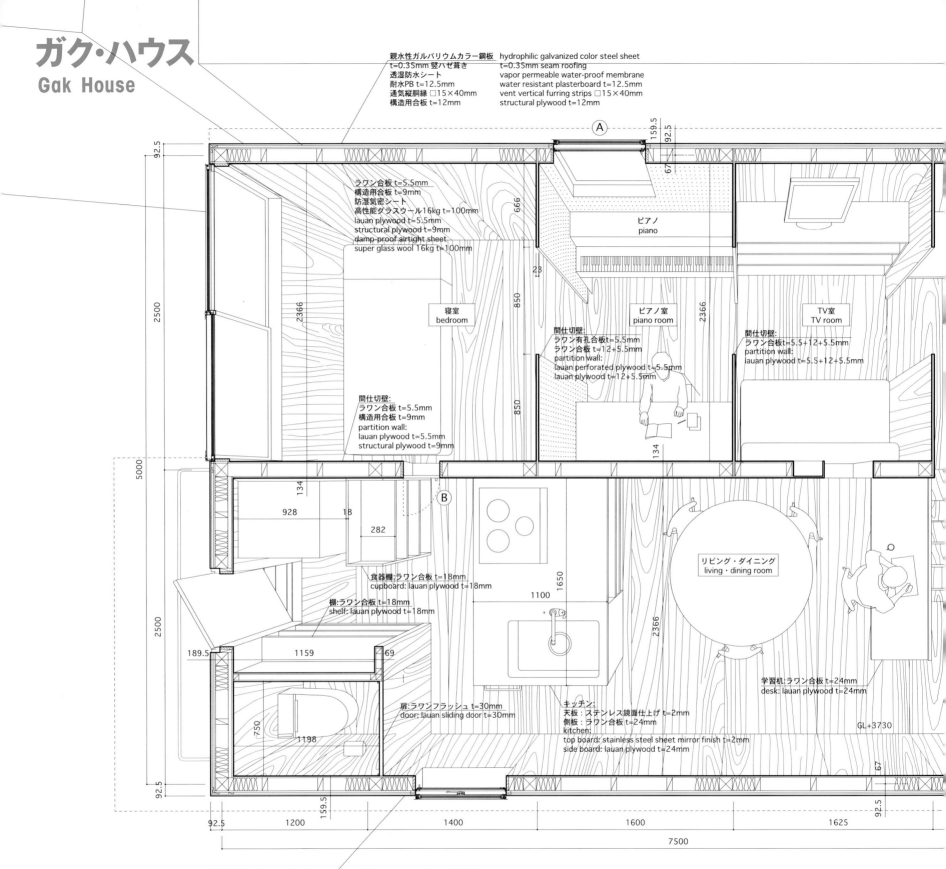

親水性ガルバリウムカラー鋼板　hydrophilic galvanized color steel sheet
t=0.35mm 竪ハゼ葺き　t=0.35mm seam roofing
透湿防水シート　vapor permeable water-proof membrane
耐水PB t=12.5mm　water resistant plasterboard t=12.5mm
通気縦胴縁 □15×40mm　vent vertical furring strips □15×40mm
構造用合板 t=12mm　structural plywood t=12mm

ラワン合板 t=5.5mm
構造用合板 t=9mm
防湿気密シート
高性能ダラスウール16kg t=100mm
lauan plywood t=5.5mm
structural plywood t=9mm
damp-proof airtight sheet
super glass wool 16kg t=100mm

ピアノ
piano

寝室
bedroom

ピアノ室
piano room

TV室
TV room

間仕切壁:
ラワン有孔合板t=5.5mm
ラワン合板 t=12+5.5mm
partition wall:
lauan perforated plywood t=5.5mm
lauan plywood t=12+5.5mm

間仕切壁:
ラワン合板 t=5.5+12+5.5mm
partition wall:
lauan plywood t=5.5+12+5.5mm

間仕切壁:
ラワン合板 t=5.5mm
構造用合板 t=9mm
partition wall:
lauan plywood t=5.5mm
structural plywood t=9mm

食器棚:ラワン合板 t=18mm
cupboard: lauan plywood t=18mm

棚:ラワン合板 t=18mm
shelf: lauan plywood t=18mm

リビング・ダイニング
living・dining room

扉:ラワンフラッシュ t=30mm
door: lauan sliding door t=30mm

キッチン:
天板:ステンレス鏡面仕上げ t=2mm
側板:ラワン合板 t=24mm
kitchen:
top board: stainless steel sheet mirror finish t=2mm
side board: lauan plywood t=24mm

学習机:ラワン合板 t=24mm
desk: lauan plywood t=24mm

GL+3730

平面詳細パース / horizontal section perspective S:1/30

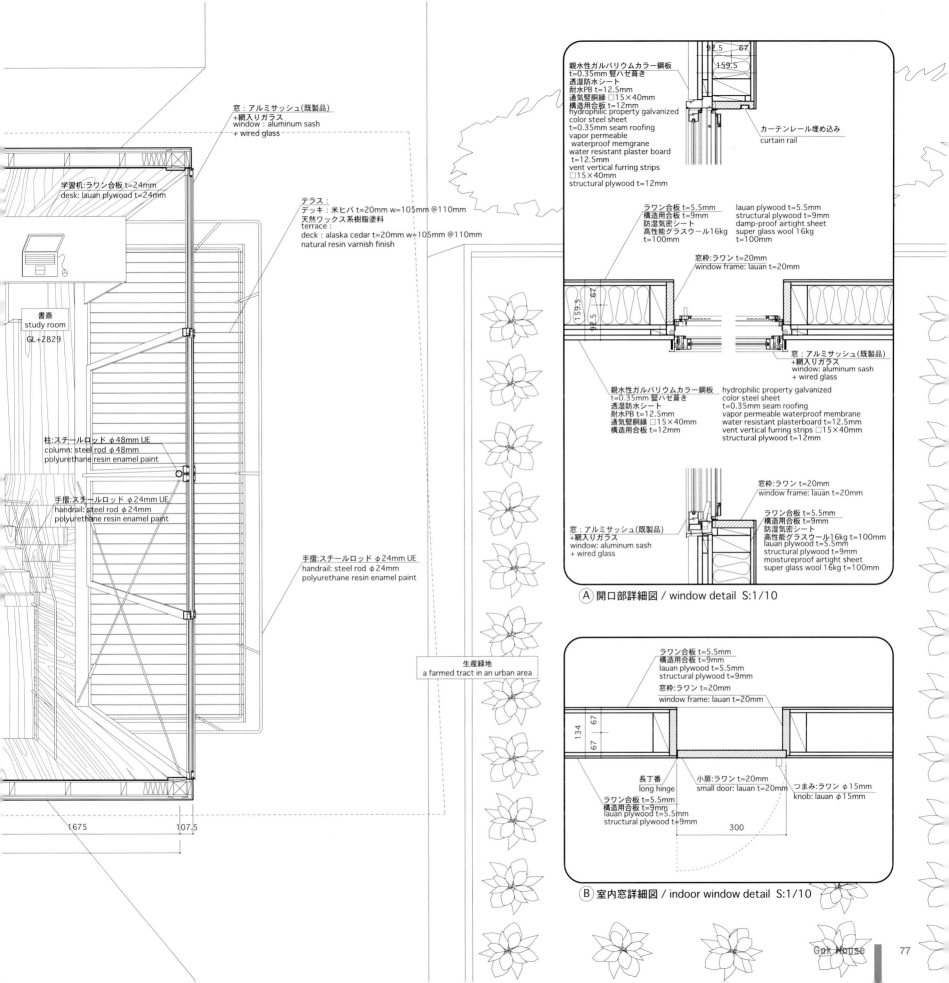

窓：アルミサッシュ（既製品）
+網入りガラス
window : aluminum sash
+ wired glass

学習机:ラワン合板 t=24mm
desk: lauan plywood t=24mm

テラス：
デッキ：米ヒバ t=20mm w=105mm @110mm
天然ワックス系樹脂塗料
terrace :
deck : alaska cedar t=20mm w=105mm @110mm
natural resin varnish finish

書斎
study room
GL+2829

柱:スチールロッド φ48mm UE
column: steel rod φ48mm
polyurethane resin enamel paint

手摺:スチールロッド φ24mm UE
handrail: steel rod φ24mm
polyurethane resin enamel paint

手摺:スチールロッド φ24mm UE
handrail: steel rod φ24mm
polyurethane resin enamel paint

1675   107.5

生産緑地
a farmed tract in an urban area

92.5   67
159.5

親水性ガルバリウムカラー鋼板
t=0.35mm 竪ハゼ葺き
透湿防水シート
耐水PB t=12.5mm
通気竪胴縁 □15×40mm
構造用合板 t=12mm
hydrophilic property galvanized
color steel sheet
t=0.35mm seam roofing
vapor permeable
 waterproof memgrane
water resistant plaster board
t=12.5mm
vent vertical furring strips
□15×40mm
structural plywood t=12mm

カーテンレール埋め込み
curtain rail

ラワン合板 t=5.5mm   lauan plywood t=5.5mm
構造用合板 t=9mm   structural plywood t=9mm
防湿気密シート   damp-proof airtight sheet
高性能グラスウール16kg   super glass wool 16kg
t=100mm   t=100mm

窓枠:ラワン t=20mm
window frame: lauan t=20mm

159.5   67
92.5

窓：アルミサッシュ（既製品）
+網入りガラス
window: aluminum sash
+ wired glass

親水性ガルバリウムカラー鋼板   hydrophilic property galvanized
t=0.35mm 竪ハゼ葺き   color steel sheet
透湿防水シート   t=0.35mm seam roofing
耐水PB t=12.5mm   vapor permeable waterproof membrane
通気竪胴縁 □15×40mm   water resistant plasterboard t=12.5mm
構造用合板 t=12mm   vent vertical furring strips □15×40mm
                            structural plywood t=12mm

窓枠:ラワン t=20mm
window frame: lauan t=20mm

窓：アルミサッシュ（既製品）   ラワン合板 t=5.5mm
+網入りガラス   構造用合板 t=9mm
window: aluminum sash   防湿気密シート
+ wired glass   高性能グラスウール16kg t=100mm
                            lauan plywood t=5.5mm
                            structural plywood t=9mm
                            moistureproof airtight sheet
                            super glass wool 16kg t=100mm

Ⓐ 開口部詳細図 / window detail S:1/10

ラワン合板 t=5.5mm
構造用合板 t=9mm
lauan plywood t=5.5mm
structural plywood t=9mm

窓枠:ラワン t=20mm
window frame: lauan t=20mm

134   67   67

長丁番   小扉:ラワン t=20mm   つまみ:ラワン φ15mm
long hinge   small door: lauan t=20mm   knob: lauan φ15mm

ラワン合板 t=5.5mm
構造用合板 t=9mm
lauan plywood t=5.5mm
structural plywood t=9mm

300

Ⓑ 室内窓詳細図 / indoor window detail S:1/10

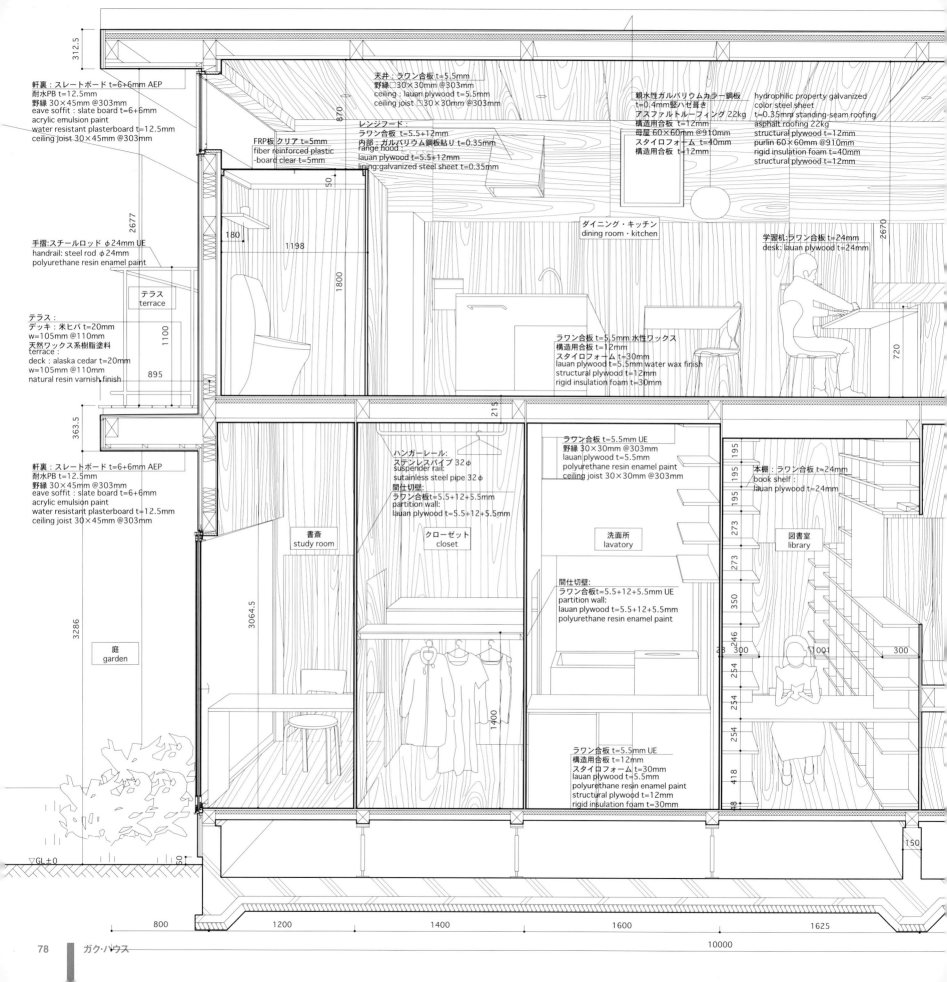

軒裏：スレートボード t=6+6mm AEP
耐水PB t=12.5mm
野縁 30×45mm @303mm
eave soffit : slate board t=6+6mm
acrylic emulsion paint
water resistant plasterboard t=12.5mm
ceiling joist 30×45mm @303mm

手摺：スチールロッド φ24mm UE
handrail: steel rod φ24mm
polyurethane resin enamel paint

テラス：
デッキ：米ヒバ t=20mm
w=105mm @110mm
天然ワックス系樹脂塗料
terrace :
deck : alaska cedar t=20mm
w=105mm @110mm
natural resin varnish finish

テラス
terrace

FRP板 クリア t=5mm
fiber reinforced plastic
-board clear t=5mm

天井：ラワン合板 t=5.5mm
野縁 □30×30mm @303mm
ceiling : lauan plywood t=5.5mm
ceiling joist □30×30mm @303mm

レンジフード：
ラワン合板 t=5.5+12mm
内部：ガルバリウム鋼板貼り t=0.35mm
range hood :
lauan plywood t=5.5+12mm
lining:galvanized steel sheet t=0.35mm

親水性ガルバリウムカラー鋼板
t=0.4mm竪ハゼ葺き
アスファルトルーフィング 22kg
構造用合板 t=12mm
母屋 60×60mm @910mm
スタイロフォーム t=40mm
構造用合板 t=12mm

hydrophilic property galvanized
color steel sheet
t=0.35mm standing-seam roofing
asphalt roofing 22kg
structural plywood t=12mm
purlin 60×60mm @910mm
rigid insulation foam=40mm
structural plywood t=12mm

ダイニング・キッチン
dining room・kitchen

学習机：ラワン合板 t=24mm
desk: lauan plywood t=24mm

ラワン合板 t=5.5mm 水性ワックス
構造用合板 t=12mm
スタイロフォーム t=30mm
lauan plywood t=5.5mm water wax finish
structural plywood t=12mm
rigid insulation foam t=30mm

軒裏：スレートボード t=6+6mm AEP
耐水PB t=12.5mm
野縁 30×45mm @303mm
eave soffit : slate board t=6+6mm
acrylic emulsion paint
water resistant plasterboard t=12.5mm
ceiling joist 30×45mm @303mm

ハンガーレール：
ステンレスパイプ 32φ
suspender rail:
sutainless steel pipe 32φ
間仕切壁：
ラワン合板 t=5.5+12+5.5mm
partition wall:
lauan plywood t=5.5+12+5.5mm

ラワン合板 t=5.5mm UE
野縁 30×30mm @303mm
lauan plywood t=5.5mm
polyurethane resin enamel paint
ceiling joist 30×30mm @303mm

本棚：ラワン合板 t=24mm
book shelf :
lauan plywood t=24mm

書斎
study room

クローゼット
closet

洗面所
lavatory

図書室
library

間仕切壁t=5.5+12+5.5mm UE
partition wall:
lauan plywood t=5.5+12+5.5mm
polyurethane resin enamel paint

庭
garden

ラワン合板 t=5.5mm UE
構造用合板 t=12mm
スタイロフォーム t=30mm
lauan plywood t=5.5mm
polyurethane resin enamel paint
structural plywood t=12mm
rigid insulation foam t=30mm

▽GL±0

800 1200 1400 1600 1625

10000

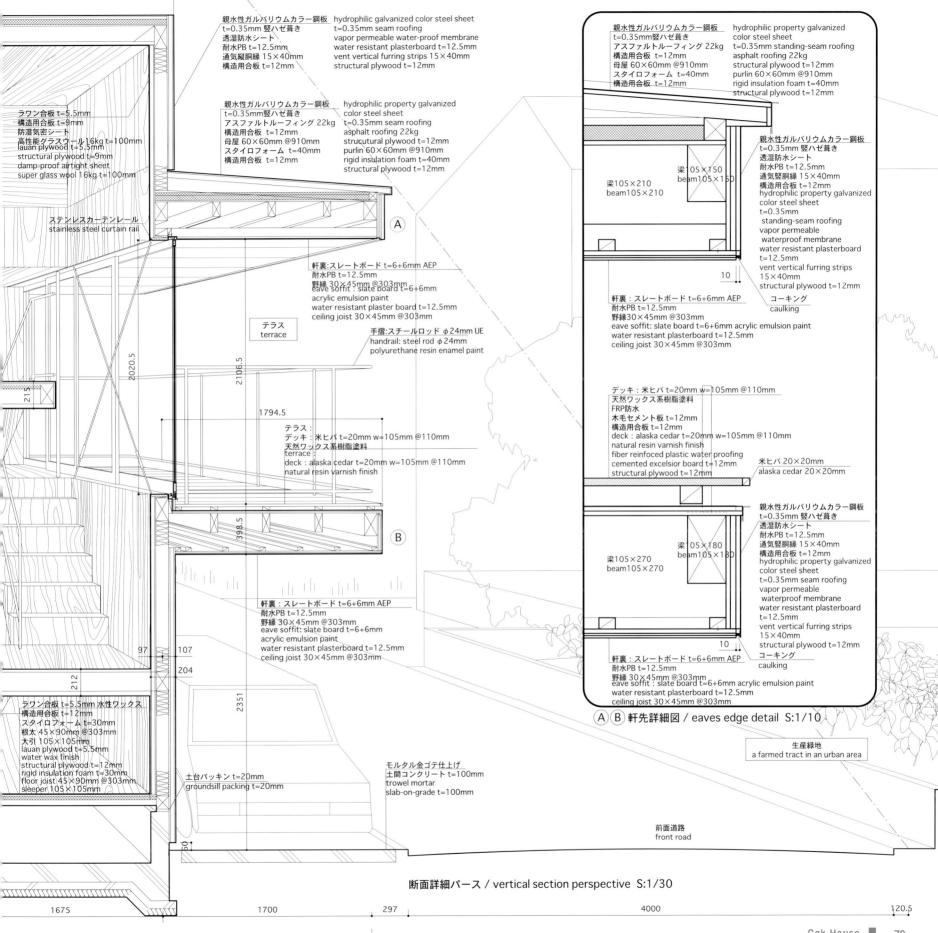

親水性ガルバリウムカラー鋼板
t=0.35mm 竪ハゼ葺き
透湿防水シート
耐水PB t=12.5mm
通気縦胴縁 15×40mm
構造用合板 t=12mm

hydrophilic galvanized color steel sheet
t=0.35mm seam roofing
vapor permeable water-proof membrane
water resistant plasterboard t=12.5mm
vent vertical furring strips 15×40mm
structural plywood t=12mm

親水性ガルバリウムカラー鋼板
t=0.35mm 竪ハゼ葺き
アスファルトルーフィング 22kg
構造用合板 t=12mm
母屋 60×60mm @910mm
スタイロフォーム t=40mm
構造用合板 t=12mm

hydrophilic property galvanized
color steel sheet
t=0.35mm seam roofing
asphalt roofing 22kg
structural plywood t=12mm
purlin 60×60mm @910mm
rigid insulation foam t=40mm
structural plywood t=12mm

親水性ガルバリウムカラー鋼板
t=0.35mm竪ハゼ葺き
アスファルトルーフィング 22kg
母屋 60×60mm @910mm
スタイロフォーム t=40mm
構造用合板 t=12mm

hydrophilic property galvanized
color steel sheet
t=0.35mm standing-seam roofing
asphalt roofing 22kg
structural plywood t=12mm
purlin 60×60mm @910mm
rigid insulation foam t=40mm
structural plywood t=12mm

ラワン合板 t=5.5mm
構造用合板 t=9mm
防湿気密シート
高性能グラスウール1.6kg t=100mm
lauan plywood t=5.5mm
structural plywood t=9mm
damp-proof airtight sheet
super glass wool 16kg t=100mm

ステンレスカーテンレール
stainless steel curtain rail

梁 105×150
beam105×150

梁 105×210
beam105×210

親水性ガルバリウムカラー鋼板
t=0.35mm 竪ハゼ葺き
透湿防水シート
耐水PB t=12.5mm
通気竪胴縁 15×40mm
構造用合板 t=12mm
hydrophilic property galvanized
color steel sheet
t=0.35mm
standing-seam roofing
vapor permeable
waterproof membrane
water resistant plasterboard
t=12.5mm
vent vertical furring strips
15×40mm
structural plywood t=12mm

軒裏:スレートボード t=6+6mm AEP
耐水PB t=12.5mm
野縁 30×45mm @303mm
eave soffit : slate board t=6+6mm
acrylic emulsion paint
water resistant plaster board t=12.5mm
ceiling joist 30×45mm @303mm

10

コーキング
caulking

軒裏:スレートボード t=6+6mm AEP
耐水PB t=12.5mm
野縁30×45mm @303mm
eave soffit: slate board t=6+6mm acrylic emulsion paint
water resistant plasterboard t=12.5mm
ceiling joist 30×45mm @303mm

テラス
terrace

手摺:スチールロッド φ24mm UE
handrail: steel rod φ24mm
polyurethane resin enamel paint

2020.5

2106.5

1794.5

215

テラス :
デッキ:米ヒバ t=20mm w=105mm @110mm
天然ワックス系樹脂塗料
terrace :
deck : alaska cedar t=20mm w=105mm @110mm
natural resin varnish finish

デッキ:米ヒバ t=20mm w=105mm @110mm
天然ワックス系樹脂塗料
FRP防水
木毛セメント板 t=12mm
構造用合板 t=12mm
deck : alaska cedar t=20mm w=105mm @110mm
natural resin varnish finish
fiber reinfoced plastic water proofing
cemented excelsior board t=12mm
structural plywood t=12mm

米ヒバ 20×20mm
alaska cedar 20×20mm

梁 105×180
beam105×180

梁 105×270
beam105×270

親水性ガルバリウムカラー鋼板
t=0.35mm 竪ハゼ葺き
透湿防水シート
耐水PB t=12.5mm
通気竪胴縁 15×40mm
構造用合板 t=12mm
hydrophilic property galvanized
color steel sheet
t=0.35mm seam roofing
vapor permeable
waterproof membrane
water resistant plasterboard
t=12.5mm
vent vertical furring strips
15×40mm
structural plywood t=12mm

B

398.5

軒裏:スレートボード t=6+6mm AEP
耐水PB t=12.5mm
野縁 30×45mm @303mm
eave soffit: slate board t=6+6mm
acrylic emulsion paint
water resistant plasterboard t=12.5mm
ceiling joist 30×45mm @303mm

10

コーキング
caulking

軒裏:スレートボード t=6+6mm AEP
耐水PB t=12.5mm
野縁 30×45mm @303mm
eave soffit : slate board t=6+6mm acrylic emulsion paint
water resistant plasterboard t=12.5mm
ceiling joist 30×45mm @303mm

Ⓐ Ⓑ 軒先詳細図 / eaves edge detail S:1/10

97   107

204

212

2351

ラワン合板 t=5.5mm 水性ワックス
構造用合板 t=12mm
スタイロフォーム t=30mm
根太 45×90mm @303mm
大引 105×105mm
lauan plywood t=5.5mm
water wax finish
structural plywood t=12mm
rigid insulation foam t=30mm
floor joist 45×90mm @303mm
sleeper 105×105mm

土台パッキン t=20mm
groundsill packing t=20mm

モルタル金ゴテ仕上げ
土間コンクリート t=100mm
trowel mortar
slab-on-grade t=100mm

生産緑地
a farmed tract in an urban area

前面道路
front road

60

断面詳細パース / vertical section perspective S:1/30

1675   1700   297   4000   120.5

ハウス＆アトリエ・ワン
House & Atelier Bow-Wow

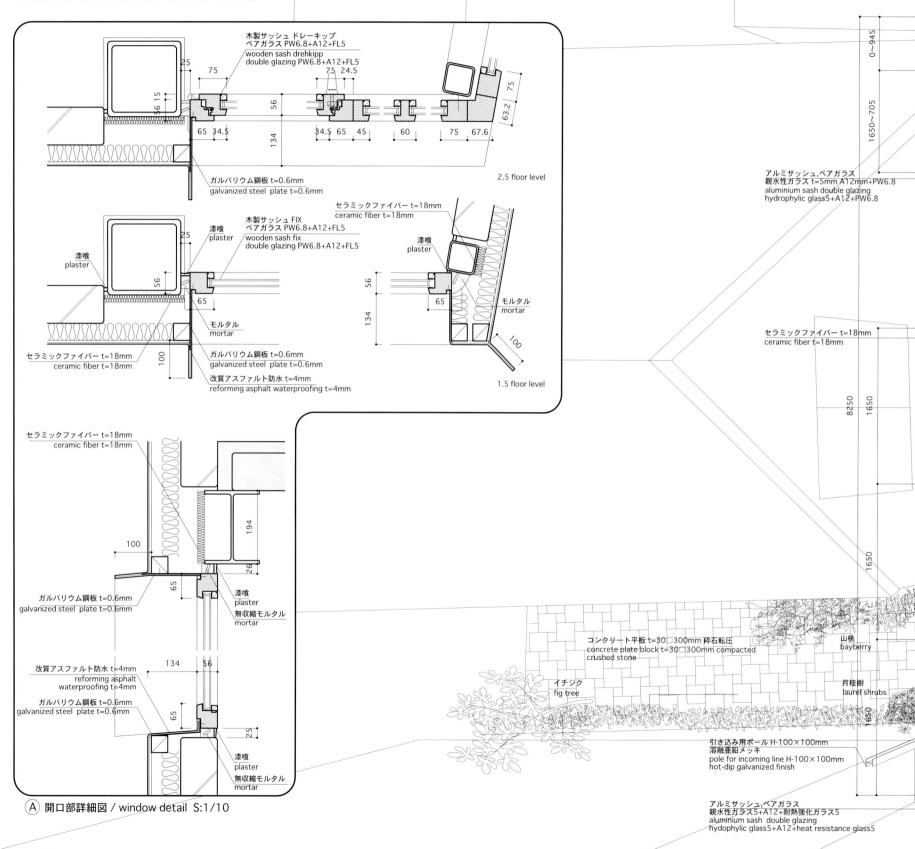

木製サッシュ ドレーキップ
ベアガラス PW6.8+A12+FL5
wooden sash drehkipp
double glazing PW6.8+A12+FL5

ガルバリウム鋼板 t=0.6mm
galvanized steel plate t=0.6mm

2.5 floor level

漆喰
plaster

漆喰
plaster

木製サッシュ FIX
ベアガラス PW6.8+A12+FL5
wooden sash fix
double glazing PW6.8+A12+FL5

セラミックファイバー t=18mm
ceramic fiber t=18mm

漆喰
plaster

モルタル
mortar

セラミックファイバー t=18mm
ceramic fiber t=18mm

モルタル
mortar

ガルバリウム鋼板 t=0.6mm
galvanized steel plate t=0.6mm

改質アスファルト防水 t=4mm
reforming asphalt waterproofing t=4mm

1.5 floor level

セラミックファイバー t=18mm
ceramic fiber t=18mm

ガルバリウム鋼板 t=0.6mm
galvanized steel plate t=0.6mm

漆喰
plaster

無収縮モルタル
mortar

改質アスファルト防水 t=4mm
reforming asphalt
waterproofing t=4mm

ガルバリウム鋼板 t=0.6mm
galvanized steel plate t=0.6mm

漆喰
plaster

無収縮モルタル
mortar

Ⓐ 開口部詳細図 / window detail S:1/10

アルミサッシュ,ベアガラス
親水性ガラス t=5mm A12mm+PW6.8
aluminium sash double glazing
hydrophylic glass5+A12+PW6.8

セラミックファイバー t=18mm
ceramic fiber t=18mm

コンクリート平板 t=30□300mm 砕石転圧
concrete plate block t=30□300mm compacted
crushed stone

山桃
bayberry

イチジク
fig tree

月桂樹
laurel shrubs

引き込み用ポール H-100×100mm
溶融亜鉛メッキ
pole for incoming line H-100×100mm
hot-dip galvanized finish

アルミサッシュ,ベアガラス
親水性ガラス5+A12+耐熱強化ガラス5
aluminium sash double glazing
hydrophylic glass5+A12+heat resistance glass5

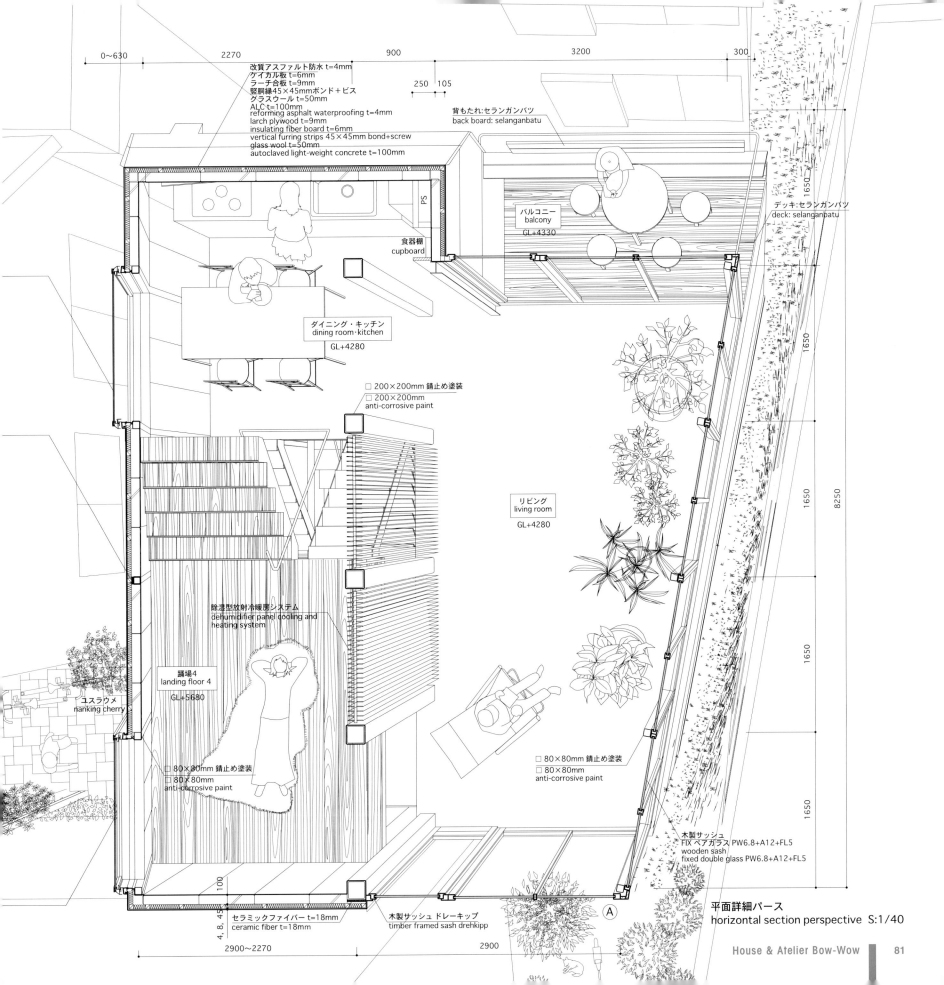

改質アスファルト防水 t=4mm
ケイカル板 t=6mm
ラーチ合板 t=9mm
竪胴縁45×45mmボンド＋ビス
グラスウール t=50mm
ALC t=100mm
reforming asphalt waterproofing t=4mm
larch plywood t=9mm
insulating fiber board t=6mm
vertical furring strips 45×45mm bond+screw
glass wool t=50mm
autoclaved light-weight concrete t=100mm

背もたれ:セランガンバツ
back board: selanganbatu

バルコニー
balcony
GL+4330

デッキ:セランガンバツ
deck: selanganbatu

食器棚
cupboard

ダイニング・キッチン
dining room·kitchen
GL+4280

□ 200×200mm 錆止め塗装
□ 200×200mm
anti-corrosive paint

リビング
living room
GL+4280

除湿型放射冷暖房システム
dehumidifier panel cooling and
heating system

踊場4
landing floor 4
GL+5680

ユスラウメ
nanking cherry

□ 80×80mm 錆止め塗装
□ 80×80mm
anti-corrosive paint

□ 80×80mm 錆止め塗装
□ 80×80mm
anti-corrosive paint

木製サッシュ
FIX ペアガラス PW6.8+A12+FL5
wooden sash
fixed double glass PW6.8+A12+FL5

セラミックファイバー t=18mm
ceramic fiber t=18mm

木製サッシュ ドレーキップ
timber framed sash drehkipp

平面詳細パース
horizontal section perspective S:1/40

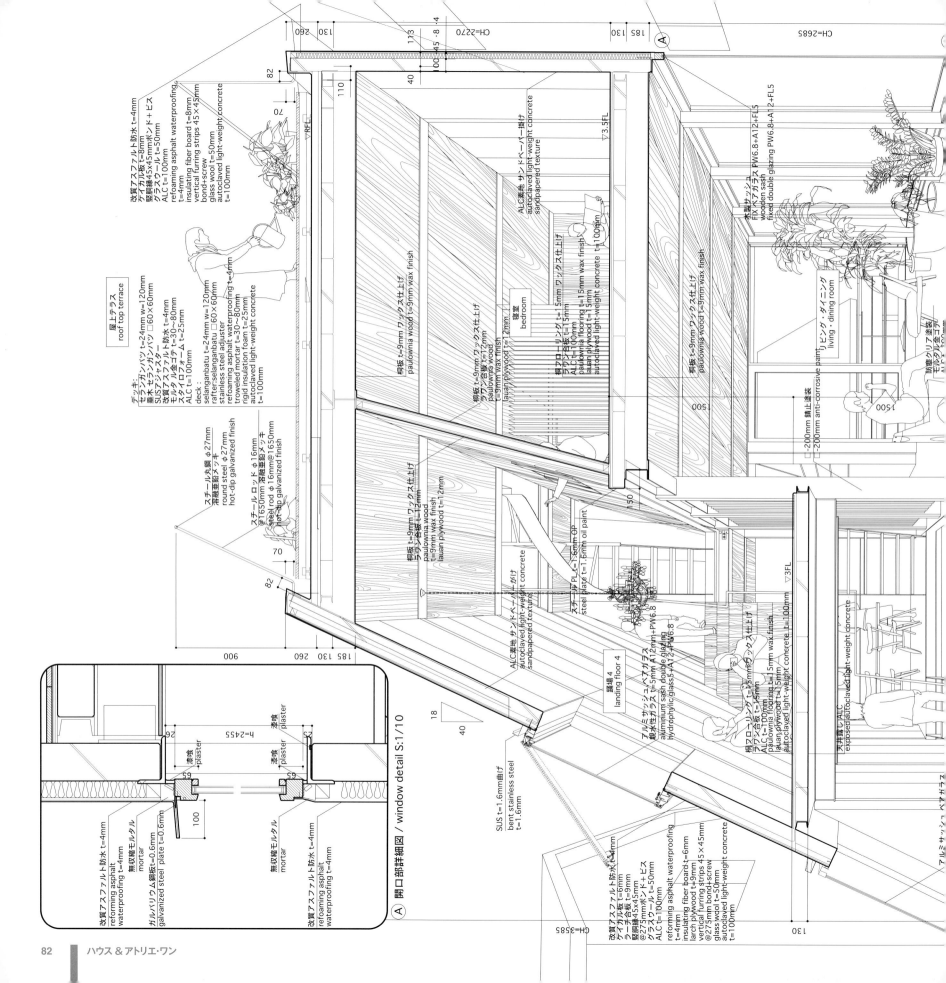

屋上テラス
roof top terrace

デッキ：
セランガンバツ t=24mm w=120mm
垂木:セランガンバツ □60×60mm
SUSアジャスター
モルタル金ゴテ t=4mm
スタイロフォーム t=30〜80mm
改質アスファルト防水 t=4mm
ALC t=100mm

deck :
selanganbatu t=24mm w=120mm
rafter:selanganbatu □60×60mm
stainless steel adjuster
troweled mortar t=4mm
rigid insulation foam t=30〜80mm
refoaming asphalt waterproofing t=4mm
autoclaved light-weight concrete
t=100mm

スチール丸鋼 φ27mm
溶融亜鉛メッキ
round steel φ27mm
hot-dip galvanized finish

スチールロッド φ16mm
@1650mm 溶融亜鉛メッキ
steel rod φ16mm@1650mm
hot-dip galvanized finish

改質アスファルト防水 t=4mm
ケイカル板 t=8mm
竪胴縁45×45mmボンド＋ビス
グラスウール t=50mm
ALC t=100mm
refoaming asphalt waterproofing,
insulating fiber board t=8mm
vertical furring strips 45×45mm
bond+screw
glass wool t=50mm
autoclaved light-weight concrete
t=100mm

ALC素地 サンドペーパー掛け
autoclaved light-weight concrete
sandpapered texture

桐板 t=9mm ワックス仕上げ
paulownia wood t=9mm wax finish

桐板 t=9mm ワックス仕上げ
ラワン合板 t=12mm
paulownia wood
t=9mm wax finish
lauan plywood t = 12mm

寝室
bedroom

桐フローリング t=15mm
ラワン合板 t=15mm
ALC t=100mm
paulownia flooring t=15mm
lauan plywood t=15mm
autoclaved light-weight concrete t=100mm

桐板 t=9mm ワックス仕上げ
paulownia wood t=9mm wax finish

木製サッシュ
FIX ペアガラス PW6.8+A12+FL5
wooden sash
fixed double glazing PW6.8+A12+FL5

リビング・ダイニング
living・dining room

防錆クリア塗装
-200mm 錆止塗装
-200mm anti-corrosive paint

天井露しALC
exposed autoclaved light-weight concrete

桐フローリング t=15mm ワックス仕上げ
ラワン合板 t=15mm
ALC t=100mm
paulownia flooring t=15mm wax finish
lauan plywood t=15mm
autoclaved light-weight concrete t=100mm

桐板 t=9mm ワックス仕上げ
ラワン合板 t=12mm
paulownia wood
t=9mm wax finish
lauan plywood t=12mm

ALC素地 サンドペーパー掛け
autoclaved light-weight concrete
sandpapered texture

踊場 4
landing floor 4

アルミサッシュ ペアガラス
親水性ガラス t=5mm A12mm+PW6.8
aluminium sash double glazing
hydrophylic glass5+A12+PW6.8

スチール PL t=1.6mm OP
steel plate t=1.6mm oil paint

SUS t=1.6mm曲げ
bent stainless steel
t=1.6mm

改質アスファルト防水 t=4mm
ケイカル板 t=6mm
ラーチ合板 t=9mm
竪胴縁45×45mm
@275mmボンド＋ビス
グラスウール t=50mm
ALC t=100mm
reforming asphalt waterproofing
t=4mm
insulating fiber board t=6mm
larch plywood t=9mm
vertical furring strips 45×45mm
@275mm bond+screw
glass wool t=50mm
autoclaved light-weight concrete
t=100mm

Ⓐ 開口部詳細図 / window detail S:1/10

漆喰 plaster
漆喰 plaster
漆喰 plaster

改質アスファルト防水 t=4mm
reforming asphalt
waterproofing t=4mm

無収縮モルタル
mortar

ガルバリウム鋼板 t=0.6mm
galvanized steel plate t=0.6mm

無収縮モルタル
mortar

改質アスファルト防水 t=4mm
reforming asphalt
waterproofing t=4mm

CH=2685

CH=2270

▽RFL
▽3.5FL
▽3FL
▽3.5BL

h=2455

断面詳細パース / vertical section perspective S:1/30

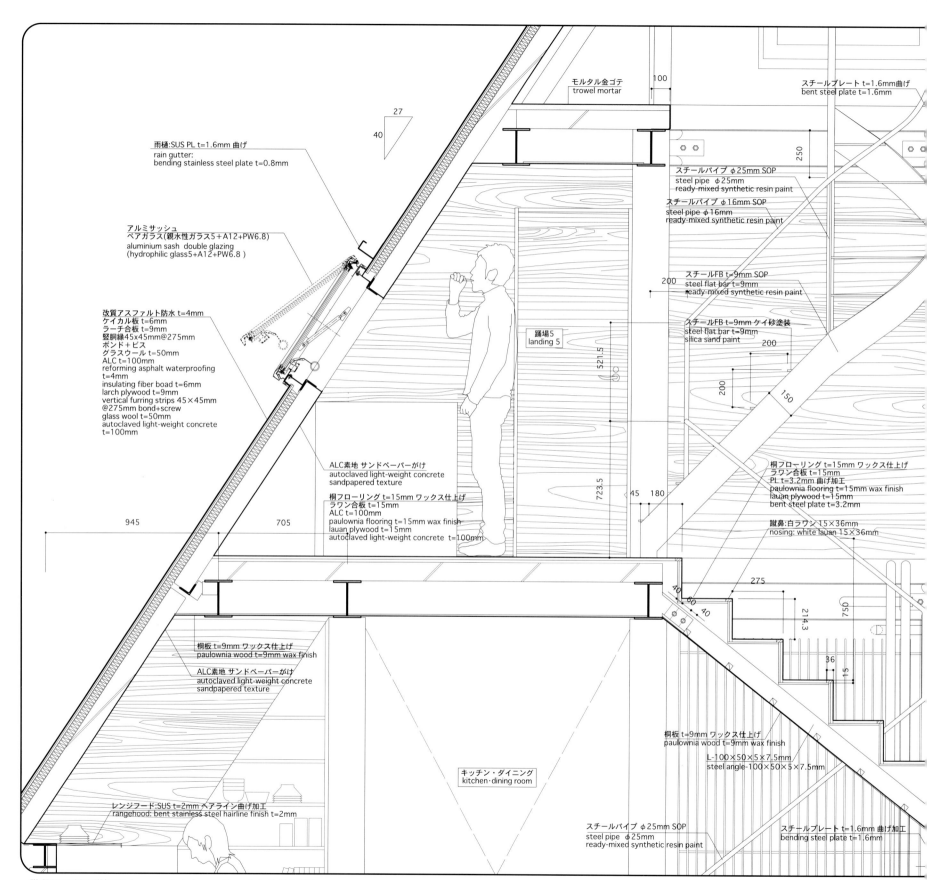

雨樋:SUS PL t=1.6mm 曲げ
rain gutter:
bending stainless steel plate t=0.8mm

アルミサッシュ
ペアガラス(親水性ガラス5+A12+PW6.8)
aluminium sash double glazing
(hydrophilic glass5+A12+PW6.8)

改質アスファルト防水 t=4mm
ケイカル板 t=6mm
ラーチ合板 t=9mm
竪胴縁45x45mm@275mm
ボンド+ビス
グラスウール t=50mm
ALC t=100mm
reforming asphalt waterproofing
t=4mm
insulating fiber boad t=6mm
larch plywood t=9mm
vertical furring strips 45×45mm
@275mm bond+screw
glass wool t=50mm
autoclaved light-weight concrete
t=100mm

27
40

100

モルタル金ゴテ
trowel mortar

スチールプレート t=1.6mm曲げ
bent steel plate t=1.6mm

250

スチールパイプ φ25mm SOP
steel pipe φ25mm
ready-mixed synthetic resin paint

スチールパイプ φ16mm SOP
steel pipe φ16mm
ready-mixed synthetic resin paint

200

スチールFB t=9mm SOP
steel flat bar t=9mm
ready-mixed synthetic resin paint

スチールFB t=9mm ケイ砂塗装
steel flat bar t=9mm
silica sand paint

200

150

200

踊場5
landing 5

521.5

723.5

45   180

ALC素地 サンドペーパーがけ
autoclaved light-weight concrete
sandpapered texture

桐フローリング t=15mm ワックス仕上げ
ラワン合板 t=15mm
ALC t=100mm
paulownia flooring t=15mm wax finish
lauan plywood t=15mm
autoclaved light-weight concrete t=100mm

桐フローリング t=15mm ワックス仕上げ
ラワン合板 t=15mm
PL t=3.2mm 曲げ加工
paulownia flooring t=15mm wax finish
lauan plywood t=15mm
bent steel plate t=3.2mm

蹴鼻:白ラワン15×36mm
nosing: white lauan 15×36mm

275

40 60 40

214.3

750

桐板 t=9mm ワックス仕上げ
paulownia wood t=9mm wax finish

ALC素地 サンドペーパーがけ
autoclaved light-weight concrete
sandpapered texture

945   705

36

15

キッチン・ダイニング
kitchen・dining room

桐板 t=9mm ワックス仕上げ
paulownia wood t=9mm wax finish

L-100×50×5×7.5mm
steel angle-100×50×5×7.5mm

レンジフード:SUS t=2mm ヘアライン曲げ加工
rangehood: bent stainless steel hairline finish t=2mm

スチールパイプ φ25mm SOP
steel pipe φ25mm
ready-mixed synthetic resin paint

スチールプレート t=1.6mm 曲げ加工
bending steel plate t=1.6mm

階段廻り断面詳細図 / around stairs section detail S:1/20

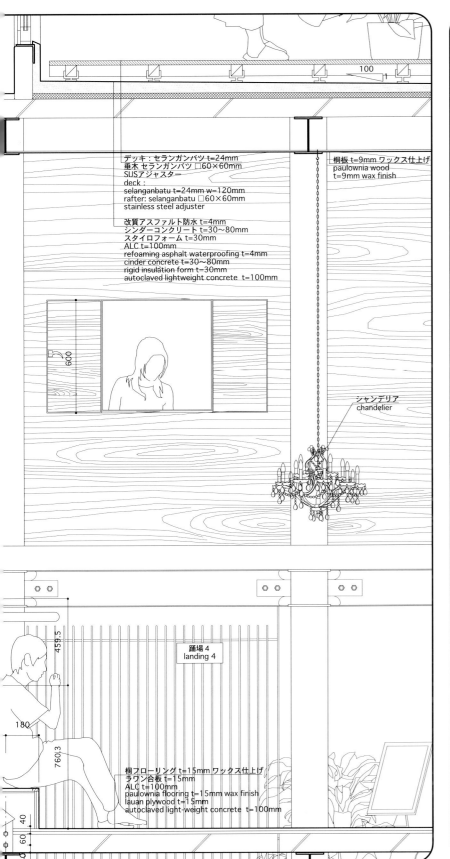

デッキ：セランガンバツ t=24mm
垂木 セランガンバツ □60×60mm
SUSアジャスター
deck:
selanganbatu t=24mm w=120mm
rafter: selanganbatu □60×60mm
stainless steel adjuster

改質アスファルト防水 t=4mm
シンダーコンクリート t=30〜80mm
スタイロフォーム t=30mm
ALC t=100mm
refoaming asphalt waterproofing t=4mm
cinder concrete t=30〜80mm
rigid insulation form t=30mm
autoclaved lightweight concrete t=100mm

桐板 t=9mm ワックス仕上げ
paulownia wood
t=9mm wax finish

シャンデリア
chandelier

600

踊場 4
landing 4

459.5

180

760.3

桐フローリング t=15mm ワックス仕上げ
ラワン合板 t=15mm
ALC t=100mm
paulownia flooring t=15mm wax finish
lauan plywood t=15mm
autoclaved light-weight concrete t=100mm

40
40
60
40

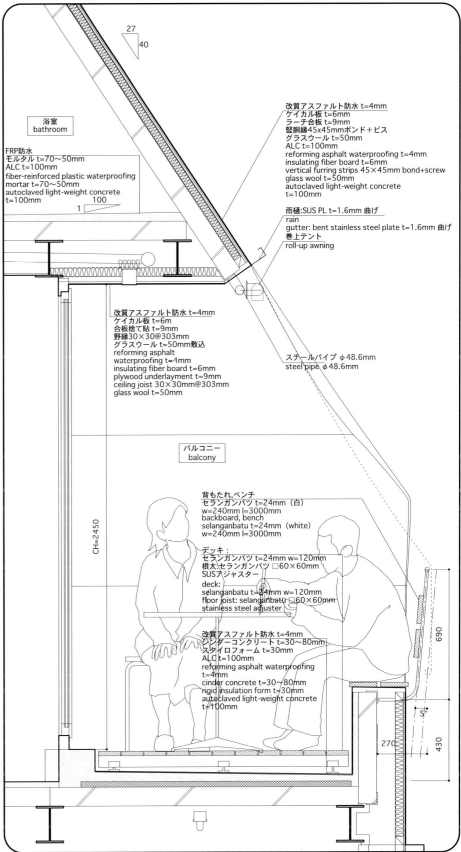

27
40

浴室
bathroom

FRP防水
モルタル t=70〜50mm
ALC t=100mm
fiber-reinforced plastic waterproofing
mortar t=70〜50mm
autoclaved light-weight concrete
t=100mm

1 100

改質アスファルト防水 t=4mm
ケイカル板 t=6mm
ラーチ合板 t=9mm
竪胴縁45x45mmボンド＋ビス
グラスウール t=50mm
ALC t=100mm
reforming asphalt waterproofing t=4mm
insulating fiber board t=6mm
vertical furring strips 45×45mm bond+screw
glass wool t=50mm
autoclaved light-weight concrete
t=100mm

雨樋:SUS PL t=1.6mm 曲げ
rain
gutter: bent stainless steel plate t=1.6mm 曲げ
巻上テント
roll-up awning

改質アスファルト防水 t=4mm
ケイカル板 t=6m
合板捨て貼 t=9mm
野縁30×30@303mm
グラスウール t=50mm敷込
reforming asphalt
waterproofing t=4mm
insulating fiber board t=6mm
plywood underlayment t=9mm
ceiling joist 30×30mm@303mm
glass wool t=50mm

スチールパイプ φ48.6mm
steel pipe φ48.6mm

バルコニー
balcony

CH=2450

背もたれ,ベンチ
セランガンバツ t=24mm （白）
w=240mm l=3000mm
backboard, bench
selanganbatu t=24mm (white)
w=240mm l=3000mm

デッキ：
セランガンバツ t=24mm w=120mm
根太:セランガンバツ □60×60mm
SUSアジャスター
deck:
selanganbatu t=24mm w=120mm
floor joist: selanganbatu □60×60mm
stainless steel adjuster

改質アスファルト防水 t=4mm
シンダーコンクリート t=30〜80mm
スタイロフォーム t=30mm
ALC t=100mm
reforming asphalt waterproofing
t=4mm
cinder concrete t=30〜80mm
rigid insulation form t=30mm
autoclaved light-weight concrete
t=100mm

690

5°

270

430

バルコニー断面詳細図 / balcony section detail S:1/20

ハウス・タワー
House Tower

モルタル金ゴテ仕上げ t=30mm〜(水勾配1/100)
硬質スタイロフォーム t=50mm
防水シート
trowel mortar t=30mm〜 (drainage slope 1/100)
rigid insulation foam t=50mm
waterproof membrane

コンクリート打放し
exposed concrete

コンクリート仕上げ t=30mm
(増打15mm)
exposed concrete

納戸2
storage 2

モルタル金ゴテ仕上げ t=150mm
撥水材塗布
コンクリート t=30mm
water-repellent paint finish
concrete t=150mm

▽4FL GL+9160

コンクリート打放し
exposed concrete

洗面カウンター:
コンクリート t=120mm
撥水材塗布
counter:
concrete t=120mm
water-repellent paint finish

家事室
utility room

モルタル金ゴテ仕上げ t=30mm
撥水材塗布
コンクリート t=150mm
trowel mortar t=30mm
water-repellent paint finish
concrete t=150mm

▽3FL GL+6940

コンクリート打放し
exposed concrete

本棚:
ラワン合板 t=15mm
(棚板t=21mm)
天然ワックス系樹脂塗料
book shelf:
lauan plywood t=15mm
natural resin varnish finish

書斎
study room

CH=4160

CH=1790

CH=2040

▽RFL GL+11190〜

カーテンレール埋込
curtain rail

スチールプレート(打込)UE
t=9mm(打込)
steel plate t=9mm
polyurethane resin
enamel paint

カーテンレール埋込
curtain rail

スチールプレート(打込)UE
t=9mm(打込)
steel plate t=9mm
polyurethane resin
enamel paint

スチールプレート(打込)UE
t=9mm(打込)
steel plate t=9mm
polyurethane resin
enamel paint

屋上テラス
roof top terrace

ベンチ:
ニヤトー材 t=18mm
天然ワックス系樹脂塗料
bench: nyatoh t=18mm
natural resin varnish finish

カーテンレール埋込
curtain rail

浴室
bathroom

モルタル金ゴテ仕上げ t=30mm〜(水勾配1/100)
撥水材塗布
防水シート
trowel mortar t=30mm〜
(drainage slope 1/100)
water-repellent paint
waterproof membrane
concrete t=170mm

カーテンレール埋込
curtain rail

内すべり出し窓:(防火設備)
木製サッシ
ペアガラス FL6+A10+PWC6.8mm
awning window:
timber framed
double glazing FL6+A10+PWC6.8mm

寝室
bedroom

スチールプレート(打込)UE
t=9mm(打込)
steel plate t=9mm
polyurethane resin
enamel paint

CH=2250

設備
maximum height

樹脂モルタル木ゴテ引き t=4mm
スタイロフォーム t=50mm(打込)
trowel finished resin mortar t=4mm
rigid insulation foam t=50mm

trowel mortar t=10mm
concrete block t=70mm
rigid insulation foam t=25mm
waterproof membrane

モルタル金ゴテ仕上げ t=10mm
スタイロブロック t=70mm
コンクリート (立上げ h=250mm)
防水シート

モルタル金ゴテ仕上げ t=40mm〜(水勾配1/100)
硬質スタイロフォーム t=50mm
防水シート
trowel mortar t=40mm
(drainage slope 1/100)
rigid insulation foam t=50mm
waterproof membrane

▽4FL GL+9250〜

コンクリート打放し
撥水材塗布
exposed concrete
water-repellent paint finish

h=570mm〜:
コンクリート打放し 撥水材塗布
exposed concrete
water-repellent paint finish

h=0〜570mm:
モルタル金ゴテ仕上げ t=15mm
防水シート
trowel mortar t=15mm
waterproof membrane

CH=1900

FIX窓:
木製サッシ
ペアガラス
FL6+A10+PWC6.8mm
fixed window:
timber fram
double glazing
FL6+A10+PWC6.8mm

コンクリート打放し
exposed concrete

モルタル金ゴテ仕上げ t=170mm
撥水材塗布
コンクリート t=30mm
water-repellent paint finish
concrete t=170mm

▽3FL GL+7110〜7160

カーテンレール埋込
curtain rail

FIX窓:
木製サッシ (防火設備)
ペアガラス
FL6+A10+PWC6.8mm
fixed window:
timber fram
double glazing
FL6+A10+PWC6.8mm

コンクリート打放し
(増打15mm)
exposed concrete

モルタル金ゴテ仕上げ t=170mm
撥水材塗布
コンクリート t=30mm
water-repellent paint finish
concrete t=170mm

▽2FL GL+4660

▽GL+11350 最高高さ maximum height

setback regulation from road width

▽GL+11350 最高高さ maximum height

道路斜線 setback regulation from road width

86 ハウス・タワー

1.25

2190   2220   4340
2100   2140   2450

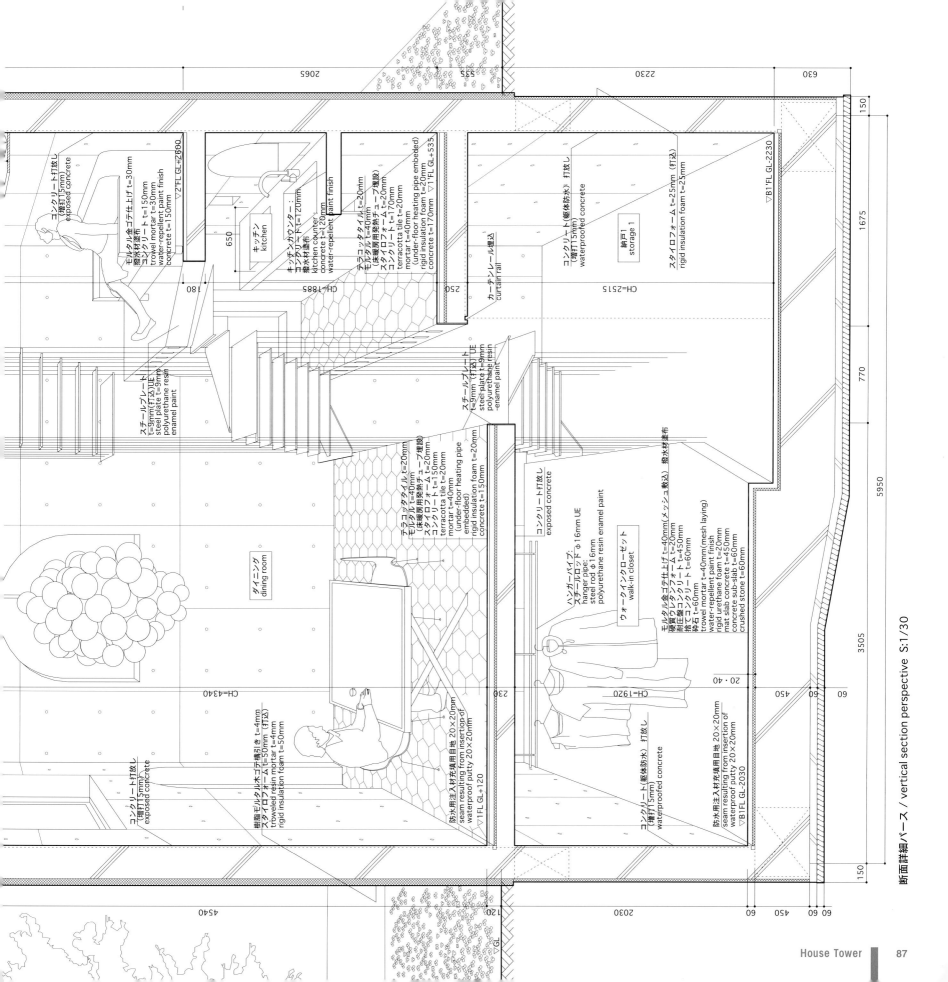

断面詳細パース / vertical section perspective S:1/30

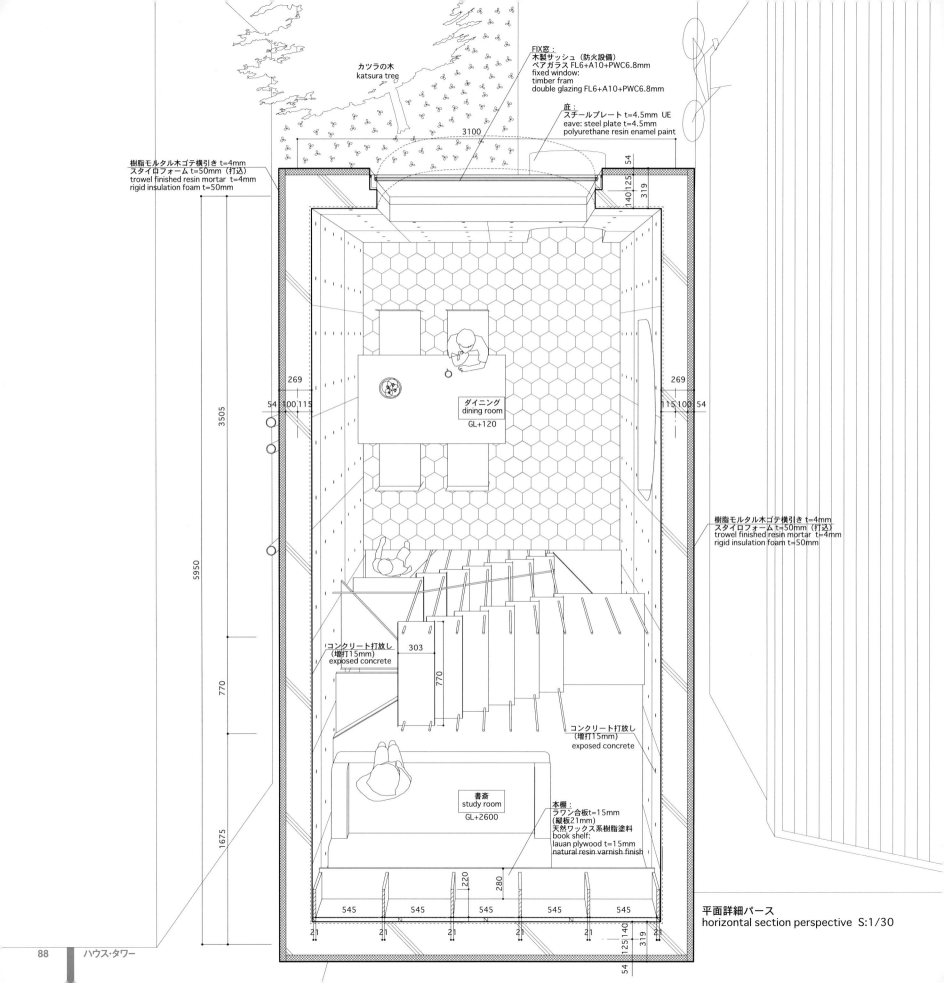

カツラの木
katsura tree

FIX窓 :
木製サッシュ（防火設備）
ペアガラス FL6+A10+PWC6.8mm
fixed window:
timber fram
double glazing FL6+A10+PWC6.8mm

庇 :
スチールプレート t=4.5mm UE
eave: steel plate t=4.5mm
polyurethane resin enamel paint

樹脂モルタル木ゴテ横引き t=4mm
スタイロフォーム t=50mm（打込）
trowel finished resin mortar t=4mm
rigid insulation foam t=50mm

3100

54
140 125
319

3505

269

54 100 115

ダイニング
dining room
GL+120

269

115 100 54

5950

樹脂モルタル木ゴテ横引き t=4mm
スタイロフォーム t=50mm（打込）
trowel finished resin mortar t=4mm
rigid insulation foam t=50mm

コンクリート打放し
（増打15mm）
exposed concrete

303

770

770

コンクリート打放し
（増打15mm）
exposed concrete

書斎
study room
GL+2600

本棚 :
ラワン合板t=15mm
（縦板21mm）
天然ワックス系樹脂塗料
book shelf:
lauan plywood t=15mm
natural resin varnish finish

1675

220
280

545 | 545 | 545 | 545 | 545

21 21 21 21 21

54
125 140
319

平面詳細パース
horizontal section perspective S:1/30

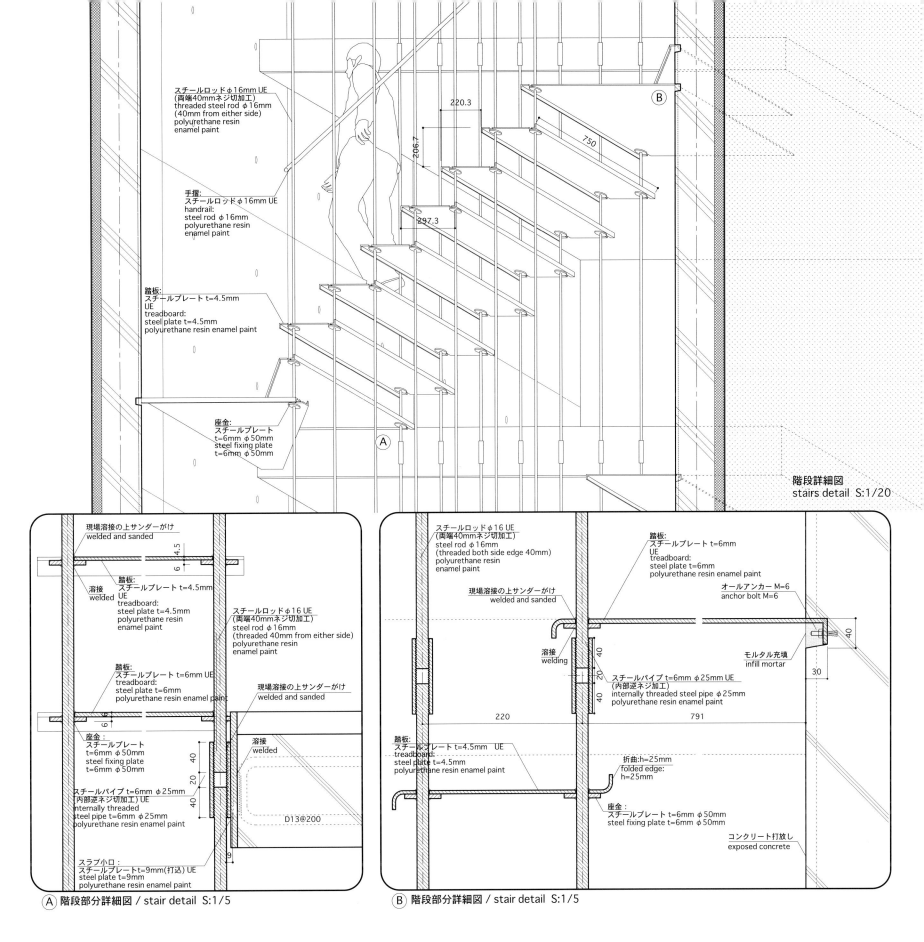

スチールロッドφ16mm UE
(両端40mmネジ切加工)
threaded steel rod φ16mm
(40mm from either side)
polyurethane resin
enamel paint

手摺:
スチールロッドφ16mm UE
handrail:
steel rod φ16mm
polyurethane resin
enamel paint

踏板:
スチールプレート t=4.5mm
UE
treadboard:
steel plate t=4.5mm
polyurethane resin enamel paint

座金:
スチールプレート
t=6mm φ50mm
steel fixing plate
t=6mm φ50mm

220.3

206.7

297.3

750

Ⓑ

Ⓐ

階段詳細図
stairs detail S:1/20

現場溶接の上サンダーがけ
welded and sanded

4.5
6

溶接
welded

踏板:
スチールプレート t=4.5mm
UE
treadboard:
steel plate t=4.5mm
polyurethane resin
enamel paint

踏板:
スチールプレート t=6mm UE
treadboard:
steel plate t=6mm
polyurethane resin enamel paint

スチールロッドφ16 UE
(両端40mmネジ切加工)
steel rod φ16mm
(threaded 40mm from either side)
polyurethane resin
enamel paint

現場溶接の上サンダーがけ
welded and sanded

座金:
スチールプレート
t=6mm φ50mm
steel fixing plate
t=6mm φ50mm

溶接
welded

40
20
40

スチールパイプ t=6mm φ25mm
(内部逆ネジ切加工) UE
internally threaded
steel pipe t=6mm φ25mm
polyurethane resin enamel paint

D13@200

9

スラブ小口:
スチールプレートt=9mm(打込) UE
steel plate t=9mm
polyurethane resin enamel paint

Ⓐ 階段部分詳細図 / stair detail S:1/5

スチールロッドφ16 UE
(両端40mmネジ切加工)
steel rod φ16mm
(threaded both side edge 40mm)
polyurethane resin
enamel paint

踏板:
スチールプレート t=6mm
UE
treadboard:
steel plate t=6mm
polyurethane resin enamel paint

現場溶接の上サンダーがけ
welded and sanded

オールアンカー M=6
anchor bolt M=6

溶接
welding

40
20
40

スチールパイプ t=6mm φ25mm
(内部逆ネジ切加工)
internally threaded steel pipe φ25mm
polyurethane resin enamel paint

モルタル充填
infill mortar

40
30

220

791

踏板:
スチールプレート t=4.5mm UE
treadboard:
steel plate t=4.5mm
polyurethane resin enamel paint

折曲:h=25mm
folded edge:
h=25mm

座金:
スチールプレート t=6mm φ50mm
steel fixing plate t=6mm φ50mm

コンクリート打放し
exposed concrete

Ⓑ 階段部分詳細図 / stair detail S:1/5

ノラ・ハウス
Nora House

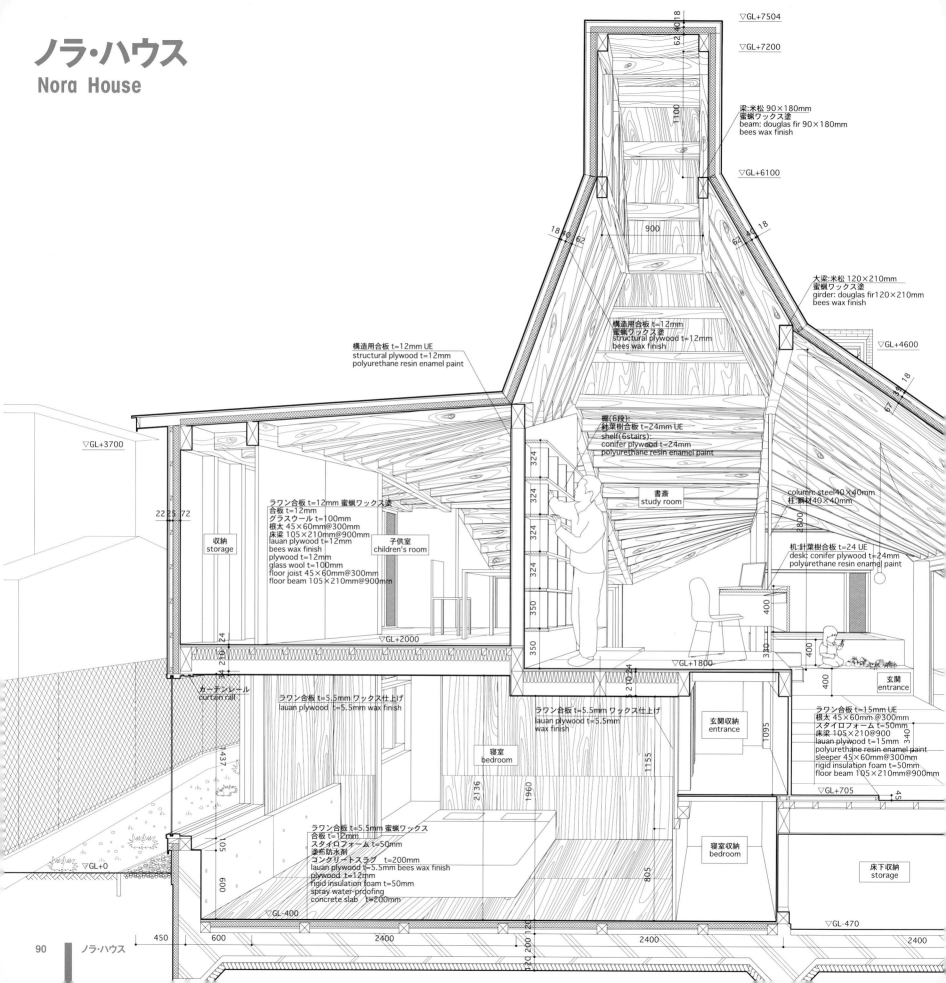

▽GL+7504

▽GL+7200

梁:米松 90×180mm
蜜蝋ワックス塗
beam: douglas fir 90×180mm
bees wax finish

▽GL+6100

大梁:米松 120×210mm
蜜蝋ワックス塗
girder: douglas fir120×210mm
bees wax finish

▽GL+4600

構造用合板 t=12mm
蜜蝋ワックス塗
structural plywood t=12mm
bees wax finish

構造用合板 t=12mm UE
structural plywood t=12mm
polyurethane resin enamel paint

棚(6段):
針葉樹合板 t=24mm UE
shelf(6stairs):
conifer plywood t=24mm
polyurethane resin enamel paint

▽GL+3700

書斎
study room

column: steel40×40mm
柱:鋼材40×40mm

ラワン合板 t=12mm 蜜蝋ワックス塗
合板 t=12mm
グラスウール t=100mm
根太 45×60mm@300mm
床梁 105×210mm@900mm
lauan plywood t=12mm
bees wax finish
plywood t=12mm
glass wool t=100mm
floor joist 45×60mm@300mm
floor beam 105×210mm@900mm

収納
storage

子供室
children's room

机:針葉樹合板 t=24 UE
desk: conifer plywood t=24mm
polyurethane resin enamel paint

▽GL+2000

▽GL+1800

玄関
entrance

カーテンレール
curtain rail

ラワン合板 t=5.5mm ワックス仕上げ
lauan plywood t=5.5mm wax finish

ラワン合板 t=5.5mm ワックス仕上げ
lauan plywood t=5.5mm
wax finish

玄関収納
entrance

寝室
bedroom

ラワン合板 t=15mm UE
根太 45×60mm@300mm
スタイロフォーム t=50mm
床梁 105×210@900
lauan plywood t=15mm
polyurethane resin enamel paint
sleeper 45×60mm@300mm
rigid insulation foam t=50mm
floor beam 105×210mm@900mm

▽GL+705

▽GL+0

ラワン合板 t=5.5mm 蜜蝋ワックス
合板 t=12mm
スタイロフォーム t=50mm
塗布防水剤
コンクリートスラブ t=200mm
lauan plywood t=5.5mm bees wax finish
plywood t=12mm
rigid insulation foam t=50mm
spray water-proofing
concrete slab t=200mm

寝室収納
bedroom

床下収納
storage

▽GL-400

▽GL-470

450 600 2400 2400 2400

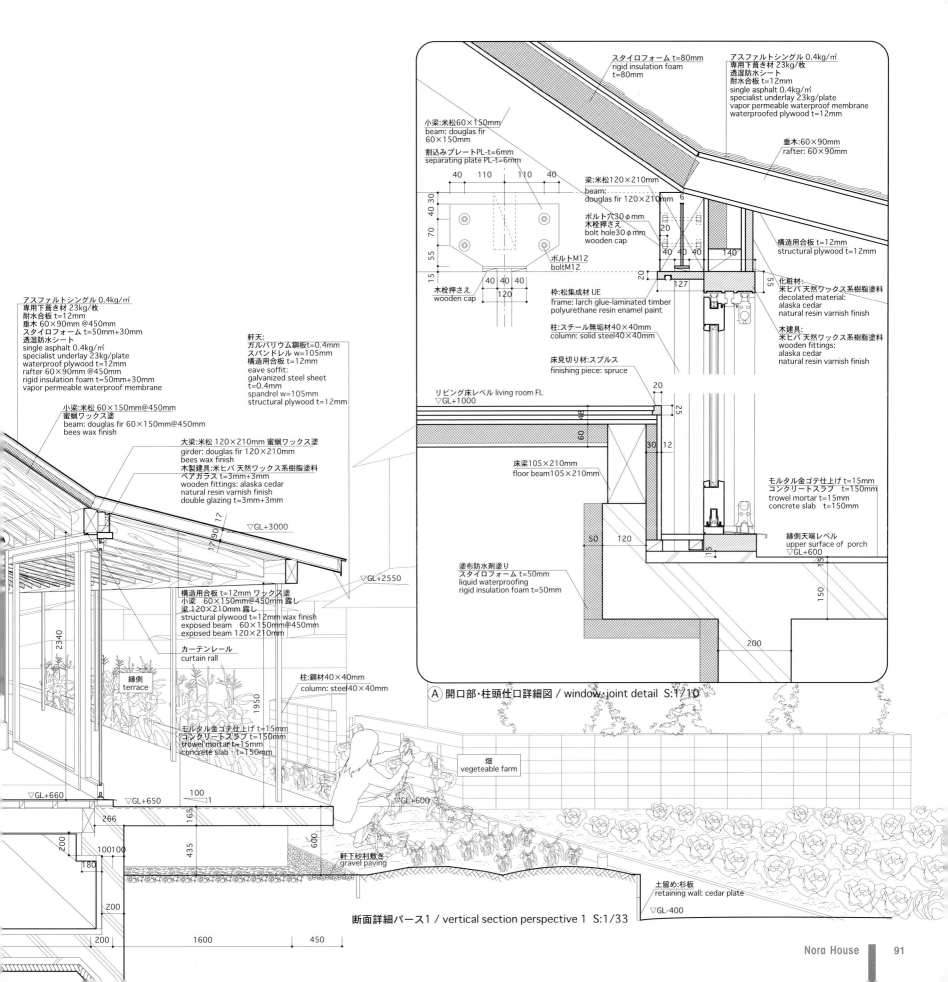

スタイロフォーム t=80mm
rigid insulation foam
t=80mm

アスファルトシングル 0.4kg/㎡
専用下葺材 23kg/枚
透湿防水シート
耐水合板 t=12mm
single asphalt 0.4kg/㎡
specialist underlay 23kg/plate
vapor permeable waterproof membrane
waterproofed plywood t=12mm

小梁:米松60×150mm
beam: douglas fir
60×150mm

垂木:60×90mm
rafter: 60×90mm

割込みプレートPL-t=6mm
separating plate PL-t=6mm

梁:米松120×210mm
beam:
douglas fir 120×210mm

ボルト穴30φmm
木栓押さえ
bolt hole30φmm
wooden cap

構造用合板 t=12mm
structural plywood t=12mm

ボルトM12
boltM12

木栓押さえ
wooden cap

化粧材:
米ヒバ 天然ワックス系樹脂塗料
decolated material:
alaska cedar
natural resin varnish finish

枠:松集成材 UE
frame: larch glue-laminated timber
polyurethane resin enamel paint

柱:スチール無垢材40×40mm
column: solid steel40×40mm

木建具:
米ヒバ 天然ワックス系樹脂塗料
wooden fittings:
alaska cedar
natural resin varnish finish

軒天:
ガルバリウム鋼板t=0.4mm
スパンドレル w=105mm
構造用合板 t=12mm
eave soffit:
galvanized steel sheet
t=0.4mm
spandrel w=105mm
structural plywood t=12mm

床見切り材:スプルス
finishing piece: spruce

アスファルトシングル 0.4kg/㎡
専用下葺き材 23kg/枚
耐水合板 t=12mm
垂木 60×90mm@450mm
スタイロフォーム t=50mm+30mm
透湿防水シート
single asphalt 0.4kg/㎡
specialist underlay 23kg/plate
waterproof plywood t=12mm
rafter 60×90mm@450mm
rigid insulation foam t=50mm+30mm
vapor permeable waterproof membrane

小梁:米松 60×150mm@450mm
蜜蝋ワックス塗
beam: douglas fir 60×150mm@450mm
bees wax finish

大梁:米松 120×210mm 蜜蝋ワックス塗
girder: douglas fir 120×210mm
bees wax finish

木製建具:米ヒバ 天然ワックス系樹脂塗料
ペアガラス t=3mm+3mm
wooden fittings: alaska cedar
natural resin varnish finish
double glazing t=3mm+3mm

リビング床レベル living room FL
▽GL+1000

床梁105×210mm
floor beam105×210mm

モルタル金ゴテ仕上げ t=15mm
コンクリートスラブ t=150mm
trowel mortar t=15mm
concrete slab t=150mm

縁側天端レベル
upper surface of porch
▽GL+600

塗布防水剤塗り
スタイロフォーム t=50mm
liquid waterproofing
rigid insulation foam t=50mm

▽GL+3000

▽GL+2550

構造用合板 t=12mm ワックス塗
小梁 60×150mm@450mm 露し
梁 120×210mm 露し
structural plywood t=12mm wax finish
exposed beam 60×150mm@450mm
exposed beam 120×210mm

カーテンレール
curtain rall

柱:鋼材40×40mm
column: steel40×40mm

2340

縁側
terrace

1950

モルタル金ゴテ仕上げ t=15mm
コンクリートスラブ t=150mm
trowel mortar t=15mm
concrete slab t=150mm

Ⓐ 開口部・柱頭仕口詳細図 / window joint detail S:1/10

畑
vegeteable farm

▽GL+660
▽GL+650
100

266

165
435

600

GL+600

軒下砂利敷き
gravel paving

200

100 100

180

200

200 1600 450

土留め:杉板
retaining wall: cedar plate
▽GL-400

断面詳細パース1 / vertical section perspective 1 S:1/33

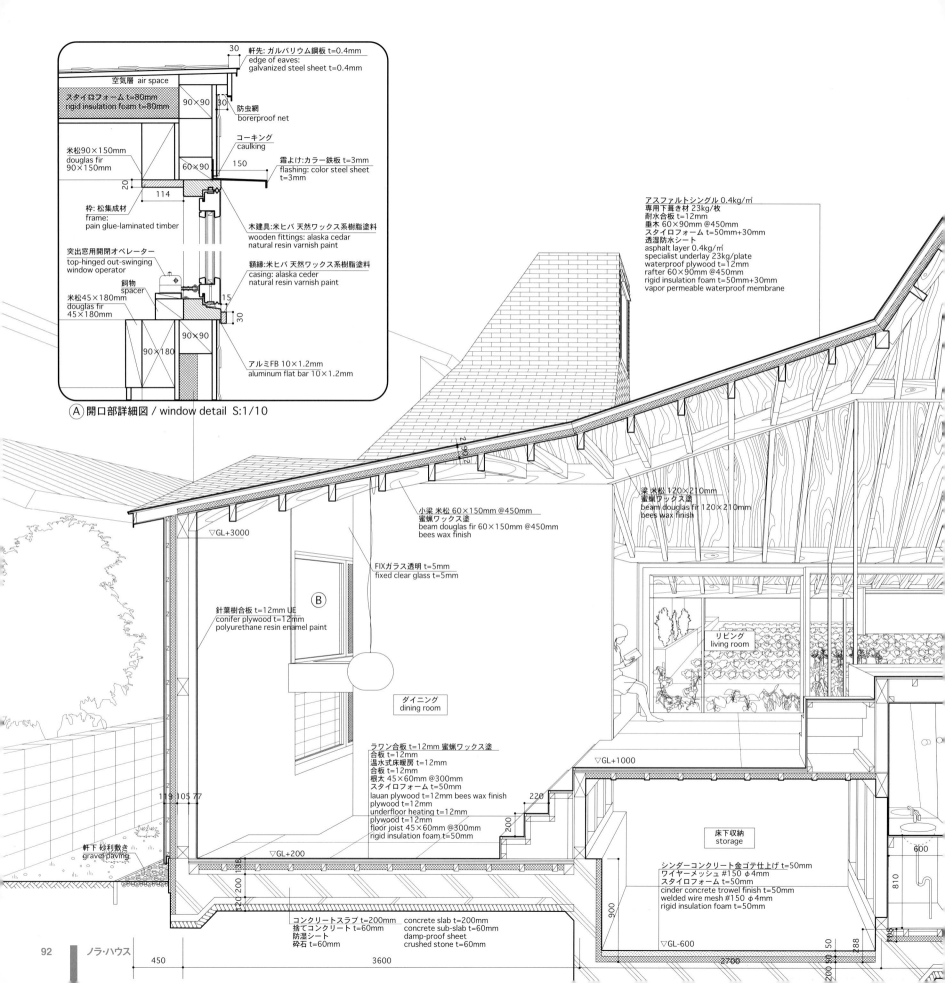

軒先: ガルバリウム鋼板 t=0.4mm
edge of eaves:
galvanized steel sheet t=0.4mm

30

空気層 air space

スタイロフォーム t=80mm
rigid insulation foam t=80mm

90×90

30

防虫網
borerproof net

コーキング
caulking

米松90×150mm
douglas fir
90×150mm

60×90   150

霜よけ:カラー鉄板 t=3mm
flashing: color steel sheet
t=3mm

20

114

枠: 松集成材
frame:
pain glue-laminated timber

木建具:米ヒバ 天然ワックス系樹脂塗料
wooden fittings: alaska cedar
natural resin varnish paint

突出窓用開閉オペレーター
top-hinged out-swinging
window operator

額縁:米ヒバ 天然ワックス系樹脂塗料
casing: alaska ceder
natural resin varnish paint

飼物 spacer

米松45×180mm
douglas fir
45×180mm

90×90

15

30

90×180

90×180

アルミFB 10×1.2mm
aluminum flat bar 10×1.2mm

Ⓐ 開口部詳細図 / window detail S:1/10

アスファルトシングル 0.4kg/㎡
専用下葺き材 23kg/枚
耐水合板 t=12mm
垂木 60×90mm @450mm
スタイロフォーム t=50mm+30mm
透湿防水シート
asphalt layer 0.4kg/㎡
specialist underlay 23kg/plate
waterproof plywood t=12mm
rafter 60×90mm @450mm
rigid insulation foam t=50mm+30mm
vapor permeable waterproof membrane

梁 米松 120×210mm
蜜蝋ワックス塗
beam douglas fir 120×210mm
bees wax finish

小梁 米松 60×150mm @450mm
蜜蝋ワックス塗
beam douglas fir 60×150mm @450mm
bees wax finish

▽GL+3000

FIXガラス透明 t=5mm
fixed clear glass t=5mm

Ⓑ

針葉樹合板 t=12mm UE
conifer plywood t=12mm
polyurethane resin enamel paint

ダイニング
dining room

リビング
living room

▽GL+1000

220

200

床下収納
storage

軒下 砂利敷き
gravel paving

119 105 77

ラワン合板 t=12mm 蜜蝋ワックス塗
合板 t=12mm
温水式床暖房 t=12mm
合板 t=12mm
根太 45×60mm @300mm
スタイロフォーム t=50mm
lauan plywood t=12mm bees wax finish
plywood t=12mm
underfloor heating t=12mm
plywood t=12mm
floor joist 45×60mm @300mm
rigid insulation foam t=50mm

200

▽GL+200

200

シンダーコンクリート金ゴテ仕上げ t=50mm
ワイヤーメッシュ #150 φ4mm
スタイロフォーム t=50mm
cinder concrete trowel finish t=50mm
welded wire mesh #150 φ4mm
rigid insulation foam t=50mm

600

810

900

120

コンクリートスラブ t=200mm   concrete slab t=200mm
捨てコンクリート t=60mm   concrete sub-slab t=60mm
防湿シート   damp-proof sheet
砕石 t=60mm   crushed stone t=60mm

▽GL-600

2700

450   3600

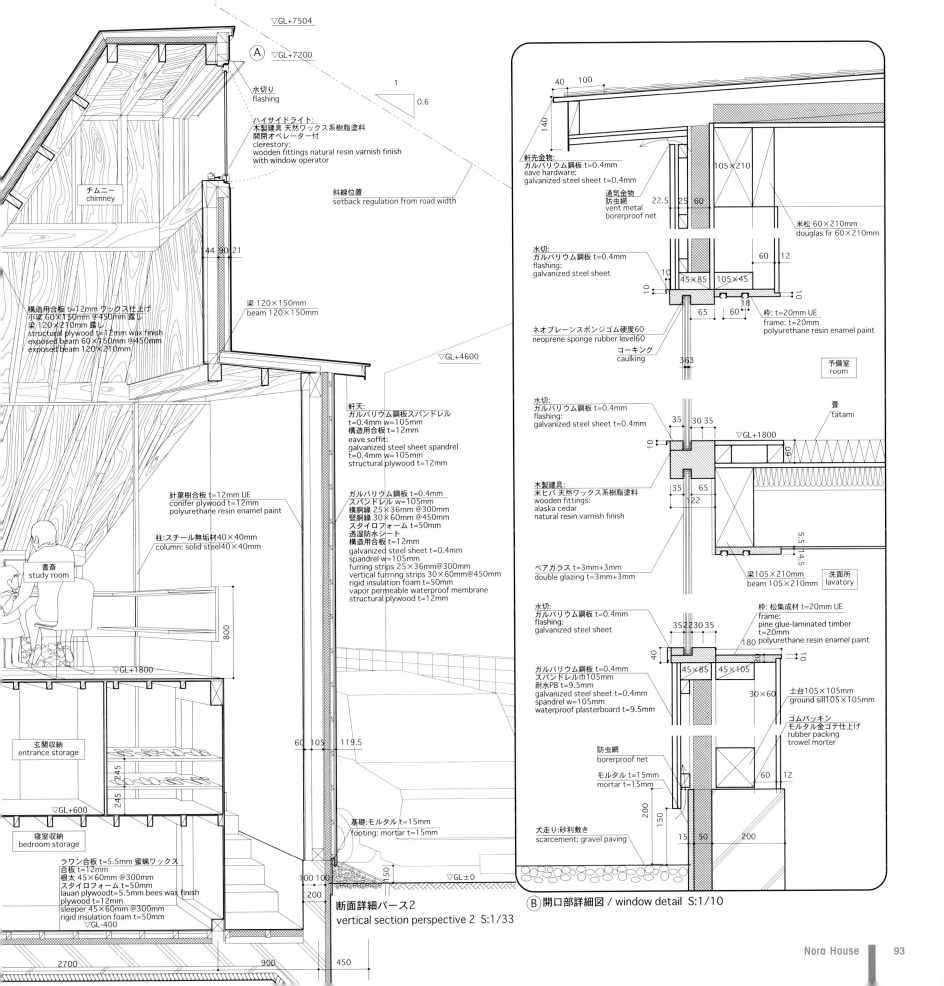

▽GL+7504

Ⓐ ▽GL+7200

1
0.6

水切り
flashing

ハイサイドライト:
木製建具 天然ワックス系樹脂塗料
開閉オペレーター付
clerestory:
wooden fittings natural resin varnish finish
with window operator

斜線位置
setback regulation from road width

チムニー
chimney

梁 120×150mm
beam 120×150mm

44 90 21

構造用合板 t=12mm ワックス仕上げ
小梁 60×150mm @450mm 露し
梁 120×210mm 露し
structural plywood t=12mm wax finish
exposed beam 60×150mm @450mm
exposed beam 120×210mm

▽GL+4600

軒天:
ガルバリウム鋼板スパンドレル
t=0.4mm w=105mm
構造用合板 t=12mm
eave soffit:
galvanized steel sheet spandrel
t=0.4mm w=105mm
structural plywood t=12mm

針葉樹合板 t=12mm UE
conifer plywood t=12mm
polyurethane resin enamel paint

柱:スチール無垢材40×40mm
column: solid steel40×40mm

書斎
study room

ガルバリウム鋼板 t=0.4mm
スパンドレル w=105mm
横胴縁 25×36mm @300mm
竪胴縁 30×60mm @450mm
スタイロフォーム t=50mm
透湿防水シート
構造用合板 t=12mm
galvanized steel sheet t=0.4mm
spandrel w=105mm
furring strips 25×36mm@300mm
vertical furrring strips 30×60mm@450mm
rigid insulation foam t=50mm
vapor permeable waterproof membrane
structural plywood t=12mm

800

▽GL+1800

玄関収納
entrance storage

245

▽GL+600

寝室収納
bedroom storage

60 105 119.5

ラワン合板 t=5.5mm 蜜蝋ワックス
合板 t=12mm
根太 45×60mm @300mm
スタイロフォーム t=50mm
lauan plywoodt=5.5mm bees wax finish
plywood t=12mm
sleeper 45×60mm @300mm
rigid insulation foam t=50mm

基礎:モルタル t=15mm
footing: mortar t=15mm

100 100

▽GL±0

150

200

▽GL-400

2700   900   450

断面詳細パース2
vertical section perspective 2 S:1/33

40 100

140

軒先金物
ガルバリウム鋼板 t=0.4mm
eave hardware:
galvanized steel sheet t=0.4mm

105×210

通気金物
防虫網
vent metal
borerproof net

22.5 25 60

米松 60×210mm
douglas fir 60×210mm

水切:
ガルバリウム鋼板 t=0.4mm
flashing:
galvanized steel sheet

60 12

10 45×85 105×45

10

10

65   60 18

枠: t=20mm UE
frame: t=20mm
polyurethane resin enamel paint

ネオプレーンスポンジゴム硬度60
neoprene sponge rubber level60

コーキング
caulking

363

予備室
room

水切:
ガルバリウム鋼板 t=0.4mm
flashing:
galvanized steel sheet t=0.4mm

35 30 35

畳
tatami

10

▽GL+1800

60

木製建具:
米ヒバ 天然ワックス系樹脂塗料
wooden fittings:
alaska cedar
natural resin varnish finish

35   65
122

5.5 14.5

ペアガラス t=3mm+3mm
double glazing t=3mm+3mm

梁105×210mm
beam 105×210mm

洗面所
lavatory

水切:
ガルバリウム鋼板 t=0.4mm
flashing:
galvanized steel sheet

35 22 30 35

枠: 松集成材 t=20mm UE
frame:
pine glue-laminated timber
t=20mm
polyurethane resin enamel paint

40

180

60

10

ガルバリウム鋼板 t=0.4mm
スパンドレル巾105mm
耐水PB t=9.5mm
galvanized steel sheet t=0.4mm
spandrel w=105mm
waterproof plasterboard t=9.5mm

45×85   45×105

30×60

土台105×105mm
ground sill105×105mm

ゴムパッキン
モルタル金ゴテ仕上げ
rubber packing
trowel morter

防虫網
borerproof net

モルタル t=15mm
mortar t=15mm

60 12

200

150

犬走り:砂利敷き
scarcement: gravel paving

15 50   200

Ⓑ 開口部詳細図 / window detail S:1/10

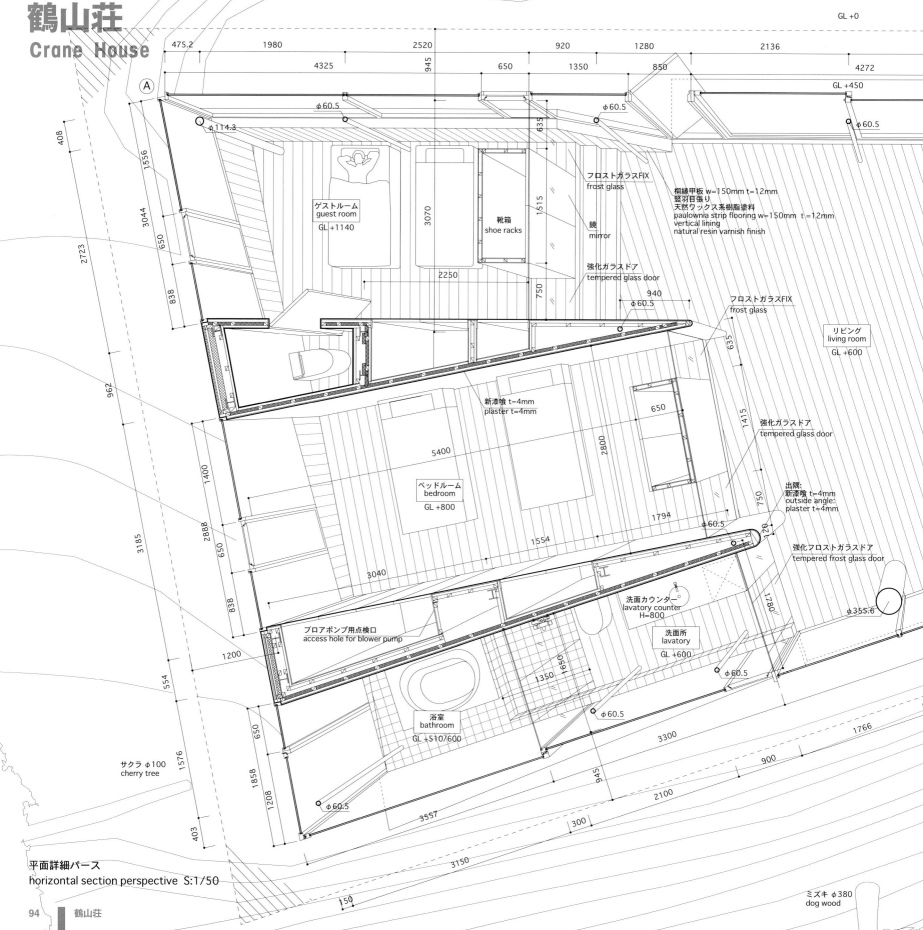

GL +0
GL +450

Ⓐ

φ60.5
φ114.3
φ60.5
φ60.5

ゲストルーム
guest room
GL +1140

靴箱
shoe racks

フロストガラスFIX
frost glass

鏡
mirror

桐縁甲板 w=150mm t=12mm
竪羽目張り
天然ワックス系樹脂塗料
paulownia strip flooring w=150mm t=12mm
vertical lining
natural resin varnish finish

強化ガラスドア
tempered glass door

フロストガラスFIX
frost glass

φ60.5

リビング
living room
GL +600

新漆喰 t=4mm
plaster t=4mm

ベッドルーム
bedroom
GL +800

強化ガラスドア
tempered glass door

出隅;
新漆喰 t=4mm
outside angle;
plaster t=4mm

φ60.5

強化フロストガラスドア
tempered frost glass door

ブロアポンプ用点検口
access hole for blower pump

洗面カウンター
lavatory counter
H=800

洗面所
lavatory
GL +600

φ355.6

φ60.5

浴室
bathroom
GL +510/600

φ60.5

サクラ φ100
cherry tree

φ60.5

平面詳細パース
horizontal section perspective S:1/50

ミズキ φ380
dog wood

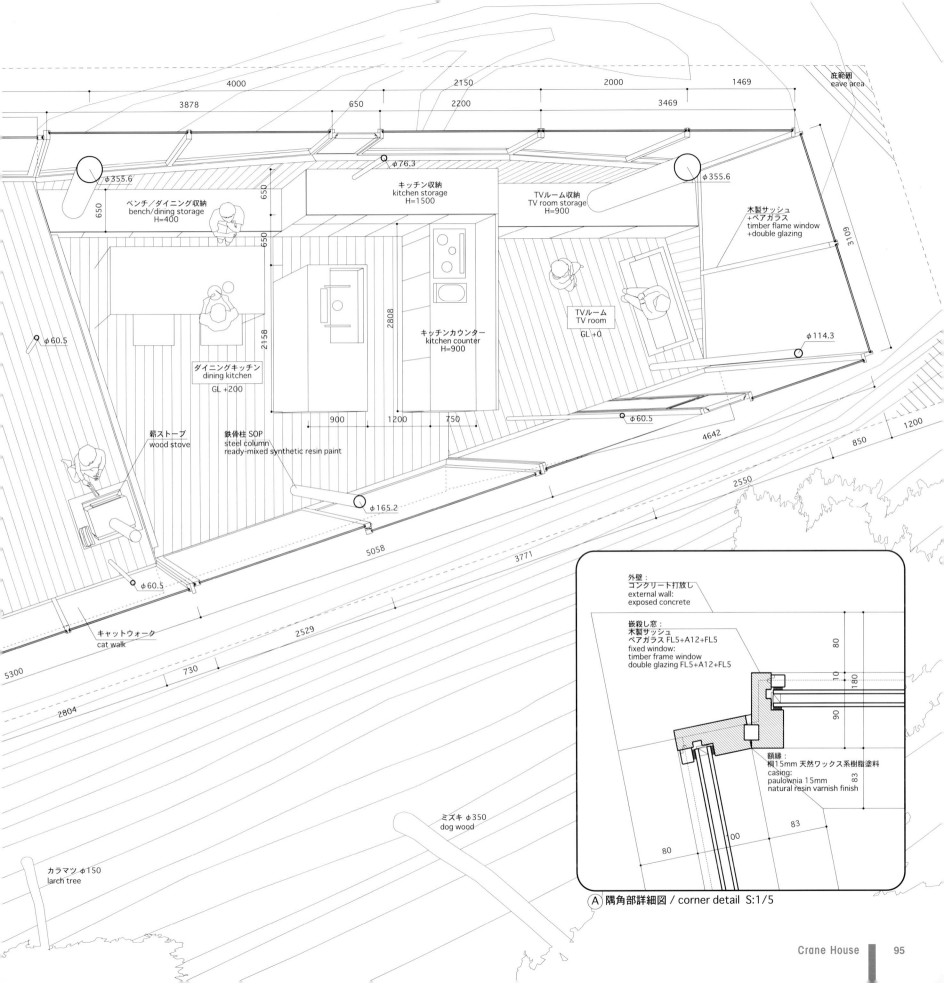

4000
2150
2000
1469

庇範囲
eave area

3878
650
2200
3469

φ76.3

φ355.6

φ355.6

キッチン収納
kitchen storage
H=1500

TVルーム収納
TV room storage
H=900

木製サッシュ
+ペアガラス
timber flame window
+double glazing

650

ベンチ／ダイニング収納
bench/dining storage
H=400

650

650

3109

φ60.5

2158

2808

TVルーム
TV room
GL +0

φ114.3

ダイニングキッチン
dining kitchen
GL +200

キッチンカウンター
kitchen counter
H=900

1200

φ60.5

薪ストーブ
wood stove

鉄骨柱 SOP
steel column
ready-mixed synthetic resin paint

900
1200
750

4642

φ165.2

2550

5058

3771

1200

850

キャットウォーク
cat walk

2529

730

5300

2804

ミズキ φ350
dog wood

Ⓐ 隅角部詳細図 / corner detail S:1/5

カラマツ φ150
larch tree

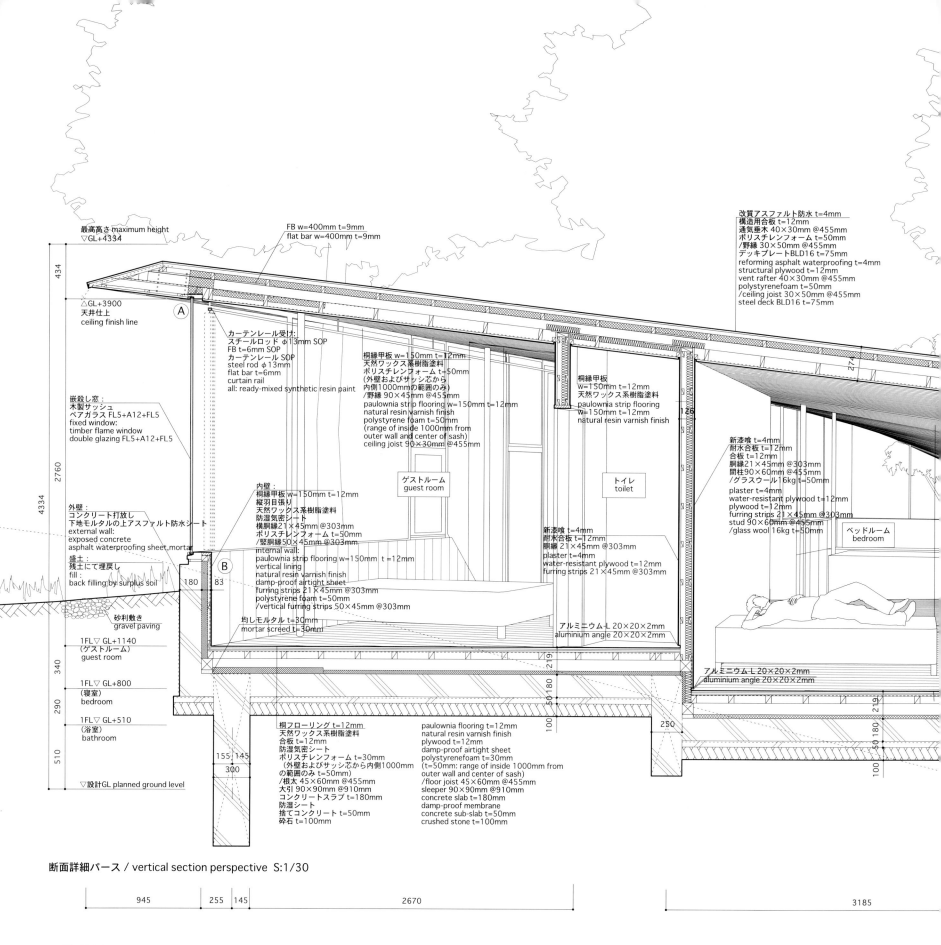

最高高さ maximum height
▽GL+4334

△GL+3900
天井仕上
ceiling finish line

嵌殺し窓：
木製サッシ
ペアガラス FL5+A12+FL5
fixed window:
timber flame window
double glazing FL5+A12+FL5

外壁：
コンクリート打放し
下地モルタルの上アスファルト防水シート
external wall:
exposed concrete
asphalt waterproofing sheet,mortar

盛土：
残土にて埋戻し
fill :
back filling by surplus soil

砂利敷き
gravel paving

1FL▽ GL+1140
（ゲストルーム）
guest room

1FL▽ GL+800
（寝室）
bedroom

1FL▽ GL+510
（浴室）
bathroom

▽設計GL planned ground level

FB w=400mm t=9mm
flat bar w=400mm t=9mm

改質アスファルト防水 t=4mm
構造用合板 t=12mm
通気垂木 40×30mm @455mm
ポリスチレンフォーム t=50mm
/野縁 30×50mm @455mm
デッキプレートBLD16 t=75mm
reforming asphalt waterproofing t=4mm
structural plywood t=12mm
vent rafter 40×30mm @455mm
polystyrenefoam t=50mm
/ceiling joist 30×50mm @455mm
steel deck BLD16 t=75mm

カーテンレール受け：
スチールロッド φ13mm SOP
FB t=6mm SOP
カーテンレール SOP
steel rod φ13mm
flat bar t=6mm
curtain rail
all: ready-mixed synthetic resin paint

桐縁甲板 w=150mm t=12mm
天然ワックス系樹脂塗料
ポリスチレンフォーム t=50mm
（外壁およびサッシ芯から
内側1000mmの範囲のみ）
/野縁 90×45mm @455mm
paulownia strip flooring w=150mm t=12mm
natural resin varnish finish
polystyrene foam t=50mm
(range of inside 1000mm from
outer wall and center of sash)
ceiling joist 90×30mm @455mm

桐縁甲板
w=150mm t=12mm
天然ワックス系樹脂塗料
paulownia strip flooring
w=150mm t=12mm
natural resin varnish finish

内壁：
桐縁甲板 w=150mm t=12mm
縦羽目張り
天然ワックス系樹脂塗料
防湿気密シート
横胴縁21×45mm @303mm
ポリスチレンフォーム t=50mm
/竪胴縁50×45mm @303mm
internal wall:
paulownia strip flooring w=150mm t=12mm
vertical lining
natural resin varnish finish
damp-proof airtight sheet
furring strips 21×45mm @303mm
polystyrene foam t=50mm
/vertical furring strips 50×45mm @303mm

均しモルタル t=30mm
mortar screed t=30mm

ゲストルーム
guest room

トイレ
toilet

新漆喰 t=4mm
耐水合板 t=12mm
胴縁 21×45mm @303mm
plaster t=4mm
water-resistant plywood t=12mm
furring strips 21×45mm @303mm

新漆喰 t=4mm
耐水合板 t=12mm
合板 t=12mm
胴縁21×45mm @303mm
間柱90×60mm @455mm
/グラスウール16kg t=50mm
plaster t=4mm
water-resistant plywood t=12mm
plywood t=12mm
furring strips 21×45mm @303mm
stud 90×60mm @455mm
/glass wool 16kg t=50mm

ベッドルーム
bedroom

アルミニウム-L 20×20×2mm
aluminium angle 20×20×2mm

アルミニウム-L 20×20×2mm
aluminium angle 20×20×2mm

桐フローリング t=12mm
天然ワックス系樹脂塗料
合板 t=12mm
防湿気密シート
ポリスチレンフォーム t=30mm
（外壁およびサッシ芯から内側1000mm
の範囲のみ t=50mm）
/根太 45×60mm @455mm
大引 90×90mm @910mm
コンクリートスラブ t=180mm
防湿シート
捨てコンクリート t=50mm
砕石 t=100mm

paulownia flooring t=12mm
natural resin varnish finish
plywood t=12mm
damp-proof airtight sheet
polystyrenefoam t=30mm
(t=50mm: range of inside 1000mm from
outer wall and center of sash)
/floor joist 45×60mm @455mm
sleeper 90×90mm @910mm
concrete slab t=180mm
damp-proof membrane
concrete sub-slab t=50mm
crushed stone t=100mm

断面詳細パース / vertical section perspective S:1/30

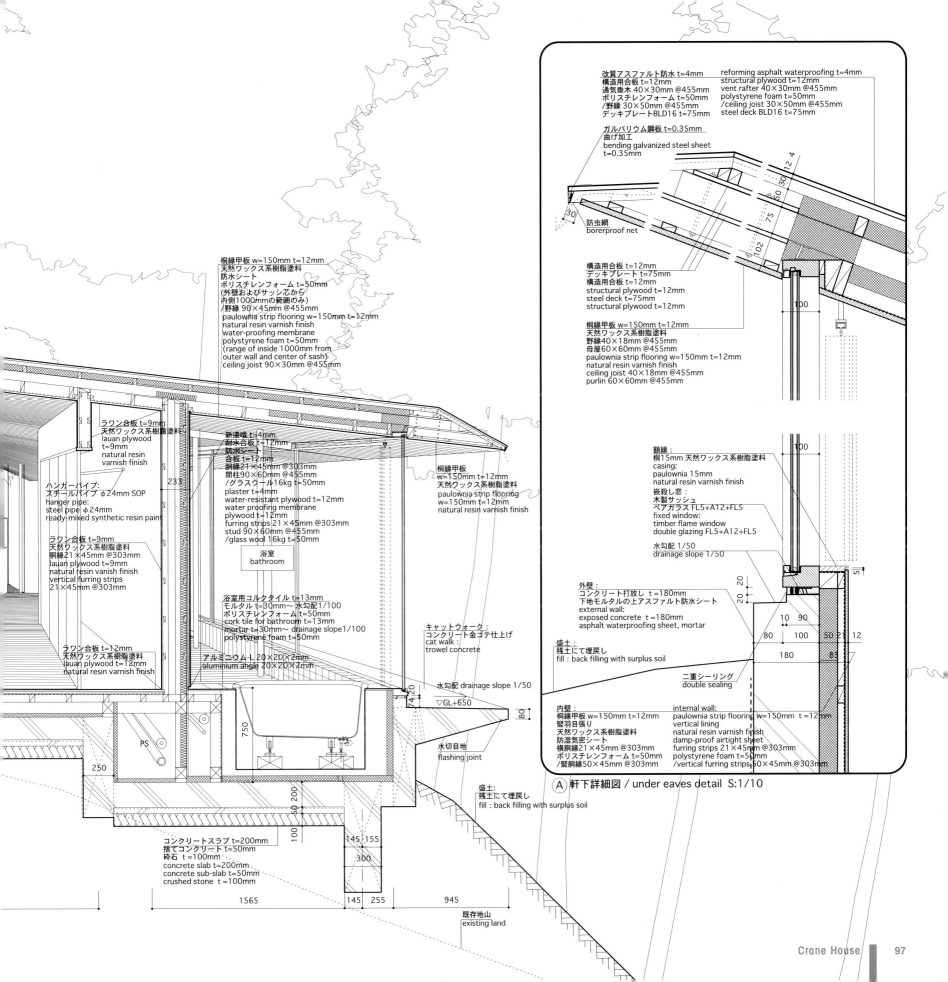

改質アスファルト防水 t=4mm
構造用合板 t=12mm
通気垂木 40×30mm @455mm
ポリスチレンフォーム t=50mm
/野縁 30×50mm @455mm
デッキプレートBLD16 t=75mm

reforming asphalt waterproofing t=4mm
structural plywood t=12mm
vent rafter 40×30mm @455mm
polystyrene foam t=50mm
/ceiling joist 30×50mm @455mm
steel deck BLD16 t=75mm

ガルバリウム鋼板 t=0.35mm
曲げ加工
bending galvanized steel sheet
t=0.35mm

防虫網
borerproof net

構造用合板 t=12mm
デッキプレート t=75mm
構造用合板 t=12mm
structural plywood t=12mm
steel deck t=75mm
structural plywood t=12mm

桐縁甲板 w=150mm t=12mm
天然ワックス系樹脂塗料
野縁40×18mm @455mm
母屋60×60mm @455mm
paulownia strip flooring w=150mm t=12mm
natural resin varnish finish
ceiling joist 40×18mm @455mm
purlin 60×60mm @455mm

桐縁甲板 w=150mm t=12mm
天然ワックス系樹脂塗料
防水シート
ポリスチレンフォーム t=50mm
(外壁およびサッシ芯から
内側1000mmの範囲のみ)
/野縁 90×45mm @455mm
paulownia strip flooring w=150mm t=12mm
natural resin varnish finish
water-proofing membrane
polystyrene foam t=50mm
(range of inside 1000mm from
outer wall and center of sash)
ceiling joist 90×30mm @455mm

ラワン合板 t=9mm
天然ワックス系樹脂塗料
lauan plywood
t=9mm
natural resin
varnish finish

新漆喰 t=4mm
耐水合板 t=12mm
防水シート
合板 t=12mm
胴縁21×45mm @303mm
間柱90×60mm @455mm
/グラスウール16kg t=50mm
plaster t=4mm
water-resistant plywood t=12mm
water proofing membrane
plywood t=12mm
furring strips 21×45mm @303mm
stud 90×60mm @455mm
/glass wool 16kg t=50mm

桐縁甲板
w=150mm t=12mm
天然ワックス系樹脂塗料
paulownia strip flooring
w=150mm t=12mm
natural resin varnish finish

ハンガーパイプ:
スチールパイプ φ24mm SOP
hanger pipe:
steel pipe φ24mm
ready-mixed synthetic resin paint

ラワン合板 t=9mm
天然ワックス系樹脂塗料
胴縁21×45mm @303mm
lauan plywood t=9mm
natural resin vanish finish
vertical furring strips
21×45mm @303mm

浴室
bathroom

額縁:
桐15mm 天然ワックス系樹脂塗料
casing:
paulownia 15mm
natural resin varnish finish

嵌殺し窓:
木製サッシ
ベアガラス FL5+A12+FL5
fixed window:
timber flame window
double glazing FL5+A12+FL5

水勾配 1/50
drainage slope 1/50

ラワン合板 t=12mm
天然ワックス系樹脂塗料
lauan plywood t=12mm
natural resin varnish finish

浴室用コルクタイル t=13mm
モルタル t=30mm～ 水勾配1/100
ポリスチレンフォーム t=50mm
cork tile for bathroom t=13mm
mortar t=30mm～ drainage slope1/100
polystyrene foam t=50mm

アルミニウム-L 20×20×2mm
aluminium angle 20×20×2mm

キャットウォーク:
コンクリート金ゴテ仕上げ
cat walk :
trowel concrete

外壁:
コンクリート打放し t=180mm
下地モルタルの上アスファルト防水シート
external wall:
exposed concrete t=180mm
asphalt waterproofing sheet, mortar

盛土
残土にて埋戻し
fill : back filling with surplus soil

二重シーリング
double sealing

水勾配 drainage slope 1/50

内壁:
桐縁甲板 w=150mm t=12mm
竪羽目張り
天然ワックス系樹脂塗料
防湿気密シート
横胴縁21×45mm @303mm
ポリスチレンフォーム t=50mm
/竪胴縁50×45mm @303mm
internal wall:
paulownia strip flooring w=150mm t=12mm
vertical lining
natural resin varnish finish
damp-proof airtight sheet
furring strips 21×45mm @303mm
polystyrene foam t=50mm
/vertical furring strips 50×45mm @303mm

▽GL+650

水切目地
flashing joint

PS

盛土
残土にて埋戻し
fill : back filling with surplus soil

Ⓐ 軒下詳細図 / under eaves detail S:1/10

コンクリートスラブ t=200mm
捨てコンクリート t=50mm
砕石 t=100mm
concrete slab t=200mm
concrete sub-slab t=50mm
crushed stone t=100mm

既存地山
existing land

インビー・ハウス
YIMBY House

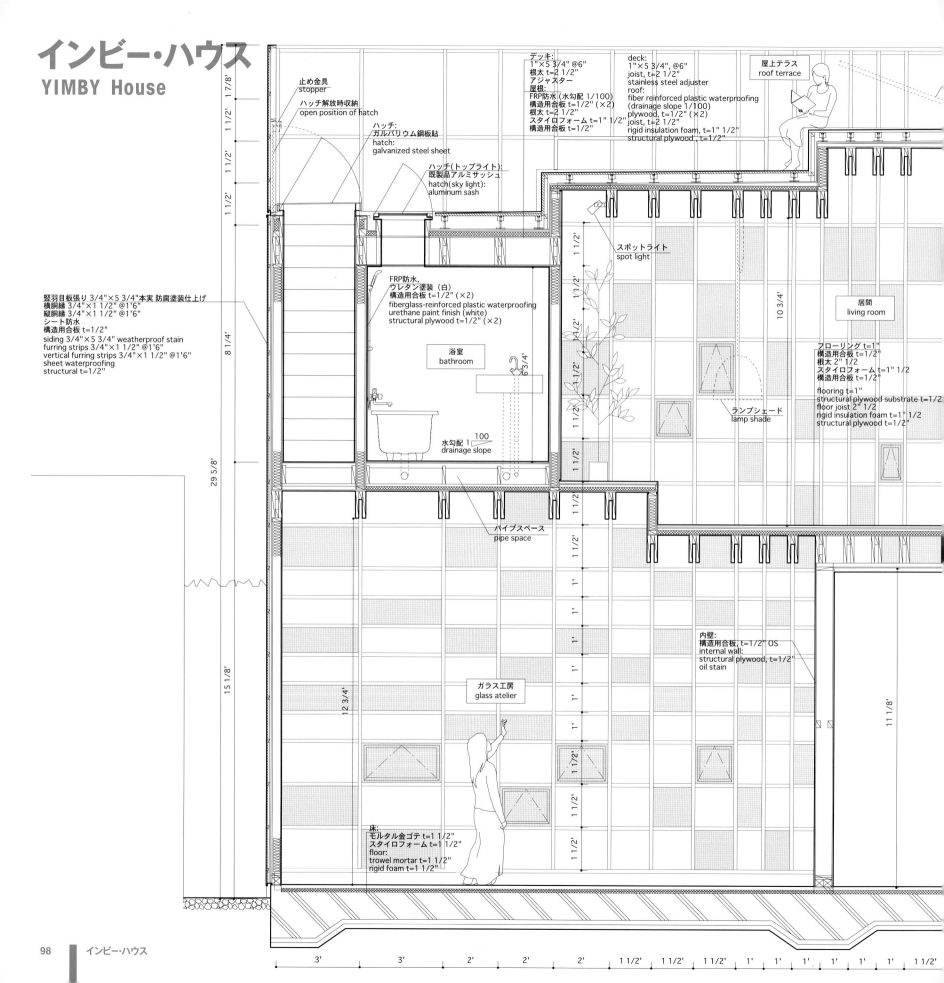

止め金具
stopper

ハッチ解放時収納
open position of hatch

ハッチ:
ガルバリウム鋼板貼
hatch:
galvanized steel sheet

ハッチ(トップライト):
既製品アルミサッシュ
hatch(sky light):
aluminum sash

デッキ:
1"×5 3/4" @6"
根太 t=2 1/2"
アジャスター
屋根:
FRP防水 (水勾配 1/100)
構造用合板 t=1/2" (×2)
根太 t=2 1/2"
スタイロフォーム t=1" 1/2"
構造用合板 t=1/2"

deck:
1"×5 3/4", @6"
joist, t=2 1/2"
stainless steel adjuster
roof:
fiber reinforced plastic waterproofing
(drainage slope 1/100)
plywood, t=1/2" (×2)
joist, t=2 1/2"
rigid insulation foam, t=1" 1/2"
structural plywood, t=1/2"

屋上テラス
roof terrace

竪羽目板張り 3/4"×5 3/4"本実 防腐塗装仕上げ
横胴縁 3/4"×1 1/2" @1'6"
縦胴縁 3/4"×1 1/2" @1'6"
シート防水
構造用合板 t=1/2"
siding 3/4"×5 3/4" weatherproof stain
furring strips 3/4"×1 1/2" @1'6"
vertical furring strips 3/4"×1 1/2" @1'6"
sheet waterproofing
structural t=1/2"

FRP防水,
ウレタン塗装 (白)
構造用合板 t=1/2" (×2)
fiberglass-reinforced plastic waterproofing
urethane paint finish (white)
structural plywood t=1/2" (×2)

浴室
bathroom

水勾配 1/100
drainage slope

スポットライト
spot light

居間
living room

ランプシェード
lamp shade

フローリング t=1"
構造用合板 t=1/2"
根太 2" 1/2
スタイロフォーム t=1" 1/2
構造用合板 t=1/2"

flooring t=1"
structural plywood substrate t=1/2"
floor joist 2" 1/2
rigid insulation foam t=1" 1/2
structural plywood t=1/2"

パイプスペース
pipe space

内壁:
構造用合板, t=1/2" OS
internal wall:
structural plywood, t=1/2"
oil stain

ガラス工房
glass atelier

床:
モルタル金ゴテ t=1 1/2"
スタイロフォーム t=1 1/2"
floor:
trowel mortar t=1 1/2"
rigid foam t=1 1/2"

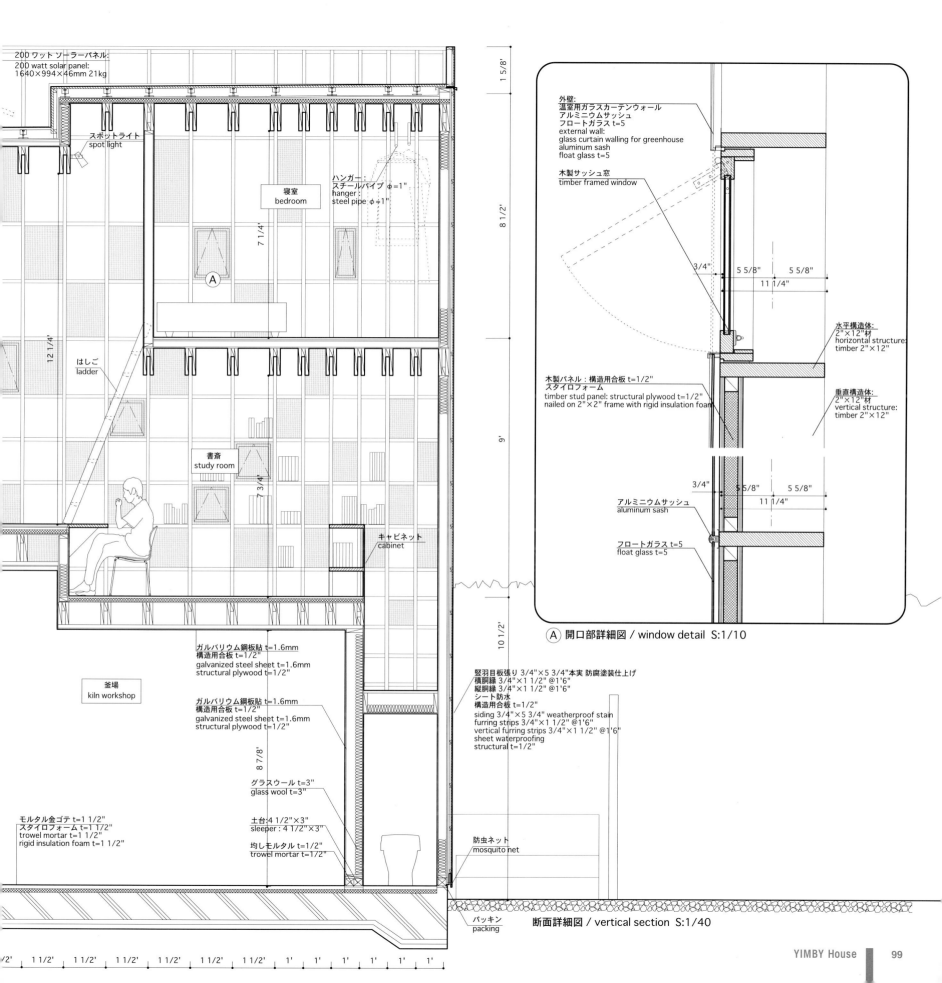

200 ワット ソーラーパネル:
200 watt solar panel:
1640×994×46mm 21kg

スポットライト
spot light

寝室
bedroom

7 1/4'

ハンガー:
スチールパイプ φ＝1"
hanger :
steel pipe φ＝1"

12 1/4'

はしご
ladder

書斎
study room

7 3/4'

キャビネット
cabinet

釜場
kiln workshop

ガルバリウム鋼板貼 t=1.6mm
構造用合板 t=1/2"
galvanized steel sheet t=1.6mm
structural plywood t=1/2"

ガルバリウム鋼板貼 t=1.6mm
構造用合板 t=1/2"
galvanized steel sheet t=1.6mm
structural plywood t=1/2"

8 7/8'

グラスウール t=3"
glass wool t=3"

モルタル金ゴテ t=1 1/2"
スタイロフォーム t=1 1/2"
trowel mortar t=1 1/2"
rigid insulation foam t=1 1/2"

土台:4 1/2"×3"
sleeper : 4 1/2"×3"

均しモルタル t=1/2"
trowel mortar t=1/2"

防虫ネット
mosquito net

パッキン
packing

1 5/8'

8 1/2'

9'

10 1/2'

外壁:
温室用ガラスカーテンウォール
アルミニウムサッシュ
フロートガラス t=5
external wall:
glass curtain walling for greenhouse
aluminum sash
float glass t=5

木製サッシュ窓
timber framed window

3/4" 5 5/8" 5 5/8"
11 1/4"

水平構造体:
2"×12"材
horizontal structure:
timber 2"×12"

木製パネル：構造用合板 t=1/2"
スタイロフォーム
timber stud panel: structural plywood t=1/2"
nailed on 2"×2" frame with rigid insulation foam

垂直構造体:
2"×12"材
vertical structure:
timber 2"×12"

3/4" 5 5/8" 5 5/8"
11 1/4"

アルミニウムサッシュ
aluminum sash

フロートガラス t=5
float glass t=5

Ⓐ 開口部詳細図 / window detail S:1/10

竪羽目板張り 3/4"×5 3/4"本実 防腐塗装仕上げ
横胴縁 3/4"×1 1/2" @1'6"
縦胴縁 3/4"×1 1/2" @1'6"
シート防水
構造用合板 t=1/2"
siding 3/4"×5 3/4" weatherproof stain
furring strips 3/4"×1 1/2" @1'6"
vertical furring strips 3/4"×1 1/2" @1'6"
sheet waterproofing
structural t=1/2"

断面詳細図 / vertical section S:1/40

1 1/2' 1 1/2' 1 1/2' 1 1/2' 1 1/2' 1 1/2' 1' 1' 1' 1' 1' 1' 1'

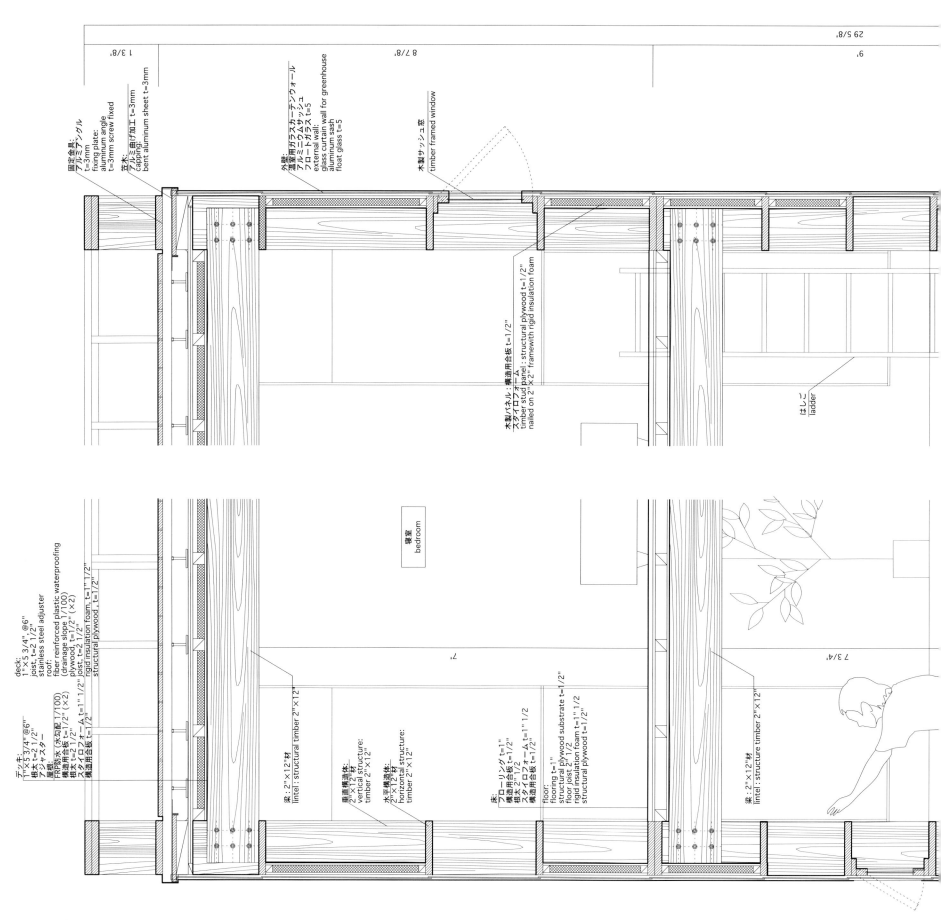

固定金具：アルミアングル
t=3mm
fixing plate:
aluminum angle
t=3mm

笠木：アルミ三曲げ加工 t=3mm
capping:
bent aluminum sheet t=3mm

外壁：温室用ガラスカーテンウォール
アルミニウムサッシュ
フロートガラス t=5
external wall:
glass curtain wall for greenhouse
aluminum sash
float glass t=5

木製サッシュ窓
timber framed window

木製パネル：構造用合板 t=1/2"
スタイロフォーム
timber stud panel : structural plywood t=1/2"
nailed on 2"×2" framewith rigid insulation foam

はしご
ladder

寝室
bedroom

デッキ：
1"×5 3/4", @6"
根太 t=2 1/2"
アジャスター
屋根：
FRP防水（水勾配1/100）
構造用合板 t=1/2"（×2）
根太 t=2 1/2"
スタイロフォーム t=1" 1/2"
構造用合板 t=1/2"
deck:
1"×5 3/4", @6"
joist, t=2 1/2"
stainless steel adjuster
roof:
fiber reinforced plastic waterproofing
(drainage slope 1/100)
plywood, t=1/2" (×2)
joist, t=2 1/2"
rigid insulation foam, t=1" 1/2"
structural plywood, t=1/2"

梁：2"×12"材
lintel : structural timber 2"×12"

垂直構造体：
2"×12"材
vertical structure:
timber 2"×12"

水平構造体：
2"×12"材
horizontal structure:
timber 2"×12"

床：
フローリング t=1"
構造用合板 t=1/2"
スタイロフォーム t=1/2"
floor:
flooring t=1"
structural plywood substrate t=1/2"
floor joist 2" 1/2
rigid insulation foam t=1" 1/2
structural plywood t=1/2"

梁：2"×12"材
lintel : structure timber 2"×12"

29 5/8'

1 3/8'

8 7/8'

9'

7'

7 3/4'

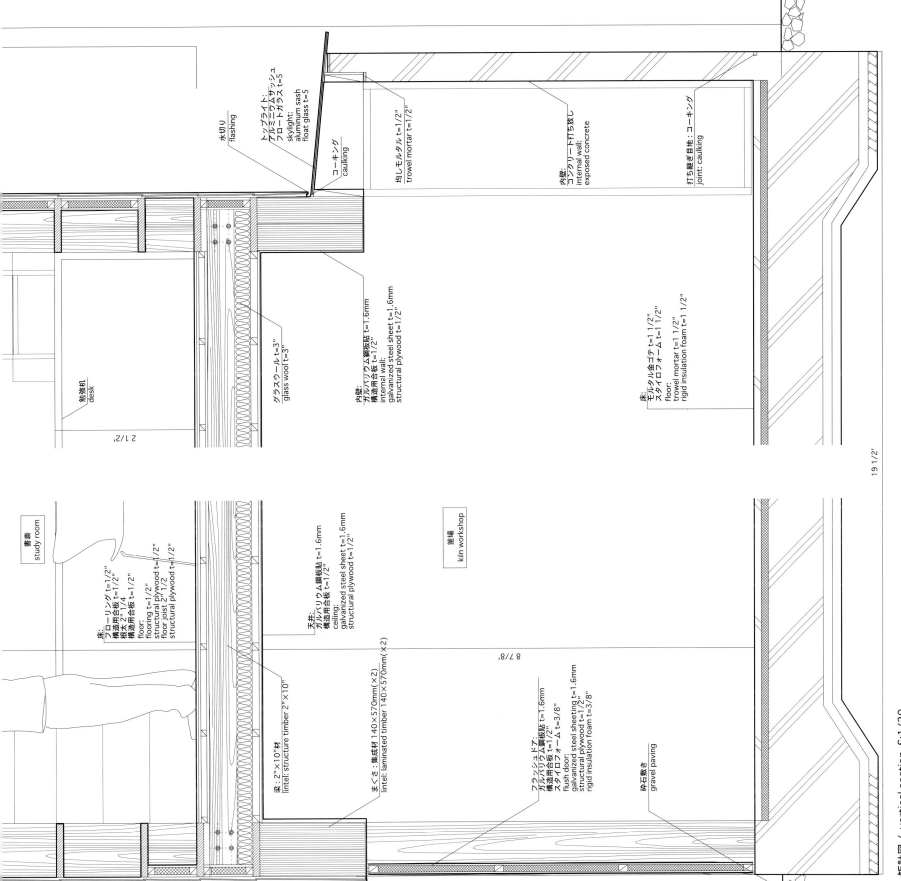

水切リ
flashing

トップライト：
アルミニウムサッシュ
フロートガラス t=5
skylight:
aluminum sash
float glass t=5

コーキング
caulking

均しモルタル t=1/2"
trowel mortar t=1/2"

内壁：
コンクリート打ち放し
internal wall:
exposed concrete

打ち継ぎ目地：コーキング
joint: caulking

勉強机
desk

2 1/2'

グラスウール t=3"
glass wool t=3"

内壁：
ガルバリウム鋼板貼 t=1.6mm
構造用合板 t=1/2"
internal wall:
galvanized steel sheet t=1.6mm
structural plywood t=1/2"

床：
モルタル金ゴテ t=1 1/2"
スタイロフォーム t=1 1/2"
floor:
trowel mortar t=1 1/2"
rigid insulation foam t= 1 1/2"

19 1/2'

書斎
study room

床：
フローリング t=1/2"
構造用合板 t=1/2"
根太 2"1/4
構造用合板 t=1/2"
floor:
flooring t=1/2"
structural plywood t=1/2"
floor joist 2"1/2
structural plywood t=1/2"

天井：
ガルバリウム鋼板貼 t=1.6mm
構造用合板 t=1/2"
ceiling:
galvanized steel sheet t=1.6mm
structural plywood t=1/2"

釜場
kiln workshop

梁：2"×10"材
lintel: structure timber 2"×10"

まぐさ：集成材 140×570mm(×2)
lintel: laminated timber 140×570mm(×2)

8 7/8'

フラッシュドア：
ガルバリウム鋼板貼 t=1.6mm
構造用合板 t=1/2"
スタイロフォーム t=3/8"
flush door:
galvanized steel sheeting t=1.6mm
structural plywood t=1/2"
rigid insulation foam t=3/8"

砕石敷き
gravel paving

矩計図 / vertical section S:1/20

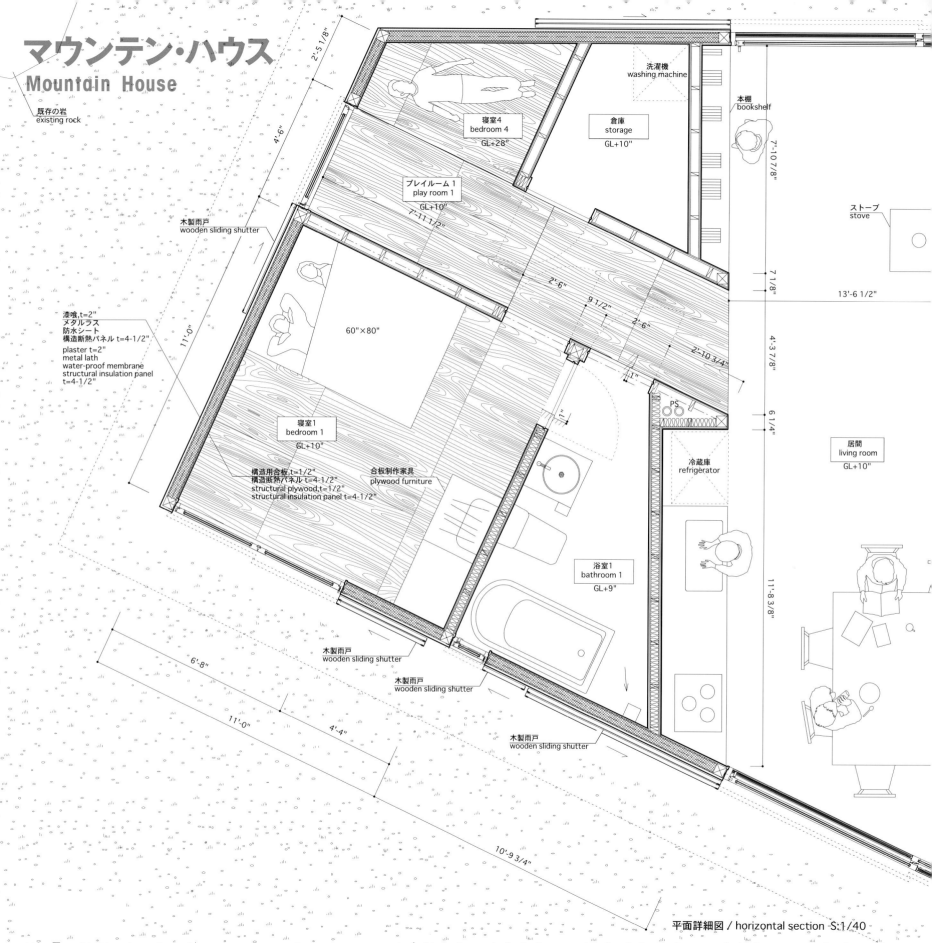

マウンテン・ハウス
Mountain House

既存の岩
existing rock

木製雨戸
wooden sliding shutter

漆喰,t=2"
メタルラス
防水シート
構造断熱パネル t=4-1/2"
plaster t=2"
metal lath
water-proof membrane
structural insulation panel
t=4-1/2"

2'-5 1/8"

4'-6"

11'-0"

6'-8"

11'-0"

4'-4"

10'-9 3/4"

寝室4
bedroom 4
GL+28"

プレイルーム 1
play room 1
GL+10"

7'-11 1/2"

60"×80"

寝室1
bedroom 1
GL+10"

構造用合板,t=1/2"
構造断熱パネル t=4-1/2"
structural plywood,t=1/2"
structural insulation panel t=4-1/2"

合板制作家具
plywood furniture

浴室1
bathroom 1
GL+9"

木製雨戸
wooden sliding shutter

木製雨戸
wooden sliding shutter

木製雨戸
wooden sliding shutter

倉庫
storage
GL+10"

洗濯機
washing machine

本棚
bookshelf

ストーブ
stove

2'-6"

9 1/2"

2'-6"

2'-10 3/4"

1"

7"

PS

冷蔵庫
refrigerator

7'-10 7/8"

7 1/8"

13'-6 1/2"

4'-3 7/8"

6 1/4"

11'-8 3/8"

居間
living room
GL+10"

平面詳細図 / horizontal section S:1/40

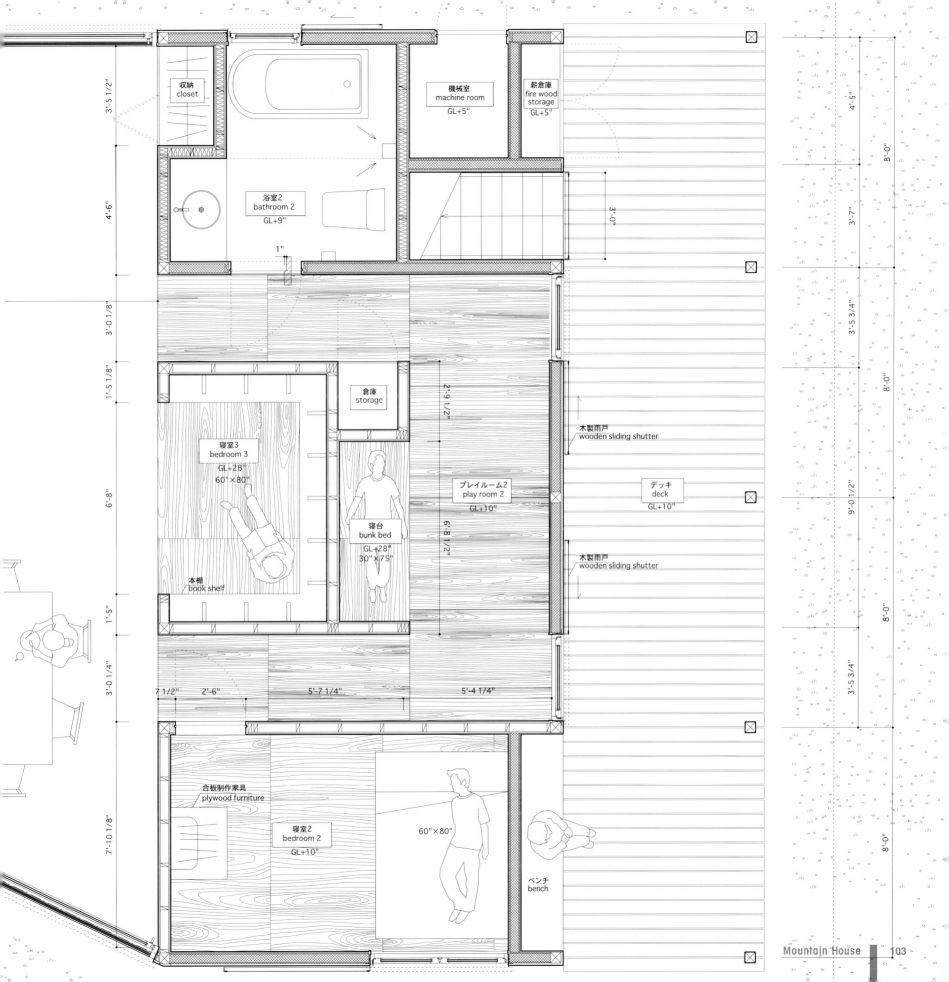

収納
closet

浴室2
bathroom 2
GL+9"

機械室
machine room
GL+5"

薪倉庫
fire wood
storage
GL+5"

1"

木製雨戸
wooden sliding shutter

倉庫
storage

寝室3
bedroom 3
GL+28"
60"×80"

寝台
bunk bed
GL+28"
30"×75"

プレイルーム2
play room 2
GL+10"

デッキ
deck
GL+10"

本棚
book shelf

木製雨戸
wooden sliding shutter

合板制作家具
plywood furniture

寝室2
bedroom 2
GL+10"

60"×80"

ベンチ
bench

3'-5 1/2"
4'-6"
3'-0 1/8"
1'-5 1/8"
6'-8"
1'-5"
3'-0 1/4"
7'-10 1/8"

7 1/2"
2'-6"
5'-7 1/4"
5'-4 1/4"

3'-0"
2'-9 1/2"
6'-8 1/2"

4'-5"
3'-7"
3'-5 3/4"
8'-0"
8'-0"
9'-0 1/2"
8'-0"
3'-5 3/4"
8'-0"

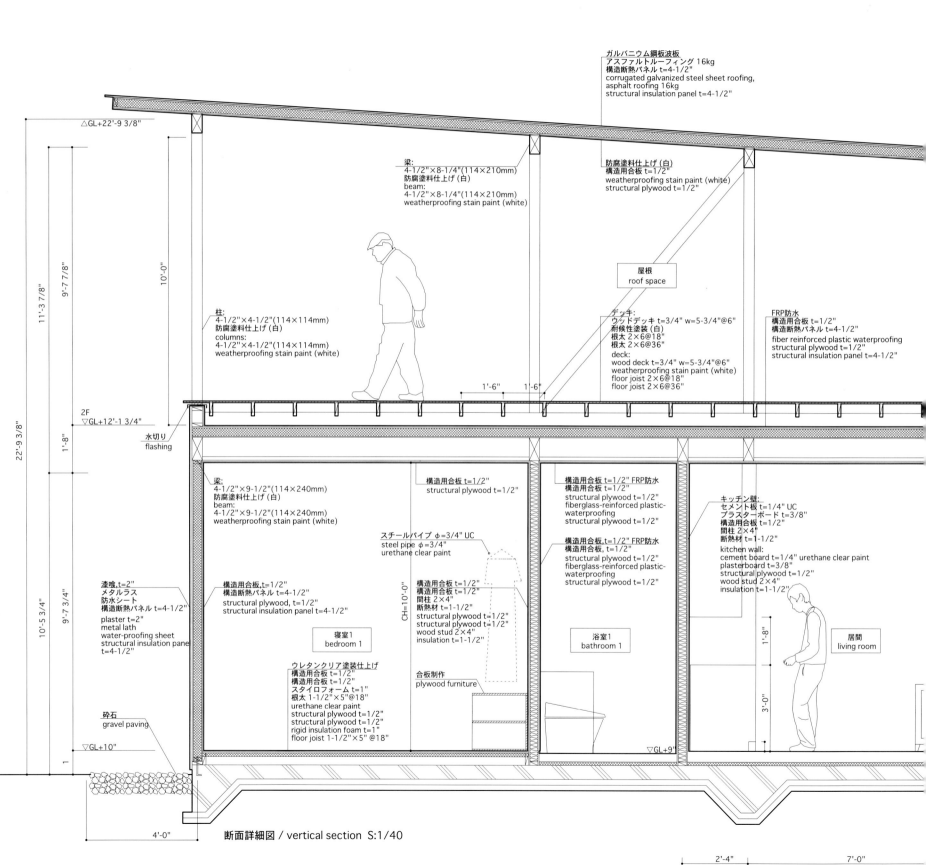

ガルバニウム鋼板波板
アスファルトルーフィング 16kg
構造断熱パネル t=4-1/2"
corrugated galvanized steel sheet roofing,
asphalt roofing 16kg
structural insulation panel t=4-1/2"

梁:
4-1/2"×8-1/4"(114×210mm)
防腐塗料仕上げ（白）
beam:
4-1/2"×8-1/4"(114×210mm)
weatherproofing stain paint (white)

防腐塗料仕上げ（白）
構造用合板 t=1/2"
weatherproofing stain paint (white)
structural plywood t=1/2"

屋根
roof space

FRP防水
構造用合板 t=1/2"
構造断熱パネル t=4-1/2"
fiber reinforced plastic waterproofing
structural plywood t=1/2"
structural insulation panel t=4-1/2"

柱:
4-1/2"×4-1/2"(114×114mm)
防腐塗料仕上げ（白）
columns:
4-1/2"×4-1/2"(114×114mm)
weatherproofing stain paint (white)

デッキ:
ウッドデッキ t=3/4" w=5-3/4"@6"
耐候性塗装（白）
根太 2×6@18"
根太 2×6@36"
deck:
wood deck t=3/4" w=5-3/4"@6"
weatherproofing stain paint (white)
floor joist 2×6@18"
floor joist 2×6@36"

△GL+22'-9 3/8"

2F
▽GL+12'-1 3/4"

水切り
flashing

22'-9 3/8"
11'-3 7/8"
9'-7 7/8"
10'-0"
1'-8"

1'-6" 1'-6"

梁:
4-1/2"×9-1/2"(114×240mm)
防腐塗料仕上げ（白）
beam:
4-1/2"×9-1/2"(114×240mm)
weatherproofing stain paint (white)

構造用合板 t=1/2"
structural plywood t=1/2"

構造用合板 t=1/2" FRP防水
構造用合板 t=1/2"
structural plywood t=1/2"
fiberglass-reinforced plastic-
waterproofing
structural plywood t=1/2"

キッチン壁:
セメント板 t=1/4" UC
プラスターボード t=3/8"
構造用合板 t=1/2"
間柱 2×4"
断熱材 t=1-1/2"
kitchen wall:
cement board t=1/4" urethane clear paint
plasterboard t=3/8"
structural plywood t=1/2"
wood stud 2×4"
insulation t=1-1/2"

スチールパイプ φ=3/4" UC
steel pipe φ=3/4"
urethane clear paint

構造用合板 t=1/2" FRP防水
構造用合板 t=1/2"
structural plywood t=1/2"
fiberglass-reinforced plastic-
waterproofing
structural plywood t=1/2"

漆喰,t=2"
メタルラス
防水シート
構造断熱パネル t=4-1/2"
plaster t=2"
metal lath
water-proofing sheet
structural insulation panel
t=4-1/2"

構造用合板,t=1/2"
構造断熱パネル t=4-1/2"
structural plywood, t=1/2"
structural insulation panel t=4-1/2"

構造用合板 t=1/2"
構造用合板 t=1/2"
間柱 2×4"
断熱材 t=1-1/2"
structural plywood t=1/2"
structural plywood t=1/2"
wood stud 2×4"
insulation t=1-1/2"

寝室1
bedroom 1

浴室1
bathroom 1

居間
living room

CH=10'-0"

1'-8"
3'-0"

ウレタンクリア塗装仕上げ
構造用合板 t=1/2"
構造用合板 t=1/2"
スタイロフォーム t=1"
根太 1-1/2"×5"@18"
urethane clear paint
structural plywood t=1/2"
structural plywood t=1/2"
rigid insulation foam t=1"
floor joist 1-1/2"×5"@18"

合板制作
plywood furniture

砕石
gravel paving

▽GL+10"

▽GL+9'

10'-5 3/4"
9'-7 3/4"

4'-0"

断面詳細図 / vertical section S:1/40

2'-4"   7'-0"

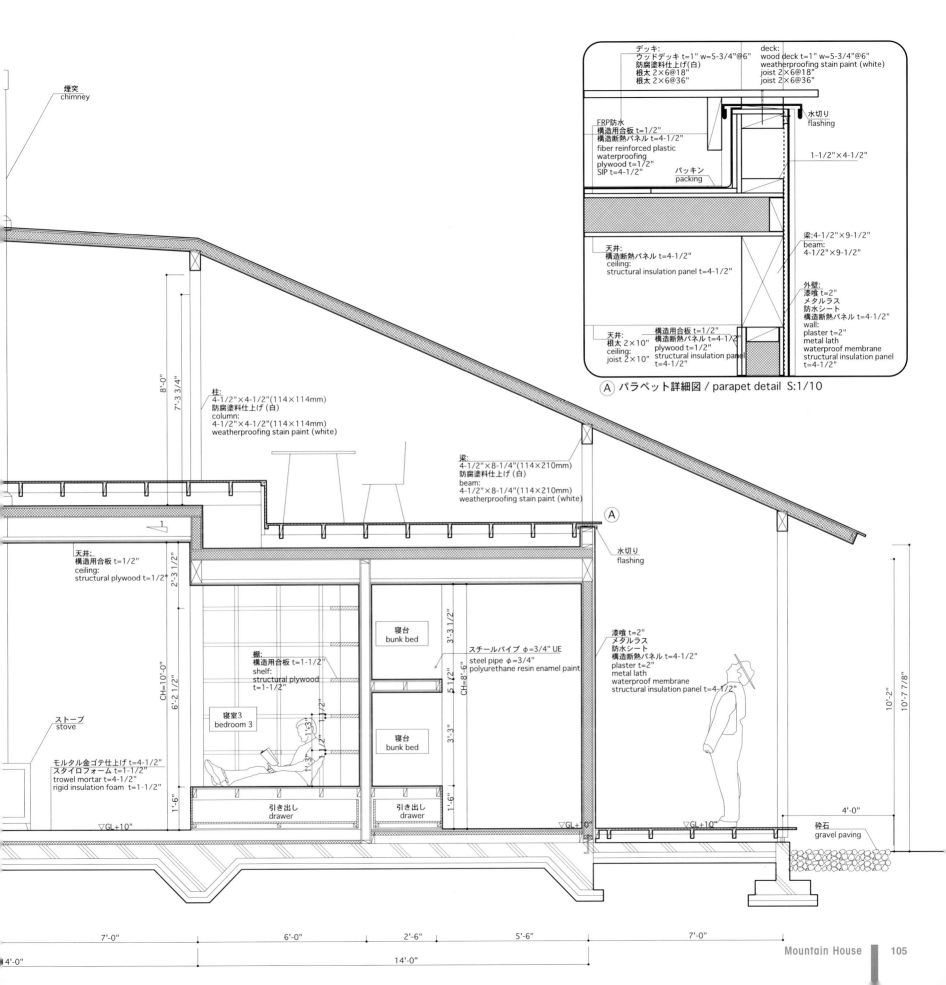

煙突
chimney

デッキ:
ウッドデッキ t=1" w=5-3/4"@6"
防腐塗料仕上げ(白)
根太 2×6@18"
根太 2×6@36"
deck:
wood deck t=1" w=5-3/4"@6"
weatherproofing stain paint (white)
joist 2×6@18"
joist 2×6@36"

FRP防水
構造用合板 t=1/2"
構造断熱パネル t=4-1/2"
fiber reinforced plastic
waterproofing
plywood t=1/2"
SIP t=4-1/2"

水切り
flashing

パッキン
packing

1-1/2"×4-1/2"

天井:
構造断熱パネル t=4-1/2"
ceiling:
structural insulation panel t=4-1/2"

梁:4-1/2"×9-1/2"
beam:
4-1/2"×9-1/2"

天井:
根太 2×10"
ceiling:
joist 2×10"

構造用合板 t=1/2"
構造断熱パネル t=4-1/2"
plywood t=1/2"
structural insulation panel
t=4-1/2"

外壁:
漆喰 t=2"
メタルラス
防水シート
構造断熱パネル t=4-1/2"
wall:
plaster t=2"
metal lath
waterproof membrane
structural insulation panel
t=4-1/2"

Ⓐ パラペット詳細図 / parapet detail S:1/10

8'-0"

7'-3 3/4"

柱:
4-1/2"×4-1/2"(114×114mm)
防腐塗料仕上げ(白)
column:
4-1/2"×4-1/2"(114×114mm)
weatherproofing stain paint (white)

梁:
4-1/2"×8-1/4"(114×210mm)
防腐塗料仕上げ(白)
beam:
4-1/2"×8-1/4"(114×210mm)
weatherproofing stain paint (white)

Ⓐ

水切り
flashing

天井:
構造用合板 t=1/2"
ceiling:
structural plywood t=1/2"

2'-3 1/2"

棚:
構造用合板 t=1-1/2"
shelf:
structural plywood
t=1-1/2"

寝台
bunk bed

寝台
bunk bed

スチールパイプ φ=3/4" UE
steel pipe φ=3/4"
polyurethane resin enamel paint

漆喰 t=2"
メタルラス
防水シート
構造断熱パネル t=4-1/2"
plaster t=2"
metal lath
waterproof membrane
structural insulation panel t=4-1/2"

CH=10'-0"

6'-2 1/2"

3'-3 1/2"

5'-1/2"

CH=8'-6"

3'-3"

ストーブ
stove

寝室3
bedroom 3

モルタル金ゴテ仕上げ t=4-1/2"
スタイロフォーム t=1-1/2"
trowel mortar t=4-1/2"
rigid insulation foam t=1-1/2"

引き出し
drawer

引き出し
drawer

1'-6"

1'-6"

▽GL+10"

▽GL+10"

▽GL+10"

10'-2"

10'-7 7/8"

4'-0"

砕石
gravel paving

7'-0"

6'-0"

2'-6"

5'-6"

7'-0"

4'-0"

14'-0"

住宅の振る舞いについて

ON THE BEHAVIOR OF HOUSES

住宅の振る舞いについて

キャラクターのある住宅

　アトリエ・ワンはこれまで20件ほどの戸建住宅や別荘を設計してきたが、それらにはそれぞれ独特のキャラクターがあるとよく言われる。特に意識してそうしたわけではないのだが、小住宅が多いということが一定の条件となって、スタイルというよりも違いの方が浮き上がってきているようである。変なたとえかもしれないが、小住宅のそういうキャラクター性というのは、握り寿司に似ていると思う。「握り」というコンパクトな形式が、あらゆる魚介類の味を比較可能にし、味、かたち、色、食感といった、素材の持つ違いを豊かさや楽しみに変えている。では小住宅の場合にキャラクターの違いを生むのものは何だろうか？　先に結論を言うと、それぞれの住宅が計画されるそれぞれの場所と、施主のパーソナリティが少しと、それらに基づいた建物の振る舞いが、キャラクターの違いを生むようである。だが場所については様々な読み方や解釈があるし、建物の振る舞い方も一通りではない。だからこそ、その対応関係は十分な説得力を持たなければならないだろう。

　こうした住宅の振る舞いを問題にする理由は、東京の住宅地の現在の状況から、「戸建住宅による都市」という仮説を導きたいからである。例えばヨーロッパの都市の市街地では、その都市なりの街のテクスチャーや調和した構成秩序があり、それを背景とした個々の建物の振る舞いというものを捉えることができる。建築家だけでなく、市民がそこにある共通の建築言語を理解しているので、一つひとつの建物の振る舞いの意味を読み取ることができるし、新しくつくられる建築は振る舞いを介して歴史や現在と対話できる。日本の街にもかつてはそうした建物と都市との対話があったはずなのだが、近代化と工業化が直結し、建築が産業化して経済成長を牽引する間に忘れ去られ、さらに今東京では規制緩和によって決定的な断絶がつくられている。だからもう建物の振る舞いなど気にする必要はないのかもしれないが、こうした振る舞いは類型化されたかたちで今の住宅のつくり方の中に残っていたり、個別の試みの中に断片として存在したりしている。この振る舞いを一つひとつ検討し、その違いに体系を与えることは、個々の建築を都市空間の実践に繋げるマイクロアーバニズムの基礎を築くことになるのではないか。

　ここでは、アトリエ・ワンの住宅を比較しながら、主に場所と建物の振る舞いの関係を解題し、建物の振る舞いの方法と意味を位置づけていきたい。

郊外住宅地の場合

　はじめに、典型的な郊外住宅地での建物の振る舞いを、アニ・ハウス、ミニ・ハウス、ガエ・ハウスを例に見てみ

On the behavior of houses

Houses with character

Atelier Bow-Wow has up until now designed about twenty detached houses and holiday villas, yet we are often told that they each have a unique character. Although we're not aware of any particular reason for this, the predominance of small houses is a constant condition, and more than a style, it is the differences in approach that have become conspicuous. This might be a strange simile, but we think that the characters of these small houses are like *nigiri* (hand-rolled) sushi. The compact format of a *nigiri* allows the flavors of all kinds of fish to be compared, and differences in the taste, shape, color, and texture of materials are converted into pleasure and richness. So in the case of small houses, how are these differences in character produced? To begin by stating our conclusion, the differences in character are produced by basing the building behavior on the place for which each house is planned, along with a dash of the client's personality. However, there are various ways of reading and interpreting a place, and there is no typical way for a building to behave. Precisely because of this, their mutual relationship must be sufficiently convincing.

The reason for addressing the behavior of these houses is that we want the current condition of Tokyo's residential districts to guide our hypotheses about the "city consisting of detached houses." For example, in the urban districts of European cities we can perceive the behavior of each individual building against the background of the texture of streets and the harmonious compositional orders. This common architectural language is understood by ordinary citizens, not just architects, so the meanings of these behaviors are decipherable, and newly built architecture can have a behavior that maintains a dialogue between history and the present day. A dialogue between architecture and city once existed in the towns of Japan, but this was completely disregarded during the period of high economic growth and development, directly linked to modernization and industrialization. Moreover, in Tokyo it has now finally become extinct as a result of deregulation. Because of this, perhaps it's unnecessary to be concerned about things like building behavior, yet this kind of behavior even now remains as stereotypical patterns in the way houses are built, and exists as fragments in particular experiments. Examining each one of these behaviors and giving a system to their differences might be the basis for assembling a micro-urbanism, allied with the implementation of individual works of architecture as urban spaces. Here, while making comparisons between the houses of Atelier Bow-Wow, we primarily want to assess the relationships between building behavior and place, and to locate the methods and meanings of building behavior.

The case of suburbia

To begin with, let's look at the Gae House, the Ani House, and the Mini House as examples of build-

よう。こうした敷地では、南側に庭を確保して北側に建物を寄せるのが共通した振る舞いとして見られるが、敷地が細分化されてくると、南側以外は隣家との距離が近くなりすぎて、建てれば建てるほど息苦しくなってしまう。この3つの作品が目指しているのは、そうした悪循環から抜け出すために、小さな敷地に即していて、かつ反復に耐えられるような、新たな振る舞いを見つけることである。

　まず、建ぺい率を使い切るという、小さな敷地での住宅設計の常套手段を一度忘れて、一敷地一建物の原則を字義通り実践するように、小さめのヴォリュームを敷地中央にポンと置く。そのために建物を3層とし、建ぺい率を低めに抑える。小さい敷地を余計に狭く感じさせる塀をなくすことで、道路から敷地の奥まで視線が通るようにする。そのために建物を半階地下に埋めて、道路と室内の視線をずらす。さらに各層をワンルームとすることで、どの方向にも開口が取れるようにする。これら3作品に共通する方法によって、周囲の環境との距離を確保した上で、改めて全方向に対して関係をつくっていくのがここでの原則である。3作品の違いは周囲との関係のつくり方の違いに現れている。

　アニ・ハウスの場合、関係を取り持つのは3つの立面の中央に開けられた窓である。これらは上下階の窓を組み合わせて一つの大きな窓となっており、この小さな住宅に不釣り合いな大きさを持っている。それは内部空間の分節やスケールを曖昧にすると同時に、顔のような正面性を獲得し、道路に対応するスケールにもなっている。これに対してミニ・ハウスで関係を取り持つのは、メインヴォリュームから四方に突き出したサブヴォリュームである。これは敷地が非常に小さいために、敷地境界からメインヴォリュームが引きをとったところにも床を張り出すことによって得られる構成であり、アニ・ハウスにおける窓が、居場所として外にはみ出しヴォリューム化したものと見ることもできる。サブヴォリュームは、その奥行きをメインヴォリュームから敷地境界までの距離によって、位置を既存の柿の木等との関係によって決められることで、メインヴォリューム周りの外部空間と相互依存的な関係となっている。さらにサブヴォリュームはニッチ、バルコニー、収納スペースを融合し、メインヴォリュームの外側から階にまたがって、内部空間の分節を曖昧にしている。

　さらにガエ・ハウスの場合、関係を取り持つのは軒の張り出しである。軒自体は、まずダス・ハウスにおいて試みられ、「引き」と「ため」を隣地からとる上で、その有効性を確認されていたものである。ここでの軒の張り出しは、北側斜線と道路斜線で規定される最大の屋根と、敷地中央におかれた箱形ヴォリュームのズレとして導かれている。ここで屋根を導入したのは、この住宅地には今もたっぷりした屋根を持つ田園都市住宅が残っていることから、そうした建築言語への参照を、ここでの振る舞いの原則としたからである。ミニ・ハウスにおけるサブヴォリュームの壁の垂直性が、敷地境界に腕を延ばしながらも周囲との関係を断つことになるのに対して、軒の水平性は距離をとりつつも同時に迎え入れることを可能にする。しかも軒の張り出しは、ガラスで閉じることで字義通りの水平窓になっており、隣との隙間から這い上がる反射光を室内に呼び込む。この水平窓の特徴は、外から室内がよく見えるが、見えるのは天井面ばかりであり、室内においては窓から離れると外が見えず、近寄ると隣との隙間や道路がよく見えるというように、外部との距離の選択ができるところである。

　こうした住宅地において住宅の振る舞いを決めるもう一つの要素として、自動車の取り扱いを挙げておく。小

ing behavior in stereotypical suburbia. Securing a garden to the south by pulling the building to the north can be seen as standard behavior for these sites. Except for in the southern direction, as the sites become subdivided, the distances between neighboring houses are reduced. The more construction there is, the more stifling it becomes. In order to escape this vicious circle, the intention of these three designs was to find new behaviors that are repeatable, and conform to small sites.

First of all, momentarily forgetting the habitual trick for designing a house on a small site of using the entire allowable site coverage, as a literally interpretation of the principle of one site / one building put into practice, a small volume is popped down at the center of the site. The building therefore becomes three levels high, and the site coverage is lessened. By eliminating fences, which make small sites feel excessively constricted, sightlines may pass from the street to the depths of the site. The building is therefore buried a half-level underground, offsetting the sightlines between the street and the house interior. In addition, by making each level a single open space, apertures can be opened in any direction. The principle of the method shared by these three designs is to first establish a distance from the surrounding environment, then remake relationships in every direction. The differences between the three designs are manifest in the differences in their ways of making relationships with the surroundings.

In the case of the Ani House, the relationship is mediated by the window openings in the centers of three of the elevations. These each combine upper and lower floor windows into one large window, disproportionately sized for such a small house. They obscure the divisions and scales of the internal spaces, and at the same time create face-like façades at a scale corresponding to the street.

In the Mini House, by contrast, the relationship is mediated by the sub-volumes that project from the main volume in every direction. Because the site is extremely small, the composition also includes floors projecting into the areas where the main volume has been pulled back from the site boundaries. The windows in the Ani House can therefore also be seen as locations turned into outward-projecting volumes. The distances between the main volume and the site boundaries determines the depth of the sub-volumes, and by setting their locations according to relationships with things such as existing persimmon trees, they have interdependent relationships with the external spaces around the main volume. Furthermore, these sub-volumes incorporate niches, balconies, and storage spaces, and they obscure the divisions of internal spaces by straddling the floors on the outer faces of the main volume.

Moreover, in the case of the Gae House, the relationship is mediated by the projection of the eaves. Eaves were first tested in the D.a.S House, where their efficacy was confirmed by "pulling back" and "collecting" from the adjacent lots. Here, the projection of the eaves was led by the offset between the box-shaped volume placed in the middle of the site, and the largest roof permitted by the north diagonal setback line and the street diagonal setback line. Because plenty of houses with roofs still remain in this garden city district, the introduction of a roof here follows a general rule of behavior that makes reference to this architectural language. The Mini House extends limbs to the site boundaries, but the relationships with its surroundings are also severed by the verticality of the sub-volume walls. By contrast, the horizontality of the eaves gives a separation while simultaneously permitting an embrace. Nevertheless, by sealing the eaves projections with glass, they are literally horizontal windows that draw light reflected up from the adjacent gaps into the interior. The character of this horizontal window allows the interior to be clearly seen from outside, but only the ceiling surface is visible. Inside, at a distance from the window the outside isn't visible, and the distance from the exterior can be chosen by moving closer so as to bring the adjacent gaps and the street into view.

Another example of an element that determines house behavior in this kind of residential district is

さな敷地では、自動車がその狭い間口を占めてしまうわけだが、これをできるだけ専用の駐車スペースとして定着しないようにしている。アニ・ハウスの場合では隣地境界からとった距離の一部、ミニ・ハウスでは道路側のサブヴォリュームの下、ガエ・ハウスでは街路側に伸びた軒の下が、車を受け入れたときだけ駐車スペースになる。建物の前に自動車が停まるときは、自動車の横側のシルエットが立面の中に納まるようにすると、みっともなくない。

密集住宅地の場合

　次に細分化の進む高密度な住宅地での建物の振る舞いを、アコ・ハウス、ハウス・タワー、ハウス＆アトリエ・ワンを例に見てみよう。こうした敷地では、敷地面積がさらに限られていることから、ヴォリュームは垂直方向に伸びざるを得ない。東京の住宅地の細分化によって、この手の建物は増加しているが、それらの多くは屋根やバルコニーなど郊外住宅が持っていた要素を残しているために、窮屈で寸詰まりな印象を与えるものになっている。この3つの作品が目指しているのは、敷地における最大容積の確保と、垂直方向への伸展という条件の中で、密集の中での新たな振る舞いを見つけることである。

　まず、敷地そのものを立体化して容積を最大限確保するように、地面と空を一気に繋ぐヴォリュームをつくる。郊外住宅地での振る舞いとは真逆で、隣地との距離は問わない。すると敷地への水平投影面積よりも立面の面積の方が大きくなる。さらに立面をできるだけ無分節に扱うことで、その見附面積を最大化し、密集住宅地の中に大きなファサードをたてる。これにより、周囲の住宅が持ち寄ってきた寸詰まりの建築要素の反復から距離をとり、白紙の状態をつくる。そこに窓を開けていくことによって、改めて隣接する環境を選択的に結びつけていくのがここでの原則である。また内部では、外部と対照的に、細かく分節された床や階段が、少しずつズレながら斜めに連続する構成がとられているが、これは地面に接する最下部から空に接する最上部までを、細分化された一つながりの空間とするもう一つの原則である。3作品の違いは、角地、狭小地、旗竿地という敷地の性格の違いに現れる。

　アコ・ハウスの敷地は角地で、多角的に開かれた場所である。角地というのは、街の中の特異点であり、アイ・キャッチであり、その意味で街路からの呼びかけが明確な敷地である。その呼びかけに対して、建築がどのように振る舞うかは、街路と建築を繋ぐコミュニケーションになりうる。敷地には隅切りがなされているのだが、それをそのままヴォリュームにすると、隅切り面が特別な面になってしまう。そうしたイレギュラーな要素ができないように、角の長さを同じ幅の壁面5枚で分割し、これを少しずつ角度をずらしながら屏風のように繋いだファサードとなっている。ここに限定された数の窓を開けていくことで、隣接する大ケヤキや神社へ向かう坂道などと室内が、改めて結びつけられる。

　これに対してハウス・タワーの敷地は細街路に小さな住宅が密集する住宅地にあり、周囲を建物に囲まれている。その重苦しい空気から抜け出し、かつ反復可能な住宅の振る舞いを導くために、ここでは敷地の奥行きの1／3近くまで道路から引きをとり、できるだけ高くヴォリュームを引き伸ばしている。間口3m、高さ11.4mの、法規違反かと見まごうばかりの特異なヴォリュームが立ち上がり、細々と分節された周囲の住宅地との関係が一度断

the handling of automobiles. An automobile will occupy the entire narrow frontage of a small site, so as much as possible we avoid making this a dedicated parking space. Part of the space between the house and the adjacent lot boundary lines in the Ani House, the area below the sub-volume facing toward the street in the Mini House, and the area under the eaves extending toward the street in the Gae House are used as parking spaces when a car is present. When an automobile is parked in front of the building, it's not unattractive to have the side silhouette of the automobile incorporated into the elevation.

The case of dense residential districts

Next, let's look at the Ako House, House Tower, and House & Atelier Bow-Wow as examples of building behavior in increasingly fragmented high-density residential districts. Because the surface area of such sites is even further constrained, the volumes unavoidably expand vertically. Due to the fragmentation of Tokyo's residential districts, this type of building is increasing, but because many of them retain elements of suburban houses such as roofs and balconies they give a stunted and truncated impression. The aim of these three designs was to ensure the maximum capacity that can be placed on the site, while discovering new behaviors within density and within a state of vertical expansion. First of all, in order to ensure maximum capacity the site itself is made three-dimensional, producing a volume that connects the ground to the sky with a single stroke. Utterly unlike house behavior in suburbia, the distance from the adjacent lots is not open to question. The surface area of the elevations then becomes bigger than the site footprint. By treating the elevations with a minimum of articulation in order to maximize this found surface area, large façades may be erected in overcrowded residential districts. They thereby achieve a distance from the repetitive collection of stunted architectural elements in the surrounding houses, producing a condition of blankness. Once again, the principle here is to selectively make links with the adjacent environment by inserting windows. In contrast with the exterior, the interior is a composition of small floor plates and stairs slightly offset on a continuous diagonal. Another principle is to make a finely articulated continuous space from the lowermost part, touching the ground, to the uppermost part, touching the sky. The differences between the three designs are manifest in the different site characteristics of corner lot, narrow lot, and flagpole lot.

The site for the Ako House is a corner lot, a place open in many directions. A corner lot is a significant spot in a town, one that catches the eye, and in this sense the call from the streets is a clearly defined site. With regard to this call, the issue of how the architecture behaves could become a kind of communication linking architecture and street. A corner has been sliced off the site, and by directly converted this into a volume, the surface of the sliced-off corner becomes a special surface. To avoid making an irregular element, the façade is divided into five wall surfaces of the same length with slightly shifted angles, connected like a *byobu* folding screen. By inserting a few windows, the rooms are again linked to the neighboring large zelkova tree and sloping street.

In contrast to this, the House Tower site is enclosed by surrounding buildings, located in a residential district of small houses crowded along tiny streets. In order to escape this oppressive atmosphere and derive a replicable house behavior, the design has been pulled back from the street by almost one third of the site's depth and stretched to give the tallest possible volume. With a frontage of 3m and a height of 11.4m, this bizarre volume appears as if it transgresses the regulations, and severs any relationships with the minutely fragmented surrounding residential district. Moreover, an arch window has

ち切られる。その上で地面から空まで一気に左官で仕上げられた目地なしのファサードに、慎重にアーチの窓が開けられている。ここで窓がアーチなのは、このヴォリュームに四角い窓の組み合わせが、牢獄の監視塔を思わせるのに対し、アーチ窓との組み合わせは、どこか中世の城の一部を思わせる面白さがあるからである。特にファサードの中心にある不釣り合いに大きなアーチ窓は、2階床で上下に分節されて室内のスケールに対応しつつ、外部に対しては街路からの視線を受け止め、街の空間スケールに対応し、この家の構えを堂々としたものにしている。

　旗竿敷地に建つハウス＆アトリエ・ワンの場合は、建物の四方が隣家に囲われている。ここでも制限ぎりぎりの最大ヴォリュームを旗部分に確保した上で、隣接する環境との関係を取り結ぶ開口が設けられている。但し、通常の戸建て住宅なら私的な庭などであった眺めの対象が、建物と建物の隙間、隣の建物の壁面など、東京の住宅地に共有されている独特の残余空間に置き換えられている。しかも道路に直接接していないので、かなり大きな開口で向き合うことができ、内部空間と建物の隙間の空間が、一体感を持って感じられるほどである。その振る舞いは、眺めに対する認識の変化がもたらしたものであり、それがなければ、ほとんど開口のない住宅になっていたかもしれない。

　これと同様に建物と建物の隙間に窓を集めた例としてクス・ハウスを加えておく。クス・ハウスの場合は部分的に道路に接する部分が逆に建物の隙間と捉え直されている。このため、街に対する建物の振る舞いは、窓を即物的に積み重ね立面に集約されている。

山林あるいは住農混在の場合

　これまで見た住宅は、ガエ・ハウスを除いて屋根のない建物であった。これは言い換えれば、これらの住宅ではヴォリュームの配置と窓の配置が、建物の振る舞いを決めていたということである。それに対して、ここでは屋根を持つ住宅の振る舞いを川西町コテージBとハウス・アサマとノラ・ハウスを例に見ていく。ここで建物の周囲にあるのは樹木、地形の勾配、太陽、畑などであるが、それらの一つが選ばれることで、建物全体を単独の秩序に従わせるのではなく、環境要素に応じてそれぞれ異なる建築要素が、個別に振る舞うことを認めることで、複数の秩序が並走する複合性が生み出されるところに特徴がある。

　川西町コテージBにおいて、周辺環境との関係を取り持つのは切妻屋根と高床であり、それぞれ雪と斜面に応じた異なる振る舞いをする。雪に対する切妻屋根は、棟と軒を水平に保つことを原則として、建物の幅の変化によって勾配を変える。これが食事、就寝、入浴に対応して3棟に分節され、Y字に組み合わせられている。これに対して床は、尾根から谷への降り口になる斜面を滑り降りるように段状に下がっていく。この振る舞いの中で段差は、調理、食事、団らん、就寝の姿勢の違いを、リズミカルな断面の変化に統合している。この屋根と床の二つの振る舞いのズレがコテージBの空間である。Y字は、茂みの中に見つけた作場道の跡であり、樹木の伐採を最小に留め、森との接触面を最大に引き伸ばす。窓は壁を背負う位置にあり、森に対して浅い空間をつくる。黒く塗られた内部を移動すると、輝く森の緑が左右交互に展開する。冬になると、キャンプ場は閉鎖され、この建物も冬支度をする。窓の外にある十手金物は雪囲いを取り付けるためのものである。外壁の納まりはこの雪囲いと

been discreetly inserted into the façade, which is finished from top to bottom with a seamless coat of mortar. The reason for the arch window is that combining a square window with this volume would make it reminiscent of a prison watchtower. By instead combining it with an arch window, it is interestingly reminiscent of part of a medieval castle. In particular, the imbalance of the large arch window at the center of the façade corresponds to the scale of the interior, which is divided above and below by the second level floor, yet as it attracts glances from the street, the exterior responds to the spatial scale of the town, and the house becomes somehow majestic.

In the case of House & Atelier Bow-Wow, located on a flagpole site, the building is enclosed on all sides by neighboring houses. Here also, having secured the maximum volume permitted by the building regulations on the flag part, windows are inserted in order to make relationships with the neighboring environment. If this were an ordinary detached house, however, the views would be of private gardens and the like. Here they are substituted with the shared leftover spaces that characterize Tokyo's residential districts, such as the wall surfaces of neighboring buildings and the gaps between one building and the next. Nevertheless, because it doesn't directly touch the street, quite large openings can be placed opposing each other, and the interior spaces seem to attain a sense of unity with the gap spaces between the buildings. This behavior brings about a transformation in our understanding of the view, without which it might have become a house with almost no openings.

In a similar way, the Kus House is a further example of collecting windows in the gaps between one building and the next. In the case of the Kus House, the section that partially touches the street is re-perceived as building gap. Therefore, the building behavior with regard to the town is a collection of windows pragmatically superimposed on the elevations.

The case of forests or mixed residential-agricultural regions

With the exception of the Gae House, the houses we have examined up until now are roofless buildings. Put another way, in these houses building behavior is determined by the arrangement of volumes and the arrangement of windows. By contrast, Kawanishi Camping Cottage B, House Asama, and the Nora House can be seen as examples of the behavior of houses with roofs. These buildings are surrounded by vegetation, uneven topography, sunshine, and open fields, but rather than choosing one of these to generate a single system that the entire building must follow, they are characterized by the synthesis of many systems running in parallel through observing the individual behavior of each different architectural element in response to environmental elements.

In Kawanishi Camping Cottage B, the relationship with the surrounding environment is mediated by a gabled roof and raised floor, each of which has a different behavior, corresponding to the snow and the slope. The gabled roof tackles the snow, altering in pitch according to the changing width of the building by following a general rule of keeping the ridge and eaves horizontal. It is split into three wings that correspond to eating, sleeping, and bathing, which are combined into a Y shape. In contrast with this, the floor follows a stepping shape as if sliding down the slope from the mountain ridge to the valley. The steps of this behavior integrate the different postures of cooking, eating, socializing, and sleeping into a rhythmically varying cross-section. The space of Cottage B is the gap between these two behaviors of roof and floor. The Y shape is the trace of a farm trail discovered in the bushes, which helped minimize the felling of trees and maximize the contact surface with the forest. The windows are located along the walls, making a shallow space with regard to the forest. Moving through the black painted interior, the reciprocal influence of the glistening greenery of the forest is enhanced.

連続するように考えられている。

　ハウス・アサマの敷地は軽井沢のはずれにある。軽井沢は明治時代にイギリス人宣教師によって見い出された避暑地で、その林の中に建つ別荘は、塀をつくらず、簡素で茶色く、屋根を持つ、という振る舞いを共有している。森だけでなく、そうした建物の振る舞いを含めて、軽井沢独特の雰囲気ができていると言える。その基本的な振る舞いを踏襲しつつ、敷地の雑木林の木々に包まれる感覚を室内にもたらすために、ここでは屋根と壁を焦げ茶で塗り込め、境界面として同様に扱った上で、各面に一つずつ窓が設けられている。これにより、冬なら梢の向こうの青空、夏なら木漏れ日が、多方向から室内に取り込まれる。特に屋根面は構造を兼ねる垂れ壁状の梁により5分割されており、朝夕、季節、時間とともに明暗や色の異なる様々な表情を見せる。この屋根の分割には、床の上に展開する、居間、食堂、書斎、寝室、洗面所といった使用に応じた寸法が設定され、場所によって微妙に勾配が異なる。建物の四隅にあたるこれらの領域は傾斜屋根と垂れ壁と窓の構成のセットを反復させながら、サイズ、プロポーション、位置を変えることで隣接環境の違いに応答している。

　ノラ・ハウスの敷地は、仙台郊外の畑の入り交じる住宅地にある。今後住宅地として密度を増すか、それともこのままの状態が続くのか、予測がつかないところがある。こうした不安定な状態だから、新たにつくられる住宅のあり方が、まちの未来を占うことになる。ここで目指されているのは、畑が混在する新しいタイプの住宅地を想像させるような、新しい都市の農家と呼ぶにふさわしい住宅の振る舞いを見つけることである。

　まず古い農家に見られる大屋根と縁側を、この住宅の基本的な要素として導入する。道路と敷地の若干の高低差を利用して＋1.2mに設定された縁側は、実際には低いバルコニーのようでもあり、道路から距離を確保している。郊外住宅地では不気味なほど生活が室内に閉じ込められているのに対し、ここでは道路側を全て縁側とすることで、若い夫婦が子供といっしょに家庭菜園で作業したり、食事したり、夕涼みするなど、生活の一部が街に開かれるようにしている。縁側の軒は低く水平に保たれ、道路側からは平屋の建物に見えるので、建物の正面がほぼ縁側で独占されることになる。周囲の家の屋根型と、向かい側の畑ののどかな広がりに呼応する大屋根は、縁側の低い部分から、二つのライトチムニーの高さにまで登り、敷地奥で1.5階の位置まで下がることによって、うねりとねじれを孕んだものになる。こうした屋根の動きは、縁側から徐々に高さを変えて床下収納や2階に至る床の段差を追跡し、窓の上端を水平に保ち、かつ屋根に谷を作らない、という3つの条件によって導かれたものである。この屋根によって1.5階分の高さに軒を抑え、窓を上下の階を跨いで一つに大きくまとめることで、窓の分量は大きくなり、住宅のスケールを逸脱しはじめる。大屋根をつまみ上げたようなライトチムニーは、大屋根の完結性に破れ目を入れ、室内の光と空気の挙動を活性化するとともに、二羽の鳥が寄り添うようなシルエットを建物に与えている。

呼びかけと応答

　最後に、上で導かれた場所ごとの住宅の振る舞いを比較することで、アトリエ・ワンの住宅における建物の振る舞いの方法と意味を位置づけてみたい。

When winter arrives, the campground closes down, and this building is also prepared for winter weather. The metal hardware outside the windows allows wooden snow screens to be installed. The profile of the exterior wall assembly was devised to be continuous with the snow screens.

The site for House Asama is in the outskirts of Karuizawa. During the Meiji Era, Karuizawa was discovered as a summer resort area by British missionaries, and the holiday villas built in these woods have a shared behavior, comprising roofs, simple brown coloring, and no fences. It could be said that the unique atmosphere of Karuizawa is not only due to the woods, but also to the behavior of such buildings. In order to bring indoors the sense of being enclosed by the groves of trees on the site while following this basic behavior, the roof and walls were stained a burnt tea color, treated like boundary surfaces, and a window was inserted in each surface. As a result, the blue skies across the treetops in winter, as well as the beams of sunlight streaming through the foliage in summer, are brought inside from multiple directions. Divided in five by the hanging walls that also double as structural beams, the ceiling surface shows various different expressions of light and color in concert with the day, season, and time. Dimensions have been established in the roof divisions that correspond to the functions spread across the floor – the living room, dining room, study, bedroom, and washroom – and there are subtle differences in slope depending on location. These areas meet at the four corners of the building, and while inverting the compositional set of sloping roof, descending walls, and windows, they respond to differences in the adjacent environment through differences in size, proportion, and location.

The Nora House site is on the outskirts of Sendai, in a residential district mixed with fields. There is no way to foresee whether it will continue to remain in this state, or will increase in density as a residential district. Because of this unstable situation, making a new house becomes a prediction about the future of the town. Imagining a new type of residential district mixed with fields, our intention here was to discover a house behavior appropriate for calling out to new urban farmers.

First, a large roof and veranda as seen in old farmhouses were introduced as the basic elements of the house. Using the slight difference in elevation between the street and the site, the veranda has been raised 1.2m, in effect becoming a low balcony, and also maintaining a distance from the street. In response to the somewhat uncanny indoor lifestyles of suburbia, aspects of daily life have been opened to the town by making the entire side facing the street into a veranda, where the young couple and their children work together in the home vegetable garden, eat meals, and sit outside in the cool of the evening. By keeping the eaves over the veranda low and horizontal, the building façade is monopolized by the veranda, so from the street the building appears to be a one-story house. Acting in concert with the roof shapes of the surrounding houses and the idyllic fields on the other side, the large roof ascends from the low part of the veranda to the height of the two light chimneys, and by lowering to a height of 1.5 stories in the deeper part of the site, it becomes full of undulations and twists. The motion of the roof is led by three conditions: following the gradual change in height from the veranda to the under-floor storage, following the change in floor height leading to the second level, and keeping the upper edge of the window horizontal with no valleys in the roof. This roof constrains the eaves to a 1.5-story height, gathering the windows into a single large one that straddles the upper and lower levels. This increases the quantity of glazing, and it begins to depart from the scale of a house. Like pinched, raised lumps on the large roof, the coherence of the roof is broken by the insertion of the light chimneys. As well as activating flows of light and air to the interior, they give the building a silhouette like two birds huddling together.

まず郊外住宅地では、境界から引きをとった敷地中央の箱形の主ヴォリュームと、そこから外に向けて全方位的に関係を結ぶ、窓、サブヴォリューム、軒／水平連窓が、振る舞いをつくりだしている。窓が問題にするのは、視線の制御とその対象であるのに対して、サブヴォリュームが問題にするのは内外の領域の取り合いであり、さらに水平連窓が問題にするのは内外の距離と向きである。大事なのはいずれの要素も、内部の階に正確に一致しないところである。そのズレによって、生活等の内容によって根拠づけられた内部の構成理論とは別に、外部の構成理論があることが示され、その根拠として街路や隣家からの呼びかけと応答、すなわちコミュニケーションの次元が浮かび上がる。

　密集住宅地では敷地に余裕がないので、郊外住宅地において有効であった中央への引きが許されない。これに代わって振る舞いをつくりだすのは、地面と空を一気に繋ぐヴォリュームが密集住宅地にもたらす大きな空白＝ファサードと、ここに開けられる大きな窓である。この大きな窓は、そこにある個別の具体的要素への応答というよりは、密集住宅地を風景化するところに特徴がある。それは密集住宅地の原則自体を呼びかけとして浮き上がらせている。ヴォリュームは垂直方向に筒抜けになったエンベロップを抑えられ、そこに開けられた窓にあわせるように、小さく分節された床や大きめの階段の踊場が設定される。そこが住み手の生活習慣、家具、調度品によって個々に領有されることで、身体の振る舞いに近い有機的な空間となっている。

　山林あるいは住農混在では、屋根と床が勾配（段差を含む）を扱っているところが、郊外住宅地、密集住宅地とは違う。床は外部の地形と内部の生活を調整する。屋根は外部の雪と雨、内部の空気や光の挙動や人の振る舞いを調整する。勾配には一つの連続面の中に、複数の振る舞いの場を差異化しつつ統合する働きがあり、このために床や屋根といった一つの建築要素の応答の中に、複数の呼びかけが重なり合うことになる。この場合、建築の空間は各建築要素の個別の振る舞いのズレに現れる。間に置かれた身体は周辺環境から一度距離をとった上で、改めて床や屋根や窓によって拡張され、鋭敏になった感覚によって、周囲の環境を含めたその場を知覚することになる。

　こうしてみると、アトリエ・ワンの住宅作品は、具体的な周辺環境やそれを生成する都市の原則に盲目に従うのでもないし、それを尊重せずに無関係なことをやるのでもない。あくまでもその環境やそれが生成される原則を下敷きにしながら、それと建築の間の呼びかけと応答の関係を検証し、活性化することによって、建築を通したコミュニケーションの次元を開発していく。郊外住宅地における中心配置の「引き」、密集住宅地におけるファサードの「空白」、山林あるいは住農混在における屋根と床の振る舞いの「ズレ」などは、呼びかけと応答の次元を検証し、より柔軟な関係を見い出すためのマイクロアーバニズムの方法であり、建築類型と都市形態をむすびつける批評的修辞であるとも言える。そこから改めて組み立てる建築の言語が、都市の中であろうと自然の景色の中であろうと、あらゆる建築の機会を、いきいきとした空間の実践に結びつけていくものとなっていることを願う。

Call and response

Finally, through the above comparisons of house behaviors guided by each location, we will try to map the methods and meanings of building behavior in the houses of Atelier Bow-Wow.

First of all, in suburban residential districts, behavior is produced by the windows, sub-volumes, and horizontal windows/eaves that make relationships outward in every direction from box-shaped main volumes that have been pulled back from the site boundaries into the center of the sites. The basis for this behavior is due to subtle differences in the mediating architectural elements, such as windows, sub-volumes, or horizontal glazing. The window addresses the question of controlling sightlines and their targets, the sub-volume addresses the question of the struggle for territory, and the horizontal window addresses the question of orientation and distance between inside and outside. The important point is that none of these elements are precisely aligned with the interior floor levels. Aside from an interior compositional theory based on the details of daily life, these offsets also reveal an exterior compositional theory, on the basis of which there is a call and response with the streets and neighboring houses. In other words, the dimension of communication becomes conspicuous.

There is no surplus on sites in dense residential districts, so the pull to the center and behavior toward the exterior that is valid in suburbia isn't valid. To produce a substitute for this behavior in dense residential districts, a volume connecting ground to sky with a single stroke provides a large blank space (= façade), into which big windows are inserted. Beyond responding to each concrete element in the immediate area, these big windows are characterized by the transformation of dense residential districts into a kind of scenery. This becomes conspicuous as a call to the principles of dense residential districts. Small subdivided floors and large stair landings are established as if adjusted to the windows inserted in the restrained vertical volume. By occupying each one with the inhabitants' lifestyles, furniture, and fittings, these become organic spaces close to bodily behavior.

In forests or mixed residential-agricultural areas, the difference from suburbia and dense residential districts is in the way the roofs and floors deal with slopes (including steps). The floors adjust external topography to internal daily life, and the roofs adjust external snow and rain to internal movements of air and light, as well as human behavior. The slopes act to differentiate and integrate several places within a single continuous surface, and several calls may overlap in a single response made by the architectural elements of roof and floor. In this case, the architectural space manifests the offsets in the individual behaviors of each architectural element. Having first become separated from the surrounding environment, a human body introduced here is once again extended by means of the floors, roofs, and windows, and is able to perceive the place with extreme acuity, including the surrounding environment.

Looked at in this way, the house designs of Atelier Bow-Wow do not blindly follow the concrete surrounding environment and the principles of the city that generates it, nor do they disregard these and do something completely unrelated. While persistently using this environment and the principles that produce it as an underlay, by examining and activating the relationships of call and response between it and architecture, the desire is to develop the dimension of communication through architecture. The "pull" of centralized layouts in suburbia, the "blank" of façades in dense residential districts, the "offset" of floor and roof behavior in forests or mixed residential-agricultural regions; these are methods for examining the dimension of call and response, for discovering more flexible relationships, and they could also be described as connections between architectural typology and urban morphology. By then reassembling them into an architectural language, whether in the city or in nature, we hope every architectural opportunity will be connected to the practice of lively space.

アニ・ハウス Ani House

所在地————神奈川県茅ヶ崎市
用途————専用住宅
構造設計————梅沢建築構造研究所
施工————東京鐵筋コンクリート
設計担当————塚本由晴、貝島桃代
構造・工法————鉄骨造
階数————2F+B1
敷地面積————122.32m²
建築面積————46.74m²
建ぺい率————38.21%
許容建ぺい率——60.00%
延床面積————121.85m²
容積率————70.18%
許容容積————150.00%
設計期間————1996.3-1996.10
工事期間————1996.10-1997.4
掲載ページ———10

LOCATION: CHIGASAKI, KANAGAWA PREFECTURE
PRINCIPAL USE: RESIDENCE
STRUCTURAL ENGNEERS: UMEZAWA STRUCTURAL ENGINEERS
GENERAL CONCRETE: TOKYO TEKKIN CONCRETE
ARCHITECTS: Yoshiharu Tsukamoto, Momoyo Kaijima
STRUCTURE/CONSTRUCTION METHOD: STEEL CONSTRUCTION
FLOOR: 2F+B1
SITE AREA: 122.32m²
BUILT AREA: 46.74m²
BUILT RATIO: 38.21%
MAXIMUM BUILT RATIO: 60.00%
TOTAL FLOOR AREA: 121.85m²
FLOOR-AREA RATIO: 70.18%
MAXIMUM FLOOR-AREA RATIO: 150.00%
DESIGN PERIOD: 1996.3-1996.10
CONSTRUCTION PERIOD: 1996.10-1997.4
SEE PAGE: 10

二階平面図
2F PLAN

配置図 1/1000
SITE PLAN

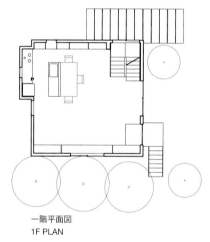

一階平面図
1F PLAN

立面図
ELEVATION

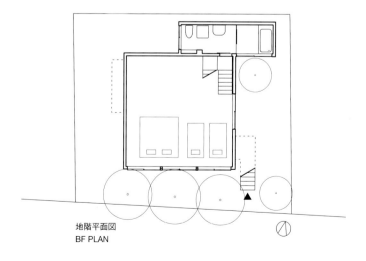

地階平面図
BF PLAN

S：1/200
0　1　2　3　4　5 (m)

ミニ・ハウス Mini House

所在地 ——————— 東京都練馬区
用途 ——————— 専用住宅
構造設計 ——————— 梅沢建築構造研究所
施工 ——————— 東京鐵筋コンクリート
設計担当 ——————— 塚本由晴、貝島桃代、
　　　　　　　　　　東京工業大学塚本研究室(武井誠)
構造・工法 ——————— 鉄骨造
階数 ——————— 2F+B1
敷地面積 ——————— 76.63m²
建築面積 ——————— 40.80m²
建ぺい率 ——————— 53.20%
許容建ぺい率 ——— 60.00%
延床面積 ——————— 90.32m²
容積率 ——————— 117.87%
許容容積 ——————— 160.00%
設計期間 ——————— 1997.9-1998.4
工事期間 ——————— 1998.4-1998.10
掲載ページ ——————— 14

LOCATION: NERIMA, TOKYO
PRINCIPAL USE: RESIDENCE
STRUCTURAL ENGNEERS: UMEZAWA STRUCTURAL ENGINEERS
GENERAL CONCRETE: TOKYO TEKKIN CONCRETE
ARCHITECTS: Yoshiharu Tsukamoto, Momoyo Kaijima
　　　　　　　+ T.I.T. Tsukamoto Lab.(Makoto Takei)
STRUCTURE/CONSTRUCTION METHOD: STEEL CONSTRUCTION
FLOOR: 2F+B1
SITE AREA: 76.63m²
BUILT AREA: 40.80m²
BUILT RATIO: 53.20%
MAXIMUM BUILT RATIO: 60.00%
TOTAL FLOOR AREA: 90.32m²
FLOOR-AREA RATIO: 117.87%
MAXIMUM FLOOR-AREA RATIO: 160.00%
DESIGN PERIOD: 1997.9-1998.4
CONSTRUCTION PERIOD: 1998.4-1998.10
SEE PAGE: 14

二階平面図
2F PLAN

配置図 1/1000
SITE PLAN

一階平面図
1F PLAN

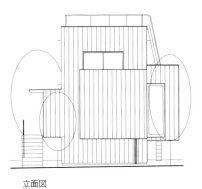

立面図
ELEVATION

地階平面図
BF PLAN

⌞―――┴――┴――┴――⌟ S：1/200
0　1　2　3　4　5 (m)

川西町コテージB Kawanishi Camping Cottage B

所在地―――――新潟県中魚沼郡川西町
用途――――――宿泊施設
構造設計――――金箱構造設計事務所
施工――――――井川・栄松特定共同事業体
設計担当――――塚本由晴、貝島桃代、東京工業大学塚本研究室(高木俊)、
　　　　　　　　共同設計者:三村大介(malo planning)
構造・工法――――木造
階数―――――――1F
敷地面積――――16,430.00m²
建築面積――――63.70m²
建ぺい率―――――0.40%
許容建ぺい率――70.00%
延床面積――――63.70m²
容積率――――――0.40%
許容容積―――――400.00%
設計期間――――1998.8-1998.9
工事期間――――1998.10-1998.12
掲載ページ―――18

TITLE: Kawanishi Camping Cottage B
LOCATION: KAWANISHI, NAKAUONUMA, NIIGATA PREFECTURE
PRINCIPAL USE: CAMPING COTTAGE
STRUCTURAL ENGNEERS: KANEBAKO STRUCTURAL ENGINEERS
GENERAL CONCRETE: JV of Igawa and Eimatsu
ARCHITECTS: Yoshiharu Tsukamoto, Momoyo Kaijima
　　　　　　　　+ T.I.T. Tsukamoto Lab.(Shun Takagi)
　　　　　　　　+ malo planning(Daisuke Mimura)
STRUCTURE/CONSTRUCTION METHOD: WOODEN CONSTRUCTION
FLOOR: 1F
SITE AREA: 16,430.00m²
BUILT AREA: 63.70m²
BUILT RATIO: 0.40%
MAXIMUM BUILT RATIO: 70.00%
TOTAL FLOOR AREA: 63.70m²
FLOOR-AREA RATIO: 0.40%
MAXIMUM FLOOR-AREA RATIO: 400.00%
DESIGN PERIOD: 1998.8-1998.9
CONSTRUCTION PERIOD: 1998.10-1998.12
SEE PAGE: 18

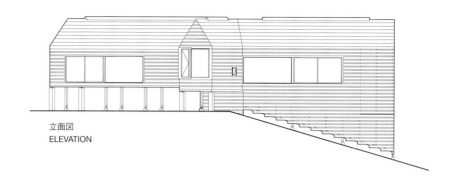

立面図
ELEVATION

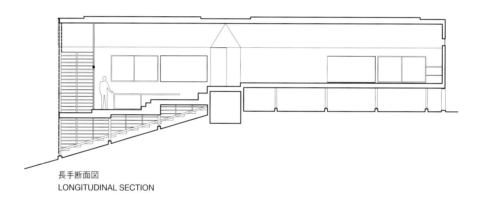

長手断面図
LONGITUDINAL SECTION

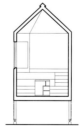

キッチン部断面図
EATING WIING SECTION

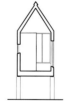

トイレ部断面図
SHOWERING WIING SECTION

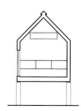

寝室部断面図
SLEEPING WIING SECTION

S：1/200
0　1　2　3　4　5 (m)

モカ・ハウス Moca House

五階平面図
5F PLAN

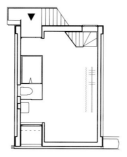

四階平面図
4F PLAN

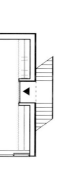

二階平面図
2F PLAN

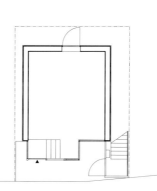

一階平面図
1F PLAN

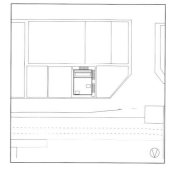

配置図 1/1000
SITE PLAN

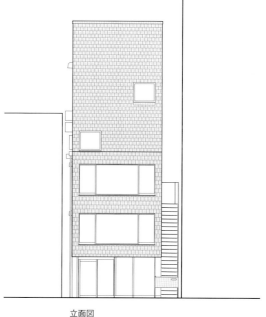

立面図
ELEVATION

所在地 ————— 東京都中野区
用途 ————— 共同住宅・店舗
構造設計 ——— 金箱構造設計事務所
施工 ————— ホームイング
設計担当 ——— 塚本由晴、貝島桃代、高木俊*
構造・工法 ——— 鉄骨コンクリート造
階数 ————— 5F
敷地面積 ——— 51.82m²
建築面積 ——— 28.76m²
建ぺい率 ——— 55.50%
許容建ぺい率 —— 90.00%
延床面積 ——— 120.25m²
容積率 ————— 232.10%
許容容積 ——— 240.00%
設計期間 ——— 1999.5-2000.1
工事期間 ——— 2000.2-2000.7
掲載ページ ——— 22

TITLE: Moca House
LOCATION: NAKANO, TOKYO
PRINCIPAL USE: APARTMENT + SHOP
STRUCTURAL ENGNEERS: KANEBAKO STRUCTURAL ENGINEERS
GENERAL CONCRETE: HOMEING
ARCHITECTS: Yoshiharu Tsukamoto, Momoyo Kaijima,
           Shun Takagi
STRUCTURE/CONSTRUCTION METHOD: REINFORCED CONCRETE
FLOOR: 5F
SITE AREA: 51.82m²
BUILT AREA: 28.76m²
BUILT RATIO: 55.50%
MAXIMUM BUILT RATIO: 90.00%
TOTAL FLOOR AREA: 120.25m²
FLOOR-AREA RATIO: 232.10%
MAXIMUM FLOOR-AREA RATIO: 240.00%
DESIGN PERIOD: 1999.5-2000.1
CONSTRUCTION PERIOD: 2000.2-2000.7
SEE PAGE: 22

S：1/200
0　1　2　3　4　5 (m)

ミツモン荘 Moth House

所在地————長野県北佐久郡御代田
用途————別荘（増改築）
施工————ホームイング
設計担当————塚本由晴、貝島桃代
構造・工法————木造
階数————1F
敷地面積————776.22m²
建築面積————72.87m²
建ぺい率————9.40%
許容建ぺい率————40.00%
延床面積————72.87m²
容積率————9.40%
許容容積————60.00%
設計期間————2000.1-2000.5
工事期間————2000.5-2000.7
掲載ページ————26

TITLE: Moth House
LOCATION: MIYOTA, KITASAKU, NAGANO PREFECTURE
PRINCIPAL USE: VILLA(extension)
GENERAL CONCRETE: HOMEING
ARCHITECTS: Yoshiharu Tsukamoto, Momoyo Kaijima
STRUCTURE/CONSTRUCTION METHOD: WOODEN CONSTRUCTION
FLOOR: 1F
SITE AREA: 776.22m²
BUILT AREA: 72.87m²
BUILT RATIO: 9.40%
MAXIMUM BUILT RATIO: 40.00%
TOTAL FLOOR AREA: 72.87m²
FLOOR-AREA RATIO: 9.40%
MAXIMUM FLOOR-AREA RATIO: 60.00%
DESIGN PERIOD: 2000.1-2000.5
CONSTRUCTION PERIOD: 2000.5-2000.7
SEE PAGE: 26

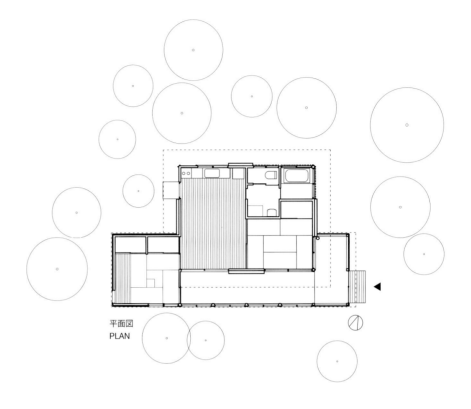

平面図
PLAN

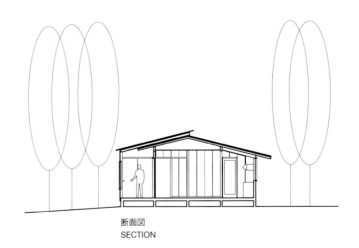

断面図
SECTION

S：1/200
0　1　2　3　4　5(m)

ハウス・アサマ House Asama

所在地―――――長野県北佐久郡軽井沢町
用途―――――別荘
構造設計―――――金箱構造設計事務所
施工―――――ホームイング
設計担当―――――塚本由晴、貝島桃代、高木俊*
構造・工法―――――木造
階数―――――2F
敷地面積―――――571.00m²
建築面積―――――84.50m²
建ぺい率―――――14.80%
許容建ぺい率―――20.00%
延床面積―――――87.00m²
容積率―――――12.20%
許容容積―――――20.00%
設計期間―――――2000.1-2000.6
工事期間―――――2000.7-2000.12
掲載ページ―――――30

LOCATION: KARUIZAWA, KITASAKU, NAGANO PREFECTURE
PRINCIPAL USE: VILLA
STRUCTURAL ENGNEERS: KANEBAKO STRUCTURAL ENGINEERS
GENERAL CONCRETE: HOMEING
ARCHITECTS: Yoshiharu Tsukamoto, Momoyo Kaijima,
           Shun Takagi
STRUCTURE/CONSTRUCTION METHOD: WOODEN CONSTRUCTION
FLOOR: 2F
SITE AREA: 571.00m²
BUILT AREA: 84.50m²
BUILT RATIO: 14.80%
MAXIMUM BUILT RATIO: 20.00%
TOTAL FLOOR AREA: 87.00m²
FLOOR-AREA RATIO: 12.20%
MAXIMUM FLOOR-AREA RATIO: 20.00%
DESIGN PERIOD: 2000.1-2000.6
CONSTRUCTION PERIOD: 2000.7-2000.12
SEE PAGE: 30

```
├─┼─┼─┼─┼─┤ S:1/200
0  1  2  3  4  5 (m)
```

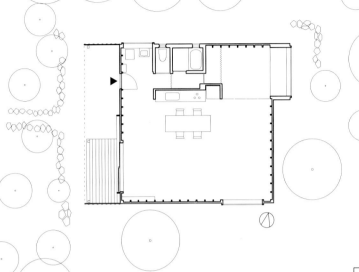

一階平面図／1F PLAN

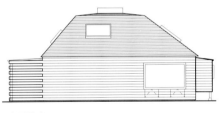

立面図／ELEVATION

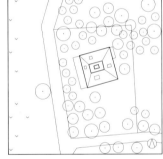

配置図 1/1000／SITE PLAN

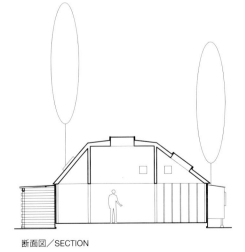

断面図／SECTION   断面図／SECTION

ハウス・サイコ House Saiko

所在地————山梨県南都留郡足和田村
用途————別荘
構造設計————金箱構造設計事務所
施工————七保
設計担当————塚本由晴、貝島桃代、東京工業大学塚本研究室(山崎徹也)
構造・工法————木造
階数————2F
敷地面積————740.90m²
建築面積————104.35m²
建ぺい率————14.08%
許容建ぺい率——50.00%
延床面積————157.96m²
容積率————21.32%
許容容積————200.00%
設計期間————2000.1-2000.6
工事期間————2000.10-2001.1
掲載ページ————34

LOCATION: ASHIWADA, MINAMITSURU, YAMANASHI PREFECTURE
PRINCIPAL USE: VILLA
STRUCTURAL ENGINEERS: KANEBAKO STRUCTURAL ENGINEERS
GENERAL CONCRETE: NANAHO
ARCHITECTS: Yoshiharu Tsukamoto, Momoyo Kaijima
        + T.I.T. Tsukamoto Lab.(Tetsuya Yamazaki)
STRUCTURE/CONSTRUCTION METHOD: WOODEN CONSTRUCTION
FLOOR: 2F
SITE AREA: 740.90m²
BUILT AREA: 104.35m²
BUILT RATIO: 14.08%
MAXIMUM BUILT RATIO: 50.00%
TOTAL FLOOR AREA: 157.96m²
FLOOR-AREA RATIO: 21.32%
MAXIMUM FLOOR-AREA RATIO: 200.00%
DESIGN PERIOD: 2000.1-2000.6
CONSTRUCTION PERIOD: 2000.10-2001.1
SEE PAGE: 34

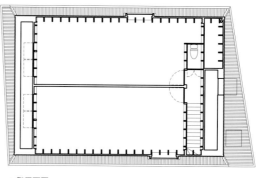

二階平面図
2F PLAN

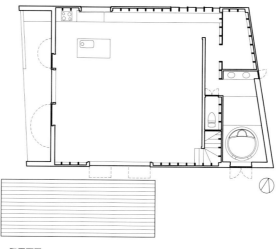

一階平面図
1F PLAN

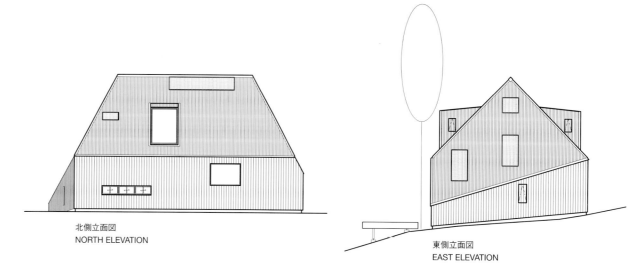

北側立面図
NORTH ELEVATION

東側立面図
EAST ELEVATION

S:1/200
0 1 2 3 4 5 (m)

ダス・ハウス D.a.S House

所在地————東京都三鷹市
用途————住居兼アトリエ
構造設計————金箱構造設計事務所
施工————飯塚建築
設計担当————塚本由晴、貝島桃代、関本丹青
構造・工法————木造
階数————2F
敷地面積————94.46m²
建築面積————36.00m²
建ぺい率————38.11%
許容建ぺい率——40.00%
延床面積————74.00m²
容積率————78.34%
許容容積————80.00%
設計期間————2000.6-2001.9
工事期間————2001.10-2002.2
掲載ページ————38

LOCATION: MITAKA, TOKYO
PRINCIPAL USE: RESIDENCE + ATELIER
STRUCTURAL ENGNEERS: KANEBAKO STRUCTURAL ENGINEERS
GENERAL CONCRETE: IIZUKA CONSTRUCTION
ARCHITECTS: Yoshiharu Tsukamoto, Momoyo Kaijima,
        Mio Sekimoto
STRUCTURE/CONSTRUCTION METHOD: WOODEN CONSTRUCTION
FLOOR: 2F
SITE AREA: 94.46m²
BUILT AREA: 36.00m²
BUILT RATIO: 38.11%
MAXIMUM BUILT RATIO: 40.00%
TOTAL FLOOR AREA: 74.00m²
FLOOR-AREA RATIO: 78.34%
MAXIMUM FLOOR-AREA RATIO: 80.00%
DESIGN PERIOD: 2000.6-2001.9
CONSTRUCTION PERIOD: 2001.10-2002.2
SEE PAGE: 38

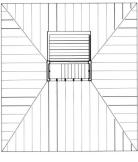

R階平面図
RF PLAN

配置図 1/1000
SITE PLAN

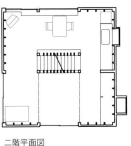

二階平面図
2F PLAN

立面図
ELEVATION

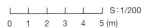

一階平面図
1F PLAN

L___I___I___I___I___I S:1/200
0   1   2   3   4   5 (m)

シャロー・ハウス Shallow House

所在地──────東京都新宿区
用途───────専用住宅
構造設計─────金箱構造設計事務所
施工───────ホームイング
設計担当─────塚本由晴、貝島桃代、田中正洋*、高木俊*
構造・工法────鉄骨造
階数───────4F
敷地面積─────47.27m²
建築面積─────35.65m²
建ぺい率─────75.42%
許容建ぺい率───100.00%
延床面積─────142.66m²
容積率──────263.82%
許容容積─────400.00%
設計期間─────2001.6-2002.1
工事期間─────2002.2-2002.7
掲載ページ────40

LOCATION: SHINJUKU, TOKYO
PRINCIPAL USE: RESIDENCE
STRUCTURAL ENGINEERS: KANEBAKO STRUCTURAL ENGINEERS
GENERAL CONCRETE: HOMEING
ARCHITECTS: Yoshiharu Tsukamoto, Momoyo Kaijima,
　　　　　　　 Masahiro Tanaka, Shun Takagi
STRUCTURE/CONSTRUCTION METHOD: STEEL CONSTRUCTION
FLOOR: 4F
SITE AREA: 47.27m²
BUILT AREA: 35.65m²
BUILT RATIO: 75.42%
MAXIMUM BUILT RATIO: 100.00%
TOTAL FLOOR AREA: 142.66m²
FLOOR-AREA RATIO: 263.82%
MAXIMUM FLOOR-AREA RATIO: 400.00%
DESIGN PERIOD: 2001.6-2002.1
CONSTRUCTION PERIOD: 2002.2-2002.7
SEE PAGE: 40

配置図 1/1000
SITE PLAN

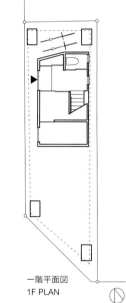

一階平面図
1F PLAN

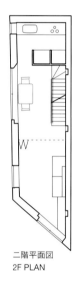

二階平面図
2F PLAN

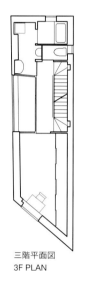

三階平面図
3F PLAN

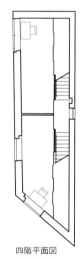

四階平面図
4F PLAN

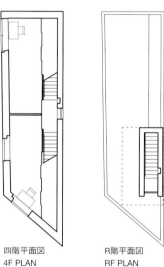

R階平面図
RF PLAN

├─┼─┼─┼─┼─┤ S:1/200
0 1 2 3 4 5 (m)

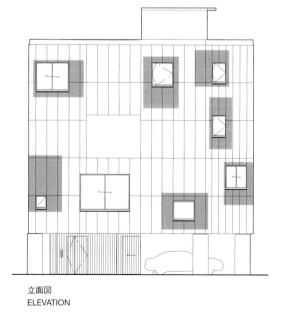

立面図
ELEVATION

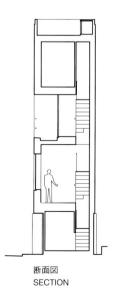

断面図
SECTION

ジグ Jig

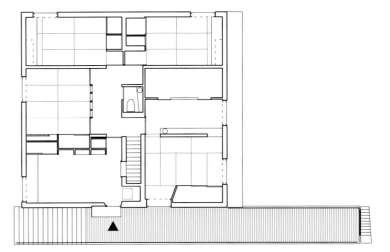

二階平面図／2F PLAN

所在地 ──────── 千葉県船橋市
用途 ───────── 専用住宅
構造設計 ─────── 金箱構造設計事務所
施工 ───────── 花実建設
設計担当 ─────── 塚本由晴、貝島桃代、山崎徹也*
構造・工法 ───── 鉄骨コンクリート＋鉄骨造、木造
階数 ───────── 2F
敷地面積 ─────── 295.22m²
建築面積 ─────── 144.23m²
建ぺい率 ─────── 48.86%
許容建ぺい率 ──── 50.00%
延床面積 ─────── 254.51m²
容積率 ─────── 86.21%
許容容積 ─────── 100.00%
設計期間 ─────── 2000.12-2002.6
工事期間 ─────── 2002.9-2003.3
掲載ページ ───── 44

LOCATION: FUNABASHI, CHIBA PREFECTURE
PRINCIPAL USE: RESIDENCE
STRUCTURAL ENGNEERS: KANEBAKO STRUCTURAL ENGINEERS
GENERAL CONCRETE: HANAMI CORPORATION
ARCHITECTS: Yoshiharu Tsukamoto, Momoyo Kaijima,
          Tetsuya Yamazaki
STRUCTURE/CONSTRUCTION METHOD: REINFORCED CONCRETE+STEEL
          CONSTRUCTION, WOODEN CONSTRUCTION

FLOOR: 2F
SITE AREA: 295.22m²
BUILT AREA: 144.23m²
BUILT RATIO: 48.86%
MAXIMUM BUILT RATIO: 50.00%
TOTAL FLOOR AREA: 254.51m²
FLOOR-AREA RATIO: 86.21%
MAXIMUM FLOOR-AREA RATIO: 100.00%
DESIGN PERIOD: 2000.12-2002.6
CONSTRUCTION PERIOD: 2002.9-2003.3
SEE PAGE: 44

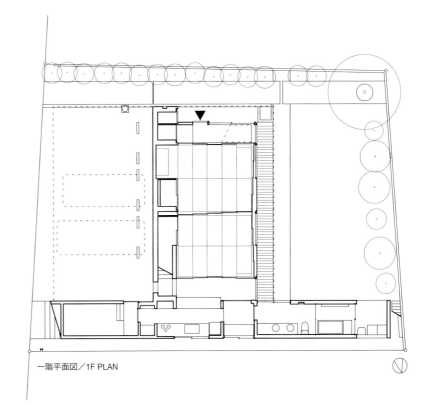

一階平面図／1F PLAN

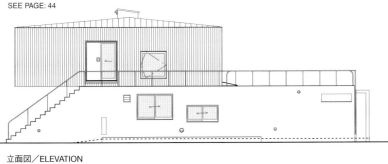

立面図／ELEVATION

断面図／SECTION

S：1/200
0　1　2　3　4　5 (m)

ガエ・ハウス Gae House

所在地————東京都世田谷区
用途————専用住宅
構造設計————オーク構造設計
施工————東京鐵筋コンクリート
設計担当————塚本由晴、貝島桃代、
　　　　　　　東京工業大学塚本研究室(斎藤理、桜井大輔、
　　　　　　　鈴木悠子、平林政道、富永大毅)

構造・工法————鉄骨造
階数————2F+B1
敷地面積————74.40m²
建築面積————36.32m²
建ぺい率————48.81%
許容建ぺい率——50.00%
延床面積————88.42m²
容積率————90.24%
許容容積————100.00%
設計期間————2001.12-2002.12
工事期間————2003.1-2003.7
掲載ページ————48

LOCATION: SETAGAYA, TOKYO
PRINCIPAL USE: RESIDENCE
STRUCTURAL ENGNEERS: STRUCTURAL DESIGN OFFICE OAK
GENERAL CONCRETE: TOKYO TEKKIN CONCRETE
ARCHITECTS: Yoshiharu Tsukamoto, Momoyo Kaijima
　　　　　　+ T.I.T. Tsukamoto Lab.(Satoshi Saito,Daisuke Sakurai,
　　　　　　Masamichi Hirabayashi, Hiroki Tominaga)
STRUCTURE/CONSTRUCTION METHOD: STEEL CONSTRUCTION
FLOOR: 2F+B1
SITE AREA: 74.40m²
BUILT AREA: 36.32m²
BUILT RATIO: 48.81%
MAXIMUM BUILT RATIO: 50.00%
TOTAL FLOOR AREA: 88.42m²
FLOOR-AREA RATIO: 90.24%
MAXIMUM FLOOR-AREA RATIO: 100.00%
DESIGN PERIOD: 2001.12-2002.12
CONSTRUCTION PERIOD: 2003.1-2003.7
SEE PAGE: 48

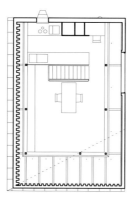

二階平面図
2F PLAN

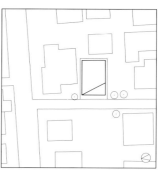

配置図 1/1000
SITE PLAN

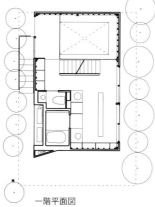
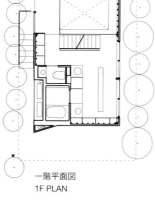

一階平面図
1F PLAN

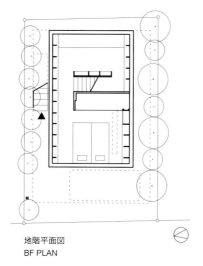

地階平面図
BF PLAN

立面図
ELEVATION

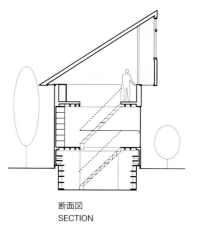

断面図
SECTION

S：1/200
0　1　2　3　4　5 (m)

クス・ハウス Kus House

所在地————東京都世田谷区
用途————専用住宅
構造設計————池田昌弘 (mias)
施工————河合建築
設計担当————塚本由晴、貝島桃代、
　　　　　　共同設計者:寺内美紀子、池田昌弘 (mias)
構造・工法————木造十鉄骨造
階数————2F+B1
敷地面積————70.90m²
建築面積————42.24m²
建ぺい率————59.58%
許容建ぺい率—60.00%
延床面積————123.18m²
容積率————154.88%
許容容積————160.00%
設計期間————2002.4-2003.6
工事期間————2003.6-2004.2
掲載ページ————52

LOCATION: SETAGAYA, TOKYO
PRINCIPAL USE: RESIDENCE
STRUCTURAL ENGNEERS: MASAHIRO IKEDA (mias)
GENERAL CONCRETE: KAWAI CORPORATION
ARCHITECTS: Yoshiharu Tsukamoto, Momoyo Kaijima
　　　　　+ Mikiko Terauchi + Masahiro Ikeda
STRUCTURE/CONSTRUCTION METHOD: WOODEN CONSTRUCTION
　　　　　　　　　　　　+STEEL CONSTRUCTION

FLOOR: 2F+B1
SITE AREA: 70.90m²
BUILT AREA: 42.24m²
BUILT RATIO: 59.58%
MAXIMUM BUILT RATIO: 60.00%
TOTAL FLOOR AREA: 123.18m²
FLOOR-AREA RATIO: 154.88%
MAXIMUM FLOOR-AREA RATIO: 160.00%
DESIGN PERIOD: 2002.4-2003.6
CONSTRUCTION PERIOD: 2003.6-2004.2
SEE PAGE: 52

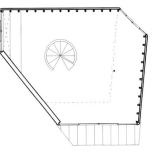

三階平面図
3F PLAN

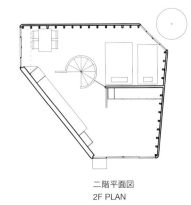

二階平面図
2F PLAN

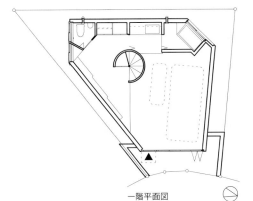

一階平面図
1F PLAN

配置図 1/1000
SITE PLAN

立面図
ELEVATION

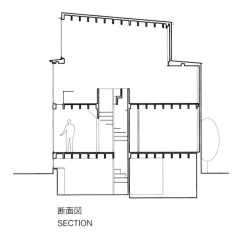

断面図
SECTION

├─┼─┼─┼─┼─┤ S:1/200
0 1 2 3 4 5 (m)

イズ・ハウス Izu House

所在地 ──────── 静岡県西伊豆
用途 ──────── 専用住宅
構造設計 ──────── オーク構造設計
施工 ──────── 大同工業
設計担当 ──────── 塚本由晴、貝島桃代、高木俊*
構造・工法 ──────── 木造＋鉄骨造
階数 ──────── 2F
敷地面積 ──────── 3,762.77m²
建築面積 ──────── 108.65m²
建ぺい率 ──────── 2.88%
延床面積 ──────── 133.08m²
容積率 ──────── 3.53%
設計期間 ──────── 2002.6-2003.8
工事期間 ──────── 2003.9-2004.3
掲載ページ ──────── 56

LOCATION: NISHIIZU, SHIZUOKA PREFECTURE
PRINCIPAL USE: RESIDENCE
STRUCTURAL ENGNEERS: STRUCTURAL DESIGN OFFICE OAK
GENERAL CONCRETE: DAIDO KOGYO CORPORATION
ARCHITECTS: Yoshiharu Tsukamoto, Momoyo Kaijima,
              Shun Takagi
STRUCTURE/CONSTRUCTION METHOD: WOODEN CONSTRUCTION
                               +STEEL CONSTRUCTION
FLOOR: 2F
SITE AREA: 3,762.77m²
BUILT AREA: 108.65m²
BUILT RATIO: 2.88%
TOTAL FLOOR AREA: 133.08m²
FLOOR-AREA RATIO: 3.53%
DESIGN PERIOD: 2002.6-2003.8
CONSTRUCTION PERIOD: 2003.9-2004.3
SEE PAGE: 56

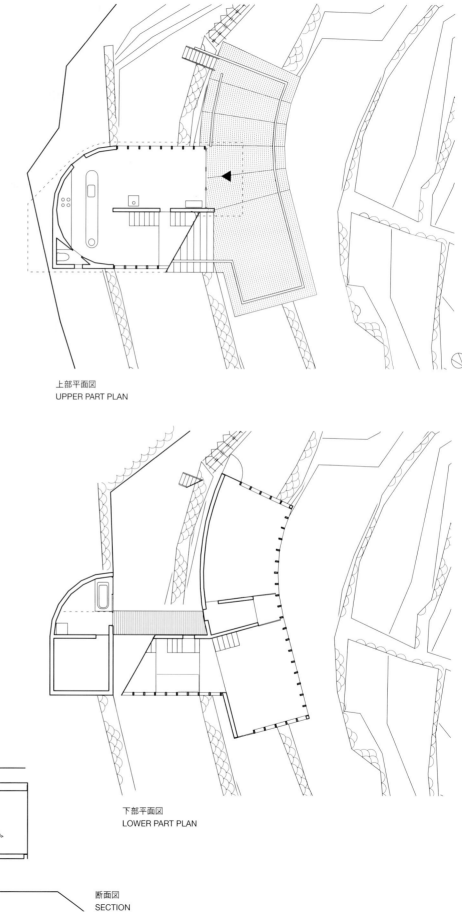

上部平面図
UPPER PART PLAN

下部平面図
LOWER PART PLAN

断面図
SECTION

S : 1/200
0 1 2 3 4 5 (m)

黒犬荘 Black Dog House

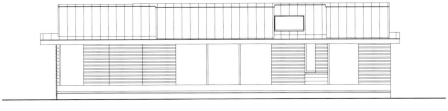

北立面図
ELEVATION

所在地————長野県北佐久郡軽井沢町
用途————週末住宅
構造設計————金箱構造設計事務所
施工————丸山工務店
設計担当————塚本由晴、貝島桃代、山本卓郎*
構造・工法————木造
階数————1F
敷地面積————1,136.03m²
建築面積————145.80m²
建ぺい率————12.83%
許容建ぺい率——30.00%
延床面積————145.80m²
容積率————11.27%
許容容積————50.00%
設計期間————2002.12-2003.8
工事期間————2003.9-2004.4
掲載ページ————60

LOCATION: KARUIZAWA, KITASAKU, NAGANO PREFECTURE
PRINCIPAL USE: WEEKEND HOUSE
STRUCTURAL ENGNEERS: KANEBAKO STRUCTURAL ENGINEERS
GENERAL CONCRETE: MARUYAMA CONSTRUCTION
ARCHITECTS: Yoshiharu Tsukamoto, Momoyo Kaijima,
            Takuro Yamamoto
STRUCTURE/CONSTRUCTION METHOD: WOODEN CONSTRUCTION
FLOOR: 1F
SITE AREA: 1,136.03m²
BUILT AREA: 145.80m²
BUILT RATIO: 12.83%
MAXIMUM BUILT RATIO: 30.00%
TOTAL FLOOR AREA: 145.80m²
FLOOR-AREA RATIO: 11.27%
MAXIMUM FLOOR-AREA RATIO: 50.00%
DESIGN PERIOD: 2002.12-2003.8
CONSTRUCTION PERIOD: 2003.9-2004.4
SEE PAGE: 60

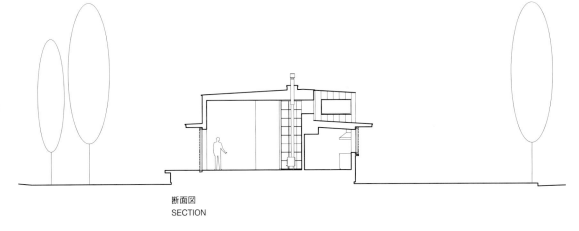

断面図
SECTION

S : 1/200
0 1 2 3 4 5 (m)

ロコ・ハウス Loco House

二階平面図
2F PLAN

配置図 1/1000
SITE PLAN

所在地————東京都八王子市
用途————住居十店舗
構造設計————金箱構造設計事務所
施工————飯塚建築
設計担当————塚本由晴、貝島桃代、山本卓郎*
構造・工法————木造
階数————2F
敷地面積————79.00m²
建築面積————40.05m²
建ぺい率————50.70%
許容建ぺい率——60.00%
延床面積————78.79m²
容積率————99.73%
許容容積————100.00%
設計期間————2004.3-2004.8
工事期間————2004.9-2005.1
掲載ページ————64

LOCATION: HACHIOJI, TOKYO
PRINCIPAL USE: RESIDENCE + SHOP
STRUCTURAL ENGNEERS: KANEBAKO STRUCTURAL ENGINEERS
GENERAL CONCRETE: IIZUKA CONSTRUCTION
ARCHITECTS: Yoshiharu Tsukamoto, Momoyo Kaijima,
　　　　　　　Takuro Yamamoto
STRUCTURE/CONSTRUCTION METHOD: WOODEN CONSTRUCTION
FLOOR: 2F
SITE AREA: 79.00m²
BUILT AREA: 40.05m²
BUILT RATIO: 50.70%
MAXIMUM BUILT RATIO: 60.00%
TOTAL FLOOR AREA: 78.79m²
FLOOR-AREA RATIO: 99.73%
MAXIMUM FLOOR-AREA RATIO: 100.00%
DESIGN PERIOD: 2004.3-2004.8
CONSTRUCTION PERIOD: 2004.9-2005.1
SEE PAGE: 64

一階平面図
1F PLAN

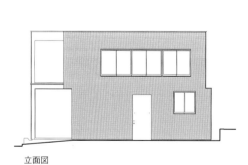

立面図
ELEVATION

断面図
SECTION

S：1/200
0　1　2　3　4　5 (m)

ジューシー・ハウス Juicy House

所在地―――――東京都世田谷区
用途――――――専用住宅
構造設計―――――金箱構造設計事務所
施工――――――花実建設
設計担当―――――塚本由晴、貝島桃代、玉井洋一
構造・工法――――鉄骨造＋鉄筋コンクリート造
階数――――――3F＋B1
敷地面積――――75.18m²
建築面積――――43.20m²
建ぺい率―――――57.46%
許容建ぺい率―――60.00%
延床面積―――――130.37m²
容積率――――――121.81%
許容容積―――――150.00%
設計期間――――2002.11-2004.6
工事期間――――2004.7-2005.2
掲載ページ――――68

LOCATION: SETAGAYA, TOKYO
PRINCIPAL USE: RESIDENCE
STRUCTURAL ENGNEERS: KANEBAKO STRUCTURAL ENGINEERS
GENERAL CONCRETE: HANAMI CORPORATION
ARCHITECTS: Yoshiharu Tsukamoto, Momoyo Kaijima,
           Yoichi Tamai
STRUCTURE/CONSTRUCTION METHOD: STEEL CONSTRUCTION
                              +REINFORCED CONCRETE

FLOOR: 3F+B1
SITE AREA: 75.18m²
BUILT AREA: 43.20m²
BUILT RATIO: 57.46%
MAXIMUM BUILT RATIO: 60.00%
TOTAL FLOOR AREA: 130.37m²
FLOOR-AREA RATIO: 121.81%
MAXIMUM FLOOR-AREA RATIO: 150.00%
DESIGN PERIOD: 2002.11-2004.6
CONSTRUCTION PERIOD: 2004.7-2005.2
SEE PAGE: 68

└─┴─┴─┴─┴─┘ S：1/200
0 1 2 3 4 5 (m)

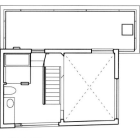

三階平面図
3F PLAN

立面図
ELEVATION

二階平面図
2F PLAN

一階平面図
1F PLAN

地階平面図
BF PLAN

アコ・ハウス Ako House

所在地―――――東京都世田谷区
用途―――――専用住宅
構造設計―――――金箱構造設計事務所
施工―――――飯塚建築
設計担当―――――塚本由晴、貝島桃代、山本卓郎*
構造・工法―――――木造
階数―――――3F
敷地面積―――――51.26m²
建築面積―――――35.51m²
建ぺい率―――――69.27%
許容建ぺい率―――70.00%
延床面積―――――84.86m²
容積率―――――165.55%
許容容積―――――200.00%
設計期間―――――2004.5-2004.12
工事期間―――――2005.1-2005.6
掲載ページ―――――72

LOCATION: SETAGAYA, TOKYO
PRINCIPAL USE: RESIDENCE
STRUCTURAL ENGNEERS: KANEBAKO STRUCTURAL ENGINEERS
GENERAL CONCRETE: IIZUKA CONSTRUCTION
ARCHITECTS: Yoshiharu Tsukamoto, Momoyo Kaijima,
            Takuro Yamamoto
STRUCTURE/CONSTRUCTION METHOD: WOODEN CONSTRUCTION
FLOOR: 3F
SITE AREA: 51.26m²
BUILT AREA: 35.51m²
BUILT RATIO: 69.27%
MAXIMUM BUILT RATIO: 70.00%
TOTAL FLOOR AREA: 84.86m²
FLOOR-AREA RATIO: 165.55%
MAXIMUM FLOOR-AREA RATIO: 200.00%
DESIGN PERIOD: 2004.5-2004.12
CONSTRUCTION PERIOD: 2005.1-2005.6
SEE PAGE: 72

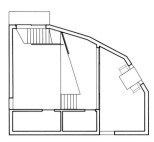

三階平面図
3F PLAN

二階平面図
2F PLAN

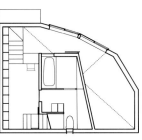

一階上部平面図
UPPER 1F PLAN

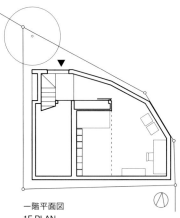
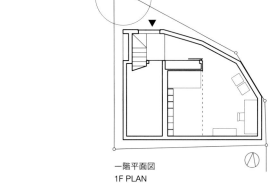

一階平面図
1F PLAN

配置図 1/1000
SITE PLAN

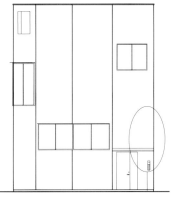

立面図
ELEVATION

S : 1/200
0 1 2 3 4 5 (m)

ガク・ハウス Gak House

所在地————東京都世田谷区
用途————専用住宅
構造設計————金箱構造設計事務所
施工————花実建設
設計担当————塚本由晴、貝島桃代、玉井洋一
構造・工法————木造
階数————2F
敷地面積————70.01m²
建築面積————41.97m²
建ぺい率————59.95%
許容建ぺい率————60.00%
延床面積————75.00m²
容積率————107.12%
許容容積————150.00%
設計期間————2004.7-2004.9
工事期間————2004.10-2005.6
掲載ページ————76

LOCATION: SETAGAYA, TOKYO
PRINCIPAL USE: RESIDENCE
STRUCTURAL ENGNEERS: KANEBAKO STRUCTURAL ENGINEERS
GENERAL CONCRETE: HANAMI CORPORATION
ARCHITECTS: Yoshiharu Tsukamoto, Momoyo Kaijima,
            Yoichi Tamai
STRUCTURE/CONSTRUCTION METHOD: WOODEN CONSTRUCTION
FLOOR: 2F
SITE AREA: 70.01m²
BUILT AREA: 41.97m²
BUILT RATIO: 59.95%
MAXIMUM BUILT RATIO: 60.00%
TOTAL FLOOR AREA: 75.00m²
FLOOR-AREA RATIO: 107.12%
MAXIMUM FLOOR-AREA RATIO: 150.00%
DESIGN PERIOD: 2004.7-2004.9
CONSTRUCTION PERIOD: 2004.10-2005.6
SEE PAGE: 76

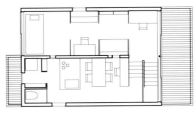

二階平面図
2F PLAN

一階平面図
1F PLAN

S : 1/200
0 1 2 3 4 5 (m)

配置図 1/1000
SITE PLAN

立面図
ELEVATION

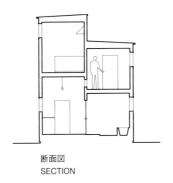

断面図
SECTION

ハウス&アトリエ・ワン House & Atelier Bow-Wow

所在地————東京都新宿区
用途————住居+事務所
構造設計————オーク構造設計
施工————日南鉄構
設計担当————塚本由晴、貝島桃代、高木俊*
構造・工法————鉄骨造+鉄筋コンクリート造
階数————3F+B1
敷地面積————109.03m²
建築面積————59.76m²
建ぺい率————54.82%
許容建ぺい率————60.00%
延床面積————211.27（172.93）m²
容積率————158.60%
許容容積————160.00%
設計期間————2004.2-2005.4
工事期間————2005.5-2005.12
掲載ページ————80

LOCATION: SHINJUKU, TOKYO
PRINCIPAL USE: RESIDENCE + OFFICE
STRUCTURAL ENGNEERS: STRUCTURAL DESIGN OFFICE OAK
GENERAL CONCRETE: NICHINAN TEKKOU
ARCHITECTS: Yoshiharu Tsukamoto, Momoyo Kaijima,
　　　　　　Shun Takagi
STRUCTURE/CONSTRUCTION METHOD: STEEL CONSTRUCTION
　　　　　　　　　　　　+REINFORCED CONCRETE

FLOOR: 3F+B1
SITE AREA: 109.03m²
BUILT AREA: 59.76m²
BUILT RATIO: 54.82%
MAXIMUM BUILT RATIO: 60.00%
TOTAL FLOOR AREA: 211.27(172.93)m²
FLOOR-AREA RATIO: 158.60%
MAXIMUM FLOOR-AREA RATIO: 160.00%
DESIGN PERIOD: 2004.2-2005.4
CONSTRUCTION PERIOD: 2005.5-2005.12
SEE PAGE: 80

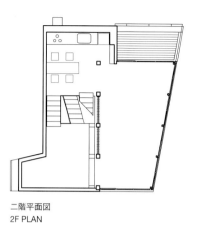

二階平面図
2F PLAN

屋上平面図
RF PLAN

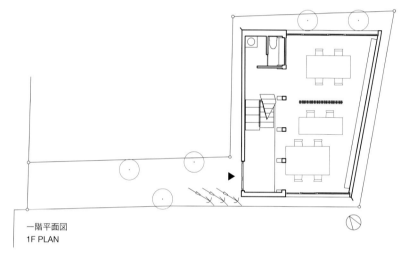

一階平面図
1F PLAN

三階平面図
3F PLAN

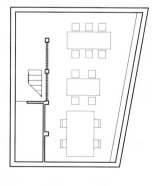

地階平面図
BF PLAN

```
├──┼──┼──┼──┼──┤ S:1/200
0  1  2  3  4  5 (m)
```

ハウス・タワー House Tower

所在地 ———— 東京都品川区
用途 ———— 専用住宅
構造設計 ———— 金箱構造設計事務所
施工 ———— TTC建設
設計担当 ———— 塚本由晴、貝島桃代、関本丹青、平井政俊
構造・工法 ———— 鉄筋コンクリート造
階数 ———— 4F+B1
敷地面積 ———— 42.29㎡
建築面積 ———— 18.44㎡
建ぺい率 ———— 43.60%
許容建ぺい率 ———— 60.00%
延床面積 ———— 65.28㎡
容積率 ———— 154.36%
許容容積 ———— 160.00%
設計期間 ———— 2005.3-2005.10
工事期間 ———— 2005.11-2006.4
掲載ページ ———— 86

LOCATION: SHINAGAWA, TOKYO
PRINCIPAL USE: RESIDENCE
STRUCTURAL ENGNEERS: KANEBAKO STRUCTURAL ENGINEERS
GENERAL CONCRETE: TTC CORPORATION
ARCHITECTS: Yoshiharu Tsukamoto, Momoyo Kaijima,
　　　　　　　Mio Sekimoto, Masatoshi Hirai
STRUCTURE/CONSTRUCTION METHOD: REINFORCED CONCRETE
FLOOR: 4F+B1
SITE AREA: 42.29㎡
BUILT AREA: 18.44㎡
BUILT RATIO: 43.60%
MAXIMUM BUILT RATIO: 60.00%
TOTAL FLOOR AREA: 65.28㎡
FLOOR-AREA RATIO: 154.36%
MAXIMUM FLOOR-AREA RATIO: 160.00%
DESIGN PERIOD: 2005.3-2005.10
CONSTRUCTION PERIOD: 2005.11-2006.4
SEE PAGE: 86

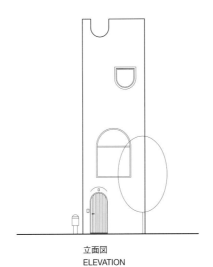

立面図
ELEVATION

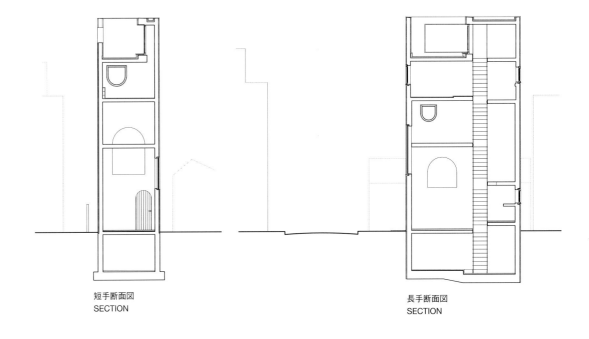

短手断面図
SECTION

長手断面図
SECTION

S:1/200
0　1　2　3　4　5 (m)

ノラ・ハウス Nora House

所在地————宮城県仙台市
用途————専用住宅
構造設計————金箱構造設計事務所
施工————橋本不動産
設計担当————塚本由晴、貝島桃代、
　　　　　　東京工業大学塚本研究室(小山敦子、金野千恵、能作文徳、吉田拓也)
構造・工法————木造
階数————2F
敷地面積————231.69m²
建築面積————90.90m²
建ぺい率————39.27%
許容建ぺい率—50.00%
延床面積————137.88m²
容積率————59.51%
許容容積————80.00%
設計期間————2005.6-2006.7
工事期間————2006.8-2006.12
掲載ページ————90

LOCATION: SENDAI, MIYAGI PREFECTURE
PRINCIPAL USE: RESIDENCE
STRUCTURAL ENGNEERS: KANEBAKO STRUCTURAL ENGINEERS
GENERAL CONCRETE: HASHIMOTO CORPORATION
ARCHITECTS: Yoshiharu Tsukamoto, Momoyo Kaijima
　　　　　　+ T.I.T. Tsukamoto Lab.(Atsuko Koyama, Chie Konno,
　　　　　　Fuminori Nousaku, Takuya Yoshida)
STRUCTURE/CONSTRUCTION METHOD: WOODEN CONSTRUCTION
FLOOR: 2F
SITE AREA: 231.69m²
BUILT AREA: 90.90m²
BUILT RATIO: 39.27%
MAXIMUM BUILT RATIO: 50.00%
TOTAL FLOOR AREA: 137.88m²
FLOOR-AREA RATIO: 59.51%
MAXIMUM FLOOR-AREA RATIO: 80.00%
DESIGN PERIOD: 2005.6-2006.7
CONSTRUCTION PERIOD: 2006.8-2006.12
SEE PAGE: 90

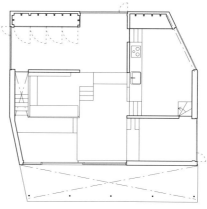

上部平面図
UPPER PART PLAN

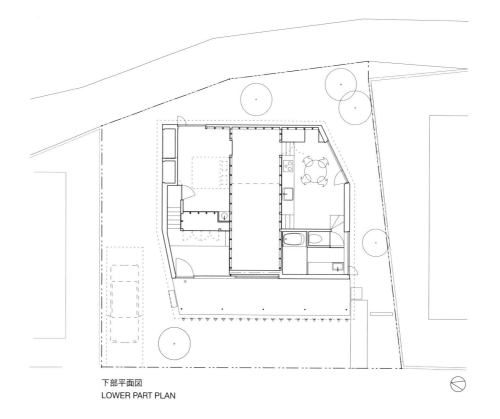

下部平面図
LOWER PART PLAN

S：1/200
0　1　2　3　4　5 (m)

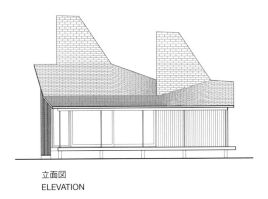

立面図
ELEVATION

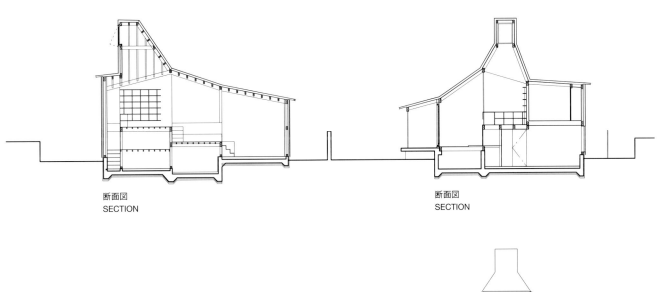

断面図
SECTION

断面図
SECTION

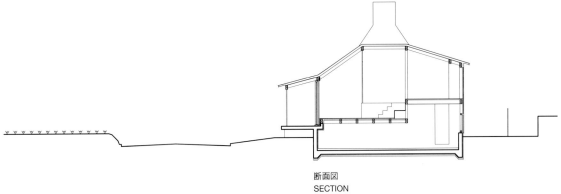

断面図
SECTION

鶴山荘 Crane House

所在地――――長野県北佐久郡軽井沢町
用途――――別荘
構造設計――――オーク構造設計
施工――――笹沢建設
設計担当――――塚本由晴、貝島桃代、平井政俊
構造・工法――――鉄骨造
階数――――1F
敷地面積――――3,561.76m²
建築面積――――142.35m²
建ぺい率――――4.00%
許容建ぺい率――20.00%
延床面積――――197.20m²
容積率――――5.54%
許容容積――――20.00%
設計期間――――2005.8-2006.8
工事期間――――2006.9-2007.4
掲載ページ――――94

LOCATION: KARUIZAWA, KITASAKU, NAGANO PREFECTURE
PRINCIPAL USE: VILLA
STRUCTURAL ENGNEERS: STRUCTURAL DESIGN OFFICE OAK
GENERAL CONCRETE: SASAZAWA CONSTRUCTION
ARCHITECTS: Yoshiharu Tsukamoto, Momoyo Kaijima,
            Masatoshi Hirai
STRUCTURE/CONSTRUCTION METHOD: STEEL CONSTRUCTION
FLOOR: 1F
SITE AREA: 3,561.76m²
BUILT AREA: 142.35m²
BUILT RATIO: 4.00%
MAXIMUM BUILT RATIO: 20.00%
TOTAL FLOOR AREA: 197.20m²
FLOOR-AREA RATIO: 5.54%
MAXIMUM FLOOR-AREA RATIO: 20.00%
DESIGN PERIOD: 2005.8-2006.8
CONSTRUCTION PERIOD: 2006.9-2007.4
SEE PAGE: 94

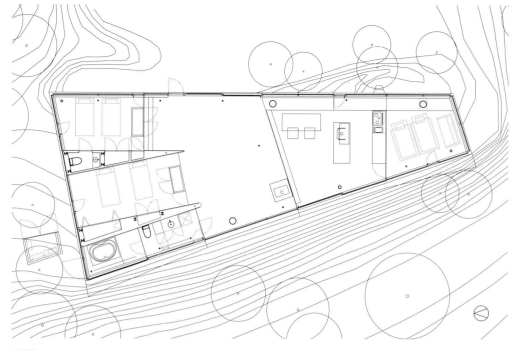

平面図
PLAN

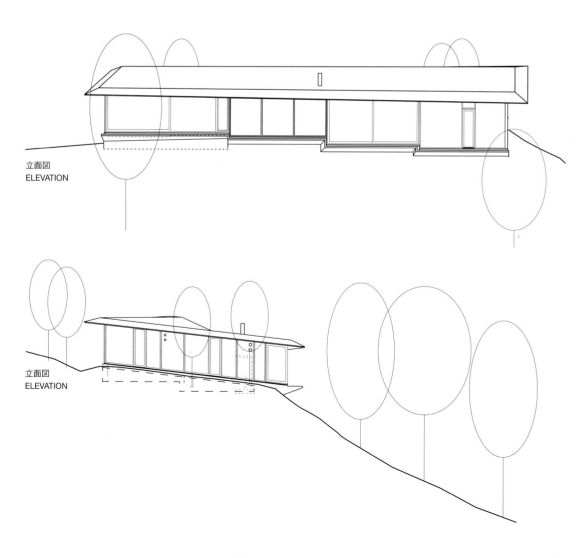

立面図
ELEVATION

立面図
ELEVATION

S：1/200
0　1　2　3　4　5 (m)

インビー・ハウス YIMBY House

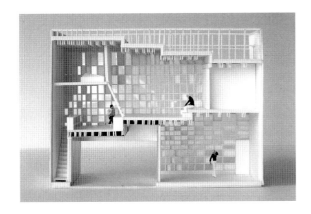

所在地————————アメリカ カリフォルニア州
用途————————住居兼アトリエ
構造設計————————金箱構造設計事務所
設計担当————————塚本由晴、貝島桃代、倉林貴彦
構造・工法————————木造
階数————————2F
敷地面積————————111.37m²
建築面積————————69.55m²
延床面積————————152.58m²
容積率————————137.00%
設計期間————————2006.3-2006.8
掲載ページ————————98

LOCATION: CALIFORNIA, USA
PRINCIPAL USE: ATELIER
STRUCTURAL ENGNEERS: KANEBAKO STRUCTURAL ENGINEERS
ARCHITECTS: Yoshiharu Tsukamoto, Momoyo Kaijima,
            Takahiko Kurabayashi
STRUCTURE/CONSTRUCTION METHOD: WOODEN CONSTRUCTION
FLOOR: 2F
SITE AREA: 111.37m²
BUILT AREA: 69.55m²
TOTAL FLOOR AREA: 152.58m²
FLOOR-AREA RATIO: 137.00%
DESIGN PERIOD: 2006.3-2006.8
SEE PAGE: 98

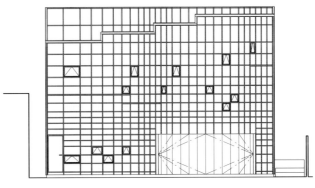

二階平面図
2F PLAN

立面図
ELEVATION

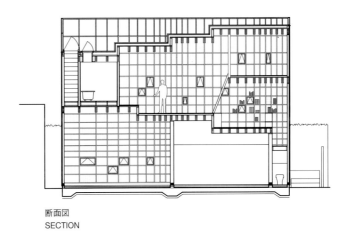

断面図
SECTION

S：1/200
0　1　2　3　4　5 (m)

マウンテン・ハウス Mountain House

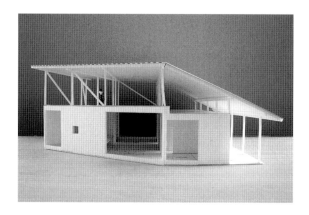

所在地————アメリカ カリフォルニア州
用途————別荘
構造設計————金箱構造設計事務所
設計担当————塚本由晴、貝島桃代、玉井洋一、倉林貴彦
構造・工法————木造
階数————2F
建築面積————178.94m²
延床面積————115.18m²
設計期間————2005.2-
掲載ページ————102

LOCATION: CALIFORNIA, USA
PRINCIPAL USE: VILLA
STRUCTURAL ENGNEERS: KANEBAKO STRUCTURAL ENGINEERS
ARCHITECTS: Yoshiharu Tsukamoto, Momoyo Kaijima,
          Yoichi Tamai, Takahiko Kurabayashi
STRUCTURE/CONSTRUCTION METHOD: WOODEN CONSTRUCTION
FLOOR: 2F
BUILT AREA: 178.94m²
TOTAL FLOOR AREA: 115.18m²
DESIGN PERIOD: 2005.2-
SEE PAGE: 102

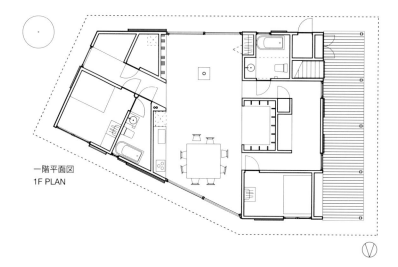

一階平面図
1F PLAN

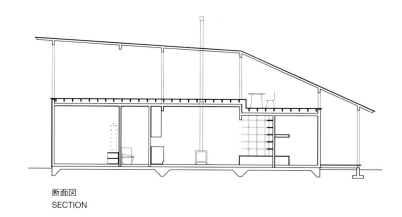

断面図
SECTION

S : 1/200

0   1   2   3   4   5 (m)

ジャングルジム・ハウス Junglegym House

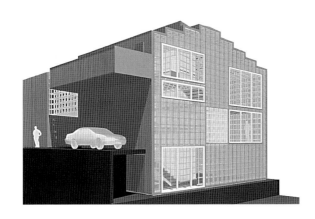

所在地————福岡県久留米市
用途————専用住宅
構造設計————オーク構造設計
設計担当————塚本由晴、貝島桃代、有岡果奈、Carlo Zuercher
構造・工法————鉄骨造
階数————3F+B1
敷地面積————215.00m²
建築面積————90.00m²
建ぺい率————42.00%
延床面積————298.00m²
容積率————138.00%
設計期間————2006.7-

LOCATION: KURUME, FUKUOKA PREFECTURE
PRINCIPAL USE: RESIDENCE
STRUCTURAL ENGNEERS: STRUCTURAL DESIGN OFFICE OAK
ARCHITECTS: Yoshiharu Tsukamoto, Momoyo Kaijima,
                Kana Arioka, Carlo Zuercher
STRUCTURE/CONSTRUCTION METHOD: STEEL CONSTRUCTION
FLOOR: 3F+B1
SITE AREA: 215.00m²
BUILT AREA: 90.00m²
BUILT RATIO: 42.00%
TOTAL FLOOR AREA: 298.00m²
FLOOR-AREA RATIO: 138.00%

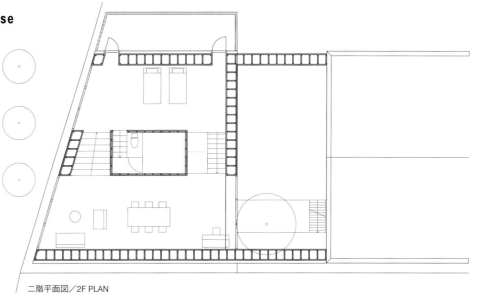

二階平面図／2F PLAN

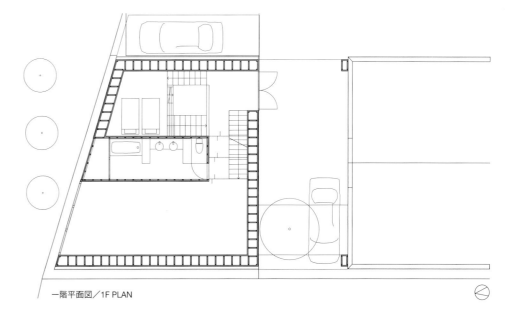

一階平面図／1F PLAN

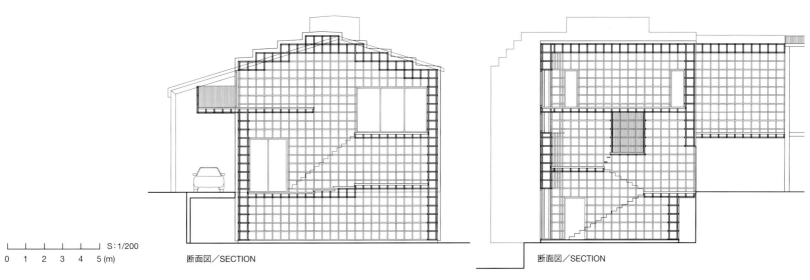

S：1/200
0　1　2　3　4　5 (m)

断面図／SECTION

断面図／SECTION

ヤオトン・ハウス／伴山人家プロジェクト Yao Tong House / Tianjin Housing Project

所在地————中国、天津市
用途————専用住宅群
構造設計————構造計画プラス・ワン
設計担当————塚本由晴、貝島桃代、
　　　　　　　東京工業大学塚本研究室(藤村龍至、片柳恭志、倉林貴彦、
　　　　　　　玉井洋一、三井祐介、杉山和也、山本幸治、吉田拓也)
構造・工法————鉄筋コンクリート造
階数————2-8F+B2
建築面積————230.13m²
延床面積————569.71m²
設計期間————2003.12-2006.11

LOCATION: TIANJIN, CHINA
PRINCIPAL USE: RESIDENCE
STRUCTURAL ENGNEERS: STRUCTURAL DESIGN PLUS ONE
ARCHITECTS: Yoshiharu Tsukamoto, Momoyo Kaijima
　　　　　　+ T.I.T. Tsukamoto Lab.(Ryuji Fujimura, Takashi Katayanagi,
　　　　　　Takahiko Kurabayashi, Yoichi Tamai, Yusuke Mitsui,
　　　　　　Kazuya Sugiyama, Koji Yamamoto, Takuya Yoshida)
STRUCTURE/CONSTRUCTION METHOD: REINFORCED CONCRETE
FLOOR: 2-8F+B2
BUILT AREA: 230.13m²
TOTAL FLOOR AREA: 569.71m²
DESIGN PERIOD: 2003.12-2006.11

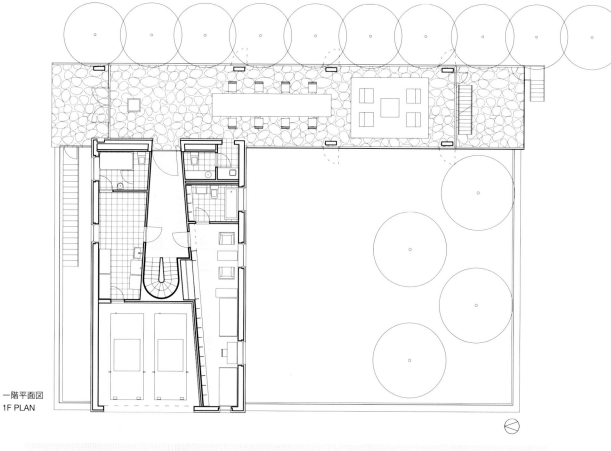

一階平面図
1F PLAN

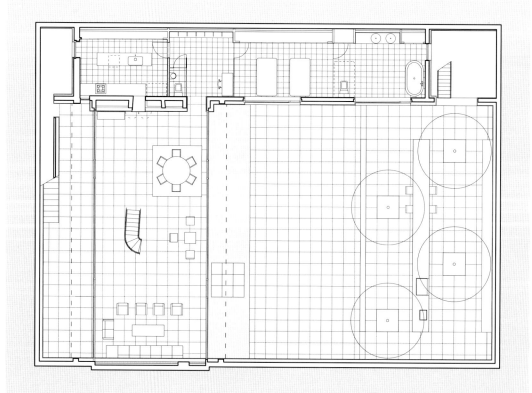

└─┴─┴─┴─┴─┘ S：1/200
0　1　2　3　4　5 (m)

地階平面図
BF PLAN

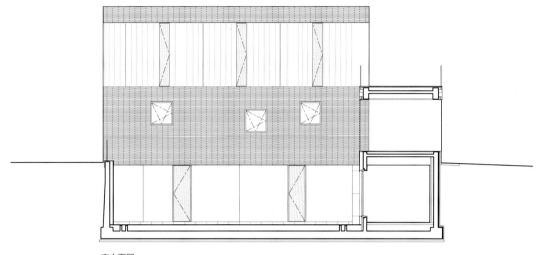

南立面図
SOUTH ELEVATION

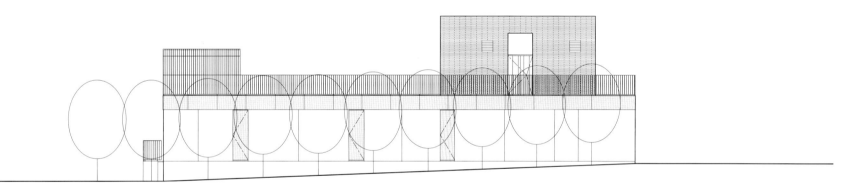

東立面図
EAST ELEVATION

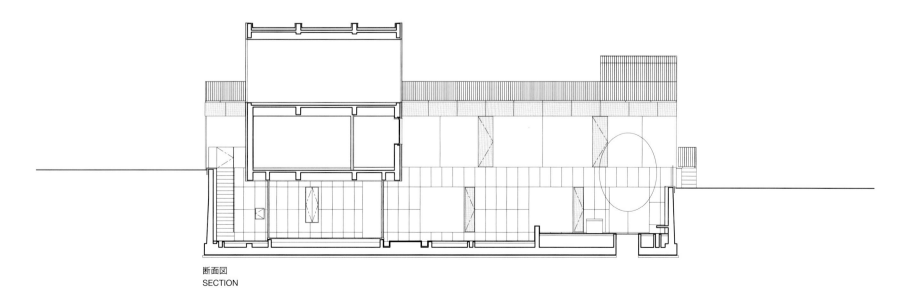

断面図
SECTION

スウェー・ハウス Sway House

所在地―――東京都世田谷区
用途―――専用住宅
構造設計―――金箱構造設計事務所
設計担当―――塚本由晴、貝島桃代、倉林貴彦、関本丹青
構造・工法―――木造
階数―――3F
敷地面積―――78.08m²
建築面積―――54.52m²
許容建ぺい率―――70.00%
延床面積―――114.30m²
容積率―――146.38%
許容容積―――160.00%
設計期間―――2006.9-

LOCATION: SETAGAYA, TOKYO
PRINCIPAL USE: RESIDENCE
STRUCTURAL ENGINEERS: KANEBAKO STRUCTURAL ENGINEERS
ARCHITECTS: Yoshiharu Tsukamoto, Momoyo Kaijima,
　　　　　　　Takahiko Kurabayashi, Mio Sekimoto
STRUCTURE/CONSTRUCTION METHOD: WOODEN CONSTRUCTION
FLOOR: 3F
SITE AREA: 78.08m²
BUILT AREA: 54.52m²
MAXIMUM BUILT RATIO: 70.00%
TOTAL FLOOR AREA: 114.30m²
FLOOR-AREA RATIO: 146.38%
MAXIMUM FLOOR-AREA RATIO: 160.00%
DESIGN PERIOD: 2006.9-

S : 1/200
0　1　2　3　4　5 (m)

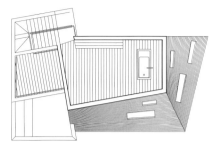

R階平面図
RF PLAN

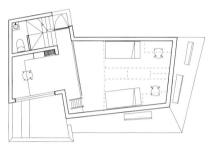

三階平面図
3F PLAN

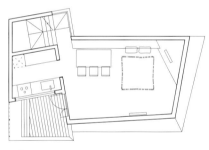

二階平面図
2F PLAN

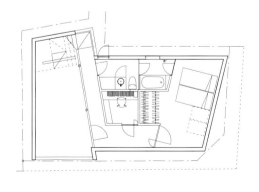

一階平面図
1F PLAN

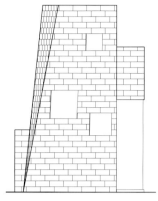

立面図
ELEVATION

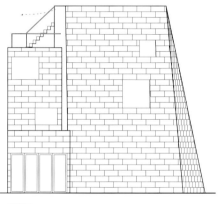

立面図
ELEVATION

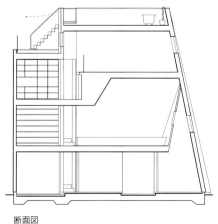

断面図
SECTION

3 in 1 ハウス 3 in 1 House

所在地 ─────── スイス チューリヒ
用途 ───────── 専用住宅
設計担当 ───── 塚本由晴、貝島桃代、玉井洋一、倉林貴彦
構造・工法 ─── 鉄筋コンクリート造
階数 ───────── 2F+B1
敷地面積 ───── 614.42m²
建築面積 ───── 137.77m²
建ぺい率 ───── 22.42%
延床面積 ───── 215.50m²
容積率 ─────── 35.07%
設計期間 ───── 2006.1-

LOCATION: ZURICH, SWISS
PRINCIPAL USE: RESIDENCE
ARCHITECTS: Yoshiharu Tsukamoto, Momoyo Kaijima,
           Yoichi Tamai, Takahiko Kurabayashi
STRUCTURE/CONSTRUCTION METHOD: REINFORCED CONCRETE
FLOOR: 2F+B1
SITE AREA: 614.42m²
BUILT AREA: 137.77m²
BUILT RATIO: 22.42%
TOTAL FLOOR AREA: 215.50m²
FLOOR-AREA RATIO: 35.07%
DESIGN PERIOD: 2006.1-

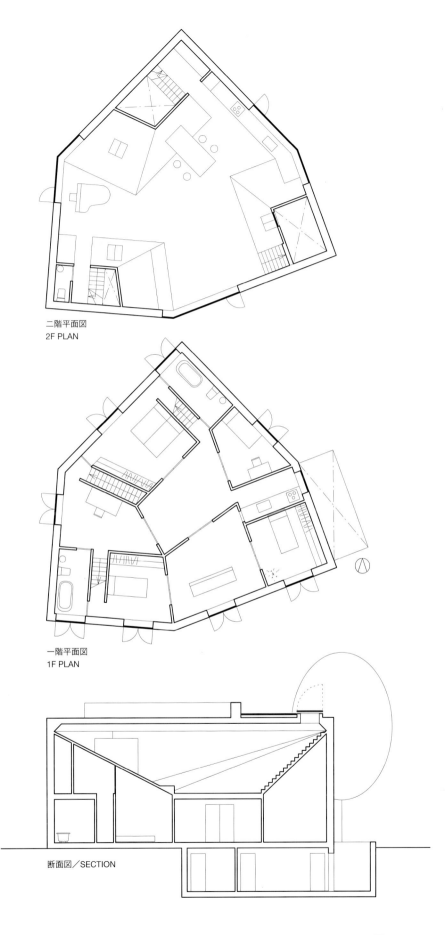

二階平面図
2F PLAN

一階平面図
1F PLAN

立面図／ELEVATION

断面図／SECTION

S:1/200

0 1 2 3 4 5 (m)

カーサ・グランツーリズモ Casa Granturismo

所在地 ――――― ポルトガル　シルベス
用途 ―――――― 専用住宅
設計担当 ――――― 塚本由晴、貝島桃代、
　　　　　　　　東京工業大学塚本研究室(Jorge Almazan、殿井環、能作文徳)
構造・工法 ――――― 鉄筋コンクリート造
階数 ―――――― 2F+B1
敷地面積 ――――― 450.00m²
建築面積 ――――― 114.48m²
建ぺい率 ――――― 25.44%
延床面積 ――――― 220.64m²
容積率 ――――― 49.01%

LOCATION: SILVES, PORTUGAL
PRINCIPAL USE: RESIDENCE
ARCHITECTS: Yoshiharu Tsukamoto, Momoyo Kaijima
　　　　　　　+ T.I.T. Tsukamoto Lab.(Jorge Almazan, Tamoki,Tonoi,
　　　　　　　Fuminori Nousaku)
STRUCTURE/CONSTRUCTION METHOD: REINFORCED CONCRETE
FLOOR: 2F+B1
SITE AREA: 450.00m²
BUILT AREA: 114.48m²
BUILT RATIO: 25.44%
TOTAL FLOOR AREA: 220.64m²
FLOOR-AREA RATIO: 49.01%

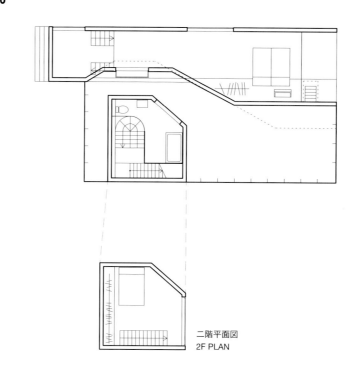

二階平面図
2F PLAN

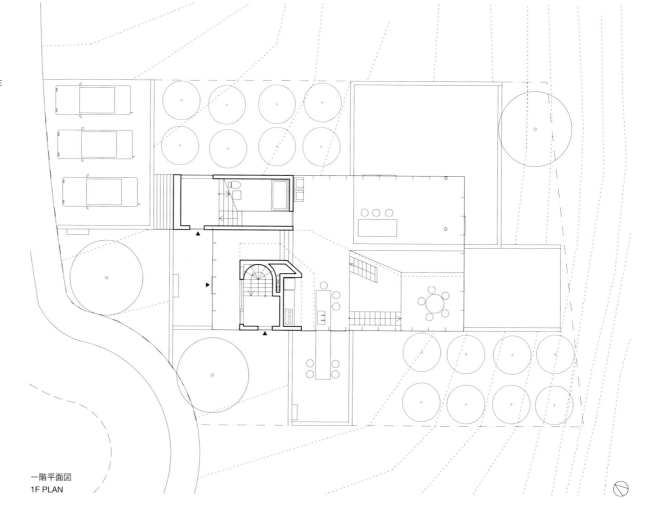

一階平面図
1F PLAN

S:1/200

0　1　2　3　4　5(m)

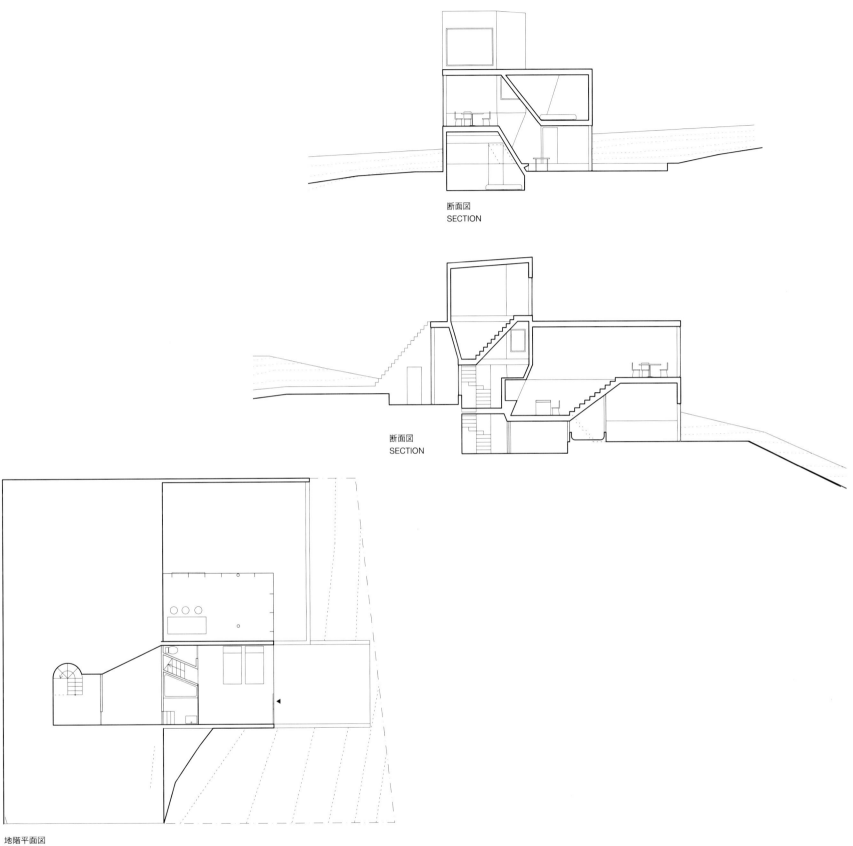

断面図
SECTION

断面図
SECTION

地階平面図
BF PLAN

アトリエ・ワン

1992年塚本由晴と貝島桃代により設立

http://www.bow-wow.jp

塚本由晴 つかもと・よしはる

1965年	神奈川県生まれ
1987年	東京工業大学工学部建築学科卒業
1987〜88年	パリ建築大学ベルビル校（U.P.8）
1994年	東京工業大学大学院博士課程修了、博士（工学）
2000年〜	東京工業大学大学院助教授
2003年	ハーヴァード大学GSD客員教員
2007年	ハーヴァード大学GSD客員教員

現在、東京工業大学大学院助教授、ハーヴァード大学GSD客員教員

貝島桃代 かいじま・ももよ

1969年	東京都生まれ
1991年	日本女子大学家政学部住居学科卒業
1994年	東京工業大学大学院修士課程修了
1996〜97年	スイス連邦工科大学チューリッヒ校奨学生
2000年	東京工業大学大学院博士課程修了
2000年〜	筑波大学講師
2003年	ハーヴァード大学GSD客員教員
2005年〜	スイス連邦工科大学チューリッヒ校客員教授

現在、筑波大学講師、スイス連邦工科大学チューリッヒ校客員教授

Atelier Bow-Wow

Established in 1992 by Yoshiharu Tsukamoto (born in 1965)
and Momoyo Kaijima (born in 1969) in Tokyo. (http://www.bow-wow.jp)

Yoshiharu Tsukamoto

1987	Graduate from Tokyo Institute of Technology
1987〜88	Guest Student of L'ecole d'architecture, Paris, Belville (U.P. 8)
1994	Graduate from Post-graduate school of Tokyo Institute of Technology
2000〜	Associate Professor of Tokyo Institute of Technology, Dr. Eng.
2003	Visiting Faculty of Harvard University GSD
2007	Visiting Faculty of Harvard University GSD

Present Associate Professor of Tokyo Institute of Technology, Dr. Eng.
Visiting Faculty of Harvard University GSD

Momoyo Kaijima

1991	Graduate from Japan Women's University
1994	Graduate from Graduate School of Tokyo Institute of Technology
1996〜97	Guest student of E.T.H. Zurich
2000	Graduate from Post-graduate school of Tokyo Institute of Technology
2000〜	Assistant Professor of University of Tsukuba
2003	Visiting Faculty of Harvard GSD
2005〜	Visiting Professor of E.T.H. Zurich

Present Assistant Professor of University of Tsukuba
Visiting Professor of E.T.H. Zurich

主な受賞

1999年 平成11年東京建築士会住宅建築賞金賞

2000年 第16回吉岡賞

2002年 American Wood Design Awards 2002

主な著作

2001年 ペット・アーキテクチャー・ガイドブック（ワールド・フォト・プレス）

2001年 メイド・イン・トーキョー（鹿島出版会）

2003年 「小さな家」の気づき（王国社／塚本由晴）

2004年 狭くて小さい楽しい家（原書房／共著：永江 朗）

2004年 現代住宅研究（INAX出版／共著：塚本由晴、西沢大良）

2006年 アトリエ・ワン・フロム・ポスト・バブル・シティ（INAX出版）

主な展覧会

2002年 第4回 光州ビエンナーレ（ビエンナーレ・ホール、光州）

2002年 第4回 上海ビエンナーレ（上海市立美術館、上海）

2003年 いかに緯度は形に姿を変えるか（ウォーカー・アート・センター、ミネアポリス）

2003年 第3回 妻有アートトリエンナーレ（十日町、新潟）

2003年 第50回 ベニス・ビエンナーレ、ゾーン・オブ・アージェンシー（アルセナーレ、ベニス）

2004年 六本木クロッシング（森アートセンター、東京）

2004年 アトリエ・ワン「街の使い方」展（キリンプラザ、大阪）

2006年 ダイナミシティ（NAi：オランダ建築博物館、ロッテルダム）

2006年 トーキング・シティ（ゼッチェ・ツォールフェライン、エッセン）

2006年 釜山ビエンナーレ2006（オンチェンジョン川、釜山）

2006年 第27回 サンパウロビエンナーレ（パビンニョ・ダ・ビエンナレ、サンパウロ）

2006年 アーキラボ「都市に巣を作る」（フラック・センター、オルレアン）

Selected Awards

1999 Gold Prize of House Architecture 1999, Tokyo Architect Society

2000 The 16th Yoshioka Prize

2002 American Wood Design Awards 2002

Selected Writings

2001 Pet Architecture Guide Book, World Photo Press

2001 Made in Tokyo, Kajima Publishing

2003 Chiisana ie no kiduki, Ohkokusha

2004 Small but Pleasant House, Hara Shobou

2004 Contemporary House Studies, INAX Publishing

2006 Atelier Bow-Wow from Post Bubble City, INAX Publishing

Selected Exhibition

2002 The 4th Kwangju Biennale, Biennale Hall, Kwangju

2002 The 4th Shanghai Biennale, Shanghai City Museum, Shanghai

2003 How Latitudes Become Forms, Walker Art Center,Mineapolis, U.S.A

2003 The 50th Venice Biennale, Zone of Urgency, Arsenale, Venice

2003 The 3rd Tsumari Art Triennale, Toka-machi, Niigata

2004 Roppongi Crossing, Mori Art Center, Tokyo

2004 Atelier Bow-Wow Solo Exhibition, Kirin Plaza, Osaka

2006 Dynamicity, NAi:Netherlands Architecture Institute, Rotterdam

2006 Talking City, Zeche Zolleverein, Essen

2006 Busan Biennale 2006, Oncheonjang River, Busan

2006 The 27th Sao Paulo Biennale, Sao Paulo

2006 Archilab "Faire son nid dans la ville", Frac Centre, Orlean

クレジット Credits

図面制作 Drawings

東京工業大学大学院理工学研究科建築学専攻塚本研究室
Tsukamoto Lab.
Department of Architecture and Building Engineering,
Graduate School of Science Engineering,
Tokyo Institute of Technology

石川徳摩　Tokuma Ishikawa

大熊克和　Yoshikazu Okuma

金野千恵　Chie Konno

千田友己　Yuki Chida

服部暁文　Akinori Hattori

五十嵐麻美　Asami Igarashi

佐々木 啓　Kei Sasaki

中村真広　Masahiro Nakamura

ファース・ギヨム　Faas Guillaume

内部美玲　Mirei Uchibe

大森彩子　Ayako Omori

立川玲香　Leica Tatekawa

小山敦子　Atsuko Koyama

能作文徳　Fuminori Nousaku

アトリエ・ワン　Atelier Bow-Wow

倉林貴彦　Takahiko Kurabayashi

関本丹青　Mio Sekimoto

玉井洋一　Yoichi Tamai

平井政俊　Masatoshi Hirai

協力 Cooperation

高木 俊　Shun Takagi／ピーネット（P-net arch.）

山崎徹也　Tetsuya Yamazaki／Shift

山本卓郎　Takuro Yamamoto
山本卓郎建築設計事務所（Yamamoto Jimusyo）

翻訳 English Translation

トーマス・ダニエル　Thomas Daniell

フォトクレジット Photo Credits

アトリエ・ワン　Atelier Bow-Wow

図解 アトリエ・ワン
GRAPHIC ANATOMY ATELIER BOW-WOW

2007年3月15日　初版第1刷発行
2007年5月25日　初版第3刷発行

企画 ──────── ギャラリー・間

著者 ──────── アトリエ・ワン（塚本由晴＋貝島桃代）

発行者 ─────── 遠藤信行

発行所 ─────── TOTO出版（TOTO株式会社 文化推進部）
〒107-0062 東京都港区南青山1-24-3
TOTO乃木坂ビル2F
［営業］TEL.03-3402-7138　FAX.03-3402-7187
［編集］TEL.03-3497-1010
URL: http://www.toto.co.jp/bookshop/

アートディレクション── 秋田 寛

デザイン ────── 秋田 寛＋森田恭行（アキタ・デザイン・カン）

印刷・製本 ───── 株式会社サンニチ印刷